Praise for
China: Fragile Superpower

"Now more than ever we need a realistic approach for dealing with China's rising power. Susan Shirk has an insider's grasp of China's politics and a firm understanding of what makes its leaders tick. *China: Fragile Superpower* is an important and necessary book."

—Brent Scowcroft,
former U.S. National Security Advisor

"Susan Shirk's lively and perceptive book examines the constraints on Chinese foreign policy in an era of rapid socio-economic change. . . . Shirk brings a wealth of experience as an astute observer of Chinese politics and as a practitioner of track I and II diplomacy toward China to illuminate the relationship between domestic legitimacy dilemmas and foreign security dilemmas."

—Alastair Iain Johnston,
The Laine Professor of China in World Affairs, Harvard

"Although other problems dominate the news today, a rising China presents America's greatest long-term challenge. Susan Shirk's excellent book argues compellingly that it also poses the greatest challenge to China's leaders. How they meet this challenge affects not only China, but also the U.S. and, indeed, the world."

—William J. Perry,
former U.S. Secretary of Defense

"In this eye-opening work, Susan Shirk details China's incredible economic progress while lifting the rug on its severe internal problems. She has injected a dose of realism into a distorted vision of China which has been promoted by gushing China watchers who focus on Shanghai's skyline."

—James Lilley,
Former American Ambassador to South Korea and China

"A major statement about the present condition of China's political system and the hidden hazards on the road ahead."

—Andrew Walder,
Stanford University

China
Fragile Superpower

Susan L. Shirk

OXFORD
UNIVERSITY PRESS

OXFORD
UNIVERSITY PRESS

Oxford University Press, Inc., publishes works that further
Oxford University's objective of excellence
in research, scholarship, and education.

Oxford   New York
Auckland   Cape Town   Dar es Salaam   Hong Kong   Karachi
Kuala Lumpur   Madrid   Melbourne   Mexico City   Nairobi
New Delhi   Shanghai   Taipei   Toronto

With offices in
Argentina   Austria   Brazil   Chile   Czech Republic   France   Greece
Guatemala   Hungary   Italy   Japan   Poland   Portugal   Singapore
South Korea   Switzerland   Thailand   Turkey   Ukraine   Vietnam

First published by Oxford University Press, Inc., 2007
198 Madison Avenue, New York, NY 10016

www.oup.com

First issued as an Oxford University Press paperback, 2008

Oxford is a registered trademark of Oxford University Press

Library of Congress Cataloging-in-Publication Data
Shirk, Susan L.
China: fragile superpower / by Susan L. Shirk.
p. cm.
Includes bibliographical references and index.
ISBN 978-0-19-537319-6 (pbk.)
1. Nationalism—China.
2. China—Politics and government—2002– I. Title.
JC311.S525 2007
320.951—dc22
2006027998

1 3 5 7 9 8 6 4 2
Printed in the United States of America
on acid-free paper

For Sam, Lucy, and David Popkin

Contents

Preface

THE PUBLICATION OF THIS PAPERBACK EDITION of *China: Fragile Superpower* follows upon and coincides with three major events in China. It follows upon the protests in Tibet and the horrific and tragic earthquake in Sichuan province, with their aftershocks and repercussions, and it coincides with the 2008 Beijing Olympics. All of them are of immense significance for China's leaders and citizens.

I'll start with the Olympics because they set the stage for the dramatic crises that have challenged China's leaders at home and abroad during the lead-up to the Games. The Chinese government set its sights on the 2000 Olympics in 1990, just a little more than a decade after it launched its highly successful economic reforms and opened itself to world trade and investment. Hosting the Olympics would honor China as a global power after more than a century of humiliating weakness. It would strengthen national pride and bolster popular support of the Chinese government and Communist Party. For three years, Beijing stirred up popular enthusiasm for its bid with rallies and billboards. But the U.S. Congress voted to oppose China's bid, and the International Olympic Committee withheld the prize. In the aftermath of the 1989 violent suppression of student pro-democracy demonstrations in Beijing's Tiananmen Square and other Chinese cities, the world appeared unwilling to grant legitimacy to a country with such an abysmal human rights record. The Chinese public felt robbed and blamed America.

In 2002 when China successfully won the bid for the 2008 Games, there was widespread public elation and a sense of vindication. Beijing spared no expense in constructing state-of-the-art stadiums and gymnasiums, airport terminals and subways, designed by the world's leading architects and engineers. In a frenetic drive for urban renewal, old neighborhoods were bulldozed to make way for glittering skyscrapers and shopping malls.

The greatest challenge was Beijing's severe air pollution. The authorities moved factories far outside the city and planned to reduce activities in surrounding provinces as well as traffic inside the city during the Games. All construction had to be completed months ahead of time to give the dust time to settle. China's leaders want the world to admire what an advanced country they have created.

As a rising power determined to reassure other countries that it isn't a threat, China has become more self-conscious about its international reputation than any other country in the world. And the Olympic Games are the best chance the nation will have in a long time to shape its image.

Yet even with the eyes of the world upon them, China's leaders have shied away from the political reforms that could have won them more praise than their beautiful facilities. The 1988 Seoul Olympics spurred South Korea's transition from an authoritarian military regime to a civilian democracy. Nothing of the sort has happened in China, however. Its leaders are too afraid of their own people to risk giving them a greater political voice.

At the 17th National Congress of the Chinese Communist Party in October 2007, there was a lot of talk about "democracy" within the Party, but no significant progress toward allowing Party members or mid-level officials to vote for the top posts within the Party as Vietnam, for example, is now doing. The Chinese oligarchy continued its traditional practice of leadership succession behind closed doors. They compromised on a package deal that elevated a number of younger leaders into the top ranks and picked Xi Jinping, the one of them conspicuously *not* associated with current leader Hu Jintao or anyone else, to become number one when Hu steps down five years from now.

Nor has electoral democracy been introduced at lower levels except in villages, which are not units of government. Elections at the next-highest level, the township, have been banned.

During the year preceding the Games, the authorities sought to ensure that there would be no unpleasant political surprises by tightening up restrictions on non-governmental organizations, including religious groups, the media and the Internet.

Despite all their focus on control, China's officials appeared to have been caught by surprise by the March 2008 demonstrations in Tibet and the Tibetan communities of Western China. When Chinese posting on the Internet reacted with outrage against not only the protestors' violent attacks on Chinese shopkeepers in Lhasa but also the feebleness of the government's response, the leaders defended themselves by getting out in front of the upsurge of nationalism. The propaganda authorities deflected people's anger away from the government onto the Tibetan "separatists" and the Western media, which they accused of biased reporting. The Chinese media vilified the Dalai Lama with rhetoric of the sort that hadn't been heard in China since the Cultural Revolution: They called the Tibetan spiritual leader a "wolf in monk's robes," "a devil with a human face but the heart of a beast," and the struggle against him "a life-and-death battle." The Chinese public loved it, but foreigners were repelled by this glimpse of China's nationalistic side, so far from the image of a cosmopolitan and harmonious society that Beijing had hoped to present to the world during the Olympics.

A second pre-Olympic shock occurred in May when an earthquake of 8.0 magnitude jolted Sichuan Province, killing more than 70,000 people and leaving millions homeless. The Chinese government's rapid and well-organized rescue and relief efforts and its willingness to accept international aid won it international approval and sympathy, especially in light of the contrast to the brutal and secretive military regime in Burma that had rejected international aid for its cyclone victims a few weeks earlier. Television images of Premier Wen Jiabao, who had rushed to Sichuan to lead the rescue efforts and encourage the children trapped under the debris, put a human face on the current Chinese leadership's "compassionate communism." The Tibet issue disappeared from the front pages of foreign newspapers and was replaced by praise for the valiant Chinese relief efforts and the unprecedented press openness and social voluntarism that accompanied them.

You can't keep an earthquake secret no matter how much effort you put into controlling the media. Journalists and editors ignored the initial ban from the Propaganda Department and rushed to the scene of the disaster because it was just too big a story for commercial media to ignore. Once the market-oriented media reported the story, the official media like the Xinhua News Service provided more detailed information than ever before. If people can't get accurate and detailed information about a disaster, they may panic and interfere with emergency response. The earthquake forced the government to permit greater transparency than ever before.

In the aftermath of the disaster, a powerful sense of identification with the victims of the earthquake evoked a spontaneous upsurge of voluntarism among ordinary Chinese. People all over the country donated food, tents, clothing, and money and drove to Sichuan in their own cars to deliver the aid and volunteer in the relief efforts. For the first time, people experienced what a genuine Chinese civil society free of government restrictions might feel like.

Will the greater openness imposed by the earthquake on Chinese leaders give them the confidence to allow it to continue after the emergency ends? Or will the bureaucracies responsible for controlling the media and social organizations go back to business as usual? It is too early to know for sure. The Tibet demonstrations and the earthquake strengthened popular identification with the Beijing government but also raised expectations for freer information and civic action that will be hard for the government to deny.

This series of domestic crises on the eve of the Olympics highlights the fragility of China's political fabric, which is the subject of this book. I believe that China's leaders sincerely desire for China to rise peacefully, without provoking conflict with the United States or other countries. On issues like North Korea or India that do not attract much public attention, Chinese foreign policies are increasingly statesmanlike. But the question that troubles me—and that motivated this book—is whether this constructive international stance is sustainable within China where nationalism is intensifying, mass protests are growing, and the availability of information through the Internet and commercial media is expanding. I hope that by better understanding the complex dynamics of China's own domestic politics, decision-makers in the United States and other countries will be able to devise wiser policies, policies that will enable China to act like the responsible power it declares itself to be.

Acknowledgments

I began writing this book as a fellow at the Center for Advanced Studies in the Behavioral Sciences, Stanford, California, during the 2004–05 academic year. I am grateful to the Center staff (especially Kathleen Much), the other fellows, and Don Lamm for encouraging my interest in writing for a broader audience beyond academia. This aspiration became reality thanks to my research assistant, Yu Zheng, my agent, Jill Marsal, of the Djikstra Agency, and my editors at Oxford University Press—Peter Ginna, who edited the manuscript, Tim Bartlett, Dedi Felman, Tim Bent, and the copyeditor, Paula Cooper. The intellectual stimulation and personal support provided by colleagues and staff at the Graduate School of International Relations and Pacific Studies, University of California, San Diego (especially Peter Cowhey, Stephan Haggard, and Barry Naughton), the University of California Institute on Global Conflict and Cooperation, and the U.S. government greatly contributed to the book. I also wish to thank Jeffrey Bader, Tai Ming Cheung, Thomas Christensen, and Andrew Walder for their helpful comments on the manuscript, and to Alastair Iain Johnston for sharing his unpublished research with me. My husband, Sam Popkin, and my children, Lucy Popkin and David Popkin (the newest China hand in the family), provided loving encouragement and good advice every step of the way.

Finally, I am deeply grateful to the many Chinese government officials, military officers, scholars, think-tank experts, journalists, and students I interviewed for informing me and my readers about China's domestic situation and foreign policy.

China
Fragile Superpower

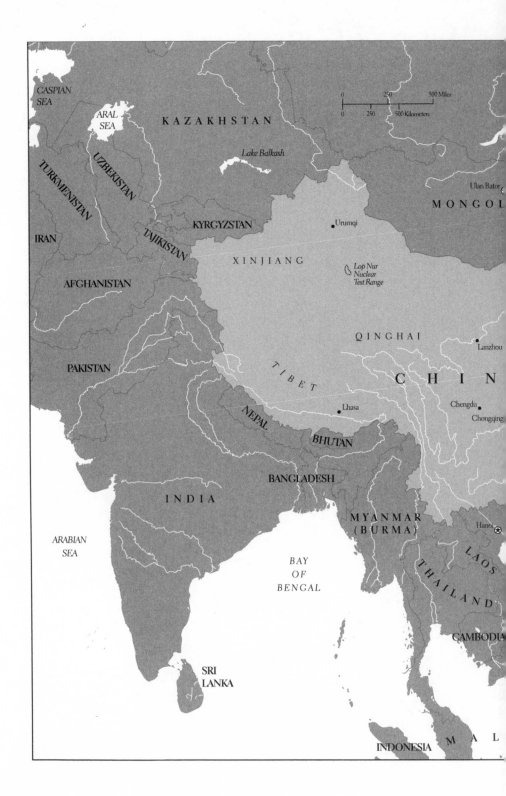

1

Strong Abroad but
Fragile at Home

A S THE DEPUTY ASSISTANT SECRETARY OF STATE responsible for American relations with China in the Clinton administration, I constantly worried about the risk of war between the two nuclear powers. A war between China and the United States is terrifying to contemplate. China's Asian neighbors would be on the front line and people all over the world would feel the shockwaves.

When I left the government and resumed my job as a university professor, these worries continued to haunt me. I can still imagine receiving the dreaded phone call from the State Department Operations Center:

"The Pentagon just informed us that a Chinese SU-27 jet fighter and a Taiwanese F-16 jet fighter have collided in the Taiwan Strait."

My heart sinks. I have heard that the military aircraft patrolling the narrow body of water between the island of Taiwan and the Chinese Mainland fly dangerously close to one another, despite U.S. warnings to the two sides.

"What about the pilots?" I ask. "Have they bailed out? Been rescued?"

"We don't know yet," says the Op Center voice.

"Has either side made a public statement? Or communicated with us? Have we seen any military moves from either side?"

"No information yet, ma'am. But CNN is just reporting it now."

I dash to my car and speed back to the State Department, using the moments of calm before entering the storm of the crisis to make a plan. What should our government do to prevent the accident from triggering a war between China and Taiwan—and very likely drawing in the United States?

I play through the various scenarios, and they all have one common thread. If CNN is broadcasting the news of the crash, it is sure to be picked up and spread by the Internet in China before the Communist Party censors can block it out. And once the news is public, China's leaders will feel compelled by the pressure of public opinion to react forcefully.

A forceful reaction is not beyond the pale. Flashpoints for military clashes between China and the United States have multiplied in recent years. And although most Americans have forgotten, China and the United States came to the brink of war in 1996. The Chinese launched massive military exercises and shot missiles into the waters outside Taiwan's ports to demonstrate their fury at our allowing Taiwan's president to visit the United States for the first time since we derecognized Taiwan and established diplomatic relations with the People's Republic of China in 1979.

Envisioning the scenario as it unfolds, when I reach my office in the State Department, I learn that President Hu Jintao has already appeared on China Central Television:

"My fellow countrymen, earlier today a Taiwan air force plane flew across the midline of the Taiwan Strait, veering into a People's Liberation Army air force jet and causing it to crash into the sea, killing its brave pilot. This flagrant and barbarous act was a deliberate provocation by the Taiwan authorities to provoke antagonism across the Taiwan Strait and undermine the status quo. The Mainland and Taiwan belong to one and the same China."

Following the pattern of previous crises, the Chinese leaders have immediately framed the situation as an intentional attack on China and boxed themselves into a corner. Now how will they prove their determination to defend the national honor against this "deliberate provocation"?

Taiwan is an issue that arouses intense nationalist emotions in China. The Japanese colonized the island from 1895 to 1945 when China was too weak to resist, during a period that the People's Republic of China (PRC) school textbooks describe as China's "century of humiliation." Ever since 1949, when the Chinese civil war ended with a Communist victory and the defeated Guomindang retreated to Taiwan, Chinese schoolchildren have been taught that the century of humiliation would finally end only when Taiwan was reunified with the Mainland.

It is widely believed in China and abroad that if the Communist regime allows Taiwan to declare formal independence without putting up a fight, the outraged public will bring down the regime. China's military and political leaders know full well that the United States, while not legally bound to intervene, has committed morally and politically to help Taiwan defend itself. They also realize that China's booming economy would be the first casualty in any military conflict with Taiwan and the United States. Nevertheless, they would use force to avoid domestic humiliation if they believed their political survival depended on it.

After consulting with the secretary of state, I call the National Security Council staff. We agree that the president should immediately telephone China's president to urge him not to mobilize the military or to make any public threats against Taiwan. Forget about using the Foreign Ministry channel. We have to get straight to China's top leader, who will be feeling the heat domestically as well as internationally. And only our president can reach their president. For our part, we will intercede with the Taiwan government and ask it not to mobilize its military forces and to return the Mainland crew promptly.

It is too late. American intelligence reports that China has mobilized not only its regular military forces but also its internal security forces. Angry Chinese students are swarming into Beijing's Tiananmen Square and the central squares of other Chinese cities, shouting, "Down with the Taiwan separatists!" Some in the crowds carry hastily made signs saying, "Down with the America-loving Chinese Communist Party toadies!" and "When will China finally stand up?"

This scene is hypothetical, but it is not a fantasy. Crises like this have happened in the past and could happen in the future. Taiwan is just a hair short of being a formal ally of the United States. We are not legally obligated to come to its defense. But an American law called the Taiwan Relations Act of 1979 does require the president to view any Chinese use of force against Taiwan as a "threat to the peace and security" of the region and to consult with Congress on how to react. American sympathies—especially those of members of Congress—have always lain much more with the small democratic island of Taiwan than with the communist giant China. The executive branch and the foreign policy community would worry that if U.S. forces fail to stand up to Chinese bullying, American credibility in Asia and the rest of the world would be harmed seriously. The United States has more than seventy thousand soldiers in uniform deployed in Asia in order to defend our allies and deter aggression. If we don't use these soldiers to defend Taiwan, wouldn't other countries view the United States as a paper tiger?

For all these reasons, any president is likely to feel compelled to respond to Chinese military actions in the Taiwan Strait by making a strong military gesture of our own in the hopes that this show of resolve will end the crisis by forcing Beijing to de-escalate just as it did in 1996. But the next crisis could escalate instead if the Chinese leaders believe that caving in to the United States would cause them to be humiliated domestically and put the survival of their regime at risk. Crisis escalation has a life of its own. War can result even if no one wants it to happen.

Taiwan is the most likely flashpoint for a military clash between China and the United States but it is not the only one. Relations between China and America's close ally, Japan, have grown dangerously acrimonious over the past several years. Chinese People's Liberation Navy vessels have begun patrolling in waters in the East China Sea near the Diaoyu Islands, which are claimed by both China and Japan. A maritime incident could spin out of control if Chinese and Japanese politicians feel pushed by hostile public opinion.

China's neighbor and former ally, North Korea, has tested long-range missiles and nuclear weapons. So far negotiations have failed to solve the problem, and international economic sanctions are squeezing the regime. If North Korea collapses violently and sends thousands of refugees fleeing into Northeast China, Beijing might send troops into the country to restore order over the objections of South Korea and the United States.

In a situation like one of these, China's leaders may not be able to manage the domestic pressures that could drive them into an eyeball-to-eyeball confrontation with the United States.

China Rising

China is reemerging as a major power after one hundred and fifty years of being a weak player on the world stage—a brief hiatus in China's long history. For two thousand years, until the late nineteenth century when it was overtaken by the United States, China had the largest economy in the world.[1] Since 1978, by shedding central planning, creating a market economy, and opening to the world, China has revived itself as an economic powerhouse and a world power. The CIA forecasts that by the middle of the twenty-first century, China's economy will once again surpass the United States economy in size, although its per capita income will still be much lower than that in the United States.[2]

History teaches us that rising powers are likely to provoke war. The ancient historian Thucydides identified the fear that a rising Athens inspired in other states as the cause of the Peloponnesian War.[3] In the twentieth century, rising powers Germany and Japan were the cause of two devastating world wars. Are China and America doomed to become enemies in the twenty-first century? Inevitably, as China moves up the economic and technological ladder, it will compete with America and expand its global reach. But a much graver danger is that as China rises in power, the United States will misread and mishandle it, so that we find ourselves embroiled in a hostile relationship with it.

Even if the two sides manage to avoid a shooting war, a cold war with China would wreak havoc in the United States and throughout the world. The two countries have become economically dependent on one another. The United States is China's largest export market (buying approximately 20 percent of its total exports) and China loans most of the dollars it earns from trade to the U.S. government, which uses the money to cover its large budget deficits. If Washington imposed economic sanctions on China and China retaliated by selling off some of the billions of dollars of American government debt it owns, American interest rates would shoot up, our economy would slow to a crawl, and a global recession could result. A hostile relationship with China would also make it impossible for our two countries to work together on the many global issues that affect the people of both countries, such as AIDS, avian flu epidemics, global warming, and terrorism.

Our best chance of avoiding antagonism with China is to open up the black box of Chinese domestic politics, look inside, and figure out what makes China act as it does on the world stage. We find a society drastically changed by economic reforms and opening to the world. China no longer resembles the bleak People's Republic of the Mao Zedong era that was the object of our Cold War fears. The China of today looks more benign and familiar. It is less totalitarian and more capitalist, less monolithic and more diverse, less drab and more colorful, less isolated and more globalized. Yet although the transformations under way inside China give it a greater stake in international peace, they also make it more dangerous as its communist leaders struggle to maintain political control. China's leaders face a troubling paradox. The more developed and prosperous the country becomes, the more insecure and threatened they feel. The PRC today is a brittle, authoritarian regime that fears its own citizens and can only bend so far to accommodate the demands of foreign governments.

A New Economic Rival

China's emergence as an economic superpower requires a difficult adjustment for Americans. As Chinese officials like to remind us, China today is still a developing country. Its annual income per capita is close to the bottom of the international rankings and a small fraction of our own.[4] Yet we feel the hot breath of this economic dragon on our backs. The steady media drumbeat of economic statistics that document China's dramatic growth is making people anxious. Every day news reports remind us that China is the fastest growing economy in the world, which has increased at roughly 10 percent annually for two and a half decades. China has surpassed the United States as the number one destination for foreign investment and the number one exporter of information technology products. China has the largest foreign reserves in the world, over $1 trillion. China is the largest consumer of steel and cement. China is the world's third-largest trading power. China exports over $200 billion more products and services to the United States than it imports from the United States according to U.S. calculations, resulting in America's largest foreign trade deficit.

As American companies move their factories offshore to China and Americans buy more imports from China, hundreds of thousands of workers in our manufacturing industries face losing their jobs. We worry about falling behind technologically as well as economically. Chinese scientists were the first to map the genome for rice, and Chinese engineers are designing new, safer nuclear power reactors and more efficient automobile engines. High-tech companies are establishing research and development facilities in China to take advantage of the brain power found there. The acquisition by a Chinese company of the personal computer unit of IBM, one of America's high-tech crown jewels, caused angst. When a Chinese oil company wanted to buy an American one, the political backlash in Washington quashed the deal. Our dependence on China to finance our huge government debt deepens our unease.

Insecure Leaders

China's growing economic might makes its leaders appear to loom over us like ten-feet-tall giants. But their self-image differs vastly. Dogged by the specters of Mao Zedong and Deng Xiaoping, the revered leaders who preceded them, China's current leaders feel like midgets, struggling desperately to stay on top of a society roiled by economic change.

China is stronger economically and more secure internationally than it has been since the nineteenth century, but paradoxically, its communist leaders have a deep sense of domestic insecurity. China may be an emerging superpower, but it is a fragile one. And it is China's internal fragility, not its economic or military strength, that presents the greatest danger to us. Unless the United States begins to understand the fears that motivate China's leaders, we face the possibility of conflict with it.

Like all politicians, China's leaders are concerned first and foremost with their own political survival. They don't have to stand for election, but they face other political risks that democratic leaders do not have to worry about. A rival leader could try to oust them. A mass protest movement could rise up and overthrow them. If China's leaders were to lose the support of the military, an opposition movement could defeat them. And unlike in a democracy, the price of political defeat to China's leaders could be crushing. Political defeat could cost them and their families their livelihoods or even their lives.

Chinese leaders are haunted by the fear that their days in power are numbered. They watched with foreboding as communist governments in the Soviet Union and Eastern Europe collapsed almost overnight beginning in 1989, the same year in which massive prodemocracy protests in Beijing's Tiananmen Square and more than one hundred other cities nearly toppled communist rule in China. Jiang Zemin, who led China during the 1990s after Tiananmen, and Hu Jintao, the current leader, know that they lack the personal prestige of Mao Zedong and Deng Xiaoping, who founded the People's Republic of China in 1949. They also recognize that two decades of economic reform and opening to the world have transformed Chinese society radically and created latent political challenges to communist rule. During his second inaugural address, President Bush spoke about expanding freedom across the world—and placed every authoritarian regime on notice. China's leaders could not have failed to take this message personally.

The worst nightmare of China's leaders is a national protest movement of discontented groups—unemployed workers, hard-pressed farmers, and students—united against the regime by the shared fervor of nationalism. Chinese history gives them good reason to worry. The two previous dynasties fell to nationalist revolutionary movements. Mass movements that accused leaders of failing to defend the nation against foreign aggression brought down the Qing Dynasty in 1911 and the Republic of China in 1949. No wonder China's current leaders are obsessed with the fear that the People's Republic of China could meet the same fate, and strive to stay ahead of the wave of popular nationalism sweeping the country.

In 1989, the regime was shaken to its roots by nationwide student protests and divisions within the leadership over how to handle them. If the military had refused to obey Deng Xiaoping's command to forcibly impose order or if it had split, the Chinese Communist Party might have followed its Soviet counterpart into the dustbin of history.

After the close call in 1989, China's leaders became fixated on what they call "social stability." They use that euphemism to convince the Chinese public that Communist Party rule is essential for maintaining order and prosperity, and that without it, a country as large as China would descend into civil war and chaos. In their speeches, the leaders make no secret of their anxieties about social unrest.

When Zhu Rongji concluded his term as premier in 2003, his farewell address emphasized social stability and called on officials to "deal correctly with inner conflicts among the people under the new situation, deal appropriately with sudden collective incidents, and work hard to resolve grass-roots conflicts and disputes to nip them in the bud."[5]

An important document issued in September 2004 by the Chinese Communist Party Central Committee openly acknowledged for the first time that Communist Party rule might not last forever in China. "The painful lesson of the loss of power by the communist parties of the Soviet Union and Eastern Europe," it said, is that "it is not easy for a proletarian political party to gain power, and even harder to exercise political power well, especially when it is held for a long time, and a party's status as a party in power does not necessarily last as long as the party does, nor is it something that once achieved is never lost."[6]

In his 2006 annual press conference, current premier Wen Jiabao advised caution in the face of the threats to China's stability. "To think about why danger looms will ensure one's security. To think about why chaos occurs will ensure one's peace. To think about why a country falls will ensure one's survival."[7]

In the face of daily reports about violent protests, Communist Party leaders will never make international considerations a priority. Their number one priority will always be the preservation of Communist Party rule. I learned this lesson in a vivid way a few years ago when I played the role of China's top leader in an unclassified "simulation"—a role-playing game designed to anticipate situations that American policymakers might face in the future. The scenario involved large-scale labor unrest in several regions of China. All of us playacting as Chinese leaders single-mindedly concentrated on calling up the police and military to quell the protests and prevent them from spreading to other groups and regions. We paid no heed at all to the world criticism being broadcast to us on TV sets around the room. Even without specific information about the personalities of individual leaders, it was obvious that the nature of our situation required us to put domestic concerns ahead of international ones. During an internal crisis, keeping the lid on at home is much more important than foreign relations.

A corollary to this general rule is that domestic considerations take precedence over foreign relations during international crises too, as we saw after the U.S. accidental bombing of the Chinese Embassy in Belgrade in 1999 and the collision of a U.S. spy plane and a Chinese fighter jet in 2001, as well as a number of Taiwan- and Japan-related crises.

Preoccupation with domestic politics is not unique to China's leaders. Even in Western democracies like our own, foreign policy is driven as much by domestic considerations as by the opinions of our allies and other foreign countries. What distinguishes China, however, is that the survival of the regime, not just the next election is at stake.

Rising Powers and the Danger of War

Unless we understand the fears that drive China's leaders' international behavior and craft our own policies accordingly, the historical odds predict war, not peace. The most notable exception to the rule that rising powers cause war occurred when the United States surpassed Britain in the late nineteenth century. The two were able to avoid war in large part because they shared the same values and culture, something that cannot be said of democratic America and communist China.

As China grows richer, it builds its military strength. China fits the classical pattern of a rising power described by historian Paul Kennedy. "Wealth is usually needed to underpin military power, and military power is usually needed to acquire and protect wealth."[8]

Since 1989, Chinese defense spending has grown at double-digit annual rates. The pace of military modernization accelerated during the 1990s in response to moves by Taiwan's leaders to establish the island as an independent sovereign country instead of a part of China. Estimates of the size of China's military spending vary widely because much of that spending is off-budget. Estimates range from a high of $80 to 90 billion (Department of Defense and the CIA)[9] to $40 billion (International Institute for Strategic Studies)[10] and $31 to 38 billion (the RAND Corporation).[11] For comparison, the United States spent $518 billion (2004); Russia spent $65 billion; Japan, $43 billion; and the United Kingdom, $38 billion (2003).[12] Chinese military experts claim they will have a modern force capable of defeating Taiwan and countering American intervention by the second half of this decade.

Misperceptions and the Risk of War

Managing the prickly relations between China, the rising newcomer on the world stage, and the United States, the established star, is a daunting challenge. China needs to reassure the United States that it isn't a threat— that it won't challenge America's dominance and is satisfied with a supporting role. And the United States needs to convince China that it is willing to share the limelight and work together as an ensemble. Both countries will have to accommodate each other. Although politicians in major countries like China and the United States understand the strategic necessity for compromise, they are tempted to use foreign threats as a foil to win domestic support as well. Superpowers want strong leaders who stand tall in the world.

Wars are caused by misperceptions—one country interpreting the behavior of another in the most threatening terms—as much as by actual conflicts of interest. The risk of misperceptions between China and the United States is heightened because we live in a unipolar world in which the power gap between the dominant power, the United States, and other countries is the largest it has ever been in world history. The American economy is the size of the economies of Japan, Germany, the United Kingdom, France, and Italy combined. And it is six times the size of the Chinese economy. American military spending is greater than the expenditures of all the other countries in the world combined, and at least six times what China spends.

Before World War II, when a number of powerful countries existed, the addition of one new power did not appear to diminish any other country's position. Today, however, many Americans see the rise of China as a direct threat to our own country's predominance in the world. And China sees the United States as the one power that can block its rise to wealth and influence. How our two countries manage this dangerous historical transition may determine whether the twenty-first century is peaceful or not.

The Two Faces of Chinese Power

The question of whether China is a threat to other countries cannot be answered just by projecting China's abilities—its growth rates, technological advances, or military spending—into the future as many forecasters do. Strength is only one part of the equation. Intentions—how China chooses to use its power—make the difference between peace and war.

The anxieties of China's Communist Party leaders about domestic challenges to their power motivate them to use their power in two very different ways. First, China generally behaves like a cautious, responsible power preoccupied with its own domestic problems and intent on avoiding conflicts that would disrupt economic growth and social stability. Keeping the economy growing by at least 7 percent per year is considered a political imperative to create jobs and prevent the widespread unemployment that could lead to large-scale labor unrest. Chinese businesses and local governments have a stake in keeping foreign trade and investment flowing. By cooperating with its neighbors, China creates a good environment for economic growth and suppresses ethnic and religious unrest in Tibet, Xinjiang, and Inner Mongolia.

Acutely conscious that its rapid rise leads other countries to view it as a threat, China's diplomats have worked hard since the 1990s to build its reputation as a good global citizen and regional neighbor. China has become a staunch supporter of the World Trade Organization and the Nonproliferation Treaty, and it demonstrates its acceptance of the international status quo by participating in many more multilateral organizations than we would expect of a country at its level of development.[13] Seeking to reassure its Asian neighbors about its benign intentions, China has resolved almost all of its border disputes, proffered free trade agreements to Southeast Asia, South Korea, and Japan, and established new forums for regional cooperation. China also has agreed to abide by a code of conduct with the Southeast Asian countries to prevent conflict over the contested territory of the South China Sea, and signed a tripartite agreement with Vietnam and the Philippines to prospect jointly for oil and gas there. Most strikingly, it has stepped forward to mediate the dangerous standoff between the United States and North Korea over North Korea's nuclear weapons program and joined with other United Nations Security Council members to impose economic sanctions on North Korea after it tested a nuclear bomb. All of this cooperative behavior boosts China's international influence and is rooted in the leaders' interest in achieving a peaceful international environment to sustain economic growth and prevent social unrest.

But in a crisis — or when dealing with a well-publicized issue that might become a crisis — China's second, more aggressive persona emerges, with potentially dangerous consequences. This is especially true if the crisis is a hot-button issue involving Japan, Taiwan, or the United States. The Communist Party has embraced nationalism as its new ideology in an age when almost nobody believes in communism anymore. China's new commercial media and the Internet, as they compete for audiences, stimulate nationalism with front-page stories hyping the threats from Japan, Taiwan, and the United States. Whenever the public pays close attention to an issue, leaders feel they have to act tough to show how strong they are. Like Chinese Clark Kents, they abandon their usual mild-mannered international demeanor, and reveal themselves as nationalist superheroes. Throwing caution to the wind, they take risks to defend China's national honor. This more emotionally volatile side of China's split personality — we might call it China's "id" — could drive China into a military confrontation.

In the following pages, I try to make sense of the way China behaves in the world and anticipate how it will behave in the future as it rises in power by looking at its foreign policy inside-out—starting with the fears of China's leaders about their own survival.

Every good diplomat knows that you can never get anywhere until you put yourself in the shoes of the person sitting across the table from you. In this book I put the reader in the shoes of China's leaders as they struggle to manage their domestic political threats while making China into an international power. Only by taking this leap of empathy and understanding the situation China's leaders face, can America and other countries influence China's rise in a peaceful direction.

2

China's Economic Miracle

WHEN I BEGAN STUDYING Chinese as a college student almost forty years ago China seemed as remote as the moon. I had no way of knowing whether I would ever be able to visit there in my lifetime. China was more mysterious and isolated then than North Korea is today. It had no diplomatic, social, or economic contacts with the United States, and almost none with other countries outside the Communist bloc.

But I was lucky in my timing. In 1971, I was one of the first Americans to visit the People's Republic of China (PRC). Our group of fifteen American graduate students toured Chinese cities and countryside for a month as guests of the government. I found a poor totalitarian country that had shut itself off from the world and was still in the throes of the Cultural Revolution, the ideological crusade Mao Zedong had launched in 1966 to shake up the country and revive its revolutionary spirit.

Mao closed the schools and summoned students to become "Red Guards" and make revolution against teachers, school principals, and other professionals who were defined as "bourgeois experts." The campaign turned society upside down. In hospitals, the doctors were forced to clean toilets and the orderlies treated patients. The Red Guards attacked the government and Communist Party officials who were "taking the capitalist road," and fought with one another using weapons stolen from military arsenals. The country was brought to the brink of total anarchy before the People's Liberation Army (PLA) restored order in 1969.

As we crossed the border from Hong Kong into the Chinese Mainland, I was stunned by the contrast between the commercial bustle and stylish skyscrapers of Hong Kong and the drab poverty of the Mainland. Mainlanders had Mao pins, Little Red Books of Mao's quotations, and little else. The tallest buildings in Beijing or Shanghai were about ten stories high. Peeling paint, rusting railings, broken windows, and unkempt parks spoke of poverty and neglect. The only cars on the street were bulky Soviet-era sedans for government officials. The soft sound of bicycle bells was frequently interrupted by political sermons blaring from loud speakers on telephone poles. The only other foreign guests at the Beijing Hotel were Cambodian soldiers there for training. Everywhere our group traveled, we attracted large crowds of curious people.

Shanghai, famous as a cosmopolitan nightspot during the 1920s and '30s, was dim and dreary at night, with no neon signs and few street lights. One evening we crossed the river from the Shanghai waterfront by the only means of transportation available, a small wooden ferry poled by a boatman, to the Pudong district where all we found were rows and rows of dilapidated worker housing.

Workers in steel mills, locomotive factories, and textile mills worked lackadaisically, ignoring the Maoist motivational slogans painted on every wall. Laborers on construction sites leaned on their shovels. Workplace absenteeism was pervasive.

The shelves of state-run department stores were sparsely stocked with uniform-type clothing made of khaki cotton or blue wool. Even in the summer season, fruit and vegetables were in short supply in the state food markets. To buy rice, eggs, meat, a bicycle, or a sewing machine, Chinese shoppers had to hand over ration coupons. As an inveterate shopper, all I could find to bring home were black canvas Mary Jane shoes and a khaki bag with Chinese writing saying "Serve the People."

The summer of 1971 was a turning point in China's stance toward the world. Chairman Mao reached out to the United States to end China's two-decade-long self-imposed isolation. While our group was in Beijing, American national security advisor Henry Kissinger arrived to arrange for President Nixon to visit China. Premier Zhou Enlai invited our group to a discussion in the Great Hall of the People and asked us to bring our tape recorders so he could communicate his explanation for this sudden shift in Chinese foreign policy both inside and outside of the country. I had spent that afternoon with Nancy Tang, the young interpreter for Zhou and Mao. Nancy and I both had grown up in New York—her father was a United Nations diplomat who had returned to China. Nancy must have talked about me to the suave premier, because he mentioned me by name several times. Explaining why the Chinese government had decided to invite President Nixon to China, he said that for the two countries to improve relations, their leaders had to meet. He said he "wished that Susan Shirk was president of the United States," but because Nixon was president, they had to invite him.

Susan Shirk and Premier Zhou Enlai, July 19, 1971.

A Rising Economic Power

The China I visit today looks and sounds like a different planet from the one I visited in 1971. The country has shed its ideological straitjacket, replaced central planning with a market economy, and opened wide to the world. Its glamorous skyscrapers, ubiquitous cell phones, traffic jams, and crowded Starbucks are indistinguishable from those of Seoul, Tokyo, or New York. China has 174 cities whose population is greater than one million people.[1] Even in the smaller cities, the skylines put my hometown of San Diego to shame, and foreigners are a common sight, no longer treated like celebrities. In Shanghai, three bridges and three tunnels, each carrying more than one hundred thousand vehicles a day, now cross the river to Pudong, which has become a financial center with one of the country's two stock exchanges and the highest hotel in the world. Economic progress also has produced some of the worst water and air pollution in the world, daily protests by laid-off workers and other discontented groups, and new class tensions between the poor and the conspicuously consuming rich.

By any measure, China is a power rising in economic strength at a remarkable pace. Since 1978, when Deng Xiaoping introduced reforms to replace Stalinist-style central planning with a market economy and to open the country to foreign trade and investment, China has grown into one of the largest and most dynamic economies in the world. By standard estimates based on current exchange rates, China as of 2005 is the fourth-largest economy.[2] Its GDP of $2.23 trillion has overtaken that of France,

Great Britain, and Italy and is behind only the United States, Japan, and Germany.[3] By estimates using a measure called "purchasing power parity" that adjusts for differences in local prices, China already is the second-largest economy behind the United States.

China has become the manufacturing workshop of the world, just as Great Britain was in the late nineteenth century. The country is the largest producer of steel, with one-third of world production.[4] Its total factory output already is right behind the United States and Japan. Chinese plants—many of them owned by foreign companies—turn out two-thirds of the world's photocopiers, microwave ovens, DVD players, and shoes. Forty percent of the consumer goods Americans buy from abroad are produced in China.[5] If each of us inventoried our clothing, furniture, and household appliances, we'd probably find that many of the items were made in China and that they cost less than what we owned twenty years ago before China started producing them. (I, for one, appreciate that cashmere, once a luxury good, is now affordable for college professors.)

Most remarkably, China has overtaken the United States to become the world's leading exporter of information and communication technology products like mobile telephones, laptop computers, and digital cameras.[6] It also is the largest producer of computer hardware, although it lags behind in software development.[7] Despite difficulties in meeting Western standards, the Zhonghua sedan, produced by automaker Brilliance China, is headed for Europe, and another Chinese automaker, Chery Automobile, has plans to bring a vehicle to the U.S. market.[8] (This trend is reminiscent of the advent of Japanese car imports to the United States in the 1970s.)

As the country that gave the world gunpowder, paper, and the compass, China is reclaiming its heritage of technological inventiveness. Its capabilities still lag behind the United States and Japan, but it is trying to catch up fast. Chinese universities graduated eight hundred thousand scientists and engineers in 2004, approximately twice as many as the United States.[9] Chinese engineers have invented new civilian nuclear reactor designs and other energy innovations.[10] *Wired* magazine dubbed China "the first cloning superpower."[11] Chinese scientists have developed bioengineered crops, and made advances in stem-cell research. China became the third nation to send a man to space when astronaut Yang Liwei went into orbit in 2003. China's research and development expenditures have grown fast (using purchasing power parity measures, $103 billion in 2004, compared with $17.9 billion in 1995) and are approaching those of Japan ($113 billion in 2004), but are still less than one-third of the United States.[12] China was among the top ten countries to submit patent applications for the first time in 2005, but its twenty-five hundred applications are still miniscule compared to the forty-five thousand applications from the United States.[13]

Foreign firms once set up research and development labs in China only if the government insisted they do so as the price of gaining access to the domestic market. But now they don't need any urging to tap into the country's burgeoning technological talent.[14] Every international high-tech communication company has established a research beachhead in China. The total number of foreign-invested R&D centers in the country has grown to seven hundred fifty from two hundred four years ago, according to the Chinese Ministry of Commerce.[15] Western venture capitalists are investing in Chinese biotech and telecom start-ups.

China's dramatic economic transformation has revived it as a regional and world power after over a century of humiliating weakness. As China grows richer, it also is building up its military strength. And as its factories move up the ladder from labor-intensive toys and shoes to technology-intensive computers and automobiles, China and the United States are starting to view one another warily as competitors. But the two economies also are deeply interconnected and interdependent. Economic ties are no guarantee that nations won't fight—for one thing, trade can introduce new bones of contention—but they do give them a stake in trying to resolve their differences peacefully.

Inside China, market reforms and rapid growth have bought the communist regime time. China remains a country with low per capita income. It is more than one hundred years behind developed countries like the United States in economic modernization, according to Chinese estimates.[16] Ma Kai, China's top economic planner, estimated in February 2006 that China still has one hundred million poor people living on less than $1 a day.

But in just twenty-five years, people have experienced a major upgrading of their living standards. According to the World Bank, since 1979, China's reforms have lifted four hundred million people out of poverty (at the $1 per day expenditure level).[17] Over the past fifteen years, according to UNICEF, China has made great strides in reducing malnutrition among children, halving its percentage of underweight children, and reducing the death rate for children under the age of five.[18] Millions of peasants have moved from the countryside to the city, expanding the urban population from 17.9 percent (1978) to 41.8 percent (2004).[19] Over ten million people own private cars and three hundred ninety-three million own cellular telephones.[20] Up until the mid-1990s, China experienced "reform without losers" —everyone became better off. Having experienced such rapid life improvements, Chinese people are now the most optimistic in the world about their futures.[21]

But menacing social problems—the by-products of rapid growth under authoritarian politics—are looming on the horizon. Growing inequality between rich and poor, the collapse of the state-run health-care system, and life-threatening environmental problems are stirring popular discontent and violent protests that could short-circuit economic development.

China's Economic Miracle

"China was one of the poorest countries in the world in the 1950s, its per capita GDP far lower than those of Europe and the United States back in the 1820s when these countries were in the early phase of industrialization," writes economist Hu Angang. Even in 1975, "China's per capita income was one of the lowest in the world."[22] Under Soviet-style central planning, collective agriculture, and isolation from the world economy, the Chinese economy still managed to grow at a respectable 6 percent annually. But because agricultural output didn't grow and population did, Chinese living standards remained stagnant—per capita food consumption was no better in the 1970s than it was in the 1950s.[23] The Great Leap Forward (1958), Mao's lunatic campaign to surpass the West overnight by forcing peasants into huge collective farms, caused the largest famine of the twentieth century anywhere in the world: twenty-five to thirty million people died and another thirty million births were postponed due to malnutrition and shortages.[24]

Mao Zedong died in 1976, and two years later Deng Xiaoping returned to power after twice having been purged by Mao. Deng was comparatively free of the ideological blinders that had warped policymaking in the Mao era. He introduced a set of bold economic changes intended to raise living standards and rebuild social support for the Communist Party after the demoralization caused by the Cultural Revolution.

The attempt to introduce market competition and profit incentives began with agriculture, the occupation of almost 80 percent of the population at the time. The collective farms were broken up into family farms, with the land still formally owned by the collective. The burst of productivity sparked by decollectivization increased food production and spurred change in the rest of the economy. Factories and farms sold whatever they produced above their plan quota and kept the profits. Managers acquired more decision-making power. And employees received bonuses based on the firm's profits. The new incentives boosted productivity.

Opening the Door

Deng Xiaoping also took the courageous step of opening China to the world after decades of self-isolation. Deng explained that "one important reason for China's backwardness after the industrial revolution in Western countries was its closed-door policy," and that opening the door would enable China "to make use of capital from foreign countries and of their advanced technology and experience in business management."[25]

Back in the Ming Dynasty (1368–1644), China had traded extensively over the Silk Road and sea routes. The Qing Dynasty, however, banned maritime trade with foreign countries until China was forced open by European imperialist powers.[26] Under Mao, the PRC walled itself off from the world and fell increasingly behind Europe, the United States, Japan, and even Korea and Taiwan.

But beginning in 1979, Deng Xiaoping opened China to the world again. China rolled out the welcome mat for foreign investors starting with special zones located on the Southern coast in close proximity to ethnic Chinese businesspeople living in Hong Kong, Taiwan, and Southeast Asia. Chinese exports, many of them manufactured in factories partially owned by foreigners, streamed out to world markets. The rigors of international competition raised the quality of Chinese products and made its businesses stronger, so that by the late 1990s China was ready to take the big step of joining the World Trade Organization (WTO) and opening up its domestic markets. China's average tariff rates dropped from 56 percent in 1982 to 11 percent in 2003.[27] The country is now the third-largest importer in the world behind the United States and Germany.[28] Its volume of foreign trade increased twenty-five times between 1978 and 2001.[29] In just twenty-five years, China went from being a closed economy to one that is highly integrated with the international economy. China today embraces globalization because it has benefited from the open global economy more than any other country during the past decades. From China's perspective, globalization is a game it can win.

How Long Can It Last?

Market reform and opening to the world sent China into a steep economic takeoff. The 1982 Chinese government goal of quadrupling the economy by 2002—which sounded ludicrously overambitious at the time—was met two years ahead of schedule. During 1978 to 2004, China's GDP grew at an average annual rate of 9.5 percent (or approximately 10 percent by the latest estimates), and even more remarkable, China's per capita GDP grew at 8 percent per year (population growth slowed as the economy grew).

Per capita growth rates above 6 percent are very rare in economic history. Japan achieved them during 1955 to 1973, and Korea, Taiwan, and Thailand did during 1982 to 1996, before they were stricken by the Asian financial crisis. But no country in world history has sustained such high rates of per capita growth for as long as China has.[30]

How long can the Chinese economic miracle last? Unless ambushed by a political or economic crisis, China is well positioned to keep growing for two more decades.[31] The Chinese economy has already rebounded from two downturns, one after the Tiananmen Square protests (1989) and one after the Asian financial crisis (1998). Unlike Japan, Korea, Taiwan, and Thailand, China has plentiful natural resources and an ample supply of low-cost educated labor. Almost half of its workers are still in agriculture. As wages rise in the coastal cities where most of the foreign-owned and export-oriented factories are located, companies can move a few hundred miles inland to find good workers willing to work for less. In a country slightly larger than the United States, companies can keep this up for a long time. Chinese savings rates—among the highest in the world at approximately 40 percent—may come down and reduce some of the investment that has been pumping into economic growth. But on the other hand, any increases in domestic consumption would stimulate the economy and make it less dependent on world export markets.

Racing the Demographic Clock

China's growth will slow after 2025 as its population ages. Right now, China is blessed with a huge working-age population—70 percent of total population in 2000—that can easily support dependent children and elderly parents.[32] As the number of people over sixty years old multiplies from one hundred twenty-eight million in 2000 to three hundred fifty million in 2030, the demographic shift will put a heavy burden on China's pension and health-care systems unless they are shored up between now and then.[33] In 2065, 54 percent of the population will be over sixty and only 22 percent will be working (unless the government starts providing incentives for people to have larger families or opens up to immigration). Other countries like Japan and Korea have grappled with the strain of an aging population. It will be harder in China, however, because as Barry Naughton observes, "China will grow old before it has had the opportunity to grow rich."[34]

This demographic timetable helps explain why China's leaders declared in 2000[35] that the two decades until 2020 were a "period of strategic opportunity." Twenty more years of rapid growth will quadruple the size of the economy once again, and create a "well-off society" (*xiaokang shehui*) with per capita income of over $3,000 (based on exchange rates), making China an upper-middle-income country according to World Bank standards. Twenty years of growth will enhance China's "comprehensive national power"[36] and its international competitiveness, thereby making China "a world power with an ability to lead."[37] China is within reach of achieving "the dream of 'making the country powerful and the people rich' (*fuqiang*) harbored by generations of Chinese leaders."[38] All today's leaders need to do is avoid any international and domestic disruptions that could trip up their race against the demographic clock.

Rich Country, Strong Army

China's economic miracle has helped turn the People's Liberation Army from a ragtag peasant army into a modern military force. But before that happened, the central government had to muster the funds to invest in a modern military. During the 1980s the central government "played to the provinces"[39]—it won over provincial officials to the reforms by allowing them to keep most of the revenues earned by their local businesses instead of remitting the money to the national treasury in Beijing. The central government was too poor to spend much on fancy military equipment or on other collective goods like roads and railroads. Deng Xiaoping was so confident of the military's support that he deferred its demands for budget increases, promising that defense spending would increase as China became more prosperous. But beginning in the mid-1990s, the central government, worried that it was on the brink of fiscal crisis and national disintegration similar to what had caused the Qing dynasty to collapse, started to rebuild its capabilities. Premier Zhu Rongji strong-armed the provinces into a tax reform in 1994 that brought more revenues into the central coffers. And Beijing began to be able to afford large investments in both defense and civilian projects.[40] Since the beginning of the 1990s, the PLA has enjoyed double-digit increases in its official budget.[41] The technological prowess nurtured in the civilian economy also is enhancing the PLA's military capabilities.

China's economic strength also translates into international political influence. China's "economic whirlpool" attracts not just money and technology, but "influence and appeal in international politics" as well, said *Global Times* (*Huanqiu Shibao*).[42] Big countries that import a lot—like the United States and China—can use their market power to get their way. No country wants to get on the wrong side of its biggest customer. Decisions on big-ticket items like purchases of aircraft, contracts for infrastructure project contracts, and the awarding of licenses for insurance companies and banks can be used to reward friends and punish enemies. Beijing retaliated against Danish companies when Denmark introduced a resolution criticizing Chinese human rights abuses at the United Nations Human Rights Commission in 1997. Internet companies like Cisco, Microsoft, Yahoo, and Google acquiesce to the demands of Chinese censors because they believe they cannot afford to forgo the world's fastest-growing market for Internet services.

Impact on World Markets

China's economic miracle has transformed it from a poor nation sitting by the sidelines into a major player in the global economy. Inevitably, when a huge, rapidly growing country like China becomes integrated into the world economy the reverberations are felt everywhere.

Mao Zedong did the workers of the world a favor by keeping hundreds of millions of Chinese laborers out of the global economy until 1978. Since the reforms began, large numbers of low-wage Chinese workers have flowed into the global labor market, competing with workers in other countries, and putting downward pressure on their wages. (According to economists, however, the size of the dampening effect on wages is less than what people think it is once macroeconomic factors and productivity increases are factored in.[43]) The brunt of competition from Chinese labor is being felt by workers in developing countries, people like the garment workers in Bangladesh and Cambodia who lost their guaranteed share of the American and European markets after January 1, 2005, when the international system of textile and garment quotas ended.[44]

On the demand side, the appetite of China's expanding economy for energy, metals, minerals, and other raw materials drives up prices on world commodity markets. Chinese demand raises costs for other countries that import these commodities, but profits the mostly poor countries that export them.[45] In 2004, China bought large shares of the world output of rubber (14 percent), cotton (15 percent), copper (18 percent), and aluminum (20 percent),[46] as well as many other commodities. When the government cooled off the overheated economy in 2005, China's imports of raw materials slowed somewhat and world prices dropped. Journalist Andrew Browne noted, "A global economy relying on China as a locomotive of growth had better get used to a lurching ride."[47]

Now that it is an automotive society, China has become the world's second-largest petroleum consumer (6.5 million barrels per day in 2004). According to the U.S. Department of Energy, China accounted for 40 percent of the demand growth over the past four years that drove the world price of oil above $60 a barrel.[48] The DOE projects that China's consumption of oil in 2025 will reach 14.2 million barrels per day. [49]

But recall that projections made in the 1970s of Japanese demand for oil were wide of the mark because they didn't anticipate the Japanese improvements in energy conservation.[50] When I met China's number one economic planner, Ma Kai, in February 2006, he explained that the Chinese are getting serious about improving energy efficiency and conservation. Today, Chinese iron and steel plants consume four times the energy U.S. plants use to produce the same amount of output. But the Chinese government is determined to reduce energy intensity (the growth of energy consumption for every unit of economic growth) by 20 percent by 2010.[51] The country's new automobile fuel economy standards are more stringent than American ones.[52] (By 2008 the standards will range from forty-three miles per gallon for the lightest cars to twenty-one miles per gallon for heavier trucks.) China is testing wind power in six hundred localities, Ma Kai said, and is doing research on other renewable energy sources, with the aim of increasing its use of renewables to 10 percent. At present China produces 94 percent of the energy it consumes, according to Ma Kai, and it intends not to let that percentage drop below 90 percent.

"Future demand on oil—especially on imports—will not be very much higher than today . . . we are going to spend a lot more on providing efficiency," the CEO of China National Offshore Oil Corporation said in a February 2006 speech.[53]

Africans and Latin Americans are seeing many Chinese arriving in their capitals these days. Chinese executives are fanning across the globe to seek secure supplies of energy and raw materials. China invests in new oil and gas fields instead of just buying energy on the market because it wants to make sure that the United States or other countries can't shut off its lights if relations sour—the same reason the United States made similar investments in the past. The logic of "oil security" is economically irrational—oil is a unified world market—but politically compelling.[54] The Chinese believe that because the energy supplies in reputable countries have already been claimed by the Americans, Europeans, Japanese, and others, they have no choice but to venture into countries that others have shunned as international outlaws. By wooing countries like Sudan, Venezuela, Iran, and Burma, China undercuts the efforts of Washington and its allies to use boycotts and other economic levers to force these countries to improve their human rights—and thereby creates new frictions in Sino-U.S. relations.

In a 2006 report, the Department of Energy stated that Chinese purchases of international energy assets were "economically neutral" and not damaging to the United States, despite the anxieties of some members of Congress about them. On the positive side, it noted that Chinese investments in developing new fields "may actually enlarge the total global oil supply."[55] China is paying a premium for these assets because current prices of oil and gas and other commodities are high. If prices drop, as they could eventually as a result of a slowdown in demand in China or elsewhere, China would suffer major losses just as Japan did after overpaying for international assets during its boom in the 1970s.

Interdependence

As a large country with an unusually high degree of openness to the world economy—foreign trade is 75 percent of its GDP[56]—China depends on other countries for its domestic prosperity and stability. It is highly vulnerable to shocks from the international economy—or from the political reactions to China's rise. If a backlash against China were to shut it out of key markets like the United States, Europe, or Japan, economic growth would slow and domestic unemployment could rise to dangerous levels. China is the target of more antidumping investigations (that accuse Chinese producers of selling their goods abroad at unfairly low prices) than any other country.[57] Seeking to head off adverse reactions that could disrupt foreign trade and investment, Chinese foreign policy makers take a cautious and accommodating stance toward most countries.

Other countries are, in turn, careful not to trip up China's growth. As Singaporean journalist Janadas Devan observes, "China has become too essential a part of the global economy for any state to contemplate a confrontation with it with equanimity."[58]

Economic interdependence has a moderating effect even on China's difficult relationships with Taiwan and Japan. China is the largest trading partner of both Taiwan and Japan.[59] Taiwanese and Japanese companies have been moving their factories to the Chinese Mainland, and Taiwan and Japan are among the largest sources of foreign investment there.[60] More than one million Taiwan businesspeople now live in the Mainland near their factories. In Taiwan politics, this group has become an important constituency for preserving the status quo in cross-Strait relations—they don't want overly assertive moves toward independence by Taiwan politicians to threaten their investments on the Mainland. And in Japan, business interests came out in opposition to Prime Minister Koizumi's visits to the Yasukuni Shrine, which honors Japanese soldiers including fourteen "Class A" war criminals convicted after World War II. Koizumi's visits to the shrine enraged people in China and South Korea where Japanese occupying forces committed atrocities, and jeopardized Japanese investments and products in China.

In nondemocratic China, however, economic interests have less influence on foreign policy. The private businesses, foreign-funded enterprises, and coastal provinces that are the prime beneficiaries of economic ties with Taiwan and Japan do not have a say in the process. Chinese leaders recognize the value of the economic ties and want to preserve them, but if public anger erupts over Taiwan and Japan, we can't count on economic pragmatism prevailing over the politicians' instincts for political survival and their own nationalist emotions.

Economic Symbiosis with the United States

China's leaders have learned that the relationship with the United States is too important to play politics with it. The symbiosis between the two giant economies gives both governments a strong incentive not to rock the relationship. The United States is China's largest overseas market and the second-largest source of its foreign direct investment on a cumulative basis.[61] America has been the chief sponsor of China's entry into the world economy, most notably in negotiating its accession into the World Trade Organization (WTO) in 2001. Sixty thousand Chinese students are studying on American university campuses.[62] China also has become one of America's main bankers, lending approximately $250 billion of its massive foreign currency reserves to the U.S. government in 2005 by buying its treasury bonds.[63] China has almost as much interest in the durability of a strong U.S. economy as the United States itself.[64] From Beijing's perspective, we are on the same economic team.

Few Americans view the economic relationship in such a rosy light, however. China sells much more to America than America sells to China. The gap between imports and exports has grown to an astounding $201.6 billion according to U.S. statistics for 2005, the largest trade deficit that the United States has ever had with any country.[65] China's currency, the *renminbi* (RMB), was pegged to the U.S. dollar at a fixed exchange rate until July 2005. The exchange rate is still set by the government instead of the market and moves within a very narrow band. Most economists agree that the renminbi presently is undervalued, which aids Chinese exports by making them cheaper. China builds up massive foreign exchange reserves from all the money it earns from its exports and from foreign investments in China—a record over $1 trillion at the end of 2006. Then it uses 70 to 80 percent of this money to buy American treasury bonds and other dollar assets.[66]

Another American complaint is that lax enforcement of intellectual property rights—widespread piracy of medicines, DVDs, CDs, and brand-name products—steals profits from many of America's marquee companies. Beijing passes laws to protect intellectual property but doesn't do enough to enforce them—many local officials are in league with the counterfeiters.

It looks like China is exploiting its economic relationship with the United States to build up its strength while weakening us. Our dependency on China to finance our budget deficit is particularly upsetting to some Americans. As former secretary of the treasury Lawrence Summers says, "There is something odd about the world's greatest power being the world's greatest debtor."[67] How could this superpower find itself in such a humiliating and potentially dangerous position? What would happen if Beijing and Washington found themselves in a crisis over Taiwan or some other issue? Mightn't China send the American economy crashing just by selling some of the U.S. securities it owns?

The United States and China certainly are economically interdependent—each country could damage the other by an economic downturn or a politically motivated action. But the real story behind the trade gap is more complicated than the simple theory that China is willfully and unfairly taking advantage of the United States.

- Most of China's exports to the United States are manufactured as foreign brands by foreign-owned companies in China, using imported components as part of cross-national production chains.[68] China actually pockets only a small part of the gain, most of which goes to the foreign companies and the consumers. According to UBS economist Dong Tao, "A Barbie doll costs $20, but China only gets about 35 cents of that."[69]
- Japan, South Korea, and Taiwan have been transplanting their manufacturing operations to China. Increasing U.S. imports from China are offset by declining shares of imports from Japan, South Korea, and Taiwan.[70] Imports from Asia accounted for 40 percent of total imports in 1998 and 40 percent of total imports in 2004.[71]
- Despite its fixed exchange rate, China's imports and exports with the world were roughly equal for a decade until 2005. (The surplus was $102 billion in 2005 and is estimated to be over $140 billion in 2006.) Even when it has a global trade surplus, however, China buys

more than it sells to its Asian neighbors and to the rest of the world excluding the United States.[72]

- Every country—not just China—runs a trade surplus with the United States. The American consumer and the American government have been spending beyond their means. Countries like China and Japan are the enablers of American profligacy. Only because these countries lend the United States money can the federal government rack up huge budget deficits without raising interest rates that would hurt consumer spending. Low-priced Chinese imports also keep inflation low so that the Federal Reserve Bank doesn't have to raise interest rates. Many analysts consider the relationship not just interdependent but "codependent" because it is unhealthy for both countries.

- China, like other countries, buys American treasury bonds not to humble or to help the United States but because it has to buy foreign exchange to keep the renminbi stable, and U.S. treasury bonds provide the safest returns for foreign exchange holdings. China would harm itself as well as the United States if it precipitously sold off a big chunk of its U.S. bonds—the value of its remaining holdings would plummet.[73]

Chinese officials are growing increasingly nervous about the risk of a protectionist backlash in the United States. They recognize that the trade gap has grown to politically intolerable proportions. Members of Congress have proposed raising tariffs on Chinese imports if China doesn't stop "manipulating" its currency. China's central bankers would like to see China's currency float because it would enable them to manage the macroeconomy without one hand tied behind their backs. They would no longer be forced to risk inflation by accumulating dollar assets to keep the renminbi's value steady and could reinvest what China earns within China instead of abroad. But China's political leaders, fearful of losing exports, slowing growth, increasing unemployment, and risking unrest keep putting off the day of reckoning. China's leaders also worry that their domestic reputations would be harmed if they appeared to be acting under foreign pressure. Although international economists believe that the Chinese currency is undervalued, they are divided about whether a change in the exchange rate would do much to reduce the U.S.-China trade gap, which is driven mostly by the fact that "China has become a leading location for the assembly of a broad range of manufactured goods, most of which previously were assembled elsewhere in Asia."[74]

China's leaders have tried to accommodate U.S. interests as best they could without throwing their own economy into a tailspin. And they keep trying to convince Americans that "a stable, prosperous, and strong China, rather than a turbulent, poor, and weak China, is more in line with U.S. interests."[75] Preserving access to their largest export market and maintaining U.S. support for China's economic development are crucial for sustaining China's growth and the Communist Party's political survival. American political reactions, however, are just one of the several huge risks looming over China's future.

Bank Insolvency

China's shaky banking system is often singled out as the country's biggest economic risk. The balance sheets of Chinese banks are weighed down by massive amounts of "nonperforming loans" that the bank will never collect because the enterprise that borrowed the money—typically a state-owned factory with good political connections—makes no profits or has gone out of business. Theoretically, if private bank customers wake up one day to the fact that their savings are not recoverable and rush in a panic to draw their money out of their accounts, the government as well as the banks could collapse.

The risk of bank insolvency has abated somewhat in recent years, however. The government reorganized the banks so they are somewhat less responsive to the pressure from local politicians to make loans to their cronies. And it has poured more than $260 billion into the banks since 1998 to improve their balance sheets. In 2005, nonperforming loans fell to 8.8 percent of total loans, down by half since the end of 2003.[76] The most hopeful sign is that the Chinese government now permits foreign banks to become part owners of Chinese banks, and they are lining up to buy in. The Bank of America's purchase of 9 percent of one of China's biggest state banks, the China Construction Bank, and its commitment to modernize the bank's loan practices and to share its risks, reduces the likelihood of bank failures in China. The Royal Bank of Scotland, Merrill Lynch, Hong Kong–Shanghai Bank Company (HSBC) Holdings, and Goldman Sachs also have invested billions of dollars buying stakes in Chinese banks in the expectation that their expertise will turn the banks into profitable enterprises.

Political Risks

The greatest risks to the Chinese economy, however, are more political than economic. The biggest question hanging over China is its political stability. As journalist Keith Bradsher observes, "Prosperity in China now has coincided with nearly three decades of the greatest social and political stability that China has seen in more than a century."[77] How long can it last?

Employment

Chinese Communist Party leaders are acutely aware that they are losing their grip on Chinese society as it is roiled by industrialization and urbanization of epoch-making proportions. In the past, a person's destiny depended on where he or she happened to be born, city or countryside. Strict household registration rules locked people permanently into their place of origin. The children of farming families—except for the few who made it to university or the army—were stuck in the countryside forever. Nowadays, however, tens of millions of Chinese are on the move in a historic exodus from countryside to city. Of the five hundred million rural labor force only one hundred million still work as farmers. Forty million farmers have lost their land to rural industrialization.[78] One hundred thirty million rural dwellers—the equivalent of one-half of the American population—have migrated to cities to find work and now constitute the main industrial workforce.[79] China's urban population has grown from 20 percent to 40 percent of the total and Chinese planners anticipate it growing to 55 to 60 percent by 2020.[80]

Within cities, the "iron rice bowl" of permanent employment in state enterprises has been shattered. Previously, the government assigned people to jobs that they held until retirement whether they liked them or not. Workers lived together in factory housing under the watchful eye of Party members. Today people find their own jobs, and four-fifths of them own their own apartments.[81] Three-quarters of urban employees work outside the state sector in private, collective, or foreign businesses where political controls are minimal.[82]

Beginning in the mid-1990s, the government stopped propping up many of the state factories that couldn't withstand market competition and let them go out of business. As the factories closed their doors, they spilled 65 million unemployed workers out on the street (1995–2001) and sparked widespread labor unrest.[83] China's official unemployment rate in 2004 was 4.2 percent.[84] But actual unemployment is much higher, reaching double-digit levels in some heavy industrial cities in the northeastern rust belt (the region historically known as Manchuria).[85] Millions more new workers enter the workforce every year searching for jobs. In 2006 the job-seeking public includes 4 million college graduates, 2.7 million graduates from vocational schools, 2.1 million graduates of secondary schools, 700,000 ex-soldiers, 2.6 million rural-urban migrants, 1 million laid-off workers, and 8.4 million urban unemployed.[86] Job creation is a political imperative. Former vice president of the CCP Party School Zheng Bijian projected that from 2006 to 2015 twenty-four million new jobs will have to be created in the cities each year. "The employment pressure will be tremendous," he said. "China's GDP must grow at a rate no slower than 7 percent annually if only to meet job creation needs."[87]

Particularly worrisome from the standpoint of political stability is the new phenomenon of unemployed college graduates. These are the individuals who would be capable of organizing and leading opposition movements. College enrollments have increased severalfold—from less than 1 million in 1978 to 11 million in 2003[88]—and many graduates are unable to find acceptable jobs. At several new privately operated colleges, students have demonstrated in large numbers when they discovered that their diplomas would have less value than school authorities had promised.[89] Increasing proportions of the hundreds of thousands of students who studied abroad are starting to return to China.[90] Although this trend is an encouraging sign that China's best and brightest have confidence in their country's future, it also makes for a tighter market for highly educated labor. The Ministry of Education expected that 25 percent of the 3.38 million students who graduated in 2005 would be unable to find jobs.[91]

Inequality

Chinese Communist Party leaders worry that growing inequality—the Chinese call it "polarization"—could provoke massive unrest or even an anti-CCP revolution. Premier Wen Jiabao, in his 2006 Lunar New Year address promised to "pay attention to maintaining social equality" and give priority to "issues concerning the immediate interests of the people."[92]

The gap between rich and poor has widened during the reform era: the richest 10 percent hold 45 percent of the country's wealth, and the poorest 10 percent have only 1.4 percent.[93] The per capita income of urban residents is now 3.23 times that of rural dwellers compared to 2.57 that of rural dwellers back in 1985.[94] The annual growth rate of urban incomes (8–9 percent) is almost twice that of rural incomes (4–5 percent).[95]

China's Gini coefficient, the internationally accepted measure of a country's income inequality (0 corresponds to complete equality and 1 to a single person having all the income), is somewhere between .46 and .49 and approaching .50 according to various Chinese official sources.[96] The Chinese define the danger line as a Gini coefficient of .40 and say that

China crossed it in 1994.[97] By comparison, according to the most recent World Bank statistics, the U.S. Gini is .41, the United Kingdom's is .36, and Germany's is .28.[98]

Premier Wen and President Hu spend much of their time traveling to China's poorer regions in the Northeast and inland provinces to show their solicitousness for the country's have-nots. The wide disparities between the affluent coastal areas and the poor interior could threaten national unity. People in China's richest areas (Shanghai, Beijing, Zhejiang province, Guangdong province, and Fujian province) make twice as much as residents of the five poorest areas.[99] Ma Kai, China's top economic planner, speaking to the 2004 meeting of China's legislature, said, "The widening wealth gap caused as cities and coastal areas race ahead of the hinterland could spark social unrest and undermine the government's authority over the country's 1.3 billion people."[100] The narrowing of economic gaps and the building of a "harmonious society" are the themes of the Hu-Wen administration as articulated in the new national five-year plan unveiled at the October 2005 Central Committee meeting.

The most politically explosive kinds of inequalities actually are the ones people can see with their own eyes, namely the extreme contrast between the lavish lifestyles of the rich and the hardships of the poor evident in every Chinese city. The official newspaper of the Communist Party, *People's Daily (Renmin Ribao)*, reports that according to an opinion survey 70 percent of people think that "the great disparity between the rich and the poor" has adversely affected social stability. It notes that people are most outraged about wealth illegitimately acquired by corrupt officials in "power-for-money transactions."[101]

Chinese researchers, at the request of Party leaders, have been studying the negative lessons of Latin American countries like Brazil and Argentina that suffer from social turmoil and economic stagnation due to the tremendous gap between the rich and the poor.[102] The populism espoused by the Hu-Wen team—its special attention to improving income distribution and addressing the needs of the poor—is designed to avoid this fate.

Corruption

It looks to many people in China as though fortunes are made not through hard work and ingenuity, but through official corruption. Wealth and political power are closely intertwined because the government still plays such an important role in economic life. According to the international surveys of the organization Transparency International, China is in the middle rankings of corruption.[103] But inside China, the perception that corruption is endemic even among the ranks of top leaders reinforces political cynicism and erodes popular support for Communist Party rule.

The prevalence of corruption also makes it harder to keep the Party leadership united. With almost every leader vulnerable to charges of corruption—even if he is clean, his relatives and associates may not be—accusations of corruption have become a useful weapon in the contest for power. High-level cases of corruption attract intense interest from the commercial media and the public. In spring 2006, the vice-mayor of Beijing in charge of all the construction projects for the 2008 Olympics was arrested on charges of massive corruption. The vice-head of the Chinese Navy, turned in by his mistress, was sacked for "economic crimes." In autumn 2006, a major corruption scandal related to Shanghai's pension funds resulted in the firing of Chen Liangyu, Shanghai Communist Party secretary and Politburo member, along with several other high-level officials.

Immorality has spread into academic life as well, as reflected in several high-profile cases of plagiarism and falsification of research results, such as the case of a researcher at Shanghai Jiaotong University who had been celebrated as a national hero for inventing a homegrown digital computer chip that turned out to be copied from a foreign model.

President Hu Jintao is portraying himself as a white knight determined to fight official corruption and clean up political life. He has described corruption as "rampant" and has vowed to wipe it out.[104] The Chinese media highlights the statistics—1932 officials convicted for corruption in 2005, including six at the minister level—to demonstrate how seriously the Communist Party is taking the problem. Chinese observers speculated that since many of the targets of investigation in 2006 were individuals with some connection to former president Jiang Zemin, the cases were prompted by current president Hu Jintao's desire to consolidate his authority in the lead-up to the political reshuffling that will occur during the Seventeenth CCP Congress in fall 2007.

Social Goods

Shortly after President Hu Jintao and Premier Wen Jiabao entered office in 2002, China was stricken by the SARS epidemic, which made frighteningly clear that the country's health-care system was in crisis. In the rush to grow the economy, the government since 1978 had neglected social goods like health care, education, and environmental protection. Government investment had concentrated on expanding industry and creating jobs instead. As one Chinese critic said, "We are just paying for jobs with tax revenues and bank credit. That is the price we pay to keep our society stable."[105] Meanwhile, little was spent on social infrastructure like health care, education, and environmental preservation.

The decollectivization of agriculture eliminated the simple clinics and "barefoot doctors" that had once provided basic health care, and left nothing in their place. Doctors and hospitals started charging more for treatment and turning patients away if they lacked the money to pay. This socialist county now has one of the most privatized health-care systems in the world. The minister of health admits that the public health system is "not sound" and that China is "unable to effectively control the spread of possible major epidemics."[106] One measure of the problem is that infant mortality has declined at a slower rate since 1990 than in India or middle-income countries despite the much slower increase in income in these nations.[107]

National spending for education, 3.28 percent of GDP (2003), is well below the 4.1 percent that is the average for developing countries, and many rural poor cannot afford the high-school fees.[108] Although China's primary-school enrollments and literacy rates are higher than the average of developing nations, the country still has eighty-five million illiterate people, most of them concentrated in the rural inland provinces.[109]

For two decades, the government treated environmental protection as a distraction from economic growth, a luxury that China could not afford until it was richer. Breakneck industrialization produced some of the worst air and water pollution in the world. According to environmental officials, acid rain is falling on one-third of the country, half of the water in its seven largest rivers is "completely useless," a quarter of China's citizens lack access to clean drinking water, one-third of the urban population is breathing polluted air, and less than a fifth of the rubbish in cities is treated and processed in an environmentally sustainable way.[110] More than 70 percent of the rivers and lakes are polluted, and ground water in 90 percent of the cities is tainted.[111]

In many Chinese cities, the air is so dirty due to the pollution from coal burning factories, charcoal stoves, and automobiles that you can't see the other side of the street. Anyone who has tried to breathe the thick, smoggy air in Beijing has to doubt whether city officials will succeed in cleaning up air pollution before the Olympic athletes arrive in 2008.

Sixteen of the twenty world cities with the worst air pollution are in China, including Beijing. Tests of the air quality of three hundred Chinese cities found that almost two-thirds fail to meet the standards set by the World Health Organization for acceptable levels of the fine particulates in the air that are the primary culprits in respiratory and pulmonary disease.[112]

The central government passes environmental laws and issues regulations, but local officials, whose promotions depend on growth rates and job creation, simply ignore them. Recent protests, however, by rural citizens outraged that chemical factories are tainting their rivers, ruining their crops, and making their families ill, have gotten the full attention of national leaders.[113] A massive chemical disaster occurred in Northeast China in 2005 when government officials waited ten days to tell the public that a factory had spilled over one hundred tons of benzene into the Songhua River causing more than ten million people living in the vicinity of the city of Harbin to lose their water for more than one week. Environmental catastrophes have the potential to produce major political upheavals—they anger a large number of people about the same issue at the same time. Even if political opposition does not materialize, continued environmental devastation and its related health effects could slow China's future economic progress.

China Needs the World

China's economic miracle has turned it into an economic super power in record time. Because its economy is enmeshed in a dense web of international production chains and financial flows, the Chinese government by and large tries to maintain good relations with its economic partners. Rapid growth under authoritarian conditions has produced a slew of daunting domestic problems. The government seeks to avoid any international conflicts that could throw its economy off course and threaten Communist Party rule.

Interdependence breeds caution, but it doesn't guarantee peace. China is having a hard time convincing Americans not to treat its economic rise as a national security threat. Chinese officials insist, as CNOOC chairman Fu Chengyu said, "China's goal is not to overturn the world order but instead to participate in this world order, and to reinforce it and even profit from it."[114] As a slogan on Chinese billboards says, "China needs the world, and the world needs China." Will Americans agree?

3

Domestic Threats

To understand the anxieties of China's leaders, it helps to remember that in 1989 the Communist dynasty almost ended in its fortieth year. For more than six weeks, millions of students demonstrated for democracy in Beijing's Tiananmen Square and 132 other cities in every Chinese province.[1] The Communist Party leadership split over how to deal with the demonstrations. And the People's Republic just barely survived.

At the center of the drama was Zhao Ziyang, the architect of China's post-1978 economic reforms and the general secretary of the Communist Party at the time. Zhao was the son of a landowner who had been killed by the Communists during land reform in the 1940s. As the leader of Sichuan Province in the 1970s he had sought to alleviate rural poverty by allowing peasants to break down large-scale agricultural collectives into small group or even family farming, experiments that later became the model for the nationwide reforms. The grateful peasants of Sichuan made up a punning rhyme: "Yao chi liang, zhao Ziyang" (If you want to eat, look for Ziyang). This thoughtful, low-key leader was the antithesis of Mao Zedong's rabble-rousing style. He had navigated the reforms through the communist bureaucracy by hammering out compromises among the vested interests, not by charisma. Still, the conservative wing of the Party had been trying to convince preeminent leader Deng Xiaoping to oust him for more than a year. The sudden death of Zhao's predecessor, Hu Yaobang, a popular leader with a reputation as a reform advocate who two years earlier had been forced from office by the conservatives, galvanized thousands of Beijing college students to march to Tiananmen Square, carrying memorial wreaths and chanting "Down with dictatorship!" and "Long live democracy and science!"

Zhao Ziyang recommended taking a gentle approach to the students by holding dialogues to persuade them that the CCP was serious about eliminating corruption and expanding democracy. But when he left town for a long-planned foreign trip, his rival Premier Li Peng engineered a Politburo meeting followed by an informal meeting with retired Party leaders in Deng Xiaoping's living room to muster support for a tough approach. In Zhao's absence, the other leaders including Deng decided to characterize the protests in an editorial in the *People's Daily* (*Renmin Ribao*) as "a well-planned plot . . . to confuse the people and throw the country into turmoil."[2]

When Zhao returned to Beijing, he sought to protect the students— and his own political skin—by proposing to meet their demands "through democracy and law." Hearing mixed signals from the leadership, students, joined now by urban residents, were emboldened to keep demonstrating. The students started a hunger strike in Tiananmen, and Beijing citizens flocked to the square to show their support. *People's Daily* journalists, for the first time ever, ignored the censors and reported what was actually happening.

The Politburo Standing Committee split on a motion to declare martial law and call in the People's Liberation Army (PLA). But another rump meeting in Deng Xiaoping's living room—Zhao didn't attend—overruled that decision, summoned the military, and blamed the "turmoil" on Zhao and on some ill-defined conspiracy backed by "hostile foreign forces." On the brink of political oblivion, Zhao went to Tiananmen in the middle of the night to apologize to the students and plead with them to end their hunger strike. "We have come too late," he said tearfully. A few days later Zhao Ziyang was fired, replaced by Shanghai Communist Party secretary Jiang Zemin, and put under house arrest.[3]

As the Chinese troops entered the city, Beijing citizens from all walks of life blocked their progress by surrounding the military vehicles. Grandmothers scolded young soldiers as "bad boys."[4] Protestors throughout the country demonstrated against martial law, Li Peng, and even Deng Xiaoping himself. Eight retired generals wrote a letter to Deng Xiaoping asking him to pull out the troops and lift martial law. The PLA sent an open letter to the public supporting the protestors' demands to "punish official profiteering, oppose corruption, and promote the construction of socialist democracy and rule of law."[5] Despite foreign speculation about mutinying troops and armed clashes among military units, in the end only one senior army commander refused to obey Deng Xiaoping's orders to forcibly disperse the protestors. (Deng had called up units from all over the country to make sure the entire military stood behind the action.) The PLA tanks rolled into the center of Beijing and killed hundreds, or possibly thousands, of students, supporters, and bystanders on the night of June 4, 1989. Crackdowns followed in other cities.

Statue of Goddess of Democracy (modeled after the Statue of Liberty in New York Harbor) towers above prodemocracy demonstrators in Tiananmen Square, May 30, 1989. (Toshio Sakai/AFP/Getty Images)

For Zhao Ziyang and the students, Tiananmen was a personal tragedy. For the Communist Party leaders it was "a life-and-death turning point for the future of our Party and state."[6] The People's Republic was almost uprooted by the split in the leadership and massive nationwide protests, and remained standing only because the People's Liberation Army stayed loyal.

From that day onward, Chinese leaders have lived with the fear that another Tiananmen might bring down the Communist dynasty. The leaders themselves never talk publicly about Tiananmen or allow the media to mention it. The CCP keeps under close supervision the mothers of the victims who have tried to organize a campaign for their children's vindication. When Zhao Ziyang died in 2005, the current leaders revealed their persistent insecurity by suppressing news of the event and restricting the funeral to a small private gathering.

The Lessons of Tiananmen

The trauma of Tiananmen left China's communist leaders hanging by a tenuous thread. Just months after the crackdown, the Berlin Wall was torn down, a popular uprising overthrew the Romanian communist dictator Nicolai Ceausescu, and communist regimes in Poland, Czechoslovakia, Hungary, and Bulgaria were toppled in rapid succession. The Soviet Union itself, the strongest communist power the world had ever seen, collapsed in 1991. Would China be next? Deng Xiaoping urged his panicked successors to remain calm and not overreact, but the anxiety surrounding the leadership compound of Zhongnanhai was palpable.

In Tiananmen's aftermath, Deng Xiaoping did a postmortem. "Of all China's problems, the one that trumps everything is the need for stability. We have to jump on anything that might bring instability. . . . And we can't care what foreigners say. . . . We will use severe measures to stamp out the first signs of turmoil as soon as they appear. This will show that we won't put up with foreign interference and will protect our national sovereignty."[7]

Deng's successors have worried obsessively that they might meet the same fate as their Soviet and Eastern European comrades. During 2005, Hu Jintao told universities and think-tanks to update the political lessons of Tiananmen by analyzing the "color revolutions" that brought down authoritarian regimes in countries like Serbia (2000), Georgia (2003), Ukraine (2004), and Kyrgyzstan (2005). ("Color revolutions" are so named for the nonviolent revolutions taking a color or flower as their symbol that have toppled authoritarian regimes in the post-Communist societies of Eastern Europe and Central Asia.) In the lead-up to the 2008 Beijing Olympics, the leaders must be worrying that Chinese students might exploit the opportunity to launch large-scale protests just as students did before the 1968 games in Mexico City and the 1988 games in Seoul.

As Deng advised, the Chinese Communist Party today puts political stability ahead of everything else. And although never publicly articulating it, the Party has come up with a formula for stability:

- Avoid public leadership splits
- Prevent large-scale social unrest
- Keep the military on the side of the Party

The three dicta are interconnected. If the leadership group remains cohesive despite the competition that inevitably arises within it, then the Communist Party and the security police can keep social unrest from spreading out of control and the regime will survive. Unless people receive some signal of "permission" from the top, protests are likely to fizzle out before they grow politically threatening. But if the divisions among the top leaders come into the open as they did in 1989, people will take to the streets with little fear of punishment.[8] And if the military splits too, or abandons the incumbent leaders, the entire regime could collapse. In all three dimensions, China's current leaders have reason to be worried.

Lesson 1: Avoid Public Leadership Splits

Inside the black box

Understanding how Chinese politics work involves a lot of guesswork. To maintain their façade of unanimity, the Chinese Communist Party and the government keep their internal deliberations secret. They allow their own citizens to see only dimly into the black box. It was big news recently when the Chinese media were permitted to report that the CCP Politburo held a meeting and what topics it discussed.[9] No Mainland newspaper or Web site dares publish leaks about what was actually said at the meetings. When Shi Tao, a Chinese journalist, e-mailed abroad the instructions from the Propaganda Department discussed at a meeting of his newspaper, he was sent to jail for ten years for leaking state secrets.[10] Zhao Yan, a Chinese employee of the Shanghai bureau of the *New York Times* accused of leaking state secrets because he obtained information from anonymous sources that Jiang Zemin planned to retire from his post as head of the Central Military Commission in September 2004, was held without trial for two years and then convicted of fraud and sentenced to three years of jail time.[11]

China's top leaders are the nine members of the Standing Committee of the Politburo of the Chinese Communist Party.[12] The number one leader, Hu Jintao, like Jiang Zemin before him, actually wears three hats—general secretary of the CCP, president of China, and chairman of the Central Military Commission—but the Party position is the real source of his power.

The Communist Party runs the country like a vast political machine, with the general secretary as Party boss. Although the Party delegates to the government much of the work of making and implementing policy, the Party appoints and promotes all government officials and military officers, almost all of whom are Party members. Control over personnel appointments creates patronage that Party officials extend to subordinates in exchange for their loyalty.

Playing to the selectorate

Communist Party leaders like Jiang and Hu don't have to stand for popular election, but neither are they absolute dictators. They have to win the support of the "selectorate," the group of people within the Party who have effective power to choose the leaders.[13] The Chinese selectorate, according to the Party constitution, consists of the CCP Central Committee, a body of approximately two hundred officials that meets twice a year and is in turn chosen by the two-thousand-member Party Congress that meets every five years. The membership of the Central Committee consists of central government and Party officials, provincial officials, and military officers who have been appointed to their jobs by the top leaders. The Central Committee, in turn, elects the top leaders—namely the Politburo, the Politburo Standing Committee, and the general secretary. (The election is by secret ballot with nominations made by the incumbent leaders.) The lines of authority between the leaders and the Central Committee go both ways, in a relationship I call "reciprocal accountability."[14] The officials who are members of the Central Committee are accountable to the Party leaders who appoint them. But at the same time the Party leaders are accountable to the officials in the Central Committee who elect them. Although top-down power is greater than bottom-up power, power flows in both directions, much like the relationship between the pope and the College of Cardinals in the Catholic Church.

How does a leader win and keep the support of the selectorate? Factional allegiances built by patronage are part of the equation. But nowadays factional loyalties are more fluid than in the past. Officials cultivate ties with a number of higher-ups instead of committing to one. Hu Jintao is a good example. He was a protégé of both Deng Xiaoping and the conservative Party elder, Song Ping.

Figure 3.1 China's Central Government Organization Chart

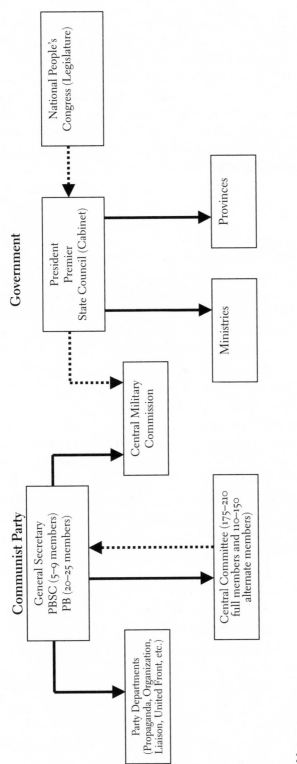

Note:
Strong Authority
Weaker Authority

PB: Political Bureau
PBSC: Political Bureau Standing Committee

As Chinese society has modernized and diversified, bureaucratic and regional interests increasingly have come into play in the political process.[15] Membership in the Central Committee is now determined by job-slot, so that every central department is represented and almost every province has two representatives. The People's Liberation Army (PLA) constitutes one of the largest blocs in the Central Committee. Government departments and provinces compete actively with one another for policies that will help them grow their economies. Party leaders play to the provinces and to departmental interests as a way of building support for themselves.[16]

The control cartel

Certain departments have disproportionate clout within the Communist Party because they are the linchpins of its control over society: the CCP Organization Department (controls personnel appointments), the CCP Propaganda Department (controls content of the media and culture), and the Ministries of State Security and Public Security (the internal police). Along with the People's Liberation Army and the People's Armed Police, the paramilitary internal security force spun off from the PLA, they constitute a "control cartel" with exceptional political independence and leverage over the top leaders.[17] A Chinese journalist said, "The CCP has two powers, the gun and the pen, and it must control both."

The propaganda apparatus has always been the preserve of the most ideologically conservative elements in the CCP. Propaganda officials are so powerful they can veto their bosses from taking public positions they disagree with. They blocked Mao (in 1966) and Deng (in 1992) from publishing their ideas (in Mao's case, the article was written by a close associate) in People's Daily and forced the leaders to find outlets outside Beijing instead. As a member of the U.S. team negotiating with China its accession to the World Trade Organization in 1999, I observed firsthand the power of propaganda officials to interdict the access of foreign movies and television shows to Chinese audiences even though other sectors were opening up. Under Hu Jintao, the propaganda cops have intensified their control over the mass media and the Internet.

The control cartel generally takes a tough line on Japan, Taiwan, and the United States. According to one Chinese participant, in 2001 when an American spy plane and a Chinese fighter jet collided off the coast of the Chinese island of Hainan and the PLA forced the American crew down and held them on the island, it was the security officials and the military who argued for holding the crew and trying them in Chinese courts instead of releasing them.

Weak voices for international cooperation

The Chinese system lacks effective checks and balances to keep its leaders from lashing out internationally to bolster themselves domestically. During 2002 through 2004 I interviewed officials and journalists in some of China's most globalized regions, Guangdong, Shanghai, and Shandong, searching for signs that provinces play as active a role in making foreign policy as they do in economic policymaking. The interests of provincial officials, as one Guangzhou journalist put it, "center on economic growth to get tax revenue, create jobs, and keep stability." Whenever domestic unrest or international tension makes foreign investors uneasy, local officials invite them for tea and try to reassure them. Yet, except for narrowly framed issues, like making it easier for Guangdong businesspeople to travel back and forth to Hong Kong, provinces never get into the act of making foreign policy. Nor do they necessarily favor a softer line. An informal poll of provincial officials enrolled in a short-term course at the Central Party School in 2001 found that they expressed surprisingly hard-line views on relations with Japan and the United States. (One possible explanation was offered by a scholar who said that the local officials "free ride on hard-line nationalism" because it helps them get promoted but is "completely disconnected from their local economic interests.") Given the clout of provincial officials in domestic policymaking, it will be important to track how their foreign policy preferences and influence evolve as their local economies become increasingly tied into global trade and investment.

Private business is the other group that has a strong stake in maintaining international economic ties and avoiding military conflict. A senior official responsible for Taiwan policy told me that a group of private business executives met with him and urged him to start a dialogue with Taiwan because their businesses were being held back by the uncertainty in the Strait. But private entrepreneurs do not yet have an institutional political voice. Jiang Zemin made a big push to allow private business people to join the Communist Party—changing the social base of the CCP would have broad ramifications for both domestic and foreign policy. But so far, only one private businessperson serves as an alternate member of the CCP Central Committee. A retired PLA general confided to me that he worries about the lack of a political counterweight to the nationalist public, military, and intelligence agencies that might push China's leaders into military action.

Making foreign policy

Foreign policymaking is more centralized and hidden from view than the making of domestic policy. Unlike domestic policy, which produces clear winners and losers, foreign policy doesn't matter as much to particular interest groups. The routine foreign policy decisions that receive little media publicity are made by the professionals in the Foreign Ministry who, like diplomats everywhere, seek to improve relations with other countries. But the politicians in the Standing Committee of the Politburo take charge of policies toward the United States, Japan, and Taiwan because they consider them "sensitive." In other words, they are domestic hot-button issues to which the public pays a lot of attention.

Under Jiang Zemin, two high-level interagency groups of ministers similar to the U.S. National Security Council—the Foreign Affairs Leading Small Group and the Taiwan Affairs Leading Small Group—became the locus for decision making.[18] Hu Jintao continues this practice, leading and regularly meeting with both groups. Since the late 1990s, some policy advisors have been trying to create a U.S.-style National Security Council that could act more promptly in a crisis, but the leaders in the Politburo Standing Committee refuse to delegate their authority over sensitive issues.

Public opinion carries much more weight than it did in the past. Any sign of popular disaffection that could imperil stability will count against the current leaders and raise the risk of leadership splits. Traditionally, the leaders got their information about public views from an elaborate system of internal intelligence gathering through bureaucratic channels, which, not surprisingly, usually told officials what they wanted to hear and therefore didn't entirely believe.

In recent years senior officials have put more credence in the information they gather by monitoring the Internet and the market-oriented mass media. Of course, the people who post opinions on the Internet usually have more extreme attitudes than those who sit safely on the sidelines. And tabloid journalism sensationalizes to excite audiences. These biases are not necessarily a problem for the Party leaders, however. Democracies pay attention to the average voters who determine the outcome of elections. But autocracies care more about the vocal extremists who are the most likely to take to the streets and mobilize others to follow them.

Jiang Zemin's surprising success

Returning to the Tiananmen crisis that traumatized Chinese politics, imagine how Jiang Zemin felt, suddenly plucked from relative obscurity as Communist Party secretary of Shanghai to become China's national leader in 1989. The future of CCP rule looked dim. The demonstrations throughout China had come close to toppling the regime. Jiang knew he was nobody's first choice to succeed Deng Xiaoping.

No one expected Jiang Zemin to last more than a few years because the engineer politician was nothing special—he had neither outstanding abilities nor the personal charisma of a Mao or Deng. China watchers predicted that like Hua Guofeng, the nonentity whom Mao Zedong chose as his successor after he had purged all his previous choices, Jiang would not survive long after the death of his patron. In unscripted situations, Jiang had an unfortunate tendency to show off, as I observed when accompanying Jiang on his 1997 visit to the United States and sitting in on meetings between senior American officials and Jiang in China. He would go off on long riffs about Chinese and Western history and culture that were not even tangentially related to the subject at hand, in an apparent effort to display his erudition and avoid serious discussion. One Chinese expert who saw Jiang at close range said, "Jiang is not only a very insecure person, like Nixon, but he also has a lot of vanity." A college student described Jiang as "a narcissist." Several policy advisors described Jiang as "emotional" and complained that his policy preferences "zigged and zagged" and "changed overnight" depending on the "people and events that influenced him." They drew a contrast with Deng Xiaoping, who maintained a "steady strategic perspective" even when "June 4, 1989, and the fall of the Soviet Union completely turned upside down our understanding of world history." One person went so far as to characterize Jiang as "psychologically unstable." President Clinton, from his very first meeting with President Jiang, was unimpressed, but he told his staff it was easy to underestimate the Chinese leader.[19]

Jiang surprised the skeptics. He used his appointment powers to build his authority beyond anyone's expectations. As general secretary of the Communist Party he had the final say on the selection of government ministers, provincial governors, and military officers. Over time, more and more people owed their jobs to him.

No one emerged as a challenger within the Standing Committee of the Politburo. Fortunately for Jiang, Zhu Rongji, the brilliant, blunt premier who is credited with China's economic restructuring during the 1990s, and who cut a more dynamic figure with the public, suppressed his own ambitions and deferred to Jiang so as to reassure him that he wasn't after Jiang's job. Jiang cleverly eliminated his major rival Qiao Shi in 1997 by introducing an unwritten retirement-at-seventy rule for Politburo-level officials. Jiang, then seventy-one, exempted himself as the preeminent leader. (According to some Chinese political experts, the retirement age for Politburo officials actually was lowered to sixty-eight in 2002 when Standing Committee member Li Ruihuan was required to step down at that age.) Li Peng, who in 1998 moved from the premiership to the chairmanship of China's quasi legislature, the National People's Congress, had been sufficiently discredited by his prominent role in the Tiananmen crackdown that he was not a serious rival to Jiang, although he was able to throw a monkey wrench in the works from time to time. Li Peng led the attack when Zhu

Rongji returned from his 1999 visit to the United States without a final agreement on China's accession to the World Trade Organization.

Deng Xiaoping, like Mao, had ruled through the force of his stature as a founding father of the People's Republic. None of Deng's successors have had the same personal sway. Jiang was never more than first among equals in the CCP oligarchy, not a politically comfortable spot to be in. The Politburo and Central Committee blocked several nominations Jiang made of his close associates from Shanghai to national office to make sure he didn't become too strong. Deng robbed him of the right to choose his own successor by anointing Hu Jintao, another cautious engineer-politician, a decade ahead of time. (Still in his forties, Hu leapfrogged to become a member of the Politburo Standing Committee in 1992 and then became vice president and vice-chairman of the Central Military Commission in 1998.) "Deng could ignore his advisors. And Mao could ignore the entire Politburo Standing Committee. But now there is no strong man," said one Chinese professor.

Hu Jintao takes few risks

Today's CCP leaders are more or less interchangeable — cautious, colorless organization men of late middle age without any special talents or

A visitor walks past portraits of four generations of China's leaders: Mao Zedong, Deng Xiaoping, Jiang Zemin, Hu Jintao (*left to right*) at a Shanghai exhibition commemorating the Chinese Communist Party's eighty-second birthday, June 26, 2003. (Liu Jin/AFP/Getty Images)

followings. As one policy advisor said with a cynical air, "Nowadays any-one can be a leader. All the Politburo Standing Committee members are the same. Anyone can sit in the chair." As leader-in-waiting, Hu Jintao knew the job was his unless he made a big mistake. Like an American judge with aspirations to serve on the Supreme Court, he avoided contro-versy by hiding his individual views so well that the officials who inter-acted with him couldn't tell what they were. The most they could say about him was that he was able to memorize facts and talking points very quickly. The most significant achievement of Hu's previous career had been to clamp down on religious and political activity in Tibet at the end of 1988 when he served in that restive region as Party secretary, which helped solidify his standing with the military and the control cartel. My observations of Hu in meetings with Americans were that he was more straightforward in his style than Jiang Zemin but that he stuck closely to his script and expressed no thoughts of his own. Even today, after four years in power, Hu holds his cards close to his chest. People in China still aren't sure what Hu stands for.

After assuming leadership in fall 2002, Hu's first actions impressed people as courageous and innovative. During the 2003 SARS epidemic Hu fired the health minister and the mayor of Beijing for the initial cover-up that had allowed the disease to spread from South China throughout the country and kill 647 people. After a Chinese submarine disaster killed all seventy sailors on board in May 2003, he fired the head of the PLA Navy and several other naval officers.[20]

But since then, Hu has reverted to business as usual. He shies away from political reform and is tightening controls over the press and the Internet. At an important Central Committee meeting in September 2004, Hu reportedly gave an old-style ideological fire-and-brimstone speech at-tacking the spread of "bourgeois liberalization" by "hostile foreign and domestic forces" and charging political reform advocates with "creating turmoil" (a loaded phrase harkening back to Tiananmen).[21] "Enemy forces inevitably take public opinion to be their point of attack," Hu reportedly warned. "The Soviet Union disintegrated under the assault of their West-ernization and bourgeois liberalization."[22] Following the meeting, CCP officials expressed worries that "some people are exploiting the Internet to attack the government and . . . the Communist Party."[23] And they made a big push to strengthen political controls over Internet content and the ideological education of youth.[24]

To make sure Party members are loyal to him and won't shift their alle-giance to one of the potential rivals who surround him in the Standing Committee, Hu Jintao reverted to old-fashioned, Mao-style methods with counterproductive results. In 2005, he launched an ideological campaign within the Party (aimed at "maintaining the advanced nature of the CCP") that for four months required all CCP members in offices, schools, and work units to spend Thursday afternoons and all day Saturday studying Party history and the speeches of the current leaders and criticizing one another and themselves for their political failings.[25] One academic said, "This campaign is rapidly eroding the popularity of Hu and Wen. We're just wasting our talents when we could be doing something worthwhile." In a stunning illustration of how the market economy has overtaken communism, Party members were able to purchase generic self-criticisms from commercial Web sites capitalizing on the campaign, which in turn necessitated a new rule that required self-criticisms in handwritten form. A former provincial Party chief explained Hu's instinct to tighten up. "The Party's authority is gradually declining, and as a result, Hu is less confident and more insecure than the leaders before him. When a leader feels insecure, he tightens controls."[26] Newspaper photos of Hu surrounded by adoring youngsters and articles praising him in lavish language are reminiscent of a Mao-style personality cult, which is unlikely to stir much public enthusiasm.[27]

Preventing open splits

As a group, the CCP leaders appear to have learned the lesson of Tiananmen. If they don't hang together, they could hang separately, as the Western saying goes.

Yet each individual politician has moments of temptation, when an interest in acquiring more power for himself might lead him to exploit a crisis situation and reach out beyond the elite selectorate to mobilize a mass following, as Zhao Ziyang tried to do during the Tiananmen crisis. Large protests increase the risk of a split by showing leaders that a following is already in place and forcing them to take a stand on the protests. Social unrest actually can create schisms at the top. The danger is not a matter of the particular personalities in the Party oligarchy at any one time, but is built into the structure of communist systems.

Changes in the mass media heighten the risk of the public being drawn into elite disagreements. Leadership splits telegraphed to the public over the Internet in other authoritarian regimes have triggered revolutionary upheavals. And while defections from the public consensus are still relatively rare in China, they are likely to increase. Seventeen high-level leaders, led by ideological hard-liner Deng Liqun, posted on the Internet a polemic against Jiang Zemin's July 1, 2001, speech that advocated the admission of private capitalists into Communist Party membership.[28] In 2006, a group of retired officials known for their liberal leanings released on the Internet their open letter protesting the closing of a newspaper. This hardly

President Hu Jintao, in military uniform, is surrounded by adoring youngsters in Beijing, May 29, 2005. (Wang Jianmin/Xinhua)

represents an epidemic of elite protest, but rather perhaps the germs of overt leadership dissent on the rise.

President Jiang was skilled at preventing splits by forcing other leaders to share with him the responsibility for controversial decisions. He put Hu Jintao, his designated successor, out in front during the crises created by the U.S. accidental bombing of the Chinese Embassy in Belgrade in 1999 and the collision between the U.S. spy plane and the Chinese fighter jet in 2001 (an act of cowardice on Jiang's part in the eyes of many of the students I've talked to). Reportedly, he also summoned more than two thousand CCP officials to a special meeting at which he required each of the members of the Politburo Standing Committee to stand up and testify that they endorsed the necessity of the campaign to eradicate the Falun Gong, the spiritual group that had organized a large sit-in around the leadership compound in April 1999, as well as the military crackdown on the Tiananmen demonstrators ten years earlier.[29] Jiang made Premier Zhu Rongji take the heat when President Clinton declined to finalize the deal for China's accession to the World Trade Organization during Zhu's visit to the United States in April 1999. As the American official traveling with Zhu on the Chinese plane I had the painful duty of witnessing Zhu's humiliation at close hand.

Beginning with Deng Xiaoping, CCP leaders have tried to reduce the risk of destabilizing leadership splits by introducing fixed terms of office, term limits, and a mandatory retirement age to regularize leadership competition. When Jiang Zemin, having reached the age of seventy-seven, retired as CCP general secretary (2002) and president (2003), it was the first time that a leader of a large communist country had ever handed down power to a successor without putting up a fight or dying. Jiang's close associate, Zeng Qinghong, praised him for "the replacement of the old by the new generation in the central leadership collective in such a stable and orderly matter. . . . From the history of the international communist movement, we can see that it is not easy to resolve this issue well."[30]

As the price of retirement, Jiang obtained promotions for several officials associated with him into the Politburo Standing Committee. As of 2006, six of the nine PBSC members are viewed as "Jiang's men."[31] Jiang also managed to hang on to his job as head of the Central Military Commission because it did not require retirement at 70. But without the institutional authority of the top Party post, Jiang's influence began to evaporate, and two years later in September 2004, he retired completely. During the two years when Jiang and Hu shared power, subordinate officials were uneasy. Foreign Minister Li Zhaoxing, on a visit to the United States, when asked a question about "China after Jiang," quipped "Not yet." The last time China had two different voices coming from the leadership they caused the near disaster of the 1989 demonstrations. Anxious to prevent any threats to stability, senior and retired leaders reportedly convinced Jiang that the best way to preserve his legacy was to retire completely.[32] Hu Jintao, not taking anything for granted, praised Jiang's "noble character, sterling integrity, and broad-mindedness."[33]

The oligarchs do everything they can to prevent divisions among themselves. The practice followed by Jiang Zemin and now by Hu Jintao, of having the top leader hold three key positions—general secretary of the CCP, president of the PRC, and chairman of the Central Military Commission— is designed to prevent destructive cleavages among the leaders. The rule that requires Politburo approval for any high-level corruption case helps keep elite contests for power within bounds. Party documents stress the importance of "a firm central leading body" in which individuals subordinate themselves to the whole to guarantee that the Party maintains its authority over society.[34] Nevertheless, this unity is hard to maintain in the face of the dramatic changes under way in Chinese society, the inevitability of competition among top leaders, and the lower penalties for political defection.[35]

Divisions at the top

On the surface, relations within the CCP's inner circle appear smooth. There is no daylight between the public positions taken by Hu and those of the premier, Wen Jiabao, a competent but pale replica of his mentor Zhu Rongji. Neither is there any evidence of a concerted challenge to Hu by the Standing Committee members who in the past were personally associated with Jiang Zemin, including his former right-hand man, Zeng Qinghong. No rival has emerged as the focal point of an opposition. Jiang himself is rarely seen, and reportedly spends most of his time in Shanghai. A Beijing professor insisted that Hu, like Jiang before him, was able to establish his authority by virtue of his formal powers as CCP general secretary. "Once you have that position and use it to do things, then you are in a solid position."

Yet ominous developments hint that divisions in the Party may be lurking beneath the surface. After two decades of policy consensus in support of market reform, Marxist critics of Western economics and market practices have launched a fierce onslaught against the reforms, blaming them for inequality, social unrest, and corruption. The critiques appear to have some official sponsorship. The broadside by the prominent elderly economist Liu Guoguang against Western-trained economists who deny the value of Marxism appeared on the *Strong Nation Forum* site of the *People's Daily*.[36] The new Left, consisting of younger intellectuals many of whom learned their Marxism in American universities, has criticized Chinese foreign policy as too accommodating. Objections to the draft law on private property for favoring the rich and violating China's constitution as a socialist nation were strong enough to cause the National People's Congress, China's quasi-legislature, to table the bill. Hu Jintao called for a major effort to learn and develop Marxist theory.[37] Some authoritative articles in CCP publications in June 2006 defended the market reforms, while others emphasized that they must be consistent with socialist values.[38] As noted earlier, an anticorruption drive is reaching into the highest level of the Party elite. Beijing's cognoscenti read these tea leaves as indications that the oligarchs in the Standing Committee of the Politburo may be pulling in opposite directions. The dominant theory is that Hu Jintao has tacked to the Left (which is concentrated largely in the control cartel) in order to defend himself from a challenge from the leaders formerly associated with Jiang Zemin, even though no one can point to any visible evidence of this challenge. The alternative theory is that someone in the Standing Committee has unleashed the leftist critics to challenge Hu. Either way, a split in the leadership puts the entire regime at risk. One policy advisor described the situation, "China can have a serious political crisis only if there is a conflict within the center, among the leaders. Now they have different ideas about the causes and remedies for the social problems that the economic changes have produced, like inequality and corruption."

Competition is heating up in the lead-up to the Seventeenth Chinese Communist Party Congress in fall 2007. (In March 2006, one of the topics that the Propaganda Department ordered the media not to report because it was considered politically sensitive was the preparations for the Seventeenth Party Congress.) No successor to Hu Jintao has been anointed—Jiang was not able to engineer the selection of his right-hand man Zeng Qinghong as Hu's successor. Zeng serves as vice president but was not appointed to the number two position in the Central Military Commission that Hu held when he was the acknowledged successor. At seventy-three, Zeng will be too old to succeed Hu in 2012. Although people assume that Hu will serve two terms as Jiang did and remain in office until 2012, he theoretically could be challenged at the end of his first term in 2007. And the contest about who will succeed him in 2012 will be intense. If past practice is a guide, that individual will need to be readied for the top job by moving up to the Politburo Standing Committee and taking up the number two position in the Military Commission in 2007.[39]

In a society undergoing explosive change, political outcomes are unpredictable because the political game is evolving too. Every day new opportunities and challenges present themselves to ambitious politicians in China. Keeping leadership competition under wraps is becoming increasingly difficult as the media and Internet compete for audiences by testing the limits on what they can report. Nationalism is a natural platform for an ambitious politician who wants to build a public reputation. We need to anticipate the very real possibility that an international or domestic crisis in the next few years could tempt a challenger to reach out to a public following and cause the CCP house of cards to collapse.

Lesson 2: Prevent Large-Scale Social Unrest

The fixation on social stability

China's leaders are obsessed with what they call "social stability," in other words, the prevention of large-scale unrest that could bring down the Communist regime. They use the euphemism "social stability" to convince the Chinese public that Communist Party rule is essential for maintaining order and prosperity, and that without it, a country as large as China would fall into civil war and chaos. Democracy is an impossibility in a country as large as China, Communist officials argue. (When pressed to explain how India, with one billion people, can be a democracy, one official explained that India, unlike China, has religion to control people.[40])

Paranoia is the occupational disease of all authoritarian leaders no matter how serious the internal threats they actually face. The Chinese suffer from a particularly acute form of the disease because of their Tiananmen trauma, the other regimes they have watched collapse, and the dramatic changes in Chinese society that surround them. In Asia, they have watched authoritarian regimes in South Korea, Taiwan, Indonesia, and Thailand be overcome by popular democratic movements as their economies modernized. Study groups analyze the "color revolutions" in Eastern Europe and Central Asia to discover how to prevent similar revolts in China. Historical memories of how the previous two dynasties—the Qing and the Republic of China—fell to opposition movements fired up by nationalist sentiments, reinforces the anxieties of the CCP leadership.

Paradoxically, the fears of Communist autocrats make them hypersensitive to public attitudes. Because the country lacks any institutions like elections to channel public opinion, a wave of discontent could sink the state. As multimillionaire businessman Li Qinfu put it to a *New York Times* journalist, "In a one-party country everything looks peaceful, but when there's a problem, it's a big problem."[41] Fearful of provoking public anger, Chinese leaders don't dare take unpopular actions—like raising gasoline taxes or electricity rates. Despite intense pressure from Washington, they are jittery about allowing China's currency to float against the dollar and other world currencies because import pressure on the prices of agricultural products could spark a modern-day peasant rebellion, a drop in manufactured exports would increase unemployment, and the pressure on the shaky financial system could cause a mass run on the banks. The uproar from young, well-educated Internet users in response to the government's 2002 move to block all access to the popular Google search engine forced it to back down after just a few days. The leaders treat any organized group, even a politically innocuous one like a church that refuses to register with the government on principle, like a potential opposition movement. The wildly popular *Supergirls* television show that whetted appetites for democracy by giving people the chance to vote for their favorite performer by sending a text message on their cell phones became the object of discussion by a worried Politburo Standing Committee.

Looking out beyond Communist Party headquarters in Zhongnanhai, internal threats appear more menacing than external ones, except for the Taiwan issue. China is more secure as a nation than it has been since World War II or even the mid-nineteenth-century Opium War, yet the CCP leadership maintains a "siege mentality"[42] in the face of potential rebellion. "Leaders are focused on domestic social unrest," one Chinese expert said. "Compared with that, the international issues are secondary."

When I asked a college student what was the greatest threat facing China today, she looked confused and asked, "Inside or outside?" "Either," I clarified. "There's no external threat that is half as serious as the threat of internal conflict," she said.

Scholar David Shambaugh observes, "The uncertainties of succession politics and perceived external threats to CCP rule combine with profound elite fears of internal social instability to produce a regime that is insular, paranoid, and reactive."[43]

All around them, the leaders see new social forces unleashed by economic reforms that could subvert the regime. Society is changing so fast that Communist politicians can't discern which groups are solidly in their camp and which groups might form the base of an opposition—so they try to satisfy them all. Having digested the experiences of other countries and been influenced by the ideas of Samuel Huntington's book, *The Third Wave*,[44] the Communist Party has concluded that "the transition period from per capita GDP of $1,000 to $3,000 [where China will be for the next twenty years] is a period when there are apt to emerge social conflicts." The Party is particularly worried that the widening income gap could cause "destabilizing social phenomena."[45] Demonstrations by laid-off workers, dissatisfied farmers, urban migrants, Muslim extremists—even retired People's Liberation Army veterans—have become an everyday occurrence. Chinese students protested not just in 1989, but also in 1985, 1986–87, 1999, and 2005. All this churning has occurred in the period since 1978, one that outside observers might consider China's most politically stable time in more than a century. The *People's Daily* rarely used the term "social stability" before 1989, but it appears with increasing frequency since then.

Jiang Zemin made stability a national priority. "It is extremely important to maintain a stable political environment and social order," he said in his report to the Communist Party Congress in 1997.[46] Current CCP leaders are even more emphatic that social stability overrides all other considerations.[47]

The Communist Party considers rapid economic growth a political imperative because it is the only way to prevent massive unemployment and labor unrest. For more than a decade, the government has based its

Figure 3.2 Mentions of "social stability" (*shehui wending*) in *People's Daily*, 1978–2005

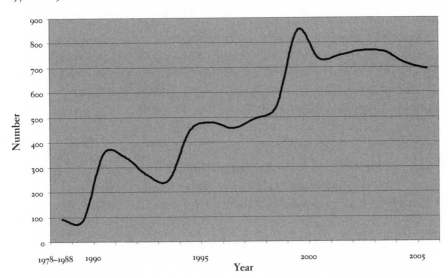

Source: *People's Daily* Electronic Version 1946–2002 and *People's Daily Online*, www.people.com.cn.

economic policies on an algorithm derived from its priority on stability. The economy must grow at an annual rate of 7 percent or more in order to create a certain number of jobs (nine million each in 2004 and 2005), and keep unemployment rates at levels that will prevent widespread labor unrest (set at 4.7 percent in 2004 and 4.6 percent in 2005).[48] These explicit growth and employment targets remain in the minds of all Chinese officials as they create foreign as well as domestic policies.

Economic flux agitates social life and frees people to form new thought and behavior patterns over which the Communist Party has no control.[49] Communications media, especially the Internet, facilitate new forms of collective action that the Party may not know about until they happen, like the Falun Gong sit-in outside Zhongnanhai in 1999. Once demonstrations erupt, people are surprised to discover that many others dislike the regime as much as they do and that the regime is weaker than they thought it was. Information about protests spreads instantaneously throughout the country now that people have cell phones and computers. In a modern version of "The Emperor's New Clothes," information cascades may create a tipping point. An apparently stable Communist regime can collapse almost overnight, as we saw in the Soviet Union and Eastern Europe, and more recently in the Ukraine.[50] A Beijing university student said to me, "The political system is so weak. One day it could erupt like a volcano."

Tracking mass protest

From the Communist Party leaders' perch in Beijing, Chinese society looks like a cauldron boiling over with unrest. The leaders follow closely—and nervously—the increasing frequency, scale, and violence of protests throughout the country. Under their direction, the sociologists and public security bureaucracies have undertaken remarkably frank scholarship on the incidence and underlying causes of social protest.[51] Everything they do—in both foreign and domestic policy—is aimed at trying to keep the lid on.

Premier Zhu Rongji revealed his obsession with unrest when he spoke with me and a group of American congressional representatives and senators in the secluded Diaoyutai state guesthouse in spring 2002. He obviously had protests by unemployed workers on his mind. "My office gets daily reports about where workers are protesting," he volunteered when the conversation began. Without referring to any notes, he continued, "Between January 1 and March 28, 2002, there were 265 protests of groups of more than fifty workers." (Zhu may have hoped to use the statistics to discourage the U.S. Congress from raising new trade barriers against Chinese exports.)

According to China's police, the number of "mass incidents" (over one hundred people) has surged from 8,700 in 1993, to approximately 10,000 in 1994, 32,000 in 1999, 58,000 in 2003, and 74,000 in 2004.[52] More than 200 protests on average occur every day.[53] The number of people involved in protests in 2004 reached 3.76 million, compared with 730,000 a decade earlier.[54]

"Mass incidents have become a major problem for social stability," Public Security Minister Zhou Yongkang said in July 2005. "Their number is on the increase and their scale is constantly expanding . . . the trend toward greater organization is clear."[55] This deluge of social unrest probably is containable unless it triggers a rupture within the ranks of the leaders. But a single leader who tries to lead the crowd instead of standing arm and arm with his comrades could cause a breach in the stability of the state.

Although the Chinese media are never allowed to report protests,[56] word spreads over the Internet and is picked up by the Hong Kong and international press. Most of the actions are small scale and uncoordinated. A sampling from a foreign perusal of reports on civil disturbances during 2004 illustrates the types of actions that occur (in approximate numbers):[57]

- Two thousand workers protest over pay arrears in a Hubei textile factory.
- One thousand residents protest against forced eviction to make way for a development project in Chongqing, Sichuan.

Figure 3.3 Estimated Number of Mass Protests in China, 1993–2004

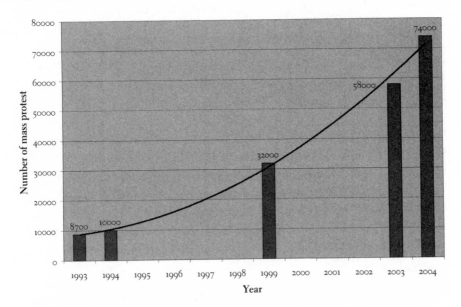

Source: The 2003 statistics are from *Liaowang*, June 7, 2004; the 2004 statistics are from *South China Morning Post*, July 7, 2005. The earlier numbers are from Murray Scot Tanner, "China Rethinks Unrest," *The Washington Quarterly* 27, no. 3 (Summer 2004), 138–39.

- One thousand workers riot after a Taiwan-owned shoe factory in Dongguan, Guangdong, refused to pay salaries.
- Six thousand taxi drivers strike to protest new taxi regulations in the capital of Ningxia.
- Hundreds of people living in a Guangdong village, who were dissatisfied with the compensation they received when the government requisitioned their land, surround police cars for almost twenty hours.
- More than three hundred villagers in Guangdong held the local Party secretary under house arrest for three days and two nights to force him to make a clean accounting of corruption.
- Five hundred striking tour guides and bus drivers from Hainan's tourist industry demonstrate for higher incomes, try to storm the Miss World Pageant, and clash with police.

National statistics about the number of protests are published in open source government reports, and the annual *China Social Blue Book* published since the early 1990s provides a surprisingly candid discussion of protest activity at a general level. The groups described as the most restive are workers laid off by state factories; farmers upset about high local taxes and fees, land seizures, or environmental damage caused by local chemical plants and other factories; and the minority groups in Xinjiang and Tibet demanding religious freedom or independence. Volatile mobs of migrant laborers are a growing concern. The sociologists who compile the *Blue Book* also watch student attitudes very closely, although their poorly worded, unscientific surveys don't lend much credence to their results. (One interesting finding: although 95 percent of Beijing college students agree that "economic development must have a stable political environment," 80 percent of them also agree that there will be political instability if the political system isn't reformed.[58]) In the *Blue Book* and in the similar studies carried out by the public security think-tanks, the analysts display what scholar Murray Scot Tanner describes as "an undisguised sympathy for the very worker and peasant protestors the police are supposed to suppress."[59]

Ethnic unrest

Some of the most violent collective action is carried out by ethnic and religious minorities in Western China. Although less than 10 percent of China's population is non-Chinese, the minority groups live in strategically important border regions—Tibet, Xinjiang, and Mongolia. In May 1993, thousands of Tibetans rioted for two days in Lhasa, and Muslim Uighurs claimed responsibility for several bombings in Xinjiang, on China's northwestern border with Central Asia. Xinjiang was rocked by violent riots and terrorist incidents throughout the 1990s. In 1997, a series of bombs exploded on buses in the Xinjiang capital of Urumchi, killing nine people, and a Uighur group took credit for a bus bombing in Beijing that injured thirty.[60] According to the Chinese government, Uighur "separatists" carried out two hundred terrorist attacks between 1990 and 2001 that killed 162 people and injured more than 440.[61] Twenty or so Uighurs were caught in Al-Qaeda training camps and fifteen are still being held at the American prison in Guantanamo Bay. Since September 11, 2001, Beijing has waged an intensive "strike hard" campaign in Xinjiang, and violence and collective action have drastically dropped off. The Chinese province of Inner Mongolia has been comparatively quiet, but Chinese authorities have canceled concerts of Mongolian-pride rock groups and shut down Mongolian language chat rooms in order to nip in the bud any Mongolian nationalist activism.[62]

Labor unrest

Communist leaders view labor unrest as the most threatening form of protest. Thanks to their Marxist education, they expect workers to be, if not the vanguard, at least a part of any future insurgency in China. Factory workers, who work and live in close proximity to one another, are easier to organize than peasants who are dispersed in the countryside. Labor protests are sure to be noticed by the media. And, most important, labor protests occur in cities like Beijing where the power holders live.

So far, most protestors have been laid-off workers dissatisfied with their unemployment benefits, rather than currently employed workers. The latter are younger and easier to organize, and they could do more damage economically and politically.[63] Demonstrations typically are small scale and limited to one enterprise. (As the government pressed state factories operating in the red to go out of business, it strategically targeted the smaller firms first, and the biggest ones have yet to be closed.)[64]

China's northeastern rust belt, particularly Liaoning Province, where unemployment approaches 40 percent in some cities, is the one region troubled by large-scale labor unrest. In a 2002 action—the largest protest since 1989—between twenty thousand and fifty thousand workers laid off by the Daqing oil field demonstrated for over two weeks to demand better severance packages. An estimated thirty thousand unemployed workers from ten different factories in a nearby city followed suit two weeks later. When nearly six thousand laid-off workers from metallurgical and machinery industries petitioned authorities in Qiqihar City, Heilongjiang Province, for larger subsistence allowances in December 2002, they used the revolutionary slogan "resistance comes where oppression is, contention rises where exploitation exists" and sang the "Communist Internationale" and the Chinese national anthem.[65]

Rural unrest

Autocrats rarely see peasants as a serious political threat—living scattered throughout the countryside they are notoriously hard to organize and their protests are likely to go unnoticed by journalists. But China, with its long history of peasant rebellions toppling dynasties, is an exception to the rule. Mao Zedong proved that "the countryside surrounds the cities" could be a successful strategy for Communist revolution in China. The revolution that brings down the Communists might follow the same formula, as one Beijing intellectual speculated to me. Because Chinese farmers lack legal property rights to their land, they have a direct interest in a democratic government that would protect property rights. And as 60 percent of the population, they certainly would gain from electoral democracy. The Beijing intellectual noted, however, that city dwellers look down on the rural masses as country bumpkins (*tu baozi*) and have some ambivalence about democratization because it would place them under the rule of the less-educated rural majority.

Chinese leaders are starting to worry about the possibility of a twenty-first-century peasant rebellion. In the past several years, rural unrest has spread, grown in scale, and attracted more notice from journalists and the central government. Land seizures and environmental pollution are the two issues that are driving farmers to violent action. In October 2004 an estimated ten thousand farmers in Sichuan Province stormed a government building and battled police over land seized for a dam project. Order was restored only after ten thousand paramilitary People's Armed Police forces were sent to the scene.

Rapidly developing coastal provinces are the site of most of the clashes over land seizures. Officials profit from lucrative commercial and residential development projects without adequately compensating villagers. The villagers feel powerless—they can't go to court because they don't legally own their land and they can't vote the officials out of office, so they have no recourse but to protest. Guangdong Province in South China was the scene of three particularly violent protests over land requisitions in 2005. In Dongzhou, Taishi, and Panlong villages security forces used deadly force to suppress the demonstrators and then put a blanket of silence over the events. The guests at a ribbon-cutting ceremony for a project in another Guangdong village called Sanzhou were trapped by thousands of villagers who objected to their inadequate compensation.[66] Hong Kong newspapers reported that Hu Jintao mentioned the Guangdong incidents in an internal speech to warn officials that they must solve rural problems instead of handing them over to the central authorities or letting them stir up social unrest.[67]

Environmental poisoning by chemical plants was the focus of several large violent incidents in the relatively affluent eastern province of Zhejiang during the summer of 2005. Thousands of villagers outside the rural town of Dongyang, led by the old people's association, lived in tents and blocked roads for more than two weeks to protest the 2001 sale of their land to chemical plants that were polluting the water supply and making people ill. An estimated three thousand police arrived with cattle prods to break up the roadblocks and found themselves defeated in a pitched battle with more than twenty thousand residents summoned from nearby villages by firecrackers. The villagers finally agreed to fold up their tents several weeks later after a compromise was worked out to close down some of the chemical plants.

News of the crisis traveled widely by cell phone and Internet even though the local government blocked chat rooms and forbade media coverage. Inspired by the success of the Dongyang resistance, fifteen thousand demonstrators in a second Zhejiang village battled with police in an effort to shut down a local pharmaceutical factory that had caused industrial accidents and polluted the water supply.[68] In a third Zhejiang village, protestors violently occupied a battery factory that they claimed was poisoning their children with lead.[69] Violent confrontations between villagers and police continued for two months.[70]

The conspicuous gap between the lifestyles of the rich and the poor rural migrants in Chinese cities also fuels populist resentments that can suddenly explode into large-scale violence. When word spread in October 2004 that a Chinese official had beaten a lowly porter, tens of thousands rioted in a city in Sichuan Province, beating police, burning cars, and storming city hall. A minor June 2005 traffic accident in Anhui Province, in which a Toyota grazed a teenager riding his bike, ignited a riot in which a mob of ten thousand attacked the police station and destroyed police cars.[71]

Student unrest

College students have been playing it safe and concentrating on their careers instead of politics. Their caution is motivated more by a lack of hope in politics and the allure of material success than by a fear that the 1989 Tiananmen Square crackdown could be repeated. The issues that arouse the greatest political activism on campuses are international ones. Nationalist emotions run strong among college youth and sometimes erupt into mass action. Most student protests are virtual in the form of online petitions, but some of them become real. Students demonstrated outside the American Embassy and consulates to protest the U.S. bombing of the Chinese Embassy in Belgrade in 1999. To prevent a repeat, the authorities locked them inside their campuses when a U.S. spy plane and a Chinese fighter jet collided in 2001. In 2003, more than one thousand Xian University students, offended by a talent show skit by Japanese exchange students doing an obscene mock striptease, demonstrated on campus and assaulted the Japanese students in their dormitory. The demonstrations spread from campus to the city, where students and ordinary citizens attacked Japanese shops until stopped by the police. Violent student demonstrations against Japan erupted in twenty-five cities in April 2005. The CCP treats the students more gently than any other group, coaxing them back to their campuses, because it wants at all costs to avoid another Tiananmen.

A PLA general candidly suggested that the students demonstrated against foreign targets to express their domestic discontents. "Demonstrations after the Belgrade embassy bombing or against Japan aren't really about foreign policy. They are the result of an accumulation of people's grievances against the Chinese government, just the same as in the Qing Dynasty and the Republican government. They are not really antiforeign. Demonstrations on foreign policy actually reflect domestic politics."

Nationalism and social unrest

National leaders in big countries like China (and the United States) use foreign policy to show domestic audiences what strong, capable leaders they are. They sometimes also use an assertive foreign policy to divert attention from domestic problems, a tactic that has become known in the West as "wag the dog." Chinese leaders are prone to public muscle flexing because they feel the need to stay out in front of a growing tide of popular nationalism. What the Chinese leaders fear most is a national movement that fuses various discontented groups—such as unemployed workers, farmers, and students—under the banner of nationalism. The lessons they learned in school about the fall of the Qing Dynasty in 1911 and of the Republic of China in 1949 have stayed with them. Any Chinese government that looks weak in the face of foreign pressure is likely to be overthrown.

The leaders recognize that popular nationalism is intensifying as the country grows stronger. In fact, they have been largely responsible for this trend. In schools and the mass media, they have promoted nationalist themes as a way to bolster the legitimacy of the Communist Party, now that almost no one believes in Communist ideology anymore.

After Tiananmen, the CCP launched a nationwide "patriotic education campaign" in schools and the mass media. Scholar Zhao Suisheng describes it as the CCP's "rediscovery of nationalism."[72] The CCP began to tout its patriotic credentials as a way to rally popular support. As Jiang Zemin said in a 1997 speech to the CCP Central Committee, "The Chinese Communists are the staunchest and most thorough patriots. The patriotism of the CCP is the supreme example of the patriotism of the Chinese nation and the Chinese people."[73] The press was filled with articles about the importance of cultivating patriotism for maintaining social stability.[74]

Beginning in 1994, schools added new courses to stimulate patriotic loyalty, and students won awards for reading the one hundred patriotic books and seeing the one hundred patriotic movies chosen by the Party. Patriotic songs, patriotic books, and patriotic versions of history became the steady diet of schoolchildren. School tours crowded historical sites established earlier, now called "patriotic education bases." The Museum of Testimony to the Crimes of Japanese Army Unit 731, the Japanese unit that experimented with chemical weapons on Chinese citizens, located in the northeastern city of Harbin, received more than three million visitors a year.[75]

To Jiang Zemin and his colleagues trying to bolster the Communist Party's popularity after the Tiananmen crackdown, it seemed like a good idea to bind people to the Party through nationalism now that Communist ideals had lost their luster. The military and the propaganda bureaucracy were particularly keen on nationalism because it enhanced their roles and potentially, their budgets. (The Foreign Ministry was most dubious because as one diplomat put it, "Those who handle foreign relations are always suspect as traitors.")

Nationalism did not have to be entirely "constructed" by the state.[76] As China grew economically and militarily more powerful, nationalist emotions were spontaneously bubbling up in the popular psyche. All the school curriculum, media, and billboards had to do was reinforce these emotions by attaching them to the common script of China's triumph under Communist leadership after the "century of humiliation" at the hands of foreign enemies. The main themes of the story are the atrocities committed by Japan during its occupation of China, the loss of Taiwan inflicted by Japanese and American military forces, and America's hegemonic interest in keeping China weak and overthrowing Communist rule through "peaceful evolution." The century of humiliation will end only when Japan apologizes sincerely for its wartime atrocities, Taiwan is brought back into the fold, and America treats China as an equal. Patriotic education nurtured popular resentments against Japan and America and an expectation that Taiwan would soon be reunified as a way of strengthening public identification with the Communist Party.

Once the official line on issues like Japan, Taiwan, and the United States became assertively nationalistic, ambitious individuals competed with one another by talking the patriotic talk. "A lot of Chinese nationalism is just a show that people put on for one another, a kind of political correctness," said a Chinese journalist. "But some of it is real."

Some Chinese intellectuals—and many foreign observers—view contemporary Chinese nationalism as something "imposed upon the people representing the will of the leader."[77] But, for most Chinese, nationalism feels like a healthy act of self-assertion, as Sinologist Edward Friedman says, "Chinese nationalists experience themselves not as victims manipulated by political interests at the state center but as pure patriots who know the truth and will not be fooled."[78]

As a U.S. State Department official, I frequently encountered aggressive questioning about American foreign policy from Chinese students—one of my roughest goings-over was by a gathering of Chinese students studying at Harvard who went after me about America's bombing of Kosovo, arms sales to Taiwan, and alliance with Japan. President Clinton received similar treatment from the student audience at Beijing University when he spoke on campus in 1998. Communist Party members—even at Harvard—prepared the students to show their patriotism in this manner.

But I also have felt the chill of genuine nationalist resentment of America in spontaneous interactions with Chinese friends. I found myself dining with a dozen university faculty in Shanghai immediately following the collision of the Chinese fighter jet and the U.S. EP-3 spy plane. One professor, a longtime friend who has visited me in my California home, couldn't bring himself to utter a word to me, so full of anger at America was he. The students I talk with express their hatred of Japan, their readiness to shed blood to keep Taiwan, and their gripes against America with proud heads held high. Patriotic passions help fill the spiritual void left by the loss of faith in communism and offer an idealistic alternative to the commercialism of Chinese society today.

The nationalist mobilization of the 1990s has boxed the CCP and its leaders into a corner. Once the authorities allow students to demonstrate outside the Japanese and American embassies, it is a struggle to restore order without the students turning on them. "The government knows that demonstrations against Japan can escalate into antigovernment demonstrations," one student told me. And if they allow people to trash the Japanese and American embassies, how can they stabilize relations with these important countries on which China's economic growth, and its political stability, depend? Once people have gotten a taste of freely protesting against the approved targets of Japan and the United States, how do you contain their demands to participate in politics? As one PLA colonel said, "Sometimes people express their domestic dissatisfactions by criticizing foreign policy. You see that a lot in China." A Beijing student observed that his classmates joined in anti-Japanese protests "because they want to participate politically." He went on to say, "It's a way of demanding rights." Nationalism could be the one issue that could unite disparate groups like laid-off workers, farmers, and students in a national movement against the regime.

Don't repeat history

Chinese history textbooks teach that dynasties fall when they are overwhelmed by the twin threats of internal unrest and foreign aggression (*nei luan wai huan*). A weak, divided state invites foreign aggression, and foreign aggression sparks domestic upheavals.[79]

The Qing Dynasty, weakened by multiple economic and administrative problems, was unable to prevent the Western powers from encroaching on Chinese sovereignty beginning in the late eighteenth century. After the British defeated China in the Opium War (1839–42), Beijing was forced to surrender a number of its key ports to the British, the French, the Americans, and other foreign governments.

Hence the Qing Dynasty was caught between constant internal rebellions (by the Taiping, Nian, Muslims, and Boxers) and the demands of the imperialist powers.[80] China's defeat by Japan in the war of 1894 was the most painful humiliation of all because the Chinese had always considered themselves superior to the Japanese. On its knees, China lost Korea and the island of Taiwan to Japan. Popular nationalism surged, and students boycotted goods from the United States (1905) and Japan (1915).[81]

The Boxer Rebellion of 1900 grew from a Shandong Province secret society that practiced martial arts into a massive antiforeign insurgency of poor peasants and itinerant laborers that killed thousands of foreigners and Chinese converts to Christianity. The Qing empress dowager vacillated on whether to back the Boxers or try to suppress them, just as today's leaders struggle with how to handle anti-Japanese or anti-American protests. The empress was reluctant to endanger herself by opposing the nationalist emotions of the people. "Today China is extremely weak. We have only the people's hearts and minds to depend upon. If we cast them aside and lose the people's hearts, what can we use to sustain the country?"[82] Finally she decided that it was safer to stand with the Boxers against the foreigners than to wind up becoming the target of the Boxers. In the end, it took a foreign expeditionary force to quash the rebellion.

The shaky new Republic of China established in 1911 found itself in much the same position as the dynasty it had supplanted. Foreign pressure was intense, and the government had little effective control over the country. The weak Chinese government acquiesced to Japan's claim to the German concessions in the Shandong peninsula at the international peace conference following World War I. Beginning on May 4, 1919, outraged college students in Beijing and other cities took to the streets to protest against the government sellout and demand political reforms. The legacy of the May 4 movement, as it came to be known, is a continuing belief on the part of Chinese students and intellectuals that nationalist resistance to a corrupt and weak government is a right and a duty.

During the 1930s and '40s, Japanese forces rolled over the Republican armies to expand Japanese military control first in Manchuria (Northeast China) and then throughout China. The strategy of the Guomindang, the ruling party of the Republic, in simple terms, was to defeat the Communist forces first, before taking on the Japanese.[83] The Communists, insisting that national salvation must come before political partisanship, kept calling for a united front with the Guomindang to resist the Japanese. By identifying itself with people's anti-Japanese nationalism, the Communist Party won their respect and went on to win the civil war.[84]

In August 2005, on the sixtieth anniversary of the end of World War II, the CCP celebrated its "miraculous victory" whereby a "weak China defeated a strong Japan," giving the Chinese people "a complete victory for the first time in more than a century in fighting foreign aggressors."[85]

Today's leaders have learned from history that nationalism is a potent but double-edged force. From the standpoint of the rulers, nationalism can be the key to managing social unrest and surviving politically. But if the rulers appear too weak to stand up to the foreigners, then their critics will turn on them and use nationalist appeals to mobilize popular support for overthrowing them.

CCP survival strategies

IDENTIFY WITH THE PROTESTORS

"The way the Chinese government manages strong popular emotions is first to join with them and then to try to do something to fix it," said a Chinese academic. Beijing has a neat formula for protecting itself from uprisings. When protests by workers or farmers break out, the central government publicly sympathizes with the protestors and blames local officials for causing the problems—then, after perfunctory trials it throws the protest leaders in jail. The central government forbids the use of force against demonstrators, but leaves it to local officials to figure out how to resolve popular dissatisfactions peacefully.[86]

The Party's effort to identify itself with the protestors—and avoid becoming their target—has reached the point that remarkably, senior government ministers now hail rural protests as a sign of democracy and praise the farmers' awareness of how to protect their rights.[87] Signaling such a tolerant attitude toward protests may protect the top leaders from personal attack, but it is bound to encourage additional unrest against the regime. The Party, therefore, from time to time feels it necessary to recalibrate its message by issuing a stern warning that no illegal protest activity will be allowed.[88] For example, in August 2005, it announced that PLA soldiers would be severely penalized and expelled from the CCP if they took part in protests.[89]

CO-OPT POTENTIAL OPPOSITION LEADERS

The Communist Party has made a concerted effort to co-opt members of the social and economic elite and prevent them from leading any political opposition.[90] The Party still controls a nationwide patronage machine, and economic growth only makes these opportunities more valuable.

College students are the most rapidly growing group within the Party. In 1990 only 1.2 percent of college students were CCP members, but as of 2003, 8 percent of them were members.[91] At Tsinghua University, considered China's M.I.T., 20 percent of the undergraduates and 50 percent of the graduate students have joined the Party.[92] Many students admit they are joining to get an edge in the competition for career opportunities, which has grown tighter because the number of graduates has increased manyfold.[93] China has twenty-three million college students, more than any country in the world. In 2006, the government decided to slow down the increase in college enrollments.[94] No group is potentially more dangerous to an authoritarian regime than unemployed college graduates.

Under Jiang Zemin, the Communist Party also began to welcome private business owners as members to keep them loyal to the regime and preempt them from demanding democracy as they have in other countries.[95] The new capitalist class has grown up in the niches of the socialist economy and prospered by colluding with local officials. So far, China's capitalists have shown little interest in becoming the vanguard of political change.

EXPAND INDIVIDUAL FREEDOM

Over the past twenty-five years, the Communist Party has relinquished its totalitarian controls over social life and allowed a multitude of politically innocuous safety valves for letting off steam. People can play video games and surf the Web to their heart's delight—the only topics filtered and blocked by the censors are political ones. Culture, fashion, sex—all are wide open. Tourism, home decorating, and driving your own car have become exciting new adventures for millions of Chinese. The Party makes a big show of inviting popular feedback on the performance of lower-level officials and petitions to reverse official misdeeds. You can go to court to sue your condominium manager if she fails to keep the garden trimmed.

STRENGTHEN COERCION

When it comes to politics, however, the CCP has retained and even strengthened its coercive muscles. Since Tiananmen, the internal security apparatus—including the ministries of State Security, Public Security, and Justice, and the military-affiliated People's Armed Police—has been beefed up and taught modern police methods. The minister of Public Security ordered cities to establish their own antiriot police beginning in 2001.[96] The minister of Public Security is a highly ranked Politburo member for the first time since the Cultural Revolution, and the top leadership includes the largest representation of security specialists it has seen for a long time. The Party appoints all the judges and has the final say over court verdicts. Any organization that fails to register with the government or that might present a political threat, including churches and other religious groups, is shut down, and sometimes its leaders are jailed.

On every occasion that might provoke public protests, such as the anniversary of May 4 (1919) or June 4 (1989), a high-profile summit meeting in Beijing, the meeting of the National People's Congress, or the death of a retired leader, well-known activists are put under police supervision.

When Zhao Ziyang (who had been under house arrest since Tiananmen) died in 2005, the CCP imposed a news blackout. Articles on Zhao's death were scissored out of overseas newspapers and magazines before they were placed on Chinese newsstands, and reports on his death from international broadcasters like CNN, BBC, and NHK (the Japan Broadcasting Corporation) were blocked. One bold magazine made a covert protest against the blackout by not publishing its regular obituary feature for a month. The Party restricted public mourning for fear it would provoke a repeat of the 1989 uprising that had been sparked by the death of another reformist leader, Hu Yaobang.

PROMISE POPULISM

President Hu Jintao and Premier Wen Jiabao have adopted a populist platform that promises to "put people first" and create a "harmonious society" by narrowing income gaps and helping farmers and the poor. Their commitment to this cause is both personal and instrumental. Wen Jiabao grew up in rural China, the son of schoolteachers, a fact that ordinary people in China are well aware of. Both Hu and Wen spent much of their careers working in the poor, neglected regions of inland China. Wen, in particular, when appearing on television visiting the rural poor, looks like he is connecting emotionally with them. Like Bill Clinton, he sometimes tears up as he listens to their tragic stories.

By raising the inequality issue themselves and channeling resources to rural needs, they hope to dampen unrest while sidestepping the underlying systemic causes of illegitimate wealth. Yet like the other tactics just discussed, this one is self-contradictory. It would be impossible for Hu and Wen to root out corruption without giving up the patronage that keeps them in power. And how could they establish a truly independent court system to punish corrupt officials without a loss of power for the Communist Party?

SUSTAIN GROWTH AND APPEAL TO NATIONALISM

By sustaining high rates of economic growth, China's leaders create new jobs and limit the number of unemployed workers who might go to the barricades. Binding the public to the Party through nationalism also helps preempt opposition. The trick is to find a foreign policy approach that can achieve both these vital objectives simultaneously.

How long can it last?

Viewed objectively, China's communist regime looks surprisingly resilient. It may be capable of surviving for years to come so long as the economy continues to grow and create jobs. Survey research in Beijing shows widespread support (over 80 percent) for the political system as a whole linked to sentiments of nationalism and acceptance of the CCP's argument about "stability first."[97] Without making any fundamental changes in the CCP-dominated political system—leaders from time to time have toyed with reform ideas such as local elections but in each instance have backed away for fear of losing control—the Party has bought itself time. As scholar Pei Minxin notes, the ability of communist regimes to use their patronage and coercion to hold on to power gives them little incentive to give up any of that power by introducing gradual democratization from above. Typically, only when communist systems implode do their political fundamentals change.[98]

As China's leaders well know, the greatest political risk lying ahead of them is the possibility of an economic crash that throws millions of workers out of their jobs or sends millions of depositors to withdraw their savings from the shaky banking system. A massive environmental or public health disaster also could trigger regime collapse, especially if people's lives are endangered by a media cover-up imposed by Party authorities. Nationwide rebellion becomes a real possibility when large numbers of people are upset about the same issue at the same time. Another dangerous scenario is a domestic or international crisis in which the CCP leaders feel compelled to lash out against Japan, Taiwan, or the United States because from their point of view not lashing out might endanger Party rule.

Lesson 3: Keep the Military on the Side of the Party

The new PLA

The People's Liberation Army (PLA) has been a key player in Chinese politics since before the founding of the People's Republic in 1949. During the Revolution, the People's Liberation Army and the Chinese Communist Party were practically merged. Mao Zedong and other CCP leaders served as commanders and the top generals were members of the Politburo. After 1949, Party commissars were part of every PLA unit, and the PLA was held up as a model of ideological commitment. The military's mission was to "serve the people" by building roads and irrigation, running state farms, preserving internal order, and preparing for people's war—although it also saw combat in Korea, Vietnam, and elsewhere. The huge "people's army" consisted mostly of conscripted peasant youth eager to escape the hardships of rural life, garbed in unimpressive baggy fatigues and sneakers, and equipped with antiquated weapons and the "spiritual atom bomb" of Mao Zedong thought.

Today's PLA has cruise missiles, submarines, fighter jets, guided missile destroyers—as well as spiffy new uniforms. The military also has begun to develop high-tech weapons to wage information warfare, and some admirals are talking about developing a fleet of aircraft carriers.[99] The PLA has transformed itself into a professional modern force. According to the Pentagon, the PLA is on its way to having capabilities that "pose a credible threat to other modern militaries operating in the region,"[100] and "put regional military balances at risk."[101] The Pentagon also envisions China as the power with "the greatest potential to compete militarily with the U.S."[102]

How did the people's army become a professional fighting force? Could the PLA exploit the domestic insecurity of China's leaders to "hijack the state" and take it in the direction of war?[103] A Party anxious to keep the military on its side might find it hard to say no to the generals. A politically powerful and independent military is a danger sign in a rising power. The military buildups and aggressive policies that drove Germany and Japan into twentieth-century wars were instigated by ambitious militaries that civilian politicians couldn't control.

The politicians and the generals

The PLA always has had political clout because of its tight relationship with the Party elite and its prestige as the victorious revolutionary army.[104] It constitutes a large bloc in the Central Committee (22 percent of full members) and has two representatives on the twenty-four-member Politburo, although for more than a decade, no general has served on the Politburo Standing Committee. Almost 10 percent of China's legislature, the National People's Congress, is in uniform.[105]

Although Mao sometimes suspected individual generals of plotting against him, the PLA as an organization never tried to usurp political power. Mao summoned the PLA to run the country and restore order after the chaos of the Cultural Revolution. After a few years, however, the PLA voluntarily returned to the barracks and handed power back to the Communist Party.[106]

Yet civilian control over the military is far from complete. The Communist Party, not the government, oversees the PLA.[107] Formally speaking, the Central Military Commission (CMC) that leads the military is both a Party and a government organ. But in reality it is led by the Party. And except for President Hu, all of the CMC's members are generals or admirals. The Ministry of National Defense is just a sign on an impressive building where foreigners are greeted, lacking the real authority of the U.S. Department of Defense. The PLA has always obeyed the Party's orders, and the Party leaders allow it a high degree of autonomy in exchange for defending the Party from potential domestic enemies. The *Liberation Army Daily* (*Jiefang Jun Bao*) describes the army's core mission as to be "a guarantor for the Party to consolidate its status as a party in power."[108] Yet the relationship between the PLA commanders and the Party's top politicians remains delicate. China turned down the Pentagon's offer to set up a military hotline between the high-level armed forces of the two countries because it was reluctant to delegate that much authority to the senior commanders.[109]

As the country's top military decision-making organ, the CMC has wide-ranging autonomy in decision making on defense matters. However, on military issues with major political, economic, and diplomatic ramifications, such as over Taiwan or on China-Russia relations, the CMC and its subordinate PLA general headquarters departments consult closely with the Politburo Standing Committee and leadership small groups.

The PLA leadership is loyal to its commander in chief, who is the CMC chairman, but only as long as he is also the head of the CCP.[110] Jiang Zemin retired from his position as Party general secretary in 2002 while retaining his CMC post. This separation of traditionally linked roles unsettled the military top brass, who began to get nervous about having two lines of authority—one to Jiang and one to Hu. Jiang reportedly had been keen to retain his CMC chairmanship for a full five-year term. But having heard the message from the generals, he gave up the position only after two years.

President Hu Jintao, in military uniform, visits with People's Liberation Army soldiers, Beijing, February 2, 2005. (Wang Jianmin/Xinhua)

Winning the support of the PLA would present a major hurdle for any rival leader trying to claim power. And assuring that the PLA is loyal to him personally is a high priority for the head of the Party.

Rewarding the protectors

The dependence of the head of the Party on the PLA to watch his back doesn't mean that the PLA always gets what it wants, which, as a Chinese journalist put it, is "a bigger budget and honor." When Deng Xiaoping (a former PLA political commissar) was the leader, he was so confident of the loyalty of the PLA that he squeezed it financially in order to concentrate on the civilian economy. Of the "four modernizations" announced in 1977, military modernization came last behind agriculture, industry, and science (the opposite of the growth path pursued by Germany and Japan during the 1930s).[111] Deng encouraged the PLA to become a more professional force, but he didn't provide the resources to accomplish it. Official defense spending stayed almost flat during the 1980s at a time when investments in the domestic economy were dramatically increasing. (If we factor in inflation, defense spending actually declined in real terms to the point by the late 1980s that PLA budget chiefs confessed that the official budget could only meet around 70 percent of the military's actual spending requirements.[112]) Official defense spending constituted an average of 6.35 percent of national income from 1950 to 1980, but dropped to 2.3 percent during the 1980s and 1.4 percent during the 1990s (of course the national income was much larger than before).[113]

The number of soldiers was cut almost in half, from 4.5 million in 1981 to 2.31 million in 2001.[114] By cutting the size of the bloated military, China's capabilities got stronger. But at the same time, military units (along with civilian units like schools, hospitals, and government offices) were told to earn money by running businesses to ease the financial burden on the state.

The period of military neglect came to an end in the 1990s. Defense spending has risen in real terms and as a percentage of GNP since 1999.[115] Official military spending has increased at double-digit rates throughout the decade and up to the present. Official military spending in 2005 increased by 12.6 percent to $29.9 billion, double the 2000 figure.[116] The 2006 budget increased military spending by 14.7 percent to $35 million.[117] The greatest infusion of new funds is going to the navy and air force, which although less politically influential than the army, are crucial to prepare for Taiwan-related contingencies.

This infusion of funds into military modernization, although a significant trend, does not match the all-out military buildups that occurred in early twentieth-century Germany and Japan and led them into war.[118] The

2005 official military budget was only 1.34 percent of China's total domestic product and 7.34 percent of total government expenditure (compared to 17.8 percent of total government expenditure of the United States, 11.4 percent of France, and 9.25 percent of Germany, according to Chinese calculations).[119] Even if China's actual military budget is two or three times the official number, as many experts believe, then its total spending amounts to $60 to $90 billion, comparable to Russia ($65 billion), but far behind the U.S. military budget of over $500 billion.[120]

Why bigger PLA budgets?

The PLA is enjoying bigger budgets at least in part because today's leaders are less politically secure and have a greater need to keep the military satisfied. As the first Chinese leaders not to have served in the military, Jiang Zemin and Hu Jintao cannot count on its automatic allegiance. Hu Jintao, like Jiang Zemin before him, lavishes resources on it to make sure that he can depend on the new, professional PLA to support him.[121]

By making the paramilitary People's Armed Police the first line of defense against domestic unrest, the CCP leaders also reduce the risk that the PLA might refuse to shoot civilians—or turn their guns on the civilian leaders—in the next Tiananmen. The PLA welcomes the beefing up of the People's Armed Police because the 1989 crackdown had seriously undermined the military's professionalism and its combat effectiveness. The Chinese know that in December 1989, when Nicolae Ceausescu ordered the army to open fire on demonstrators, the army revolted and arrested the Romanian dictator, an event that sent shivers of fear through military and Party circles in China.

Hu Jintao appears to be having some difficulty winning over the military, however. Calls for the military to show its "absolute loyalty to the Party" are unusually shrill. Hu has not appointed as many new generals as Jiang had by this time. And the chief political commissar in the PLA made the remarkable public statement that Hu Jintao is "greatly concerned" about stability in the army.[122] The 14.7 percent increase in the 2006 official budget for the PLA should help Hu keep the military not just on the Party's side, but also on his side.

The strategic rationale for increasing the military budget is that China is preparing to solve the Taiwan problem militarily if it has to.[123] The emergence of democratically elected presidents in Taiwan who appeared to be moving the island toward formal independence provided the main impetus. When the Clinton administration permitted President Lee Teng-hui to visit America to make a speech at his college reunion at Cornell in 1995, China's leaders were shocked into the realization that if they didn't make China's threat to use force to prevent Taiwan independence more credible, they might be confronted with a fait accompli. Senior PLA officers were vocal in urging a strong show of force against Taiwan.[124] After the United States responded to China's large-scale exercises and missile launches by deploying two aircraft carrier battle groups, China's leaders deescalated the crisis with a new appreciation of the country's military weakness. This was the context in which the PLA received funds to step up the acquisition of new fighter jets and destroyers from Russia, improve its training for coordinated operations among the army, navy, air force, and strategic missile forces, and begin to mobilize local civilians so that they could directly support military units in the event of war by providing fishing boats and merchant ships to transport troops across the Taiwan Strait and by activating militia and reserve units.

Senior military commanders continue to use the Taiwan issue as a central rationale to justify continued hefty increases in defense spending. At the National People's Congress annual meeting in April 2006, Rear Admiral Yang Yi, the head of a major PLA strategic think-tank, said that the main reason for the latest double-digit increase in Chinese military outlays was the need to "oppose Taiwanese separatist activities." Huang Chunping, a rocket expert affiliated with the PLA General Armament Department concurred, stating that "as I see it, with the Taiwan independence forces again raging, we will do what should be done, and despite the Olympics, the national interests and the unity of the motherland come first!"[125]

A 2006 article in the Chinese press stated the connection explicitly. "The double-digit increase [in military spending] did not take place until very recent years when tension escalated across the Taiwan Straits. As the leadership of Taiwan goes mad and provocatively edges toward splitting the island from the country, the Mainland is being pressed to get serious about the least-desired scenario of armed conflict. After all, the country has a legitimate right to safeguard its territorial integrity."[126]

Guns vs. butter

Although the Chinese military budget, like the rest of the budget, is never debated openly before it is formally approved by the National People's Congress, some intellectuals in China are starting to grumble about excessive military spending. A subterranean "guns vs. butter" debate is beginning among the policy elite, but not among the populace. A Beijing survey found more support for military vs. social spending in 2004 than in 2003.[127] Almost all (95 percent) of Chinese urban citizens surveyed by the Pew Global Attitudes Project in 2006 thought that China's rising military power was a good thing.[128]

One professor told me that at a 2005 seminar, he raised the question, "How strong a military do we actually need?" "I want China to be an economic superpower and a political superpower," he said, "but it's not necessary for it to be a military superpower." Another academic said that the issue went beyond simply taking money away from domestic priorities like developing poor inland regions or improving the availability of water in north China. "The military buildup makes the PLA more influential, so it will be impossible to make progress on domestic political reform." An economist who advocated making the budget debate more open and transparent said that the PLA and the Ministry of Construction were the major opponents of such a move.

During the 2006 meeting of the National People's Congress, the PLA felt it needed for the first time to justify its budget increase in the mass media. Articles bolstered the military's case by quoting citizen comments on the Internet, one of which advocated raising the defense budget to 10 percent of government spending because the country "stands on a weak base" of national defense.[129] Press articles pointed out that the PLA started modernizing from a very low base that was generations behind the world's strongest militaries in terms of hardware.[130] A lengthy article in the *Liberation Army Daily* replied to arguments against military spending by making the case that "the awe created by military strength" instead of causing war, actually helps "curb or postpone the outbreak of war" and guarantee a "peaceful international environment for development."[131] Another article argued that China's international influence depended on having a military force "commensurate with its international status."[132] An influential Fudan University physicist called for military competition with the United States in a "bold and confident manner." He asserted, "We do not need to spend more money on arms to bully other countries, but we do need a bigger military budget to avoid being bullied."[133]

Military hawks

The military's perspective on Japan, Taiwan, and the United States generally is more hawkish than that of civilian officials, according to interviews, and military voices constrain China's policies on these controversial issues. The PLA press typically takes a tougher line on these issues than the civilian press. According to scholar You Ji, soldiers are taught that "Taiwan presents the last unfulfilled mission of the PLA to liberate the whole country." They "would regard it as an enormous loss of face if Taiwan were to declare independence and the PLA were unable to do anything about it."[134] The Party leaders don't dare try to persuade the PLA otherwise, especially when the actual situation looks unfavorable to China. "If political relations are bad with Japan or the U.S., the PLA has more influence," said a Chinese journalist. A PLA researcher told You Ji that when he read Jiang Zemin's speeches on Taiwan, he found that Jiang talked tough to the military, emphasizing the importance of military preparations to solve the problem, but when addressing civilians, talked about the hope for a peaceful solution.[135]

In a recent example of tough talk from the military, General Zhu Chenghu, a longtime acquaintance with a sharp tongue, said in an interview with the foreign press that China was prepared to use nuclear weapons if the United States attacked China with conventional weapons in a clash over Taiwan. China, he said, was willing to sacrifice "every city east of Xian." The statement not only roiled American public opinion against China, but also was completely out of line with China's long-held position of "no first use," i.e., that it would never use nuclear weapons unless it were attacked by nuclear weapons. But the Foreign Ministry spokesman did not completely disavow Zhu's remarks. They were the general's personal views, he said, but then he added that China will never allow Taiwan to become independent.[136] (China's foreign minister, at a Washington event, did reaffirm China's position that it would never use nuclear weapons first.[137]) Five months later, General Zhu received a mild punishment for his remarks—an administrative demerit that meant no promotion for a year.[138] "He should have been fired," a researcher at a military think-tank said.

Internet commentary debated whether Zhu's statement was an officially sanctioned signal to the United States, and whether he was a brave patriot or a lunatic who "should face a firing squad." "I find punishing him quite unnecessary. Perhaps everyone has forgotten how America bombed our embassy," said one posting. "China is listed by America as one of the countries to deploy nuclear weapons against," noted another. But some others criticized Zhu as "another Hitler-esque war maniac," and said, "If Zhu wants to die, go ahead. It's not worth millions of people dying and destroying every city east of Xian for Taiwan." One optimist said that Zhu's comments were "just talk. The children of Chinese leaders studying in America will never allow a nuclear war." Another observed, "Such comments have at least the virtue of informing Americans that their current foreign policies create passionate enemies. The American people simply do not believe that they will ever suffer any serious losses on American soil." Some of the praise of the general was removed by bulletin board monitors soon after it was posted.

Domestic Politics and Foreign Policy

When today's Chinese leaders make foreign policy, they have to keep in mind the reactions of the groups upon whom their political power depends — other leaders, the mass public, and the military. When it comes to economic policy and routine matters of foreign policy, politicians do what works, i.e., what makes the economy grow at 7 percent per year or more. If they don't improve living standards and keep unemployment low, they believe they will meet the same fate as their former comrades in the Soviet Union.

Much of China's foreign policy is highly pragmatic in order to prevent international disruptions to domestic economic growth. But the foreign policy issues that receive a lot of public attention are treated symbolically, as issues of principle instead of problems to be solved: the principle that Japan must atone for its historical sins, the "one China" principle that Taiwan must accept, and the principle of opposition to American hegemonism. Communist Party leaders, as well as their ambitious subordinates hoping for promotions, show their strength by taking a firm stand on principle. Swimming against this powerful current of political correctness on Japan, Taiwan, and the United States takes unusual bravery. As one policy advisor said, "In China, when foreign policy is made by a handful of leaders, they make the right call, flexible and pragmatic. When it involves a larger group they tend to be more rigid and tough."

One professor said, "Leaders and officials need to speak the truth, not play to this popular [nationalist] mentality." He recalled how Premier Zhou Enlai, speaking to a crowd upon his return from a major international meeting in Indonesia in 1955, said "Our Southeast Asian neighbors are not afraid of the U.S. In fact they are afraid of us." "That's the kind of courage it takes," the professor said.

In the past, foreign policy rarely has been central to inner-party political contests,[139] but we may see more debates between hawks and doves in the future. In the early 1990s Deng Xiaoping had to defend rapprochement with the United States against the conservative wing of the CCP that had been strengthened by the Tiananmen crackdown.[140] Nowadays, it would be surprising if everyone agreed on the same tradeoffs between maintaining economic growth and bolstering the CCP's reputation as a defender of national honor.[141] If CCP leaders begin to compete by reaching out to ordinary citizens, or a crisis occurs that galvanizes public attention, hawkish positions are likely to dominate because they resonate more with the public than dovish ones.

By shining the light of publicity on foreign policy, the media are making it harder and harder for decision makers not to treat foreign policy as domestic politics. China's press is not yet entirely free, but it is market driven and pushing the limits of Party censorship, and the Internet amplifies its impact on public opinion. Ironically, a freer press may push leaders toward short-term grandstanding moves that damage long-term international relations—politicians in democratic countries like the United States often feel that kind of pressure to flex their muscles. A prominent Chinese expert on America said, "If China had a free press, I would be criticized all the time. The moderates never win with the public."

4

The Echo Chamber of Nationalism

Media and the Internet

IN JANUARY 2006, Li Datong, the middle-aged editor of *Freezing Point* (*Bing Dian*), found himself fired. *Freezing Point* is the weekly supplement of the national newspaper *China Youth Daily* (*Zhongguo Qingnian Bao*), the official voice of China's Communist Youth League that had transformed itself into a popular commercial newspaper. Li's error was publishing a scholarly article by Guangzhou professor Yuan Weishi challenging the orthodox version of Chinese history taught in junior-high-school textbooks.

Professor Yuan compared the accounts in PRC and Hong Kong textbooks of major conflicts with foreign powers in China's nineteenth-century history—the Opium War and the Boxer Rebellion—and found that the PRC textbooks distort history to "inflame nationalistic passions." "Since the 'foreign devils' are the invaders, the Chinese are justified and praised in whatever they do," he wrote, even the xenophobic Boxer movement that "cut down telegraph lines, destroyed schools, demolished railroad tracks, burned foreign merchandise, murdered foreigners and all Chinese who had any connection with foreign culture."[1] The article argues that this kind of uncritical antiforeign nationalism was at the root of Mao-era disasters like the Great Leap Forward and the Cultural Revolution, and that it is still being taught to Chinese children. In Yuan's words, "Our youth are continuing to drink the wolf's milk!"

Two weeks after the article was published, Communist Party Propaganda Department officials called the senior editors of the *China Youth Daily* on the carpet and ordered them to close *Freezing Point* and dismiss Li and his co-editor, Lu Yuegang. They accused the weekly of publishing an article that "attempted to vindicate the criminal acts by the imperialist powers in invading China . . . contradicted news propaganda discipline, seriously damaged the national feelings of the Chinese people . . . and created a bad social influence."[2]

Li, although a veteran journalist and Communist Party member, resisted fiercely. Refusing to bend to the propaganda authorities, the editor went over their heads to complain to top Party and government leaders that the propaganda officials' actions violated China's constitutional guarantee of freedom of speech. He also posted online an open letter protesting the "illegal stoppage" of the publication. The propaganda officials had banned all media and Internet reporting on the suspension and shut down Li's blog even before they informed Li about the suspension. But Li's letter was widely copied and circulated during the brief window before the CCP watchdogs deleted it from bulletin boards and forums.[3] Li also gave interviews to foreign journalists who reported extensively on the closing of *Freezing Point*. In a rare act of opposition, thirteen liberal-leaning retired officials, including a former secretary of Mao Zedong, a former head of the Propaganda Department, and former chief editors of the *People's Daily* and Xinhua news agency, posted a letter protesting the closing of the magazine.[4]

According to Li, the Propaganda Department officials picked an article about history textbooks as their excuse to shut *Freezing Point*, which for some time had been testing the limits by publishing articles on Taiwan democracy and other sensitive subjects, because they were confident of having public opinion on their side of the history issue. As they predicted, almost all the comments posted on popular Web sites such as sina.com and many postings by Chinese students studying abroad on mitbbs.com lambasted Professor Yuan as a traitor for taking a critical perspective on Chinese history. Support for Yuan's revisionist approach prevailed only on the liberal intellectual Web site Century China (Shiji Zhongguo at www.cc.org.cn), which itself was closed by the propaganda authorities during the summer of 2006.

President Hu Jintao stepped in to quell the controversy by means of a compromise that allowed the paper to remain open and the editors to stay on the payroll in lower positions, but muzzled its politically freewheeling style. Li Datong, having no other options left, surrendered. He told a Hong Kong television interviewer that *Freezing Point* was able to resume publication quickly because of the "open-minded act" of central senior officials.[5]

China's Media Revolution

The *Freezing Point* affair dramatizes how China's newly commercialized media and the Internet have radically transformed domestic politics and have complicated the domestic context for making foreign policy in China.

In the prereform era, China had no journalism as we understand it, only propaganda. The Communist Party was highly concerned about public opinion and invested a huge amount of resources in trying to affect it.[6] The mass media's sole purpose was to serve as loudspeakers to mobilize public support for Party policies.[7] The media was called the "throat and tongue" of the Party, a phrase that today's irreverent young journalists utter with delicious sarcasm. Chinese citizens obtained all their information about their country and the world from a few officially controlled media sources that said pretty much the same thing. In 1979, there were only sixty-nine newspapers in the country, all of them run by Party and government organs.[8] As of 2005, China had approximately two thousand newspapers and nine thousand magazines.[9]

Front-page photographs glorified local and national leaders, and every article celebrated their achievements in formulaic, ideological prose. Local news such as fires or crimes was rarely reported. What little foreign news appeared was based on the dispatches of the government's Xinhua news agency. People read, or pretended to read, the *People's Daily* and other official newspapers in the morning at work—all offices and factories were required to subscribe to them. The 7:00 PM news on China Central Television (CCTV), the country's prime-time television news program, rehashed what had been in the *People's Daily*.

To help transform China into a modern, open economy, and to save the government money, the Communist Party decided to give up its monopoly over the provision of information to the public and allowed newspapers and magazines, television and radio stations, and Internet providers to compete on the market instead of being bankrolled by the state.[10] The commercialization of the mass media began in the 1980s and picked up steam in the 1990s following a brief retrenchment after the Tiananmen crackdown.[11] Since then, media organizations have been competing with one another to sell advertisements and attract audiences by feeding the public's hunger for timely, accurate, and lively news.

Internet News

The Internet is the greatest multiplier of the new sources of information. In the decade since China was first connected to the Internet in 1995, its use has exploded. Only 10 percent of Chinese adults had even heard of the Internet in 1997. Two years later, 2 percent had gone online. By 2004,

12 percent of Chinese aged eighteen and older used the Internet, according to a Gallup national survey.[12] The estimated number of Internet users totaled one hundred thirty-two million by the end of 2006.[13] Just one household in eight actually owns a computer, but many more have access to computers at work, school, or in the more than one hundred thousand Internet cafés dotting the country.[14] China is well on its way to becoming the world's largest Internet community.

The Chinese public spends more time reading news on the Internet than engaging in other online activities.[15] Most Internet news comes from three big commercial Internet news sites, sohu.com, sina.com, and netease.com. Only 10 percent of Chinese Internet users access international media sources directly.[16]

The Chinese news sites post breaking news from the international media almost instantaneously, much faster than the print and television sources, which have to consult Party watchdogs first. The news sites also pick up exposés from local media and turn them into national news. Additionally, the sites provide roadmaps to local and international news sources. To compete, many established newspapers have created online editions. Because of its speed and wide reach, the Internet sets the agenda, forcing officials, and the print and television media, to react.

In one example, at 5:00 PM on April 1, 2001, a Chinese netizen posted a story from the Associated Press reporting that a U.S. EP-3 reconnaissance plane and a Chinese fighter jet had collided off China's southern coast, setting off an uproar in the chat rooms. It took two hours for China's official Xinhua news agency to issue its announcement of the accident. And the story didn't hit the *People's Daily* front page until April 4. Li Xiguang (the dean of the Tsinghua University Journalism School) concluded that because of its slow response during the crisis, the official press effectively abdicated its role as opinion leader to the Internet, which carried timely news from foreign sources.[17]

Between the Market and the Censors

China is still a long way from having a free press, however. As of 2004, China ranked near the bottom of world rankings of freedom of the press by the international watchdog organizations Freedom House (173 out of 192 countries) and Reporters without Borders (162 of 167 countries). The Communist Party continues to monitor and control the content of mass media, including the Internet, although at a much higher cost and less thoroughly than before. The Propaganda Department, responsible for the content of the media, remains one of the most powerful baronies within the Communist Party. Journalist He Qinglian, in her book *Media Control in China*, lambastes the Communist Party for its limits on press freedom. She describes Chinese journalists as "dancing in shackles." Yet she credits marketization for "opening a gap in the Chinese government's control of the news media."[18]

"The government is losing the levers to control the media," says Liu Junning, an academic advocate of democracy. "It is the consumers who command the loyalty of media managers now," says Liu Xiaobo, a writer who has spent years in jail for his political views. "They show fake enthusiasm for orders from above, but their efforts to curry favor with the customer are genuine."[19]

Access to Information Expands

The Communist Party's propaganda bureaucracy tries to control news content in the market-oriented media and largely succeeds in the print and television domains. Only a few journalists have dared to resist in the manner Li Datong did. Yet the Party allows reporting of many topics that were taboo in the past. And Internet communication is just too fast, too decentralized, and too internationalized for the censors to block breaking news before it reaches the online public.[20]

The Chinese people have access to more information than ever before about what is going on inside and outside the country. Keeping the Chinese people ignorant of a speech by Taiwan's president, Japan's premier, or the U.S. secretary of defense is no longer possible. Nor is it possible to suppress news about a natural or man-made disaster inside China. When authorities tried to black out news about the developing SARS epidemic in south China during February through March 2003 as the National People's Congress was meeting in Beijing, people found out about it anyway because their friends and family living abroad or in Hong Kong informed them by cell phone. *Caijing* magazine evaded the ban by reporting on the outbreak of the epidemic in Hong Kong. When a brave Chinese doctor tried to sound the alarm about the spread of the disease to Beijing, the domestic press wouldn't publish what he told them, but *Time* magazine did, and the *Time* interview was immediately posted on the Internet.

Propaganda Department Retains Clout

Two organizations within the Communist Party have the status of sacred cows because the top leaders depend on them to stay in power. The Organization Department, responsible for appointing CCP and government officials, controls patronage. And the Propaganda Department, responsible for the political content of the media, textbooks, books, and movies, controls public opinion. Together with the internal security bureaucracies and the People's Liberation Army, these organizations constitute the "control cartel," the linchpin of Party power.

The marketization of the media and the growth of the Internet, by making the job of the propaganda police more difficult and justifying their need for greater resources and authority, may have actually enhanced their clout within the CCP. No one knows how large the censorship corps actually is in China, but it undoubtedly has expanded in recent years.[21] The Party appears willing to spend whatever it takes not to lose the information battle. (In contrast, Singapore, the commercial city-state that has long practiced press censorship, decided it would be too costly to attempt to restrict the information on the Internet beyond blocking pornography and requiring sites to register.[22]) The commercial interests behind the media also have more to lose if the propaganda police put them out of business. With so much money at stake, the large Internet news sites and other large circulation publications can't afford not to defer to the propaganda authorities.

Ever since the Propaganda Department was put in charge of the patriotic education campaign, the 1990s campaign to bolster the CCP's legitimacy, it has been single-mindedly promoting nationalism. Only when the top leadership, speaking in one voice, gives it an explicit order, does it modify the message.

Stories about Japan, Taiwan, and the United States Sell

The media, competing with one another, naturally try to appeal to the tastes of their targeted audiences. Editors make choices about which stories to cover based on their judgments about what will sell commercially. That means a lot of reports about Japan, Taiwan, and the United States, the international relationships that are the objects of intense interest and emotion. The publicity given to these topics makes them domestic political issues and constrains the way China's leaders and diplomats deal with them. Most foreign policy issues—those involving China's relations with countries other than the big three—get little media publicity and are handled by the professional diplomats in the Foreign Ministry. Even relatively minor events involving China's relations with Japan, Taiwan, or the United States, however, become front-page news and must be carefully managed by the politicians in the Communist Party Politburo Standing Committee.

Media Stoke Nationalism

News media, competing for audiences but "guided" by the propaganda authorities, reinforce nationalist myths.[23] Chinese journalists have a saying, "There are no small matters in foreign affairs." Foreign affairs topics are considered politically sensitive and potentially dangerous territory for journalists. Journalists also have to satisfy two masters: their audiences and the Propaganda Department. A nationalist slant on news events works for both of them. Nationalism has become the politically correct point of view, enforced by the marketplace as well as the censors, as the public reaction to the *Freezing Point* article on history textbooks illustrates. But encouraging nationalism can backfire, as Chinese leaders learned from the anti-American demonstrations that followed the Belgrade embassy bombing in 1999. After that crisis, Chinese leaders ordered the Propaganda Department to moderate the media message about the United States to calm public opinion and protect the relationship with Washington.

Officials Get Information about Public Opinion

The nationalist views expressed in the media and the Internet blow back on policymakers. Chinese officials read the tabloids and the Internet to find out what the public is really thinking, and come away with the impression that nationalism is sweeping the country. They feel under public pressure to take tough stands toward Japan, Taiwan, and the United States because what they are reading is highly skewed in the nationalist direction.

Media Facilitate Opposition

The commercial media and the Internet could enable a political opposition to emerge. Interactive technologies like cell phones and the Internet enable individuals to coordinate collective action such as the Falun Gong sit-in in 1999 and the anti-Japanese student demonstrations of 2005. Although news sources are forbidden to publish reports of protests, word gets out anyway, emboldening others to join in. In the old days, when all news was communicated through Communist Party mouthpieces, the Party used the media to mobilize support for its policies and had few worries about popular opposition to them. Thomas Schelling made this point with an apt analogy. "The participants of a square dance may all be thoroughly dissatisfied with the particular dances being called, but as long as the caller has the microphone, nobody can dance anything else."[24] Today, as the number and variety of microphones have increased, so have the force of public opinion and the possibility of coordinated opposition.

Global Times

Newspaper market research indicates that international news is second to sports as the most popular topic. In 1992, the Communist Party's flagship newspaper, *People's Daily*, struck gold when it founded *Global Times*, a profitable newspaper devoted to international news that now claims a readership of almost two million, the second largest in the country.[25] *Global Times* has the unique advantage of having access to the *People's Daily's* foreign correspondents and the political protection of the Communist Party leadership. It is a tabloid, but an authoritative one. "We try to represent the national interest," said the editor. "We don't want to make problems for China's foreign policy. The American press considers itself a watchdog of the government, but in China the press has a more cooperative spirit toward the government." Unlike some other tabloids whose editors get fired frequently for stepping over the line, *Global Times* has never lost an editor because it has close relations with the Communist Party and knows what the Party wants it to say. Thanks to its special connections, it breaks stories that other newspapers don't dare to report. For example, it was the first to report on the North Korean famine in 1997.

At a special seminar on the *Global Times* phenomenon sponsored by *People's Daily*, CCP propaganda officials praised the publication for taking the "art of propaganda" to a high level. Tsinghua University Journalism dean Li Xiguang noted that the paper's huge commercial success proved that it was giving readers what they wanted. It took international news stories and reframed them from the standpoint of China's national interests.[26] One *Global Times* editor said that the Party leaders use the newspaper to communicate some of the "undertones" of their policies to the public.

Global Times began timidly, publishing once a week and covering mostly soft international news topics, such as Princess Diana, Arafat's wedding, the Japanese royal family, Chinese film stars in Hollywood, World Cup football, and the Olympics. During the 1995–96 crisis in the Taiwan Strait following President Lee Teng-hui's visit to the United States, only one front-page story dealt with Taiwan. The paper covered positively President Clinton's visit to China in June 1998, but it devoted more ink to his scandalous behavior in the White House with Monica Lewinsky.[27]

In 1999 *Global Times* began to feature harder news from a brash nationalist angle, starting with sympathetic stories on Yugoslavia's resistance to bombing by NATO and the United States. This trend toward harder news stories accelerated after the May 1999 bombing of the Chinese Embassy in Belgrade. (It is no wonder people in China believed that NATO's bombing of the Chinese Embassy in Belgrade was intentional. Based on the slant of *Global Times* reporting, they must have inferred that China was covertly assisting the Yugoslav government.) Since that time, about half of the newspaper's front-page stories—which always include a sensational headline and photograph—deal with the United States because, as a *Global Times* editor said, "People care most about China's national security and U.S.-China relations." "You have to have a front page that will make people want to buy the paper," he continued. "A good way to attract readers is to have an exciting cover story on the United States, Japan, or Taiwan, or if possible, two or more." Another editor acknowledged, "Our reporting is very critical of Japan on the history issue. We react with a story whenever the Japanese right wing says or does something that shows its support of militarism."

Sensitive to the criticism from abroad and from Chinese academics that *Global Times* promulgates xenophobic nationalism, its editors insist they promote "patriotism" (*aiguo zhuyi*), not "nationalism" (*minzu zhuyi*). To reach audiences who are put off by jingoism and want a more moderate approach, the newspaper publishes debates between experts with different points of view. Professor Yan Xuetong, whose sharp sound bites on international power politics have made him a television star, proposed the idea of the debates to the *Global Times* editors and hosts them on a regular basis at Tsinghua University where he teaches. *Global Times* also has pioneered the practice of publishing interviews and dialogues with foreigners, including diplomats from the U.S. Embassy in Beijing and academics like me. In 2004 the newspaper published my dialogue with America expert Wang Jisi about the way Chinese school textbooks mold students' attitudes.

Other newspapers focused on international news, like *World News Journal* (*Shijie Xinwen Bao*) compete with *Global Times*, but have failed to surpass it in authoritativeness or circulation.

Television

Most Chinese get their news from television. China Central Television (CCTV) has expanded to 16 channels, and cable carries over forty provincial channels nationwide. 95 percent of the population owned TV sets as of 2000, about two-thirds of them are connected to cable, and three times as many adults watch television daily as read a newspaper or listen to the radio combined.[28] The countryside, where the Internet has not yet penetrated, is almost entirely dependent on television for news.

China Central Television is considered the most authoritative television network and the best place for advertisers to win consumer trust for their products.[29] CCTV carries commercial advertising on all its channels and competes energetically with the cable stations. CCTV-2 and many local cable channels have home shopping. Many television channels are required to broadcast the CCTV nightly news at 7:00 PM. Following this old-fashioned exercise in propaganda, however, comes a news discussion program called Focus introduced in 1994 that breaks new ground with its investigative reporting of wrongdoing by local officials. Focus is widely regarded as the most influential media voice in China.[30] Because the program's muckraking attracts the attention of top national officials, hours after each exposé airs local government and Party officials meet to swiftly resolve the problems that were criticized.[31] A day or two later, Focus proudly announces how the local officials have resolved the problems, including firings. One Chinese television critic told me that the show has lost much of its bite recently, but the programs I watched during the summer of 2006 harshly criticized local officials' failures to respond adequately to destructive typhoons. The show sometimes invites experts to discuss foreign policy questions, but its focus is largely domestic.

For timely news during an international crisis, however, China Central Television lags behind the local cable channels and Hong Kong-based Phoenix Television. During the terrorist attacks on New York City and Washington, D.C., on September 11, 2001, the popular Hunan and Chongqing channels broadcast live CNN reports from America. (CNN otherwise is available in China only in international hotels, government offices, and some high-end residential developments. Some individuals rented hotel rooms for several days to watch the CNN coverage of the 9/11 attacks.) Central Television, however, after a brief news bulletin right after the first attack and a slightly expanded report an hour later, went silent on the event until it ran a full report with prerecorded footage three hours later. According to one Chinese media expert, CCTV drove the audience away by being overcautious in its reporting.[32] Presumably CCTV had to get clearance from the political authorities before it could broadcast the footage. Viewers complained strenuously on the Internet about the delay in CCTV coverage.

Phoenix Television, a Hong Kong joint venture founded in 1996 between Rupert Murdoch's Star TV and several Chinese investors including the government-owned Bank of China, officially available only in nearby Guangdong Province and international hotels, according to one estimate actually reaches one hundred forty-seven million people on the Mainland and has about 20 percent of the television market in China's largest cities.[33] The Hong Kong channel, which features slick, international-style news shows, got its big break in 1999 when the United States mistakenly bombed the Chinese Embassy in Belgrade. Phoenix Television's timely and fervently nationalist reporting over seven days drew a large audience and turned its anchor people into celebrities.[34] During the September 2001 terrorist attacks on America, Phoenix Television reported round the clock, playing and replaying the footage of the planes colliding into the Trade Center towers, as its newscasters compared it to scenes in American disaster movies like *Pearl Harbor* and *Air Force One*.[35] More recently, Beijing students are following the war in Iraq closely on Phoenix TV.

Phoenix Television is the television equivalent of *Global Times*—splashy and nationalistic and favored by its ties with the Communist Party. But it is highly believable to Chinese viewers because it sounds nothing at all like old-style propaganda. The channel, which has to appeal to Hong Kong audiences as well as Mainland ones, is more daring in covering Taiwan-related issues than *Global Times*—it even carried the inauguration address of Taiwan's president, Chen Shui-bian.[36]

Central Television tried to win back audiences (and advertisers) during the U.S.-led invasion of Iraq.[37] Its coverage was so extensive—fourteen hours a day on the first three days of the war—that one Chinese academic joked to his friends, "I didn't realize that it was a Chinese war."[38] (Market competition also motivated many newspapers that had never before sent correspondents abroad to dispatch reporters to Iraq. The journalists were furious that the Chinese government ordered them to leave Iraq because of safety concerns when the invasion began, forcing them to report from the sidelines in Jordan.) CCTV established its own twenty-four-hour news channel to complete with Phoenix in May 2003, and is authorized to broadcast breaking news before, not after, obtaining the approval of the Party authorities.

Controls over Media Content

If you peruse the Chinese blogosphere or even a newsstand, you will be amazed at the fascination with Western cultural icons like Madonna and

Britney Spears and shocked at the images of violent and sexually explicit acts. As Xiao Qiang, director of the China Internet Project at the University of California–Berkeley said, "It's a wild place. Outside of politics, China is as free as anywhere."[39] The CCP lacks the manpower and resources to control everything, so it keeps its thumbs on the types of information that officials believe could arouse political opposition and subvert the Party's power. When it comes to sports, technology, lifestyles, movie and music stars, health, and sex, almost anything goes, especially on the Internet. Chinese Web surfers have access to the same information about these politically innocuous subjects that people in other countries do.

The CCP also has opened up space for the media to report on domestic issues like environmental problems, economic inequality, and weaknesses in health care and education. Corruption by local officials was also fair game for journalists as long as they went after political figures in provinces other than their own before 2004 when provincial leaders complained to the Politburo and convinced it to ban this practice of investigative reporting in other provinces. The bold muckraking of business-oriented publications like *Caijing* magazine on business corruption, poor corporate governance, and stock market manipulation has not run into serious flack from the CCP censors.

But anything related to individual leaders, the Communist Party, democracy, political reform, protests, discussions in government meetings, the 1989 Tiananmen demonstrations, human rights, Falun Gong, religion, corruption at the top, Taiwan, Tibet, and other topics that the Propaganda Department considers politically sensitive because they could subvert Party power, is forbidden. Mass protests, such as the anti-Japanese student demonstrations in April 2005 or the winter of 2005 through 2006 demonstrations by villagers in the southern province of Guangdong, are blacked out. Chinese journalists who report on topics in the closed zone can find themselves fired or imprisoned for years on charges of subversion or revealing state secrets.

Censorship of the market-oriented media relies primarily on old-fashioned communist methods: administrative oversight, personnel appointments, and self-censorship by career-minded journalists.[40] Every publication must obtain a government license, and licenses are limited in number and monopolized by high-ranking, state-owned organizations.[41] Most commercial newspapers and magazines are part of media conglomerates headed by an official publication and supervised by a government or Party entity. The chief editors of the newspapers and magazines are appointed from above. The chief editor of *Global Times*, appointed by the editors and Communist Party committee of *People's Daily*, acknowledged, "If we veer too far away from the general direction of the upper level [Party leadership], I will get fired. I know that." *Strong Nation Forum (Qiangguo Luntan)*, the fiercely nationalistic Internet bulletin board focusing on international issues, is located on People's Web (Renmin Wang at www.people.com.cn), a Web site owned and managed by *People's Daily*. Every publication and Internet news site has a government or Party entity responsible for the contents of its news. Central Television reports to Communist Party central authorities and television stations in provinces and cities report to local party authorities.

China's system of monitoring and censoring of the contents of the mass media is highly fragmented but dominated by the CCP Propaganda Department. The Propaganda Department has authority over the contents of the print media, television, and radio, which also must be licensed by the General Administration of Press and Publications and State Administration of Radio, Film, and Television. The State Council Information Office is in charge of the content of Internet news sites but as an agency much less powerful than the Propaganda Department, generally follows its lead. The Ministry of the Information Industry controls the Internet, including the blocking and filtering. The Ministry of State Security (China's CIA) and the Ministry of Public Security (China's FBI) police Internet bulletin boards, blogs, and e-mail.

Internet Censorship

Political optimists had high hopes for the Internet in China. As Xiao Qiang notes, because the Internet is "an inherently free technology with a decentralized, end-to-end architecture" many people believed it would make government censorship impossible.[42] But in fact, the Chinese censors have showed themselves highly capable of controlling Internet content and people's access to information on the Internet.

The daunting challenge of extending censorship to the Internet has stimulated a burst of Chinese technological innovation. According to Harvard University's Berkman Center, China operates the most extensive and technologically sophisticated system of Internet filtering in the world.[43] Filters installed on the Internet backbone and the servers of Internet providers, as well as on instant messaging client software, reject searches using banned keywords and block out some overseas and local Web sites entirely. Chinese hackers in 2004 discovered the list of approximately one thousand taboo keywords and posted it on the Internet: 15 percent of the terms were about sex, the rest were about politics (5 percent of the keywords were internationally related like "Defend the Diaoyu Islands" and "sell out the country," in keeping with the Party leaders' desire not to let ultranationalism get out of hand).[44]

The CCP also employs a large network of Internet "nannies"—managers of Web sites, bulletin boards, and blog platforms, assisted by government Internet monitors and citizen vigilantes—who are responsible for policing content.[45] The State Council Information Office, the lead agency at the central level, is in almost constant contact with the editors of thirty-two large Internet news sites—by instant messenger, no less—to orchestrate their coverage of important events, and the large sites in turn guide the smaller ones.[46]

(The State Council Information Office [SCIO] acquired the responsibility for managing the content of the Internet news sites because its head, Zhao Qizheng, was a former nuclear physicist and an early enthusiast of the Internet. When he came to Beijing from Shanghai to head the SCIO, he hired some Internet experts and established a Web site and internal network for his organization. So when the commercial Web sites got started in 1999, his agency was given the responsibility to oversee Internet news content.)

The human element means the control is far from airtight. It usually takes an hour or more for controversial postings to be erased. The article on history textbooks that prompted the Propaganda Department to close *Freezing Point* remained on the *China Youth Daily* Web site for a week or so after the print publication was closed. When Pope John Paul II died in 2005, the news sites first allowed and then deleted prayers and discussion about his death because as a sohu.com official said, "Religious issues are special. We are afraid of problems arising."[47] Even when the large sites block out a story such as the anti-Japanese demonstrations or the police shooting of rural protesters in the southern town of Dongzhou, the news spreads through e-mail, instant messaging, blogs, and bulletin-board forums.[48] Clever netizens evade the nannies by using coded substitutes for banned terms while retaining the meaning of the posting, or by using historical cases as surrogates for contemporary targets. Sophisticated netizens, moreover, can bypass the "Great Firewall" of China by doing searches through proxy-servers abroad. Still, the CCP has succeeded to a surprising and depressing degree in restricting people's access to politically relevant information through the Internet. Although many people may not even be aware that their searches are being blocked, others can see the visible hand of the censors as stories considered politically sensitive disappear mysteriously from news sites after minutes or hours. A 2005 poll by the Chinese Academy of Social Sciences found that only 7.6 percent of Chinese Internet users believe that political content on the Internet should be controlled.[49]

In spring 2005 Party authorities ordered university Internet bulletin boards, which had become platforms for freewheeling discussion, to deny access to individuals who were not university students. The students, afraid to express their resentment against the Party for dampening their discussions, took to the streets against the Japanese instead—a linkage that some students brought to my attention. A number of other chat rooms and bulletin boards that discuss political topics were shut down in 2006.

China's censorship of the Internet has caused an uproar in the U.S. Congress and media. American companies like Cisco, Yahoo, Microsoft, and Google, in order to do business in the lucrative China market, have swallowed their scruples and cooperated with the Chinese government in censoring searches. Yahoo came under the heaviest fire for helping Chinese security agencies track down Shi Tao, a Chinese journalist who had sent an Internet message leaking the Propaganda Department's instructions prohibiting articles on the anniversary of Tiananmen. Shi was sentenced to a steep ten years in prison.

The U.S. government (Voice of America and Radio Free Asia) helps fund the efforts of "hacktivists" like Bill Xia, a brilliant expatriate and Falun Gong adherent, to develop software that allows Chinese citizens to break through the CCP firewall to access information outside China, including information about human rights abuses inside China. Xia says one hundred thousand users a day use his Freegate software or two other censorship-defeating systems he developed.[50] The cyber war between the Chinese censors and U.S. human rights activists has so far not spilled over into relations between the two governments. But someday China's leaders may start complaining about what they certainly must view as a hostile violation of their virtual state sovereignty.

The Propaganda Department

As a department of the Communist Party Central Committee, the Propaganda Department outranks government ministries or the State Council Information Office, and dominates the process of media censorship. The CCP Propaganda Department has changed its English name to the "Publicity Department" to sound more forward looking. In Chinese, however, it is still called the Propaganda Department, and its functions as chief of the information police are much the same despite the broadening of its beat to include the new commercialized media. Operating through its national network of provincial and municipal branches, the Propaganda Department sends instructions to publications several times a week by fax or telephone about what topics not to report on and what topics to play up. The instructions are posted on editorial room bulletin boards. Typically, about one-third of the instructions come directly from the center, and two-thirds from the local propaganda authorities who according to journalists often are more restrictive than the central ones.

The central Propaganda Department and its regional branches have committees of about ten retired officials called "Critical Reading Groups" who critique news reporting and mete out penalties after the fact. After *Freezing Point* editor Li Datong publicly questioned the authority of these groups, someone knowledgeable about them leaked detailed information about their activities to the Hong Kong press. In the ten years since it was established in 1994, the central Critical Reading Group published 8,136 critiques, or an average of about two per day.[51]

In the Jiang Zemin era from 1990 to 2003, observers attributed the power of the Propaganda Department to its longtime head, Ding Guangen, a veteran Long March leader and ideological conservative who had been a bridge-playing pal of Deng Xiaoping. Rumors suggested that Jiang gave Ding and the propaganda apparatus free rein because Deng Xiaoping, before he died, had left a letter to Jiang asking him to protect his friend Ding.

After Ding retired in 2002, Guangdong provincial Party secretary Li Changchun took over the propaganda portfolio within the Standing Committee of the Politburo. Journalists were hopeful when Li, having just assumed his post, gave a major speech advocating that the media stay close to the public and to real events instead of mechanically following Party directives.[52] The new leadership team of President Hu Jintao and Premier Wen Jiabao handled the SARS crisis in a way that appeared to herald a new style of press openness—giving candid press conferences and criticizing the blackout of information on SARS that they could conveniently blame on the previous leaders.

These positive signs were short-lived, however. A few months later, the Propaganda Department began reverting to form, closing newspapers and firing journalists. It also backtracked on allowing foreign companies to participate in the operations and production of content for China's TV stations, much to the disappointment of Rupert Murdoch and other international media executives.[53]

Since then, numerous editors have been punished for pushing the limits of press freedom. Some of them bravely fought back. One fired editor posted a broadside on an academic Web site defending himself, and the editorial staff at another popular Beijing paper whose editors had been sacked went on strike.[54] Li Changchun, who when serving as Guangdong provincial leader had never been viewed as a friend by the local journalists, started sounding and acting like another Ding Guangen. One theory blames Li Changchun's ambitions. As the youngest member of the Politburo Standing Committee he may be trying to make a name for himself to win a promotion in 2007. Some journalists, however, blame the retrograde trend on the entrenched bureaucracy within the Propaganda Department itself—most of its senior officials who have been there for decades resist change. Other journalists and political observers attribute the crackdown to Hu and Wen and the other members of the Standing Committee who still have the traditional communist preference for more control over information reaching the public.

During a crisis, the Propaganda Department often goes off on its own without coordinating with decision makers. For example, after the collision of the Chinese fighter jet and the American spy plane in 2001, the Propaganda Department put out the line that the American plane had "entered China's territory without permission," when in fact it was flying over waters that according to international law give China some special economic rights but are considered international waters. "The line in the early press reports on the crisis made it difficult to make flexible decisions later on," according to a Chinese political insider. Uncoordinated directives from the Propaganda Department made it hard to avoid what is called a "commitment trap" that limits options for resolving the crisis. In other situations as well, the Propaganda Department has been the object of complaints by the senior officials in the leading groups responsible for foreign affairs and Taiwan. An expert who observed the Taiwan Affairs Leading Group said the group criticized the Propaganda Department for instructing newspapers to run articles criticizing the then president of Taiwan, Lee Teng-hui—articles that hadn't been authorized by the authorities responsible for Taiwan policy, but were then taken to be stating government positions.

The State Council Information Office

The State Council Information Office—China's international public relations department—was created in 1990 to improve China's overseas image. The SCIO manages relations with the foreign press corps, oversees China's international radio service, and tries to help the world see China in a positive light, in addition to its responsibilities over the Internet news sites. The SCIO holds frequent press conferences and trains press spokesmen to talk like real people instead of ideological automatons.[55] SCIO officials also coach leaders on how to handle their public appearances when they travel abroad. When I met SCIO head Zhao Qizheng, a former colleague of Jiang Zemin's in Shanghai, he spoke proudly of Jiang's polished appearance with Mike Wallace on 60 *Minutes*.

Beginning in the late 1990s, the SCIO realized that the inflamed rhetoric of China's domestic media was aggravating China's relations with the United States, Japan, and Taiwan. The U.S. government had begun to push back—for example, Secretary of Defense William Cohen complained about the way the media was slanted against America in a 2000 speech at Tsinghua University. The Japanese government also complained about the virulent anti-Japanese tone of the Internet and popular media. When *Global Times* published a piece that deviated from government policy and attacked the pro-independence Taiwan businessmen running operations on the Mainland, the piece was reprinted in the overseas edition of the *People's Daily* and caused an economic panic in Taiwan.[56]

The SCIO began to brief foreign news editors of the major domestic media on international issues and urge them to use less charged language in their reports on the United States, Japan, and Taiwan. Some time later, however, the Propaganda Department slapped down the SCIO for usurping its authority over the content of the domestic media and ordered the office to limit itself to international P.R.

The Foreign Ministry

The Chinese Foreign Ministry has established its own Web site and discussion forum to educate public opinion to be more reasonable and less emotional. China's ambassadors to various countries and even Foreign Minister Li Zhaoxing himself have been offered up on the Foreign Ministry Web site for online question-and-answer sessions.[57]

Extensive media coverage of the war in Iraq aroused intense public interest and created a difficult public relations problem for the Foreign Ministry. In the lead-up to the U.S. invasion, Chinese academics, emboldened by the government's equivocation on the invasion, organized both anti- and prowar online petitions. The antiwar camp was much larger, however. On one day after the invasion nine hundred thousand mostly anti-U.S. messages were posted on a forum dedicated to the war on *Xinhuanet*, part of the official news agency.[58] The police forced antiwar activists to cancel a planned protest march. Afterward, the organizers complained about China's lack of democracy and its unprincipled foreign policy that was to "be a friend with everybody as long as there is money to be earned."[59] The government presumably was worried that large-scale antiwar demonstrations would turn against the government. The Foreign Ministry published a defense of itself on the *People's Daily* Web site claiming that Chinese diplomats had been doing important "back-

Japanese Prime Minister Junichiro Koizumi pays respect to the Chinese soldiers who died in the war against Japan in War Memorial Hall at Marco Polo Bridge outside Beijing, where the war began in 1937, October 8, 2001. (Hu Haixin/ Xinhua)

stage work" and claiming that massive demonstrations are part of Western culture and don't really change anything.[60]

Foreign Ministry diplomats have learned to become more media savvy to build public support for their policies. For example, when Japan's prime minister Koizumi visited a war memorial outside Beijing during his last visit in 2001, one official moved the memorial wreath closer to the statue so that the photographers could capture Koizumi's bow. "Millions of Chinese people saw the image of Koizumi bowing down before the statue of the big Chinese soldier at the Marco Polo Bridge. It was a very powerful image."

Toning Down the Message

Competition for audiences drives news media to concentrate on stories that are exciting and compelling. Just like journalists in other countries, Chinese journalists have a preference for conflict and war. As one television producer said, "News shows get more viewers in a crisis, so the media like crises the best." Even minor statements or actions from Taiwan, Japan, or the United States attract audiences because people are intensely interested in these tension-ridden relationships. And when the media reports it, the government has to react to it.

For example, when President Bush in an obvious slip of the tongue, used the term "Republic of Taiwan" that implied recognition of Taiwan as a sovereign country, the Chinese government spokesman had to criticize the remark as if Bush had actually meant it. Referring to this incident, a journalism professor noted, "Taiwan sells, especially any story about Taiwan and the U.S. The government now can't afford to ignore any U.S. mistake on Taiwan because people will see it as acquiescence, so the government spokesman has to respond."

I asked a Chinese think-tank expert why China couldn't ignore the many small slights against the People's Republic made by Taiwanese figures. He sighed and said, "We are the hostages to our own propaganda. Our propaganda makes it hard for us not to react when Taiwan or the U.S. do things. People don't know anything about the world that isn't filtered through the Chinese media. Only international relations experts access Western news directly through Western Web sites. Everyone else either reads about it in the official or popular press or reads reports about it on Chinese Web sites. All the information comes through Chinese lenses."

In the aftermath of the 1999 Belgrade embassy bombing and the student protests against the American Embassy and consulates that followed, Chinese leaders directed the media to tone down their harsh rhetoric toward America. Too much patriotism can be a bad thing if it triggers protests that imperil CCP rule or forces the government into a confrontation with the American superpower. The censors banned all press criticism of the American president and directed the media to report on the United States in a less hostile manner. Scanning the electronic archive of the *People's Daily*, we can see that mentions of the polemical anti-American terms "hegemonism" (referring to American dominance in the world) and "multipolarity" (referring to the goal of reducing American power) peaked in 1999, and then declined afterward except for a minor upturn after the 2001 aircraft collision.[61] Mentions of the cooperative term "win-win" increased over the same period.

When the air collision of the American spy plane and the Chinese fighter jet occurred, journalists were frustrated by their instructions to keep their reporting subdued even while the Internet chat rooms were hyperventilating. One CCTV producer objected to the way the Propaganda Department controlled the framing of stories about the accident. "People don't like it," he said. "They want to make money, make attrac-

Figure 4.1 Mentions of "hegemonism" (*baquan zhuyi*), "multipolarity" (*duoji hua*), and "win-win" (*shuangying*) in *People's Daily*, 1978–2005

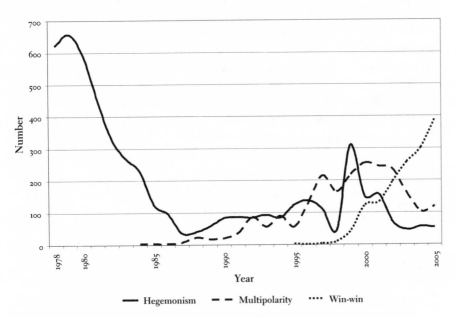

Source: *People's Daily* Electronic Version 1946–2002 and *People's Daily Online*, www.people.com.cn.

tive and interesting shows. People worry about ratings because the companies that buy commercials watch to see which stations and shows have more viewers." A university expert who appeared on a CCTV talk show a few days after the collision to discuss it found that all the panel participants were handed the themes they were supposed to address. When he asked who had prepared the points, he was told "the Party center."

Since the end of 1999, Party leaders have been using their control over the media to protect the country's crucially important relationship with the United States from negative public opinion. Party leaders forbid the media from raising issues that could arouse public emotions against the United States before or after summit meetings with the American president or during other high-level meetings. For example, the media was silent when the Pentagon issued the Nuclear Posture Review, which talks about building new nuclear weapons, because as one think-tank expert noted, "Jiang Zemin laid down the line that nothing should disrupt positive momentum in relations with the U.S. before or after his visit [to Crawford, Texas] to see Bush." The American abuse of Iraqi prisoners in Abu Ghraib was the target of much more vehement media criticism in the United States than in China.[62] When President Bush visited Beijing in fall 2005, the Chinese side turned down the American request for a live press conference between the two presidents because it wanted to hide any conflicts between the two leaders from public view.

Still, Chinese politicians know that using the media to play to the public's resentment of the United States makes them more popular. In 2005, when U.S. commerce secretary Donald Evans met his new counterpart, the handsome and ambitious Bo Xilai, in Beijing, Bo violated diplomatic protocol by criticizing Evans personally to his face while the media were present. During the photo opportunity, when officials usually make polite chitchat, Bo volunteered an assessment of Evans's job performance as 70 percent good and 30 percent bad.[63] Later, when the two of them were walking into the meeting room, Bo turned to the Chinese press staked out at the door and repeated this mild criticism while the TV cameras whirred. An embarrassed Evans was left to find his way into the room himself.

Blowback: Media Information about Public Opinion

China's foreign policymakers pay close attention to the media and believe that unlike the canned propaganda in the official press, *Global Times* and the Internet reflect what the public is genuinely thinking.[64] Every foreign policy official I have interviewed describes him- or herself as feeling under increasing pressure from nationalist public opinion. "How do you know," I ask, "what public opinion actually is?" "That's easy," they say, "I find out from *Global Times* and the Internet."

Summaries of Internet news and discussions are prepared by the State Council Information Office and the Information Department of the Foreign Ministry, as well as by the personal secretaries of foreign policy officials. Senior officials themselves also increasingly go online to sample public opinion. During the SARS crisis, both President Hu Jintao and Premier Wen Jiabao mentioned publicly that they had gone online to read what people were saying. The official English-language newspaper *China Daily* observed, "Cyberspace has, to some extent, gradually evolved into a valuable place to gauge public opinion. Obviously, the public has one more channel to interact with the government. . . . We have seen cases of public opinion expressed in cyber space being taken into consideration by the government."[65] Articles in the official press seek to enhance their credibility by quoting statements that people have posted on the Internet, for example on the public's support for increases in military spending,[66] or on the prisoner abuse at Abu Ghraib prison.[67]

Before the advent of the commercial media and the Internet, Chinese politicians and officials obtained information on social attitudes from an elaborate bureaucratic system of internal reporting that still exists.[68] The local bureaus of Xinhua news service and *People's Daily*, along with provincial and municipal Party newspapers and television stations, are tasked with providing reports to the Communist Party leaders. Journalists in these organizations are assigned to produce a certain number of internal reports, and receive substantial financial awards if their reports are significant enough to reach the top leaders.[69] Education officials are also required to report on student attitudes. Foreign Ministry officials also travel outside Beijing to give speeches and sample mass opinion, just as U.S. State Department officials do.

Today, however, officials get more of their information about public opinion directly from the popular media and the Internet, as well as from letters and e-mail. They rely less on the information filtered through the bureaucracies who previously acted as their ears and who might bias the information in order to please them. Directly obtained information is more vivid and believable, and has a sharper impact. Based on the information that blows back to them from the media and the Internet, officials have a strong impression that nationalist views are intensifying and spreading like wildfire. That picture forms the political context in which they make policy decisions.

(Jiang Zemin, in a 2001 interview with the *New York Times*, said that he didn't surf the Web himself because it was difficult for him to work the mouse. But he learned the views of the public from press reports and from telephone calls from "private friends like a worker who . . . perhaps forty years ago was working with me," and from "professors, and engineers, people from many professions who are my friends."[70])

Foreign Ministry officials like to repeat an anecdote about ordinary citizens mailing them calcium pills to urge them to show more backbone in standing up against the United States. This story may be apocryphal, a bureaucratic myth created to counterbalance the common American negotiating ploy of referencing pressures from Congress. But it also reflects the new reality of making foreign policy with one eye on domestic public opinion.

According to Foreign Ministry officials, the issue on which public opinion has the greatest impact is policy toward Japan. The diplomats who handle Japan issues in the Asia Department of the Foreign Ministry read the bitter Internet attacks on Japan themselves.[71] In 2003 one construction worker was killed and forty-three injured when they accidentally dug up canisters of mustard gas left by the Japanese army after World War II in the northeastern city of Qiqihar. Chinese diplomats knew that in order to preempt a firestorm of Internet criticism, they had to deliver a strong protest to the Japanese ambassador and post it on the Foreign Ministry Web site immediately before the story hit the news. They also believed that they had to obtain compensation from the Japanese to satisfy the public.

According to one think-tank expert, right before Jiang Zemin paid a state visit to Japan in 1998, Foreign Minister Tang Jiaxuan made a statement about Japanese aggression being past history and China needing to look forward in its relationship with Japan. People heard about Tang's statement on the Web, where it was vehemently criticized. The very next day, the expert heard people at a seminar at a private bookstore vilify Tang based on what they had learned on the Web. That is why the Foreign Ministry needed its own Web site, the expert said, to communicate directly to people.

The most vivid example of the impact on policy of Internet opinion regarding Japan occurred in March 2005 when a petition with almost thirty million names demanding that the Chinese government block Japan's bid to join the U.N. Security Council was publicized without government interference by links on the main pages of China's major Internet news sites sina.com, sohu.com, and netease.com. The petition mobilized the April student protests and resulted in the Chinese government's official announcement that it opposed Japan's membership.

Skewed Feedback

Officials acknowledge that the information about public opinion that Chinese leaders and officials get from the *Global Times* and the Internet is skewed toward more extreme nationalist views. *Global Times* wins audiences by exaggerating the threats from Japan, Taiwan, and the United States. And in China as in the West, the people who express their views on the Internet usually are those with more extreme points of view. Individuals with more moderate views do not express them with the same emotional intensity and are less eager to publicize them. In China, posting your political opinions on the Internet also carries the danger of attracting retribution from the Party.

Students I have interviewed at China's elite universities—Beijing University, Tsinghua University, and the Chinese Foreign Affairs College where Chinese diplomats are schooled—said that although they spent hours reading chat-room discussions, they never dared post messages themselves because their careers would be ruined if Party authorities traced the remarks back to them. The rules require individuals to use their own names when joining online discussions, making it all the more risky.

Why do the Chinese Communist Party and the government pay so much attention to the extreme xenophobic views that dominate the

Internet bulletin boards and discussion forums when they know they are unrepresentative? One explanation may lie in the nature of politics in authoritarian countries. Politicians in democracies rely on public opinion polls with scientifically selected representative samples because they need to know what the average voter is thinking in order to win elections. But politicians in authoritarian countries like China don't worry about losing elections. Their political survival depends instead on being attentive to the people who feel so strongly about something that they might come out on the streets to protest. Individuals willing to risk fulminating on the Internet are the ones likely to take the greater risk of participating in, or even organizing, mass protests.

Responding to Internet Opinion

Throughout world history, every advance in communication technologies has made it easier for insurgent groups to organize collective action and harder for states to prevent them from doing so. The massive pro-democracy demonstrations in Tiananmen and a hundred other Chinese cities in 1989 were facilitated by the fax machine. The 1999 Falun Gong sit-in was organized by means of e-mail and cell phones. Coordination of the anti-Japanese demonstrations in 2005 occurred mysteriously without any evident leadership or organization through obscure Internet sites, e-mail, and cell-phone text messages. Organizing protest letters and petitions nowadays is much easier thanks to the Internet, as Chinese dissident Liu Xiaobo details in a 2006 online essay, "Me and the Internet."[72] In this paean to the Internet, Liu writes, "The Internet provides an information channel that the Chinese dictators cannot completely censor, it allows people to speak and communicate, and it offers a platform for spontaneous civilian organizations."

An army officer offered the view that "the Internet is an outlet for people to express themselves. If you didn't have it, you would have extreme action instead. It's a way to relieve tension, but it also can arouse the feelings of a large group of people and put pressure on the government to do something. Then people feel they have really accomplished something so it reduces the necessity to protest." It's by no means clear whether the Party oligarchs agree that online venting is relatively harmless. Is virtual activism a substitute or a prelude to the real thing?

The leadership clearly does realize, however, that it can no longer control the spread of information, and that to survive politically it must respond to the news. In domestic politics, the emergence of the Internet and commercial media has dramatically increased government responsiveness. When a disaster occurs, officials' instinctive reaction still is to suppress the news. But when the information eventually leaks out as it always does, officials apologize, fire subordinates, and try to fix the problem to restore public support.

In 2001, Premier Zhu Rongji became the first PRC leader to apologize to the public when he took responsibility for an explosion that killed forty-seven children and staff in a rural school where the students were producing fireworks. The premier initially had publicly endorsed the far-fetched explanation offered by the local officials of a deranged suicide bomber. But when, despite a blackout of the Chinese media, the accounts of Hong Kong and foreign journalists who had interviewed villagers by phone spread over the Internet, Premier Zhu offered his apology in a televised press conference.[73]

When it comes to international news, however, the reactions of senior officials are less constructive. Information about the Japanese prime minister visiting the Yasukuni Shrine or the Taiwan president taking another step toward legal independence sparks a firestorm of online protest demanding that the government take a tough stand. It has become increasingly difficult for China's leaders not to react by making ultimatums that they later might have to deliver on. The CCP's ability to control the information that reaches the public is declining at the same time as the country's military capabilities are improving. And these two trends combine dangerously to intensify the pressure to use force to defend China's honor.

5

The Responsible Power

O NE BALMY DAY IN MAY 1994, twenty Chinese strategic thinkers from military and government think-tanks and an equal number of Asians and Americans sat stiffly around a large rectangle, empty except for some large potted plants. The high-ceilinged meeting room was draped with red velvet. Over the head of Foreign Minister Qian Qichen, who opened the session, hung a bright red sign, "Post–Cold War Security Situation in the Asia-Pacific and its Prospects." It was the first conference on regional security that China had ever hosted. China's policymakers were waking up to the fact that the country's growing economic and military might was making its neighbors apprehensive. Diplomatic and public channels were abuzz with talk of the China threat. If Asian countries joined with the United States to try to contain China and keep it weak, it would wreak havoc on domestic stability in China. How could the Chinese government head off the regional backlash? This conference was intended to try to find a solution.

After the fall of the Soviet Union, Deng Xiaoping gave an instruction that China should lie low internationally to avoid conflicts. Literally translated, Deng's words were "Hide our capacities and bide our time, but also get some things done" (*tao guang yang hui you suo zuo wei*). Deng's cryptic instruction is often repeated but was never published—perhaps because it was intended to deceive foreign countries that China was weaker than it actually is, or because it might be misconstrued as intended to deceive. Chinese officials take Deng's instruction to mean that until China is strong, it should adopt a low-key foreign policy instead of attracting suspicion by asserting itself. Avoiding international conflicts that could throw the country off course domestically has been the lodestar of Chinese foreign policy in the post-Deng era—with the exception of the more hard-edged policies toward Japan, Taiwan, and sometimes the United States.

At the conference, Chinese participants, heeding Deng's advice, denied over and over that China was, or would ever be, a threat to anyone. Foreign Minister Qian Qichen professed that "even when China becomes a strong and developed country, it will continue to refrain from aggression and expansion."[1] Chinese speakers blamed "the China threat theory" on "countries searching for a new enemy to replace the Soviet Union."

I presented a paper floating the idea of a "concert of powers" for Asia— an arrangement by which China, Russia, Japan, and the United States would coordinate to keep the peace in Asia the way the Austria, Britain, Prussia, Russia, and France did in Europe during 1815 through 1848.[2] The Chinese participants objected to my calling China a "power." "How about 'leading country'?" I suggested instead. They rejected it out of hand. China is still a weak, developing country, they insisted.

The Chinese self-effacing denials rang hollow, defensive, and unconvincing. Major General Pan Zhenqiang from China's National Defense University was the only person who acknowledged that China was becoming a power. "We have to assure countries around us, including the United States that we have no aggressive intentions, that we want a peaceful environment to concentrate on economic development. We have to have others believe us, and that is a problem."

A Nation's Reputation Clearly Is Very Important

China's effort to ease the world's concerns about its intentions has become much more sophisticated since that conference in 1994. The government has orchestrated an impressive campaign to reassure its Asian neighbors, the United States, and the rest of the world that it will behave cooperatively even as it grows stronger—that China is a "responsible power." Crafting the strategy is a new generation of cosmopolitan diplomats in the Chinese Ministry of Foreign Affairs (MFA), who by and large operate below the radar of the mass media and public attention. Chinese politicians delegate most foreign policy decision making to the diplomats, except for the issues related to Japan, Taiwan, and the United States that arouse more domestic interest and controversy. The politicians agree with the diplomats that overall, a cooperative approach to foreign policy is the best way to reduce the risk of international reactions that could lead to domestic political problems.

With a remarkable self-consciousness about how its own actions and words are perceived by others, the Chinese government has set about keeping peace at home by cultivating a benign reputation abroad. Chinese international relations experts like Nankai University professor Pang

Zhongying have discovered "a nation's reputation is clearly very important," just as important as its economic or military power.[3]

To burnish its international image and make its foreign propaganda sound more believable, the PRC established the State Council Information Office. Unfortunately, the external and internal propaganda are not always in sync. Asia Department diplomat Fu Ying, in a recent speech, said, "I oppose the idea of saying things differently internally and externally. We need to speak the same inside and outside—after all, it is now the information age."

As one PLA colonel said, "We are learning that we have to do a better job of explaining China to foreigners. We can't just show the good things, we have to show the not-so-good as well, to let people decide for themselves. It's like when you serve a meal to people. You can't tell them before they eat it how delicious it is."

Responsible Power, Status Quo Power

Nowadays Chinese denials and poor-mouthing have been replaced by a candid acknowledgement that the country is a rising power. Chinese scholars admit that "China is now turning from a regional to a world power."[4] Appropriating the language the Clinton administration used in its China policy speeches, the Chinese government has begun to refer to itself as "a responsible power." Think-tank scholar Wang Yizhou, who originated use of the term in China, wrote in 1999, "Maintaining a proactive and constructive posture, China will enter the twenty-first century with the image of a responsible big power. With the passing of time, the so-called 'China threat theory' will be defeated automatically."[5]

"It's funny to hear people say 'responsible power,' since it's what Americans used to say when criticizing China [for acting irresponsibly]," said one Beijing scholar. "Chinese say this now because after twenty years of reform and opening, China has become an insider in the international system, a status quo power that wants to work to maintain the system." Increasingly, China accepts the values of the international system and acts in support of existing international arrangements.[6] One academic said, "China doesn't support bad guys like Saddam Hussein or Kim Jong Il any more, it goes with mainstream standards." (Beijing, however, is willing to overcome its scruples and make friends with countries the West considers rogue states when its drive for secure energy supplies requires it.)

"Trade officials say that if you join the WTO or another international organization, you have to follow the rules," said an international relations expert. "The military says that the rules are to limit China, they were made by the United States so we have to change the rules. But the Foreign Ministry has adopted the new thinking." Although Party leaders may have their own suspicions that the United States has rigged the international game against China, by and large, they share the Foreign Ministry view that China gains by acting like a team player.

Foreign Minister Tang Jiaxuan gave an internal speech arguing that it had been a mistake for China to support Slobodan Milosevic and Saddam Hussein because they were tyrants who had little support from their own people and "we shouldn't give the world the impression that we only care about our own interests, we should show that we also care about morality." Having a moral foreign policy is essential for China to have international "credibility and trust" said the scholar who told me about the Tang speech.

Why shouldn't China support the status quo? It certainly has flourished under it. Chinese experts often observe that China has benefited more than any other country from the World Trade Organization and the open international economy. By supporting the Comprehensive Test Ban and the Nuclear Nonproliferation Treaty China protects its status as a recognized nuclear power and prevents others from going nuclear. Some Chinese critics of Bush-administration foreign policies say it is not China but the United States that is "a nation which alters the status quo,"[7] a view with which many American critics of the administration would agree.

Peaceful Rise

When the Hu Jintao–Wen Jiabao team came into office in 2002, they put into currency a new term, "peaceful rise." President Hu launched a research project on "the rise of China" led by Zheng Bijian, a veteran CCP theoretician who had worked for Hu at the CCP Party School for training high-level officials. Premier Wen used the term in December 2003 when he spoke at Harvard University,[8] and President Hu used it at an incongruous occasion—a celebration of the 110th anniversary of the birth of Mao Zedong.[9] Hu organized a collective study session of the CCP Politburo to discuss "the development path of peaceful rise," and universities and think-tanks explored the concept in research projects.[10] The phrase, adopted from Western discussions about China as a rising power, sparked controversy in elite circles, however. Some people worried that "rise" might make foreigners view China as more threatening and that "peaceful development" was a more innocuous phrase. Others objected that "peaceful" undercut China's threat to use force if Taiwan declared independence. As a result, the leaders now use the term "peaceful development," and leave it to the nongovernmental experts to talk about "peaceful rise." (State

Council Information Office head Zhao Qizheng reportedly said, "The 'peaceful' is for foreigners, and the 'rise' is for us.")

Hu Jintao's speech at the 2004 Boao Forum (the China-hosted version of the elite conference held every year in Davos, Switzerland), didn't use the term "peaceful rise," but as China's official news service observed, it was what the speech was all about. Hu referenced China's ancient "tradition of sincerity, benevolence, kindness, and trust toward the neighbors," and noted that "China always practices what it preaches," namely, "We pursue a policy of bringing harmony, security, and prosperity to neighbors and dedicate ourselves to strengthening mutual trust and cooperation with the fellow Asian countries, easing up hot-spot tensions, and striving to maintain peace and tranquility in Asia."[11]

China's expressions of peaceful intentions are more credible, however, when they are conveyed through actions as well as words. China's recipe for establishing its reputation as a responsible power has three main ingredients:

- Accommodating its neighbors
- Being a team player in multilateral organizations[12]
- Using economic ties to make friends

China's efforts to prove that it is a responsible power have succeeded impressively in Asia and beyond. International opinion polls indicate that people around the world view China positively, more positively than the United States.[13] But how permanent is China's commitment to international cooperation? Will its growing global role and its search for the raw materials necessary to keep its economic juggernaut going pit it in a geopolitical contest with the United States? If despite all its efforts to prove its good intentions, other countries still treat it as an enemy, can China keep turning the other cheek or will it respond in kind? And does China have the domestic "political capital" to maintain this responsible approach to foreign policy or will it, as scholar Pei Minxin predicts, be "constantly tempted to sacrifice long-term diplomatic objectives for short-term [domestic] political gains"?[14]

The Asia Department of the Ministry of Foreign Affairs

You can find the best and brightest Chinese diplomats in the Asia Department, the Foreign Ministry's largest and most important section. Much of the credit for China's stunningly successful Asia policy belongs to Fu Ying (current ambassador to Australia and previous head of the Asia Department and one of the handful of women in the senior ranks of the ministry), her mentor, Wang Yi (current ambassador to Japan and previous vice–foreign minister for Asia), and to the brood of talented youngsters they have raised to follow them.

I first encountered the then-forty-year-old Fu Ying in 1995 when she attended a meeting of the Northeast Asia Cooperation Dialogue (NEACD), the unofficial six-party talks on regional security issues for government officials and scholars from China, the United States, Japan, South Korea, North Korea, and Russia that I lead. When we held the first meeting of the group at the University of California–San Diego campus in 1993, we had a harder time persuading the Chinese to come than the North Koreans—the highest level official authorized to attend was a second secretary from the Chinese Embassy in Washington, D.C. For the first few meetings of the group, the Chinese officials acted reluctant and uneasy, showing up because they didn't want to be left out, but raising objections to study projects, group statements, or anything that would move beyond just talk. When they spoke, they sounded like a stale *People's Daily* editorial.

Fu Ying, however, was a breath of fresh air—articulate, stylish, and relaxed with foreigners. She had studied in England and served with the U.N. peacekeeping mission in Cambodia in the early 1990s, a valuable apprenticeship in international cooperation.

It didn't take long for Fu Ying to realize that regional dialogues provided opportunities for China to show its neighbors that it was sincere about cooperating with them. She became a kind of co-leader of NEACD—the two of us put our heads together every night to figure out the next day's agenda. For Fu Ying, the challenge was to work around the cautious approach toward multilateral organizations laid down by the government to follow her own instincts to move faster. Thanks to Fu Ying's proactive attitude, NEACD established a subgroup for discussions among military and defense officials, and drafted a set of principles for Northeast Asian cooperation that included human rights, military transparency, and freedom of navigation on the seas. Today, NEACD, fourteen years old, serves as a useful informal venue for hashing out issues on the agenda of the on-again, off-again official six-party talks on the North Korean nuclear program and is laying the ground work for eventually establishing a permanent multilateral organization for Northeast Asia.

After participating in NEACD and the official multilateral groups like the ASEAN Regional Forum that were just starting, Fu Ying became an advocate within the bureaucracy for regional multilateral cooperation. As she moved up the career fast track in the Asia Department, China's approach toward regional cooperation became increasingly proactive. Fu succeeded in bringing Wang Yi (then head of the Asia Department) on board with the multilateral approach, as I learned when she arranged for me to talk with him after the 1996 NEACD meeting in Beijing. A dashing

Japanese speaker, Wang Yi later visited me in San Diego, spent six months at Georgetown University to prepare for future promotions by improving his English, and enrolled as a part-time Ph.D. student at the university attached to the foreign ministry. This bold and bureaucratically nimble duo brought a new spirit of confident cooperation to China's Asian diplomacy.

Accommodate Neighbors

Hu Jintao

China's efforts to warm its relationships with its neighbors began in 1979, ten years before the end of the Cold War, and were driven more by the start of its economic reforms than by a change in global alignments. Deng Xiaoping believed that to concentrate on economic modernization, China needed a peaceful, stable environment that would involve a reorientation of China's foreign policies away from promoting revolution to stabilizing relations with the governments in its neighborhood. For the first time in China's modern history, the country developed a coherent, integrated, and omnidirectional Asia regional policy, consisting of improved ties with all the countries surrounding it.[15] Over the 1980s and 1990s China restored or established diplomatic relations with Indonesia (1990), Singapore (1990), Brunei (1991), and South Korea (1992); elevated relations with India (1988) and the Philippines (2000); normalized relations with Russia (1989), Mongolia (1989), and Vietnam (1991); began to build bilateral and multilateral ties with Kazakhstan, Tajikistan, Kyrgyzstan, Uzbekistan, and Turkmenistan (1992). Although Jiang Zemin supported this regional effort, his highest priority was major power relations, particularly with the United States. Under Hu Jintao, however, China's grand strategy focuses on relations with Asian neighbors to "concentrate attention on managing the periphery."[16]

China's leaders recognize that as China grows economically and militarily more powerful, its neighbors, worried about its intentions, might join together and with the United States try to contain it. To head off "a counterbalancing alliance,"[17] they take a prudent and accommodating approach reminiscent of the skillful way Chancellor Otto von Bismarck managed Germany's rise in the late nineteenth century.[18]

For centuries in the past, imperial China was feared and respected as the dominant power in Asia. As its strength revives, the surrounding countries watch anxiously to see if it intends to re-create a China-centered hierarchy. Countries like Vietnam and Mongolia with a history of unhappy subordination to China are particularly suspicious of China's imperial ambitions, as I heard when I talked with their officials. Their suspicions struck me as somewhat exaggerated until I had a telling conversation with the hotel doorman one day as I stood outside my Beijing hotel waiting for a ride to the airport to fly to Ulan Bator, the capital of Mongolia. He asked where I was traveling, and I answered, "Mongolia." "Oh, that used to be ours," was his immediate response.

Japan and India, as major Asian powers, believe that China intends to keep them in a second-class status and reclaim the number one position for itself, and that a rising China represents a threat to their national security. Although China has more historical grievances against Japan than it does against India, India is even more mistrustful of China than Japan is. Japan has been a U.S. ally for sixty years while India is just now getting over its Cold War animosity against the United States. Despite these differences, as Bismarck would have predicted, both countries now are strengthening relations with the United States as a counterweight to the Chinese threat, which creates a new set of foreign policy problems for Beijing.

Geography as well as history make China's diplomacy with its neighbors particularly challenging. "China is a country with the longest land border lines and the largest number of neighbors in the world," a senior Foreign Ministry official reminded me. It has twenty-two thousand kilometers of land boundaries with fourteen different countries. As of 2005, it had managed to get demarcation agreements for 90 percent of them including the forty-three-hundred-kilometer-long border with Russia.[19] A major study of these border negotiations by scholar Taylor Fravel shows that despite its traditional concern about territorial sovereignty, China accepted compromises that divided contested territory and gave China a smaller share of land in the settlement.[20] China has been willing to give up territory in order to stabilize relations with the countries on its land borders, although the maritime territorial disputes have been more difficult to settle.

China's "good neighbor policy" goes beyond the favors large countries usually bestow on their smaller neighbors: high-level visits, gifts of foreign aid, and foreign direct investment. What distinguishes the Chinese approach is its willingness to accommodate the interests of its neighbors in order to build trust and increase Chinese influence. In key bilateral relationships with Southeast Asia and India, for example, China has been willing to make compromises to create what its diplomats, adopting the Western lingo, call "win-win" outcomes.

Southeast Asia

China views Southeast Asia as its traditional sphere of influence and a strategic backdoor through which a hostile outside power could penetrate and disrupt China's development. During the Mao era, Southeast Asian governments in Thailand, Malaysia, Singapore, Indonesia, and the Philippines distanced themselves from China because the Chinese Communists were bankrolling and training insurgencies in their countries. "Relations with Southeast Asia have changed a lot," according to a retired senior official in the southern province of Guangdong, "China used to have a wall around it, and Southeast Asians used to fear that China would export revolution to them." By 1991, China had established diplomatic relations with all ten Southeast Asian countries (Thailand, Malaysia, Indonesia, Philippines, Brunei, Singapore, Vietnam, Cambodia, Laos, Myanmar) and severed aid to all rebel groups. Yet the Southeast Asian countries still viewed China with deep mistrust because of the history of Chinese dominance and because of fears that China's economic juggernaut would roll over their own smaller economies.

In less than a decade, China's skillful diplomacy has turned this situation around. According to a 2004 report from the U.S. National Defense University, "The days of Southeast Asia viewing China as a problem are over. Increasingly, the region sees China as a partner and market opportunity rather than as a potential threat."[21] Public opinion polls in Southeast Asia indicate positive views of China. One poll found that 76 percent of Thais chose China as Thailand's closest friend. In contrast, only 9 percent of Thais chose the United States.[22] A Chinese expert on Asia policy reported, "China's leaders feel more confident because they are seeing relations with their neighbors improve from their own efforts."

Despite Beijing's preference for dealing with countries one by one in direct bilateral relations, to endear itself to the Southeast Asians it supported the regional leadership role of the Association of Southeast Asian Nations (ASEAN), a multilateral grouping of the ten Southeast Asian countries. Foreign Minister Qian Qichen attended the ASEAN foreign ministers meeting in 1991, and was a founding member of the regionwide security forum led by ASEAN, the ASEAN Regional Forum (ARF) in 1994. The Southeast Asian countries are small only by comparison to their giant neighbor to the north—Indonesia is the fourth-largest country in the world, with a population of 207.4 million people—nevertheless they enjoy the enhanced clout that ASEAN gives them.

South China Sea Disputes

A major bone of contention between China and Southeast Asia is the territorial dispute over the hundreds of miniscule islands in the South China Sea that sit astride the major sea-lanes and may have rich deposits of oil and gas under the seabed. China claims that almost the entire South China Sea belongs to it. Taiwan, Vietnam, the Philippines, Brunei, and Malaysia also claim particular islands and waters around the Spratly Islands.

Up until the late 1990s, China used force to enforce its expansive claims. In a 1974 naval battle, it drove the Vietnamese out of the Paracel Islands in the northern part of the sea. A 1988 skirmish between the two navies over a reef in the Spratly Islands in the south killed seventy-two Vietnamese.[23] Following the 1988 clash, China physically occupied several islets for the first time. In February 1992, China passed a law proclaiming that 80 percent of the South China Sea belonged to China and that China had the right to restrict foreign military activities in the sea, although the U.S. Navy continues to sail and conduct exercises there.

In a brazen move, China in 1994 built new structures (judged by Western intelligence to be for military use) on Mischief Reef, an islet claimed by the Philippines. When the Philippine armed forces arrested fifty-five Chinese fishermen fishing in the area, the Chinese retaliated by sending nine naval vessels to retake the reef. The Philippines was unable to reverse the situation.[24]

China's bullying in the South China Sea alarmed its Southeast Asian neighbors and undercut the conciliatory noises Beijing was making at the same time. Beginning in 1990, Chinese leaders said repeatedly that China was prepared to shelve the question of sovereignty and jointly develop the Spratly Islands.[25] In informal negotiations organized by Indonesia, China agreed with the other claimants that matters should be resolved peacefully and that unilateral action should be avoided. But as a retired Chinese ambassador told me in 1995, "No one will believe us until we make a concrete proposal." China refused to discuss the matter with ASEAN as a group, preferring bilateral discussions in which it had more leverage.

After the seizure of Mischief Reef, the ASEAN ministers told China just how unhappy they were about its unilateral actions and what they implied about China's hostile intentions toward its neighbors. What's more, the United States started paying attention to the issue—the State Department made public statements and raised the question at an ASEAN Regional Forum meeting, in a challenge to China's objection to discussing it in a multilateral setting.

China got the message and made an about-face in the late 1990s. Although it maintained its formal claim to sovereignty over the South China Sea, it negotiated with ASEAN a code of conduct for all the claimants. The text was less explicit about what kinds of actions were ruled out of bounds than the ASEANs would have preferred. Yet it did stipulate that the claimants will "exercise self-restraint in the conduct of activities that would complicate or escalate disputes and affect peace and stability including, among others, refraining from action of inhabiting on the presently uninhabited islands."[26] The South China Sea has been calm ever since. China also has mended its disputes with Vietnam and the Philippines. In a 2005 breakthrough, when Vietnam raised objections to plans by oil companies from China and the Philippines to undertake joint seismic exploration in the Spratlys, the two countries simply invited Vietnam to join them.[27] China's relations with Vietnam have improved so much that its navies are jointly patrolling the fishing grounds in Beibu Bay.[28]

Southeast Asian countries do not want to have to choose between the United States and China. As they grow closer to China, they hedge their bets by trying to keep the United States engaged in the region.[29] China's attentions spark "cooperation competition" from Japan, South Korea, and India, as well as the United States, who rush to sign agreements with Southeast Asia.[30] China has not pressed the Southeast Asian countries for an exclusive relationship. The only thing it asks of the Southeast Asians is that they hold the diplomatic line against Taiwan. Chan Heng Chee, Singapore's ambassador to Washington, described the relationship this way: "ASEAN's approach to China has been to bring Gulliver to shore, but to tie him down with many strings of engagement, in multilateral forums, protocols, and declarations. Gulliver seems not at all to mind, and never being asleep is also tying a few strings around ASEAN."[31]

India

China's conciliatory attitude toward India is another striking example of its willingness to compromise to mend fences in Asia and stands in vivid contrast with its much more emotionally volatile approach to Japan. India is a potential rival—comparable to China in its important historical role in Asia, population size, land scale, and growth rates. The two giants had a hostile relationship during the Cold War and fought a short but bitter border war in 1962. China formed a close relationship with Pakistan and sold it nuclear and missile technology in order to balance India, which was then under the patronage of the Soviet Union. China's military and political ties with Pakistan remain close. Up until recently, only a trickle of trade (a mere $3 billion in 2000) flowed between China and India.[32] There were no direct flights between the countries until 2002. The disputed border between India and China was a serious source of friction.

India infuriated the Chinese government when it tested its nuclear weapons in 1998 for the first time since its "peaceful nuclear explosion" in 1974—not because of the test itself, but because Prime Minister Vajpayee wrote a letter to President Clinton (which became public) that blamed the test on the threat from China.

China's effort to warm its relations with India began in 1979, as part of its omnidirectional good neighbor campaign in Asia. The relationship got a major boost from the 1988 visit to China of Indian prime minister Rajiv Gandhi. Deng Xiaoping told Gandhi, "Let both sides forget the unpleasant period in our past relations, and let us treat everything with an eye on the future."[33] The two countries agreed to decouple overall bilateral relations from their unresolved border dispute, and in 1996 their armies started a number of confidence-building measures along the border.

China's most significant compromise to promote rapprochement was to change its position on Kashmir, the fiercely contested region where Pakistani and Indian forces have shed blood time and time again. Beginning in 1980, China abandoned its support for the Pakistani position that the fate of Kashmir should be decided by a plebiscite held under United Nations auspices to determine the wishes of the Kashmiri people, and adopted instead the neutral position that the Kashmir dispute should be solved peacefully by Pakistan and India.[34]

The Indian nuclear tests, and the Pakistani tests that followed, caused only a brief hiatus in the Chinese government's efforts to engage India. The U.S. government sought China's help in trying to salvage the global nonproliferation regime by attempting to persuade the two South Asian countries to give up their nuclear ambitions.

On the eve of President Clinton's June 1998 visit to China I had the task of negotiating a joint statement on the South Asian nuclear crisis with the head of China's Foreign Ministry Arms Control Department, Sha Zukang. The Chinese side had welcomed the administration's idea of making such a statement as a "deliverable" for the summit because it would highlight strategic cooperation with Washington. (The Indians felt disparaged by the statement and blamed it mostly on Beijing.) The usually irascible Sha agreed with alacrity to most of the points in the U.S. draft, including agreeing to condemn the tests, and urging India and Pakistan to sign the Nuclear Nonproliferation Treaty and the Comprehensive Test Ban Treaty. Most significantly from the American perspective, he agreed to the promise that neither China nor the United States would provide nuclear or missile technologies to India or Pakistan, a nonproliferation pledge that China had never before formally made. But Sha's mood darkened when we discussed having China commit itself to ratifying the Comprehensive Test Ban Treaty. He said that the hawks in the military would be angry if he committed China to ratify the treaty, especially since the U.S. Congress hadn't ratified it. "If China moved first, it might shame the Congress into acting," I suggested. But Sha was not persuaded.

But the Asia Department in the Foreign Ministry was much less concerned about the nuclear tests than the Arms Control Department was and more eager to restore diplomatic momentum. (Interestingly, I found the same difference in perspective between the regional bureau and the arms control bureau in the U.S. State Department.) Just a few months after the May tests, the Asia Department resumed its meetings with Indian counterparts. Nor did the nuclear tests shake China's accommodating position on Kashmir. Shortly after the tests, China had floated the idea of a multilateral meeting to help negotiate the dispute (a position closer to Pakistan's), but a month later it reverted to the more equidistant stance of recommending direct negotiations between the two sides.[35] During the fighting in the Kargil region of Kashmir in 1999, China's public statements were almost as evenhanded as those of the G-8 Western powers, according to a senior Indian official.[36]

At the same time as it cultivates better relations with India, China is also improving relations with the countries surrounding India (Nepal, Burma, Bangladesh, and Sri Lanka), which makes India uneasy. Underlying the rapprochement of the two rising powers, a sense of competition for influence in the region remains.

China's calm turning of the other cheek toward the Indian nuclear affront contrasts sharply with its fevered reactions toward any slight from Japan, its other potential rival in Asia. The Chinese have no historical gripes with India other than a disputed border. India is barely mentioned in Chinese textbooks. China takes Japan's capabilities much more seriously than India's, with the exception of the dynamic Indian software industry that China would like to emulate. The Chinese media also pay much more attention to Japan than to India because the public is largely indifferent toward India, but passionately interested in Japan.[37] Because India policy—unlike Japan policy—is formulated away from the spotlight of public attention, officials risk no public censure when they make concessions to India.

The two faces of Chinese power—its accommodating approach to most of its neighbors and its unyielding approach to Japan—were on display when Premier Wen Jiabao visited India in April 2005. At the time, Chinese students were demonstrating against Japan back home. Wen endorsed India's bid for permanent membership in the United Nations Security Council, but stood with the students in opposing Japan's bid. (When the Indian bid ultimately was packaged together with those of Brazil, Germany, and Japan, China apologized to India and withdrew its support.)

The Bush administration's obvious desire to cultivate India as a counterweight to China has gotten India more play in the Chinese press. According to *Global Times*, "The United States simply wants to help India become a major power to contain China."[38] Particularly galling to Chinese officials is the Bush administration's support for India's nuclear energy program even though it has not signed the Nuclear Nonproliferation Treaty. ("How can we not feel this is hostile to us?" one Chinese general said heatedly.) But the Chinese are sanguine that India will not allow itself to be used as a pawn against China because, as *Global Times* put it, "It is very hard to imagine that India would blindly become an appendage to another nation and lose its diplomatic independence."[39] What's more, the Chinese believe that the Indians are growing more positive toward them because Chinese economic growth is benefiting the Indian economy.[40]

Still, American attention to India is spurring China to increase its own cooperation with India in a Bismarckian effort to make sure India doesn't form an anti-China alliance with the United States. The two sides are intensifying their border negotiations, and in the meantime, have agreed to accept the actual line of control as the de facto border. The two fast-growing economies are encouraging their oil companies to submit joint offers for oil and gas assets in other countries as a way to prevent their competition for energy from becoming cutthroat. China and India worked together and with the United States to defuse the spring 2006 political crisis in Nepal by persuading King Gyanendra to step down.[41] Most remarkably, the navies of these former antagonists held joint maneuvers off the Shanghai coast in 2003 and in the Indian Ocean in 2005.

Embrace Multilateralism

Chinese officials used to be highly skeptical about the value of participating in multilateral organizations in Asia. They relished China's status as a permanent member of the U.N. Security Council. In their immediate neighborhood, however, they worried that because China was the biggest kid on the block, the other countries would gang up on it.[42]

Over the past decade, however, China has become a born-again believer in regional multilateralism. It has moved from the sidelines to participate actively in every grouping. It has helped found new groups of its own, ASEAN Plus Three (China, Japan, and South Korea and the ten countries of Southeast Asia) and the Shanghai Cooperation Organization (China, Russia, Tajikistan, Kyrgyzstan, Kazakhstan, and Uzbekistan). As the convener of the six-party talks on the North Korean nuclear issue, it has emerged as the leader of Northeast Asian multilateral cooperation. And it has made multilateral cooperation a core tenet of its national security doctrine. Thanks largely to China's newfound enthusiasm, Asia is now bound together by almost as many regional organizations as Europe has.

Starting with the ASEAN Regional Forum (ARF) was a safe way for China to ease itself into regional cooperation. The so-called ASEAN way is to improve trust through informal dialogue rather than pursue formal agreements and concerted action, and to operate by consensus so that the most cautious member sets the pace. The nondemocratic countries of ASEAN insist that the organization not interfere in any member's domestic political situation, which suits China just fine. As its comfort level has increased, however, China has moved out in front and tried to make ARF more than just a talk-shop. Beijing surprised the other ARF members by proposing that the organization start to address military issues, and hosted the first meeting of defense officials in 2004.[43]

China has never been particularly enthusiastic about the Asia Pacific Economic Cooperation (APEC) forum led by the United States. When financial markets in Thailand, Indonesia, and South Korea crashed during the 1997 Asian financial crisis, China joined with Japan, Korea, and ASEAN to create a new mechanism for financial stabilization instead, called ASEAN Plus Three.

Because China's currency (the renminbi) was not internationally traded, the country was protected from the financial storm that buffeted the rest of the region. China's leaders chose not to get a competitive edge on their suffering neighbors by lowering the relative value of their currency—thereby showing up Japan, which did devalue at the height of the crisis. China also contributed to the International Monetary Fund package to help Thailand recover.[44] China's high-profile altruism earned it lavish praise from President Clinton when he visited China in June 1998, as well as an invitation to meet with the G-8 finance ministers in Europe.[45]

China's response to the crisis exceeded the expectations of the other Asian countries, while the American and the IMF response disappointed them for being too skimpy and too doctrinaire. The Asians decided that they needed their own regional insurance scheme to protect them from future financial crises. Overcoming American objections, the finance ministers of the ASEAN Plus Three established a web of bilateral currency-swap agreements for nations in crisis (tied to IMF conditions in order to appease the United States) and agreed to share information to provide an early warning of short-term movements of capital.

China uses the ASEAN Plus Three as a mechanism for improving relations with Japan in areas that are not noticed by anti-Japanese public opinion in China.[46] China, Japan, and South Korea are carrying out joint projects to aid the poorer ASEAN countries in Indochina, conduct environmental training, and improve rice stocks. Even more ambitiously, China is trying to persuade Japan and South Korea to join it in developing common East

Asian standards for future generations of digital telephones and other information and communication technologies, in the hope of strengthening the international competitiveness of Chinese industries. Since 1999, the leaders of the big three have been meeting together at the margins of the ASEAN Plus Three summits. (These high-profile meetings, however, are affected by public opinion at the grassroots level. Public anger in China and South Korea over Prime Minister Koizumi's controversial visits to the Yasukuni Shrine drove Beijing and Seoul to cancel the three-way encounter in 2005.)

China has promoted the strengthening of ASEAN Plus Three to the point where it appears likely to eclipse the less effectual organizations that have American participation. In addition to ASEAN Plus Three's annual leaders' meetings, the ministers of finance, economics, foreign affairs, agriculture, public health, labor, and science and technology meet regularly to coordinate their efforts. A network of think-tank experts—the East Asia Vision Group—recommends specific actions to the leaders.

The ASEAN Plus Three countries held an East Asian Summit in Malaysia in December 2005 that looked like a Chinese ploy to exclude the United States from Asia, although Chinese officials insist it actually was the Malaysians' idea, not theirs. The foreign ministries of China and some ASEAN countries would prefer that the summit not become a regular event because it smacks of anti-Americanism and is redundant with the busy schedule of meetings under the ASEAN Plus Three umbrella.

The Shanghai Cooperation Organization

Pride of ownership makes the Shanghai Cooperation Organization (SCO) China's favorite regional organization and a useful precedent for expanding its role in other organizations. According to Foreign Ministry Asia Department then-head Fu Ying, the two focal points of China's regional cooperation framework are the SCO and ASEAN Plus Three.[47]

The Shanghai Cooperation Organization grew out of the lengthy negotiations between China, the Soviet Union, and the Central Asian Soviet republics to resolve their border disputes. When the Soviet Union dissolved and Kazakhstan, Kyrgyzstan, Tajikistan, and Uzbekistan became independent countries, China sought their agreement not to harbor Muslim terrorists who might threaten Xinjiang and the other western provinces.[48] The charter of the group, signed in 1996, pledges to combat "terrorism, separatism, and extremism," which in China's eyes are more or less synonymous. China also coveted oil and gas from Central Asia to help develop its poor provinces in the western part of the country.

Thanks to China's sponsorship, the Shanghai Cooperation Organization has become more institutionalized than any other Asian organization, with a secretariat in Beijing and a counterterrorism center in Bishkek, Kyrgyzstan. Its charter envisioned joint military exercises, something China had never before agreed to. The first set of exercises was held in 2003. As a homegrown organization, the SCO has helped to build bureaucratic support within China for extending multilateral cooperation into the military sphere.

When the United States beefed up its military presence in Central Asia after the 9/11 terrorist attacks—by stationing troops at bases in Kyrgyzstan and Uzbekistan as staging areas for the war in Afghanistan and showing no signs of leaving anytime soon—neither the SCO countries nor the Chinese or the Russians objected at first. Chinese experts explained that they viewed the area as part of Russia's traditional sphere of influence, so if the Russians weren't worried, why should they be? One specialist noted, on the other hand, that the U.S. bases in Uzbekistan and Kyrgyzstan are only 400 kilometers—a one-hour plane trip—from the capital of China's western province of Xinjiang. Still, a PLA general sent to investigate reported that the U.S. military presence was modest, the Central Asian countries welcomed it, and it shouldn't affect China's interests in any significant way.

But the sudden collapse of the authoritarian regime in Kyrgyzstan and the violent suppression of a protest in Uzbekistan (as well as the regime changes that occurred almost simultaneously in Georgia and the Ukraine) awakened Central Asian leaders to their vulnerability and changed their attitudes toward the American presence. They blamed the "color revolutions" on prodemocracy efforts by the United States and the Europeans, a perspective shared by China.[49] In reaction, the 2005 SCO summit called on the United States to set a timetable for its military withdrawal from the region, and Uzbekistan told the United States to leave its air base. According to Chinese sources, although the United States blamed China and Russia for evicting it, the prime movers actually were Kyrgyzstan and Uzbekistan.[50] Nevertheless, Beijing is having an increasingly difficult time convincing Washington that the organization isn't an anti-American club. For one thing, Iran's virulently anti-American president Mahmed Ahmadinejad was invited to be one of five observers at the 2006 summit meeting in Shanghai.

Multilateral Military Cooperation

The Chinese People's Liberation Army, despite its traditional secretiveness and reluctance to reveal its weaknesses to other countries, has been prodded by the Foreign Ministry to get on the regional cooperation band-wagon. The PLA started using bilateral military exercises as a way to make friends, beginning with one of its Shanghai Cooperation Organization partners, Kyrgyzstan, in 2002, and following with Pakistan, India, France, Britain, Australia, and Russia.[51] Joint exercises always have nontraditional missions like search and rescue or counterterrorism—to show that China doesn't have hostile intent toward any neighbor, and to preserve the se-crecy of preparations for actual combat.[52] The PLA invites other countries to observe the joint exercises, and some of China's own exercises as well, as a way to show itself more open and transparent.[53]

Some forward-looking officials in the Asia Department of the Foreign Ministry and military officers in the foreign affairs office of the Defense Ministry had the idea that if China participated in the regionwide exer-cises organized by the U.S. Pacific Command and its allies, it would sig-nal that China was not interested in challenging the American military presence in Asia, a message that would be reassuring to both Americans and Asians. The PLA Navy also was eager to join "the family of navies in the region and the world," as one officer put it. But could they get high-level political and military agreement for such a bold departure from the PLA's traditional practice?

The internationalists in the Defense Ministry adopted the ingenious approach of hooking their proposal to the precedent of the Shanghai Cooperation Organization. Jiang Zemin had signed off on multilateral military exercises in the SCO charter, so extending his decision to autho-rize other multilateral exercises should not be difficult. They argued in their memo, "Just as the WTO will make China stronger economically, participating in joint exercises will make the PLA stronger militarily." Once the memo went up the military and Foreign Ministry chains and Jiang Zemin himself had chopped off on it, the PLA in 2002 started to send observers to the large regional exercise called Cobra Gold hosted by Thai-land and organized by the U.S. Pacific Command, as well as to regional mine-sweeping and submarine rescue exercises.[54] Since then, China's military cooperation has gone much farther than anyone could have an-ticipated. In 2006, China actually joined in a joint naval exercise orga-nized by the United States in the Sea of Japan with Japan and four other countries aimed at preventing the spread of nuclear weapons.[55] After many years of discussion, the PLA and the Pentagon announced plans for a joint maritime rescue exercise. By participating in U.S.-led joint exer-cises, China sends a signal that it wants to be on the same team with its Asian neighbors and the United States, even militarily.

The Six-Party Talks

China emerged from the wings and claimed the diplomatic spotlight on the world stage for the first time in 2003 when it launched an effort to prevent conflict between the United States and the Democratic People's Republic of Korea (DPRK, North Korea's formal name) over the North Korean nuclear weapons programs. As a Chinese scholar wrote, "Never in the diplomatic history of the PRC has the country been so deeply or extensively involved in a controversial regional issue to which it was not a direct party."[56]

"The Korea Peninsula is a 'test stone' for rising China," according to one policy advisor, using a term from the Chinese game Go to describe a feint to test the reactions of your opponent. "We can see if we can play a more active role and succeed and thereby play a responsible and constructive role in the region and the world. The fourth generation leaders [Hu and Wen] want to be more active. They are very ambitious for China's role in the world. They want China to play a constructive role. Taiwan is another 'test stone' but we will put it off until later."

The Chinese government assumed an unprecedented leadership role in resolving the crisis because the hostile interactions between the United States and North Korea were endangering China. President Bush had publicly declared that he "abhorred" Korean leader Kim Jong Il[57] and condemned the North Korean regime in his 2002 State of the Union speech as part of an "Axis of Evil." Pyongyang announced in January 2003 that it was withdrawing from the Nuclear Nonproliferation Treaty and subsequently that it was producing nuclear weapons. The Bush administration was refusing to talk face to face with the North Korean government and China feared it might attack North Korea just as it had attacked Iraq. As one of China's America experts put it, "One of the two might go crazy. This would cause big problems for China. So China had to do something." Dreading chaos on China's borders and the domino-like spread of nuclear weapons to South Korea, Japan, and even to Taiwan, the Chinese leaders felt they had no choice but to step forward to mediate the conflict.

The Bush administration insisted that any talks with North Korea involve other Northeast Asian countries too. The administration's goal was to line up China, Russia, Japan, and South Korea on its side to exert pressure on Pyongyang to abandon its nuclear ambitions, or if North Korea resisted, to use sanctions or military force against it. China's diplomats therefore began shuttling back and forth between Asian capitals in an attempt to start a multilateral negotiation.

To assume the role of mediator, China had to distance itself from its Communist ally. Ever since PLA troops fought side by side with the North Koreans against the United States in the Korean War (1950–53), the Chinese have viewed the North Koreans as their revolutionary blood brothers. Military and Communist Party contacts remain frequent and friendly, although since the early 1990s, China has shifted more of its attentions to the economically dynamic South Korea. (Chinese tourists visit North Korea for a nostalgic reminder of how bleak life in China used to be before its economic modernization.) Chinese experts and diplomats are just as perplexed by North Korean leader Kim Jong Il's mentality as are their American counterparts. Although they can empathize with Kim's sense of insecurity in the face of American hostility, they can't understand why Kim pursues nuclear brinksmanship instead of following their successful path of market reform. China has economic leverage over North Korea if it chooses to use it. The pitifully weak economy in North Korea depends on China for almost all of its imported fuel, and Chinese businesses have invested in North Korean plants. Former secretary of defense Bill Perry believed that Chinese intervention was one of the factors responsible for bringing Pyongyang back into the Nuclear Nonproliferation Treaty after it had threatened to quit it in 1993.[58]

To bring North Korea to the negotiating table in the nuclear crisis ten years later, China provided extra economic aid and investment and signaled a new willingness to get tough with its erstwhile ally. China publicly demanded denuclearization of the Korean Peninsula, closed for three

China's President Jiang Zemin (*left*) with North Korea's leader Kim Jong Il in Beijing, January 20, 2001. (AFP/Getty Images)

days an oil pipeline to the DPRK (ostensibly for technical reasons), arrested for tax evasion the Chinese entrepreneur whom Pyongyang had selected to run a special economic zone near the Chinese border, and voted in favor of referring to the United Nations Security Council the International Atomic Energy Agency's report on North Korean violations of the Nonproliferation Treaty.

I was in China in August 2003 when the first round of the six-party talks met for the different sides to present their initial proposals. Although little was accomplished, the Chinese media touted the event as a diplomatic triumph for China. CCTV's twenty-four hour news channel provided CNN-style constant coverage that filled the time with profiles of each country's representatives, interviews with experts, summaries of press coverage by the *New York Times* and other foreign press that emphasized China's central role in the historic event, and old footage of Premier Zhou Enlai, as if the talks were the continuation of a glorious tradition of Chinese diplomacy. A banner running under the television picture said, "The eyes of the whole world are on the Beijing meeting." Taxi drivers, even outside Beijing, expressed pride in China's achievement. At the suggestion of the Asia Department of the Foreign Ministry, which suddenly realized it had scored a public relations coup, the meeting room in the Diaoyutai state guesthouse with the six-sided table arrangement was opened to the public for weekend viewing for one hundred yuan ($12) admission. The international media, as well, were dazzled by China's new style of international leadership.

The six-party talks on the North Korean nuclear issue at Diaoyutai state guesthouse in Beijing, July 26, 2005. (Guang Niu/AFP/Getty Images)

At the fourth round of talks in 2005, the six countries agreed to a general statement of common goals including the denuclearization of the Korean Peninsula—a triumph for the Chinese negotiators who held the pen in the drafting of the agreement and obtained the critical compromises from the parties.

At that point, however, the situation began to deteriorate again. The U.S. Treasury Department advised a bank in Macao (the former Portuguese colony that in 1999 returned to Chinese rule) to freeze North Korean accounts because of suspected money laundering related to counterfeiting and other criminal activities, and North Korea refused to return to the table until the financial "sanctions" were lifted. Kim Jong Il then proceeded to test missiles in the direction of Japan in May 2006 and, three months later, to flaunt world opinion by testing a small nuclear bomb.

The nuclear test forced China's leaders to choose sides. It could stand by North Korea or join an international effort to impose sanctions led by the United States. Most foreign observers predicted that Beijing would never squeeze North Korea hard because it is more fearful of triggering the violent collapse of the country and driving thousands of refugees across the border into northeast China (a region already troubled by massive unemployment and labor unrest) than it is of a North Korea armed with nuclear weapons. It also wants to prevent Korean reunification under a government led by Seoul that could place U.S. armed forces right on China's border.

This time, however, China's leaders decided to get tough with Kim Jong Il.[59] The Chinese Foreign Ministry's statement following the test reflected more anger than that of any other country. The statement denounced the test as "brazen" (*hanran*), a highly loaded term in Chinese that the government has only used five times in the past—in each instance reacting to a provocation related to Taiwan, Japan, or the United States.

Even prior to North Korea's nuclear blast, China had raised the price it was charging Pyongyang for oil and it was reported to have cut off all oil sales to Pyongyang following the missile tests during September 2006.[60]

After the nuclear blast, China voted "yes" on a muscular U.N. Security Council resolution. The resolution rules out the use of force for the time being. But it was much stronger than anything that China (a longtime opponent of sanctions especially in its own neighborhood) had been willing to swallow in the past. American secretary of state Condoleezza Rice was impressed. "I cannot conceive of even a short time ago China agreeing to call North Korea's behavior a threat to international peace and security," she said.[61]

China began inspecting some trucks at the border and went beyond the requirements of the resolution to order some banks to halt transactions with North Korea.[62] Propaganda authorities also started allow' loids and Internet news sites to freely criticize North Korea's a(sure sign that the Party was building popular support for a tough respons.

China's firm actions may have convinced North Korea to return to the six-party talks. (Alternatively, resuming talks might have been part of North Korea's original game plan.) Three weeks after the sanctions were imposed, the North Korean and American negotiators met in Beijing and agreed to resume the talks. Whether or not the six-party process ultimately succeeds in convincing North Korea to abandon its nuclear ambitions, it has made China the indispensable power[64] in Northeast Asia.

Multilateralism on a Global Scale

After a decade of experience, Chinese diplomats have become more and more positive about multilateral organizations as a means to enhance China's reputation as a responsible power. China behaves as a good citizen in the United Nations and other global bodies, and has signed practically every international arms-control treaty.

Overcoming a longtime aversion to international actions that involve what it calls "interference" in the internal affairs of other countries, in 1992 China started to participate in United Nations peacekeeping operations. Approximately four thousand Chinese soldiers have served in U.N. contingents since China dispatched the first batch of eight hundred engineering troops to Cambodia, and as of 2005 China had thirteen hundred soldiers throughout the world wearing U.N. blue helmets.[65] China has come under criticism for cozying up to Sudan's violently repressive regime, but over four hundred of its soldiers also serve in the country as U.N. peacekeepers. China also dispatched civilian police to a U.N. mission supporting the new nation of East Timor that seceded from Indonesia. A Chinese serving as a U.N. observer in Lebanon was killed by an Israeli air strike in July 2006.

As a permanent member of the U.N. Security Council, China is on the spot as one of the four countries in the world with the power to say no to American proposals. In the Security Council, China feels torn between its desire to show itself as a responsible power and its deep suspicion of the Bush administration's unilateral approach to foreign policy, which former foreign minister and senior statesman Qian Qichen described as "to rely on U.S. might, particularly its military might, to dominate the world."[66] Robert Zoellick, when he served as the deputy secretary of state in the second Bush administration, sent Chinese officials heading for the dictionary when he called on China to become a responsible "stakeholder" in the international system on issues like nonproliferation—a country that steps forward to help solve international problems instead of hanging back and free riding on the efforts other countries. He suggested that China's actions on Iran's nuclear program were a test of China's seriousness in its commitment to nonproliferation.[67] On issues outside its region, such as Iran's nuclear program, China usually hesitates to support tough U.N. action like sanctions because it doesn't want to make enemies (especially if the country is one of its oil suppliers) and it opposes sanctions as a matter of principle. But it also hates to use its veto, especially if it stands alone in opposition. Over time, if the United States works in concert with the Europeans and Russia on problems like Iran, China is likely to be coaxed into joining in or at least abstaining instead of vetoing. The unanimous Security Council votes in 2006 against the North Korean missile and nuclear tests are a good precedent.

In the five years since it joined the World Trade Organization, China has been an enthusiastic supporter of the organization although it keeps a low profile on contentious issues like agricultural subsidies because it doesn't want to alienate its trading partners in Europe or the developing world. China is one country that might be able to bridge the stubborn differences between these two groups that have blocked progress on further trade liberalization, but it hasn't yet been willing step into the mediator role.

To encourage constructive Chinese leadership on trade and other issues, the G-8 powers who manage the global economy are flirting with the idea of inviting China to join the select group. After all, the Chinese economy has a greater global impact than Italy, Canada, or even France does. Chinese leaders try hard not to look too eager to join this exclusive rich nation club, but a Chinese commentator argues that "the time is ripe for China to join the G-8."[68] One Beijing student raised the issue of the G-8 to complain about American treatment. "Why does the G-8 have Russia but not China? China's economy is much more important to the world economy. It's because the U.S. still doesn't trust or respect China and Russia claims to be a democracy."

New Security Concept

Beginning in 1996, Chinese scholars—encouraged by the Asia Department of the Foreign Ministry to provide a normative rationale for China's multilateral diplomacy that could help persuade skeptics in the military, government bureaucracy, and university[69]—articulated "a new security concept based on mutual trust, mutual benefit, equality, and cooperation," and contrasted it with traditional and Cold War concepts based on realpolitik and military force that they claimed the United States still adhered to. As the Chinese put it, the new concept replaces zero-sum security with the notion of mutual "win-win" security. Jiang Zemin's 1999 speech to the United Nations Committee on Disarmament in Geneva drew the distinction between "the old security concept based on military alliances and buildup of armaments" and the "new security concept that meets the need of the times."[70] Claiming credit for inventing a new paradigm, China positioned itself as the vanguard of a new era of international cooperation.

Although many foreign policy experts in China still see Asia through the lens of realpolitik—as a head-on-head contest for power between China and the United States or China and Japan—the scholars behind the new security concept rejected that approach. As one think-tank expert said, "We are not worried about the U.S. and its allies encircling China. No one can encircle China. It depends on ourselves. If we are peaceful, no one can encircle us. The domestic threat is the number one threat to China."

The Asia Department commissioned a report on the new paradigm by Zhang Yunling, the dynamic scholar heading up the Asia-Pacific Research Center at the Chinese Academy of Social Sciences. Zhang had spent nine years working at the Institute of European Studies and had models of European community building in his mind. The report frankly acknowledged that China's actions on the ground, along with its rising power, were causing other states to perceive it as a threat. China needed to demonstrate to its neighbors that it adhered to the existing rules of the international order. Greater activism in multilateral activities would signify that it was a country that supported the status quo instead of challenging it.[71]

Multilateralism and the U.S. Role in Asia

Underlying China's multilateral activism is an implicit challenge to the United States as the superpower that dominates the Asia-Pacific region and the world through its system of bilateral alliances. As one expert said, "Integration with East Asia puts China in a stronger position when dealing with the United States." Being surrounded by friendly neighbors gives China a buffer against U.S. pressure.

What's more, China's vision of a multilateral security community in Asia presents an alternative that competes with the U.S.-led arrangement of "hub-and-spokes" alliances with Japan, South Korea, Australia, and Thailand. When Premier Zhu Rongji was asked at the 2002 Boao Forum about China's views on the various multilateral organizations sprouting up in the region, he replied, "Regional organizations are like railroads, planes, and ships. They can compete. If people don't like them, they don't have to come." If Asian countries believe that a regional security community addresses their security needs better than the U.S. alliance system, then the U.S.-led system over time will wither away, and the United States will have to join the multilateral trend or find itself marginalized in the region.

China has opted not to confront American supremacy head-on. The official rhetoric euphemistically describes China's objective as "multipolarity," i.e., narrowing the power gap between the United States and the other major powers like China (but not including Japan, of course). In the Asian arena, some Chinese academic experts—and almost all military ones—advocate trying to drive the American military out of its bases in Japan and Korea because American forces are used to contain China and to keep Taiwan separated from the Mainland.[72] Many others recognize that Taiwan aside, the U.S. presence helps stabilize the Korean peninsula and prevent Japan's revival as an independent military power.

The Chinese government has never adopted an Asian version of the Monroe Doctrine to try to keep the United States out of its neighborhood. "China and all the Asian countries want to find ways to engage the United States, especially in the security sphere. It will be similar to trans-Atlantic relations," Zhang Yunling, the head of the Asia-Pacific Research Center told me. China has not put pressure on Singapore or Thailand to prevent the American navy from using their facilities, nor offered support to groups in Japan or South Korea that want to do away with U.S. bases.

Still, the Chinese government sends ambiguous signals on whether or not its ultimate goal is to exclude the United States from Asia. When Foreign Minister Tang Jiaxuan told Secretary of State Colin Powell in a private meeting in 2001 that China didn't want to push the United States out of East Asia, Washington considered it a major step forward. Vice–Foreign Minister Wang Yi, in a speech to an international seminar I attended in 2003, stated openly that "China would like to see the United States play a positive and constructive role in this region."[73] (Wang's staff, recognizing the sensitivity of the issue, originally insisted that his speech be off the record, but Wang gave personal permission for it to be published in *Global Times*.) More recently, Wang, now ambassador in Tokyo said again that China "respects the objective fact that the United States has a traditional influence on this region and has a realistic stake."[74]

Yet China turned down American requests to attend the Shanghai Cooperation Organization as an observer. Russia, but not the United States, was allowed to observe the 2005 East Asian Summit.[75] And China didn't invite the Americans to observe the massive joint exercises with Russia that although ostensibly directed at an antiterrorist mission included amphibious landings and other activities relevant to a Taiwan contingency.[76] Whenever China's actions belie its welcoming words, it fuels American suspicions that Beijing's true intentions are hostile. Deputy Secretary of State Zoellick laid down a marker in a 2005 speech. "The United States respects China's interests in the region, and recognizes the useful role of multilateral diplomacy in Asia. But concerns will grow if China seeks to maneuver toward a predominance of power."[77]

By promoting multilateralism as a way to enhance its influence in a nonthreatening way, China is taking a lesson from the rising power of the previous century, the United States. After World War II, American leaders chose to bind their hands by creating international institutions like the United Nations. They anticipated correctly that if the United States agreed to abide by the rules of international organizations, it would make other countries more comfortable with American power.[78] China is seeking to head off hostile reactions to its growing might in Asia by using much the same approach, although the organizations it has helped create so far are much less binding.

Economic Diplomacy

China's emerging economic power creates both problems and opportunities for its foreign relations. Having set a world record of 10 percent annual growth for more than two decades, China causes other countries to worry. As China sucks up more foreign direct investment than any other country, how much will be left for others? Will other exporting countries be squeezed out of their markets by a country whose share of world exports grew from 1.9 percent (1990) to 4 percent (2000) and almost 6 percent (2005)?[79] The world prices of oil, natural gas, iron ore, coal, soybeans, and other commodities raised by the voracious appetite of Chinese industry are a boon to the poor countries with these mineral resources under the ground. But in more developed countries will the inflationary effect of higher commodity prices outweigh the inflation-dampening effects of inexpensive manufactured products imported from China and thereby slow down growth? As China becomes a global economic power doing business all over the world, will it support or subvert American interests?

On the positive side, China's dynamic growth and its huge domestic market translate into a lot of benefits it can bestow on other countries to cultivate friendly relations. Trade relations are driven primarily by an economic logic, but China earns a lot of good will through its magnetic appeal to international businesspeople. A *Global Times* article urged Chinese foreign policymakers to "play the economic card well. Unlike the military or political card, everyone likes to take the economic card."[80] Chinese emperors (and American presidents) learned a long time ago that a large, vibrant economy attracts foreign emissaries who are willing to kowtow for the opportunity to trade and invest. Government and business leaders from throughout the world come to Beijing to curry commercial favor and obtain government approvals for their business ventures. The Chinese government awards its purchases of airplanes, insurance licenses, and approvals for large investment projects to various important countries, including the United States, to try to keep them all happy.

Free Trade Agreement Diplomacy

The best thing that ever happened to China's regional relations was its joining the World Trade Organization (WTO). Not only did membership signify that China had joined the club of rule-abiding countries, but it also required the country to open its markets wider to foreign products than any developing country had before—China committed to reduce its average import tariffs to 10 percent by 2005. Average tariffs in China today are only slightly higher than in developed countries and much lower than in most other developing countries.[81]

When President Clinton visited China during the Asian financial crisis and commended Premier Zhu Rongji for not devaluing China's currency, he also prodded China to open its markets to more imports so that it could serve as the engine of growth for the region. Since China joined the WTO and lowered the barriers to its domestic market, it has done just that. During 2000 to 2004, China's imports increased 149 percent (from $251 billion to $624 billion), considerably faster than its exports (which went up 128 percent, from $280 billion to $629 billion).[82] Asian economies that used to sell the largest portion of their goods to the United States and Europe increased their sales to China. China has become the number one trading partner of South Korea, Vietnam, and Japan.

Thanks to China's surging imports and its economic diplomacy with its neighbors, the Asian region has become more economically interdependent than ever before. Intra-Asian trade has grown almost two times as fast as global trade, and has become over half of the total trade for the regional economies, according to the Asian Development Bank.[83] "Rapid growth in the People's Republic of China is the driving force behind expanding intraregional trade," said ADB chief economist Ifzal Ali. "The economies of East and Southeast Asia have benefited greatly from the rise in Chinese imports."[84]

Having already swallowed the bitter pill of tariff cuts, China was in an ideal position to pursue bilateral free trade agreements with its neighbors. By promising market access to which it already had committed in order to join the WTO, it could win points for benevolence. A Chinese diplomat explained the political logic of free trade agreements. "All countries think they will benefit from a free trade area with China because of China's huge market."

The bold idea of offering free trade agreements (FTAs) to improve China's relations with its neighbors after WTO accession came from the strategic-thinking diplomats in the Asia Department of the Foreign Ministry. Originally the Foreign Ministry favored an FTA with South Korea and Japan because of the political importance of mending relations with those countries. But the economists concluded that China would lose a little from a free trade agreement with Korea and a lot from one with Japan, unless the two countries at long last opened their agricultural markets to foreign rice and other commodities, which the Chinese judged was almost impossible because of the strength of the farm lobbies in the two countries. Inside China, getting a bureaucratic consensus on a trade agreement with large trading partners like Korea and Japan would be difficult because so many sectors would be affected.

The most logical candidates for a special trade relationship turned out to be the Southeast Asian countries in China's backyard who feared the loss of foreign investment and export markets to China once it joined the WTO, and feared the effect of cheap Chinese goods flooding into their own markets.[85] As of 2000, China's trade with ASEAN was only about 8 percent of its total trade and 5 percent of ASEAN's total trade, so domestic producers wouldn't object too much about losing tariff protection.[86] Even the Chinese rubber growers, who would lose market share to higher-quality Southeast Asian rubber, didn't try to block the agreement.

At a Singapore meeting between China and ASEAN in November 2000, Premier Zhu Rongji surprised his own staff by spontaneously proposing a free trade agreement with the Southeast Asian countries before an internal decision had been made. "The Southeast Asians were all saying how much China's entry to the WTO was going to hurt them," according to one Chinese expert on Southeast Asia. "Zhu thought to himself how to reply. Without any preparation, he said, 'Why don't we consider the possibility of a long-term trade agreement?'"

China's surging imports and its free trade diplomacy have left Japan in the dust. China's return to its traditional position as the central economic player in Asia has disrupted the previous hierarchical pattern often described as a flock of "flying geese" with Japan in front, South Korea and Taiwan next, and then further back China and the Southeast Asians. In addition to ASEAN, China has signed or is negotiating preferential trade agreements with Chile, Hong Kong, Australia, New Zealand, and the Bangkok group (Bangladesh, India, Laos, South Korea, and Sri Lanka). The Chinese Foreign Ministry continues to push for a free trade agreement with Japan and South Korea. One economist observed, "It is good to get political credit for proposing a free trade agreement with Japan and South Korea but not really have to do it." China's free trade diplomacy has put pressure on Japan to throttle its powerful agricultural lobbies so it can better compete with China on the playing field of regional economic cooperation.[87]

China's New Global Reach

China has dramatically expanded its global reach in the search for supplies of oil, natural gas, and other raw materials like iron ore and copper to fuel its breathtaking economic growth. Chinese businessmen eager to diversify their export markets (right now they sell mostly to the United States, Europe, and Japan) also have branched out looking for customers in places like Africa, Latin America, and the Middle East. Chinese industrialists are exploring these economies as well in order to build factories close to the raw materials. Following close behind are Chinese diplomats with friendship agreements, foreign aid, and infrastructure construction to grease the wheels of the foreign bureaucracies that will have to approve the energy contracts and the Chinese product markets. Sales of military equipment are likely to come next because the Chinese military industrial complex will want to take advantage of the new doors that have been opened to expand its overseas sales.

Africa, a continent that has been neglected by Americans, has been targeted by China as a land of opportunity because of its rich reserves of oil, iron ore, copper, gold, and other minerals. Chinese investment in Africa, still a small share of the continent's total foreign investment, has grown from $1.5 million in 1991 to $1.2 billion in 2005. China has become the continent's third-largest trading partner. Total trade quadrupled to $40 billion between 2001 and 2005.[88] As of 2006, China obtained 30 percent of its oil from Africa.[89] Transportation links have increased too. You can now fly directly from Nairobi to Guangzhou on Kenyan Airlines.

To expand commercial ties with Africa, the Chinese government has been lavishing high-level attention on it. President Hu Jintao, Premier Wen Jiabao, and State Councillor Tang Jiaxuan all trouped to Africa during 2006, visiting fifteen different countries. I was in Beijing in November 2006 when

China hosted forty-eight African heads of state at a high-profile summit meeting (a huge gathering of several thousand delegates) that marked the climax of what the Chinese called the "Year of Africa." The Beijing authorities treated the extravaganza as a dry run for the Olympics. The city was decked out in red lanterns and posters, and the air was unusually clear because of special traffic control measures. Television and other media were saturated with reports celebrating the event as China's debut as a global leader.

The Western news media, on the other hand, emphasized that by offering unconditional aid and other favors, China subverts the efforts of the United States and other Western countries to link financial incentives to improvements in human rights and environmental protection—a criticism that has been made sharply by World Bank president Paul Wolfowitz.[90] The most contentious issue is the civilian violence by militias linked to the government in the Darfur region of Sudan, a country where China has large oil interests. The United States and its allies want to put more pressure on the Sudanese government to halt the killing, and China stands in the way.

When I met with a Chinese Foreign Ministry official responsible for Africa policy right before the summit, he insisted that China was working behind the scenes to convince the Sudanese government to "take a more pragmatic attitude" toward an international peacekeeping presence. In a newspaper interview, Vice–Foreign Minister Zhai Jun said, "We use our good relationship and cooperation with the government" to push for a settlement, "but we don't have to announce every time we do this."[91] Chinese television reported that during the summit President Hu said, "the Darfur issue is now at a critical stage" and in his meeting with Sudan president Omar al-Bashir, Hu advised him to "strengthen dialogue with all parties."[92] Less than a week after the summit ended, United Nations officials announced that it had reached agreement with the Sudanese government to send a peacekeeping force to Darfur, and credited Wang Guangya, the Chinese ambassador to the United Nations, with persuading Sudan to accept the force.[93]

African officials, many of them from nondemocratic governments, prefer China's uncritical friendship to what they view as Western hectoring. An American general testifying to Congress about China's role in Africa paraphrased a statement made to him by an Africa leader. "We love the United States. You, above all else, tell us exactly what we need and then China turns around and gives it to us."[94] A South African businessman said that China was the first big foreign power to come to Africa without acting "as though they are some kind of patron or teacher or conqueror."[95]

Like its colonial predecessors, however, China is starting to provoke a local backlash in some quarters—beginning in Zambia, where the Chinese community in the capital of Lusaka has grown tenfold to approximately thirty thousand in the past decade. When an opposition candidate for president accused China of exploiting the poor country, rioters and looters attacked Chinese shopkeepers and the candidate won more votes than predicted.[96]

Almost overnight China has turned itself from a regional power into a global one. As China's global footprint expands, so do the anxieties of Americans and others that China is "taking over the world." This is an economic version of the Cold War mind-set that caused Westerners to wring their hands every time the Soviet Union made friends with a developing country. The political backlash against China's presence in Africa, Latin America, and the Middle East creates a dilemma for Chinese policymakers. They can't survive without the resources, but neither can they rise peacefully if they sully their reputation as a responsible power.

In fact, the motivations behind China's new global activism are more economic and commercial than geostrategic. As National Defense University expert Phillip Saunders writes, "China's increasing demand for economic inputs and access to export markets follows a logic and geography independent of strategic concerns."[97] When China's own energy supplies failed to keep pace with economic growth, the country became a net oil importer beginning in 1993. Owing to its burgeoning automobile society and its surging industrial growth, it has become the second-largest oil consumer in the world and the third-largest importer of oil, even though it still depends primarily on its own coal supplies for industrial use.

Energy Security

Over the past few years, Chinese leaders have concluded that simply buying oil and gas on global markets is not a safe bet. "Rising oil prices have hurt China much more than the U.S.," a senior economic official said, "because Chinese energy use is much more inefficient." Fearing adverse reaction from middle-class car owners and the risk of inflation, the Chinese government is reluctant to pass energy price increases on to the consumers, so it bears much of the financial burden itself.

The government worries that supply disruptions and shortages caused by political instability in oil-producing countries could jeopardize economic growth, raise unemployment, and put the regime at risk. Although the global energy market works well and physical shortages of oil are very rare, South China did experience a shortage in 2005.[98] China depends on the politically volatile Middle East for 60 percent of its oil (a percentage projected to grow to 80 percent by 2010).[99] And Russia plays politics with its oil and gas customers. China thought that Russia had agreed to build an oil pipeline from eastern Siberia to northeast China, but Russia has not followed through on this commitment and may route the pipeline to its Pacific coast opposite Japan instead. What's more, from China's perspective it looks like global energy markets are dominated by the Western oil companies. And the U.S. Navy controls the vital international sea lanes on which the ships carrying China's imported oil must travel.[100] What really worries China's leaders is that the United States and its European allies could sever China's oil supplies if there were a crisis in the Taiwan Strait or elsewhere. That is why they believe that the only way to guarantee a secure flow of energy is to take physical control over oil and gas by buying up equity stakes or long-term supply contracts in producing countries.

Economists say that owning oil fields in other countries instead of buying oil in the global marketplace is irrational. Yet the Chinese are not alone in embracing the primitive concept of "energy security." The Japanese invested heavily in energy assets all over the world during the 1970s (and suffered losses when prices dropped subsequently). In the United States, members of Congress and the media often decry China's purchases of energy assets in countries like Canada and Venezuela for challenging U.S. traditional access to "secure" energy supplies.[101] A Chinese energy expert observed to a Western journalist, "A popular saying abroad is that oil is just a commodity that anyone who has money can buy. But this saying is most popular in the countries that already control the supplies."[102]

Chinese mistrust of American intentions toward them—heightened by the firestorm of American opposition to the bid by the China National Offshore Oil Company (CNOOC) to acquire the American oil company UNOCAL—makes them particularly prone to thinking of energy competition as a "great game" driven by political rivalries. "There is no free market when strategic resources are involved," a Chinese student asserted. In an ominous tone, he observed, "Japan started World War II when it felt strangled because it couldn't get access to energy supplies in China and elsewhere. It could be very dangerous if countries try to restrict China's energy supplies." Since 2002, the Hu Jintao administration has encouraged the three national oil companies as well as other state corporations to "go out," as the Chinese put it, to make investments abroad. It established a high-level interagency Energy Leading Group under Premier Wen Jiabao in 2005. The Politburo held a special session on energy security that June. And in October, a major Central Committee document highlighted the competition for global resources as a prominent international trend.[103]

China is discussing or has already concluded asset-purchase or long-term contract agreements in Africa (Sudan, Nigeria, Gabon, and Angola), Latin America (Brazil, Ecuador, and Venezuela), Russia, Central Asia (Kazakhstan), Asia (Indonesia and Myanmar), and Australia. The travel itineraries of Hu Jintao, Wen Jiabao, and other Chinese leaders reflect their overwhelming interest in energy and other raw materials. Everyone noticed when Hu Jintao's first stop after visiting the White House in 2006 was Saudi Arabia. There, among the topics under discussion were Saudi Arabia's investment in an oil refinery in Fujian Province and its offer to actually store some of its oil in China as part of China's newly created strategic oil supply—to have on hand if there are disruptions elsewhere.

As a latecomer to international energy markets, China finds that most of the good oil and gas assets in stable and respectable countries are unavailable because they are already owned by national companies in the producer countries or by Western oil companies. Therefore, China has been forced to turn to countries where U.S. sanctions forbid American companies from doing business, such as the Sudan and Iran. Americans look askance at China's increasingly cozy relations with anti-American dictators in the oil-rich countries of Africa, Latin America, and Central Asia. Chinese officials retort that China has nowhere else to go because the resources in all the "good" countries have been sewn up. But other countries inevitably exploit the competition between China and the West to get a powerful ally on their side just as they did during the Cold War contest between the Soviet Union and the United States. American and European economic pressures to force Iran to abandon its nuclear programs and Sudan to stop its tragic genocide are complicated by China's ties with these countries. China's drive for energy security has pushed it to the wrong side of these issues for a country that wants to be recognized as a responsible power.

The Responsible Face of Chinese Power

By accommodating its neighbors, cooperating in multilateral organizations, and using its market power to win friends, China appears to have gone a long way toward convincing its Asian neighbors and most of the world that it is a benign and peaceful rising power. The Bush administration has publicly acknowledged that "the China of today is simply not the Soviet Union of the late 1940s . . . most importantly [because] China does not believe that its future depends on overturning the fundamental order of the international system."[104]

✗ China's accommodating stance helps its leaders avoid clashes with other countries that could derail economic growth and threaten the CCP's hold on power. Chinese scholar Jin Canrong in a newspaper interview drew an analogy between China's current focus on internal development and American isolationism between the Civil War and World War I. Like the United States during that period, China is "industrializing rapidly, weathering a huge population shift from rural to urban areas, and grappling with enormous social problems related to rising expectations and a widening wealth gap." Because of its daunting domestic challenges, China "seeks enough time and international stability to lift its people out of poverty, ease societal stresses and keep enough money flowing to maintain the Communist Party's monopoly."[105]

But the integration of such a huge and explosively growing economy, with hundreds of millions of industrious workers and massive demands for energy and raw materials, into the world economy after three decades of separation has created a wrenching ripple effect on almost every country in the world. As China's leaders see it, they are blameless because they are merely trying to develop their own economy by doing business according to the standard practices that Western countries have used for decades. Singapore senior statesman Lee Kuan Yew defended China's approach. "They [the Chinese] will trade, they will not demand, 'This is my sphere of influence, you keep out' . . . they are not asking for a military contest for power, but for an economic competition."[106] But economic competition is easily misperceived as a geopolitical contest for power, even in this era of globalization.

Because of China's political fragility and secretiveness, moreover, nagging doubts remain about whether its leaders will be able to keep a steady hand on the tiller. Beijing's approach to international issues that garner close public attention—especially those involving Japan, Taiwan, and sometimes the United States too—is not as calm and responsible as the rest of its foreign policies. Particularly when emotionally incendiary issues are involved, public sentiment demands tough stands, not accommodation. As one chat room posting said, China should "behave strongly [and] not only behave friendly to people . . . to be a responsible great power we have to hold a rose in one hand and a gun in the other, in many circumstances to oppose and revenge."

Senior statesman Qian Qichen, when speaking at his alma mater Beijing University, was asked by a student (using Mao-era terminology) what was the "major contradiction" in China's current foreign policy. "The contradiction between China's public opinion and its constructive foreign policy," Qian answered.

6

Japan

"When the Chinese People Get Angry, the Result Is Always Big Trouble"

THE NEIGHBORHOOD OF ZHONGGUANCUN, in Beijing's northwest suburbs next to the university district, is a shiny showcase of high-tech China. Picture a more commercial version of Kendall Square in Cambridge, Massachusetts, adjacent to M.I.T and not far from Harvard. The more than one hundred thousand students who live nearby are China's best and brightest—universities in Beijing admit only the top scorers on the national entrance examination. Beijing University and Tsinghua University are the Harvard and M.I.T. of China. In Zhongguancun, technology firms spun off from academic research labs fill stylish high-rise buildings. Superstores and shopping malls sell computers, cameras, and electronic peripherals to crowds of consumers. Large video screens advertise the products inside.

On Saturday, April 9, 2005, more than ten thousand students congregated in the largest mall in Zhongguancun—not to shop, but to demonstrate against Japan and what they considered its failure to properly acknowledge the atrocities it committed when it occupied China during World War II. The students waved PRC flags and chanted "rise up, rise up," as they called for a month-long boycott of Japanese goods.

The Japanese government had recently approved a new textbook that glossed over the slaughter of civilians in the infamous Nanjing Massacre of 1937 and denied Japan's responsibility for its wartime aggression in China. And Japanese prime minister Junichiro Koizumi refused to stop visiting the Yasukuni Shrine in Tokyo that honors Japanese war dead, including fourteen war criminals.[1] All of this occurred at a time when the United Nations was considering Japan's application to become a permanent member of the Security Council.

The students targeted Japanese electronics goods displayed in store windows as the symbolic focal point of their protest. The slogan "Reject

Anti-Japanese student protestors demonstrate in Zhongguancun in Beijing's university district, April 9, 2005. (China Photos/Getty Images)

Japanese goods!" was emblazoned across their shirts or on their headbands. Exhilarated with the excitement of what for most of them must have been their first political demonstration—Chinese students have been politically quiescent since the Communist Party called in the army to put down forcibly the prodemocracy demonstrations in Tiananmen in 1989—the young people turned violent as the protest spread beyond the mall. They smashed electronic billboards advertising Canon cameras and other Japanese electronic products (while taking pictures of one another with their Japanese-brand cell phones and cameras), kicked and hammered Toyota automobiles caught in the melee, and broke the windows of Japanese banks and restaurants. The older anti-Japanese activists who evidently had organized the demonstration lost control of the young crowd.

Surging out of Zhongguancun onto the same road that the democracy demonstrators had taken in 1989, the students marched into the heart of Beijing. Onlookers cheered them along the way, and some of them joined the parade. The Beijing police and People's Armed Police (China's national paramilitary domestic security force) prevented the large march from entering Tiananmen, but allowed a small contingent to enter the foreign embassy district and diverted the rest.

Arriving at the Japanese Embassy and the ambassador's residence, the demonstrators threw bottles, tiles, stones, and eggs over the heads of the five-man-deep cordon of People's Armed Police, who stood with plastic shields and cattle prods and surrounded the buildings. The PAP allowed the students to pelt the embassy and residence but blocked entry to them. An established anti-Japanese activist proclaimed through a megaphone that this was the beginning of a new era of anti-Japanese protests. His voice had to compete with the loudspeakers on the police van that repeated the message, "Express your protest with discipline and restraint, and once you've done so, go back to your campus." Dozens of buses waited to take the students back to their schools. Around six o'clock the police, saying *"Chu chu qi, goule"* ("You have vented your spleen, enough now"), gently dispersed the crowd.[2]

The Beijing demonstration was part of a national wave of violent anti-Japanese protests that had begun the previous weekend when people protested outside Japanese supermarkets and department stores in the Sichuan provincial capital of Chengdu, and in Shenzhen, across the border from Hong Kong. In both cities, the police allowed the protestors to damage the stores, but barred them from entering. The Shenzhen protests continued on April 10 and 17, with a reported ten thousand people taking to the streets on the seventeenth.[3]

The Communist Party Propaganda Department had imposed a media blackout on April 6, before the April 9 Beijing protest. No newspapers, Web sites, or television stations had been permitted to report on the protests. Yet by the third weekend protests had grown larger and more unruly, and had spread to every corner of China, covering twenty-five cities in all.[4] The student demonstrators were joined by workers and jobless people,[5] as well as business people moved by patriotic emotion and a desire to show that they stood for something other than just making money.[6]

Most alarming from the standpoint of the Communist Party leaders was the novel way the demonstrations were organized. Organizers circumvented the government's orders to the Web masters of the major Web sites to delete announcements of planned demonstrations by using minor Web sites and blogs, as well as messages sent chain-letter style over the Internet and by cellular telephone text messages. The announcements were forwarded to me and other China watchers abroad so that we, and presumably the Chinese police, knew about the protests ahead of time. On the eve of the April 9 protests in Beijing, the Japanese government warned Japanese residents about them. But the Communist Party's usual methods to diffuse local labor or rural protests—sympathize with the protestors, arrest the organizers, and stop the protests from spreading to other regions—were useless against this decentralized, bottom-up mobilization with no visible organization or leadership.[7] The 2005 protests were the first—but certainly not the last—Chinese experiment with a new-style, technology-enabled collective action that mimicked the Ukraine's "Orange Revolution."

The demonstration on April 16 in Shanghai, China's most cosmopolitan city, was the largest and most violent. A city government spokesman estimated the size of the crowd at twenty thousand,[8] but some eyewitnesses believed it was as large as one hundred thousand. Demonstrators wore T-shirts decorated with the blood-splattered face of Japanese prime minister Junichiro Koizumi and carried signs vilifying him. They damaged the Japanese consulate, Japanese restaurants, and Japanese cars, and kicked and beat up some unfortunate people who were caught in the mob. One sign carried by demonstrators summed up what was happening: "When the Chinese people get angry, the result is always big trouble."

After three weeks of protests, the Communist Party finally sent a clear signal that it was time to stop. I was in Beijing on April 16 when the *People's Daily* published a front-page official commentary that praised patriotism as a noble sentiment, but urged young people to "cherish social stability" and express their patriotism rationally through their studies and their jobs. The commentary made only a veiled reference to the protests themselves, but the authorities had to lift the news embargo on them later in the week in order to give an explicit order to cease them.[10] I went to Beijing's

Chinese demonstrators burn a defaced portrait of Japanese Prime Minister Junichiro Koizumi during an anti-Japanese rally on April 16, 2005, in Shanghai. (China Photos/Getty Images)

Tiananmen Square on April 16 to witness a planned anti-Japan demonstration, but it fizzled out because university authorities kept the students on their campuses. All I saw were disappointed foreign journalists with their cameras and more police officers than usual. A few weeks later, on the anniversary of the famous May 4 movement—the student protests in 1919 against the treaty that handed over the German territorial concessions in China to Japan after World War I—the Beijing authorities closed Tiananmen Square and held a massive coming-of-age ceremony for eighteen-year-olds there to prevent any protests from occurring.

The Most Emotional Issue

Of the three foreign policy relationships that China's leaders consider the most "sensitive" in domestic politics—Japan, Taiwan, and the United States—Japan is the one that is the most difficult for them to handle. Japan is "the most critical zone in all aspects of China's foreign relations,"[11] requiring a skillful balancing act on the part of Chinese leaders. "Japan is the most emotional issue," a student explained. "It is the one issue on which public opinion really matters to the government."

The Chinese Communist Party's political legitimacy is bound up with its 1945 victory in the Anti-Japanese War. The founding legend of the People's Republic relates how the Chinese people, led by Mao Zedong and the CCP, finally stood up and threw off the yoke of fifty years of cruel and humiliating oppression by the Japanese.[12] Since 1949, PRC schoolbooks and propaganda have been retelling the story of Japan's victimization of China and China's heroic defeat of Japan.

Chinese politicians use Japan-related issues to mobilize support for themselves as strong leaders or to divert attention from difficult domestic problems. The less confident the leaders, the more they fan the fires of anti-Japanese nationalism. Jiang Zemin took a much tougher public stance toward Japan than Mao Zedong or Deng Xiaoping ever did. The propaganda effort to revive popular support for the Communist Party through patriotism—an effort that began after Tiananmen—took Japan's aggression against China as its main historical justification. The Party facilitates Internet-based mass petitions against Japan, and even permits small demonstrations on a regular basis outside the Japanese Embassy in Beijing. The media play to the public's appetite for anti-Japanese news and make it impossible for the CCP to control Japan-related information as thoroughly as it once did.

Whenever anti-Japanese emotions boil over into large-scale protests that threaten to spin out of control, it takes a delicate touch to halt the protests without having them turn against the CCP instead. As scholar Zheng Yongnian says, the use of nationalism is beneficial for the regime, "but it must stop at a certain point."[13] In South Korea during the 1960s, public protests against what people viewed as the weak stance of the country's dictatorial leaders in dealing with Japan fueled the movement toward democracy—the same thing could happen in China.[14]

Jiang Zemin's campaign to pump up anti-Japanese nationalist sentiment has boxed his successors into a corner. Hu and Wen don't dare to look soft on Japan. But on the other hand, if they can't find a way to cool down popular passions against Japan, during a crisis these passions might boil over into an antigovernment rebellion or make it impossible for them to duck an outright military clash with Japan.

Japanese Backlash

Until recently, stirring up popular hostility toward Japan looked safer than stirring up anger toward the United States or Taiwan, which could push the country into a shooting war with a much more powerful adversary. Some Chinese still think that venting against Japan is cost free. As a Beijing foreign policy expert explained to me during the April 2005 demonstrations, "The U.S. is a superpower, so China doesn't want to offend it. But most Chinese view Japan as a second-rate power whose economy depends on China's growth." "That's why the leaders take tough public positions against Japan," he continued. "They don't care about the actual consequences, the actual costs." On April 18, 2005, one posting on Strong Nation Forum put it succinctly. "It is alright that our relations with Japan deteriorate to the worst. However, we must not damage our relations with the United States!"

But the bolstering of domestic support by trashing relations with Japan is becoming riskier as a Japanese backlash builds. The Japanese public increasingly views China as a threat and supports the assertive stance of political leaders like Prime Minister Koizumi toward it. Perceptions of a threat from China make the public interested in revising Japan's postwar "peace constitution" and strengthening the country's military defense. The Japanese have also tired of the perpetual pressure to atone for the crimes committed in World War II and seek recognition that they too suffered greatly in the war. Koizumi, both stimulating and responding to this mood, was the first postwar prime minister to pay annual visits to the Yasukuni Shrine, and the first openly to acknowledge Japan's Self-Defense Forces as a real military.

Japanese public opinion has soured on China. It took a sharp nosedive in 2004 after Japan defeated China in the Asian Cup soccer match in Beijing and an angry Chinese crowd assaulted a Japanese diplomat's car, breaking the rear window (the diplomat was uninjured).[15] A poll by *Yomiuri Shimbun*, one of Japan's leading newspapers, conducted after the April 2005 anti-Japanese demonstrations showed that overwhelming majorities favored taking a tough stance against China.[16] Six months after the protests, Japanese polls found that approximately 65 percent of Japanese felt unfriendly toward China, a larger proportion than that of Chinese who feel unfriendly to Japan (53.6 percent), according to Chinese polls.[17] As of 2006, only 28 percent of the Japanese and 21 percent of the Chinese had positive views of each other, and people in both countries consider the other competitive, greedy, and arrogant.[18]

Japanese politicians are playing to the anti-Chinese mood. Koizumi issued two different statements on the 2005 anniversary of the end of World War II—one for foreign consumption that included an apology and an acknowledgement of Japan's "colonization and aggression" and one for domestic consumption that left them out.[19] In the 2005 parliamentary election, the opposition party's critique of Koizumi's frequent visits to the Yasukuni Shrine got little traction with the voters. Instead Koizumi's anti-Chinese attitude helped reelect the Liberal Democratic Party with an increased majority. When Koizumi retired as prime minister in September 2006, the majority Liberal Democratic Party chose Shinzo Abe, a politician known for his hawkish anti-China attitude, to succeed him. Japan has reduced its development aid to China because its public resents China's lack of gratitude and worries about fueling China's military buildup.[20] (The Chinese government has not publicized the aid.) Also, after years of ignoring Chinese vessels exploring off the coast of Japan, ostensibly for research purposes, the Koizumi government started to challenge them publicly. It's becoming clear that the interplay between the domestic politics of the two sides is dragging the relationship into a downward spiral.

People in China see every Japanese act through the lens of history and fail to recognize the impact of China's own actions on Japan. A Chinese student complained that Japanese politicians were pandering to anti-Chinese sentiments. "Public opinion matters, but the leaders can influence back," he said, with no apparent appreciation that the same could be said of China. An October 2005 poll done jointly by Chinese and Japanese organizations found that 90 percent of Chinese blamed Japan for the poor relations between the two countries, while more than half the Japanese respondents said it was hard to tell which side was to blame.[21]

Koizumi

Diaoyu

International Risks

The possibility of military conflict between China and Japan, the two largest economies and largest militaries in Asia, no longer seems as remote as it once did. With the price of oil sky-high and both countries dependent on imported fuels, the long-simmering territorial dispute over the East China Sea that lies between the two countries is becoming an active conflict of interest. For years, the two governments tried to keep nationalist hotheads from stirring up popular emotions over the disputed Diaoyu Islands (called the Senkakus by the Japanese) and the surrounding waters of the East China Sea. Japan took control of the islands in 1895 when it acquired Taiwan and Korea. After the end of World War II, the United States administered them, and returned them to Japan in 1972. But the Chinese believe that the islands have been theirs for centuries.

The Chinese have begun drilling and the Japanese have given approval to a company to drill for oil and gas in the waters. Chinese warships have begun to patrol nearby in what one Japanese politician denounced as "gunboat diplomacy."[22] In 2004, a noisy nuclear-powered Chinese submarine entered Japanese waters and provoked a rare military alert on the part of the Japanese self-defense forces; the Chinese apologized later. According to a Japanese newspaper, between July 2004 and June 2005 China deployed naval surveillance aircraft 146 times and patrol boats eighteen times to the disputed boundary area in the East China Sea. And the Japanese Air Self-Defense Forces are intercepting the Chinese aircraft with increasing frequency. They scrambled them approximately thirty times in the six months before February 2006.[23] The two governments would like to head off a military confrontation over the oil and gas fields through quiet negotiations. But China's porousness to information from abroad and the aggressiveness of its own media have put the talks on the front burner of public attention, which will make compromise much harder to achieve, and a military face-off a dangerous possibility.

In the six hours after sina.com, the Chinese Internet news portal, posted the news about the Japanese government's decision to allow an oil and gas company to start drilling in the area in July 2005, twenty-four hundred people posted messages of "strong indignation and condemnation," saying things like "it is an encroachment on China's foremost interest," and "Japan intends to hinder China's development by the act." The official Xinhua news agency reported on the outraged online reactions, which guaranteed that senior officials would hear about them. It also quoted a Zhejiang University professor who said, "Japan's ambition of seizing oil and gas resources on the continental shelf of the East China Sea is a new form of its expansionist and invading ideology during World War II."[24]

Foreign ministry officials made strong protests to the Japanese government both in Beijing and in Tokyo that were prominently reported in *People's Daily* and other outlets.[25]

From a domestic political perspective, getting satisfaction on the intangible issues related to Japan's World War II history is a higher priority than negotiating a solution to the tangible dispute over drilling in the East China Sea. Foreign Minister Li Zhaoxing reportedly told Japanese diplomats in October 2005, "If the problem of Japan's historical awareness and [the prime minister's] worship at Yasukuni Shrine is resolved, we can absolutely resolve the East China Sea problem through friendly agreement."[26]

Objectively, it would best serve China's long-term national interests to set history aside and cultivate good relations with Japan, not to feud with it. But China's leaders have consistently sacrificed those interests in order to win domestic points for pressing symbolic issues. The clearest example of the leaders' priority on protecting themselves from the public's anti-Japanese emotions is the fact that they have refused to invite Prime Minister Koizumi to visit China since 2001, and that President Hu Jintao declined to meet with him even outside of China because of his annual visits to the Yasukuni Shrine. According to one Beijing student, "For the leaders to be responsible to our people, they cannot invite Koizumi at this time. Japan has to do something first because it is Koizumi who caused the problem." Another student observed, "Hu Jintao is afraid that he will lose the support of the people if he invites Koizumi to visit China while he is still visiting Yasukuni."

"What if the next Japanese prime minister continues to visit the shrine?" I asked a third student. "Relations will be frozen. It will be very dangerous," he replied. "China will make a big policy change because it will be clear that there is no sincerity on Japan's side."

Economic Costs

China's economic growth—essential for the Communist Party to maintain power—benefits from trade and investment from Japan, even though both sides view Japan as more economically dependent on China than China is on Japan.[27] Japan was China's largest trading partner until 2004 when the European Union moved ahead of it, and it is the fourth-largest source of foreign direct investment. According to the Japanese government, the number of Chinese students studying in Japan (70,814) has surpassed the number studying in the United States (64,757 in 2002 to 2003).[28]

The anti-Japanese mood in China worries Japanese executives about the political risk of doing business there. A poll of almost seven thousand

Japanese companies conducted after the April 2005 demonstrations found that two-thirds said they had concerns about investing in China and another 13.5 percent said they had serious concerns about the economic impact of anti-Japanese attitudes on the Mainland. Of the companies who had plans to invest, 30 percent were considering putting them off.[29] A poll of Japanese companies who already had operations in China indicated that although only 10 percent of them felt their business had suffered from the protests, the number of firms planning to expand had dropped substantially.[30] Yet when the 2005 statistics were released, they showed that Japan's direct investment in China actually had risen almost 20 percent to a record $6.53 billion despite the anti-Japanese demonstrations. Even so, Chinese leaders remained worried that repeated violent protests against Japan or boycotts of Japanese products would eventually drive Japanese businesspeople away.

The U.S.-Japan Security Alliance

In terms of global realpolitik—that is, if nationalist emotion were not a factor—China clearly would benefit by wooing Japan away from its long-time security alliance with the United States. Picking fights with Japan only drives the island nation to embrace the United States more closely. The U.S.-Japan alliance, originally designed to defend against Soviet expansion in Asia, has not withered after the fall of the Soviet Union. Instead the alliance has actually grown stronger, fed by Japan's fears of an antagonistic China, a nuclear-armed North Korea, and America's desire to share with Japan the burden of deterring Chinese and North Korean military action. In 1997, Washington and Tokyo revised the guidelines that govern how they would cooperate militarily during a regional crisis. Japan also agreed to develop a costly theater missile defense system jointly with the United States, justifying the investment as a necessary line of defense against attacks from North Korea. But, in fact, the China threat also was a major consideration.

Japan As a Military Power

Chinese analysts once viewed the U.S.-Japan alliance as a "useful constraint on Japan's remilitarization," or colloquially, "the cork in the bottle." Since the mid-1990s, however, they believe the alliance is "driving rather than constraining Japan's rearmament."[31]

China's hostile stance has motivated Tokyo to expand its own military reach and power, a trend that Washington has encouraged. Japan's self-defense forces served in Iraq in noncombat roles, and its naval ships—including state-of-the-art Aegis destroyers acquired from the United States—are in the Indian Ocean supporting American operations in Afghanistan.[32] Japanese naval development is driven by the fact that almost all of Japan's imports of oil and other commodities travel by ship around the southeast coast of Taiwan. If China remains hostile to Japan and reclaims Taiwan, it could cut Japan's economic lifeline. As the retired head of the Japanese navy put it, "The sea lanes would all turn red."[33]

Most remarkably, the Japanese parliament is moving toward revising the Constitution to eliminate Article 9, the linchpin of the postwar "peace constitution" in which Japan renounced the use of force and the establishment of a real military. China's unfriendly attitude toward Japan is provoking the perverse result of motivating Japan to abandon its postwar pacifism.

A People's Liberation Army officer noted another potential cost to anti-Japanese demonstrations that alienate Japanese public opinion. "In the past we had hoped Japan would stand aside in the defense of Taiwan, but now we can't assume that it will."

Regional Reactions

Beijing is cooperating with and accommodating every country in Asia other than Japan because of its interest in reassuring its neighbors that it is a cautious power with peaceful intentions. However, relations with Japan are the glaring exception. When Pyongyang tested seven missiles on July 4, 2006, President Hu and Prime Minister Koizumi each consulted by telephone with President Bush and other world leaders, but they didn't dare pick up the telephone to talk with one another. When other Asians see China and Japan dueling, they worry about the possibility of a military conflict that could tear the region apart. South Korean president Roh Moo-hyun has said that South Korea may need to become the "balancer" between China and Japan. Southeast Asians worry about the possible emergence of two hostile blocs in Northeast Asia: China and South Korea vs. Japan and the United States.[34] Singapore's prime minister Lee Hsien Loong urged China and Japan to "moderate nationalist sentiment . . . work toward reconciliation . . . and come to terms with the history of the Second World War the way Germany and France have done in Europe."[35] Political friction between China and Japan retards efforts to build regional economic cooperation as well. China and Japan constitute more than 80 percent of the total size of the economies of the thirteen East and Southeast Asian countries who are hoping eventually to build a free trade zone.[36]

The diplomats in the Asia Department of the Chinese Foreign Ministry can recite all the reasons that China would gain by improving relations with Japan. They want to build ties with Japan that, in the words of one rising young diplomat, are more about "interests" than about "face." But their hands are tied not only by the Communist Party politicians who treat Japan policy as a form of domestic politics, but also by the open hostility of the Chinese public toward Japan.

Meanwhile worries about Sino-Japanese conflict continue to grow. As Xu Dunxin, a former Chinese ambassador to Japan, said, "When neighbors cannot get on well with each other, they can move out. However, when neighboring countries cannot get on well with each other, they cannot move away. Japan and China are close neighbors separated only by a strip of water."[37]

Chinese Public Opinion

A scientifically reliable survey of Beijing citizens between 2000 and 2003 indicates that people have more negative feelings toward Japan than toward the United States, and that these feelings are strong across the entire population—they vary less according to income, age, or gender than do feelings toward the United States.[38] Hostile attitudes toward Japan have grown in recent years, according to the national surveys conducted by the Institute for Japanese Studies of the Chinese Academy of Social Sciences. In 2002 43.3 percent of people said they had unfriendly feelings against Japan. By 2004 the number had risen to 53.6 percent. Interestingly, the proportion of people who say they are "neutral" is very large and the proportion of those who say they are friendly is tiny. The researchers explain that when relations with the United States are strained, people still are willing to say their own opinion is "friendly." But even when relations with Japan are relatively good, people hesitate to say they are friendly to Japan.[39]

Much of the Chinese antipathy toward Japan is genuine and historically rooted. Young people in particular seek an idealistic cause that replaces the communist values they have abandoned and transcends the commercialism that pervades Chinese life today. But political correctness also is a factor. Any politician who advocates setting historical issues aside had better begin by blaming Japan for causing all the problems in the first place and argue that by provoking nationalist overreactions, Japan is trying to divert China from its priority goal of self-strengthening.[40] Social pressure to conform to the nationalist line operates with respect to relations with the United States and Taiwan too, but it is strongest on Japan. The pressure isn't felt only among politicians. A young netizen I interviewed said that when posting any online opinion regarding Japan, you have to begin by saying how much you hate Japan, otherwise the Web site manager will usher you off. Some people told me right after the April 2005 protests that social pressure would discourage them from buying major Japanese appliances or traveling to Japan. One family had already canceled its May holiday trip to Tokyo Disneyland. Another person said that although she still planned to travel to Japan, she wouldn't tell anyone about it. Almost two years after the protests, many college students say that if there is a choice, they will not buy Japanese products. Others admit, as one student said, "China is in an embarrassing situation. We can't live without Japanese products."

I have my own unscientific method of comparing popular views of Japan, Taiwan, and the United States. Whenever I speak to an audience of Chinese students, local officials, or journalists I ask for a show of hands on whether Beijing's policy toward each is "too tough," "too weak," or "just right." Consistently, more people criticize the government's policy toward Japan as "too weak" than criticize its policy toward Taiwan or the United States as weak.

A survey of young people conducted in summer 2005 found that more than half said they hated or disliked Japan. Nearly 80 percent said they had never met anyone from Japan. More than 60 percent said they formed their opinions about Japan through the press, TV, and the Internet. The three Japanese people most familiar to the Chinese young people were Prime Minister Junichiro Koizumi and the World War II military leaders later condemned as war criminals, General Hideki Tojo and Admiral Yamamoto Isoroku.[41] Most of the Chinese students I have met report that they avoid the Japanese students on their campuses. One Chinese student who had studied in the United Kingdom said that even abroad the Chinese students shunned their Japanese classmates—only the Taiwanese students would talk to them.

As one newspaper editor put it, "Relations with Japan are a matter of patriotism, but relations with the United States are a matter of ideology. That's why it's more difficult to make any concessions to Japan." A Chinese netizen measured the intensity of his feelings another way. "I would like to donate one month's salary if our army fought against Taiwan. I would like to donate one year's salary if our army fought against America. I would like to donate my life if our army fought against Japan."

The Burden of History

Why are Chinese emotions toward Japan so raw? The Japanese attacked Pearl Harbor and killed many American GIs during World War II, but most Americans have forgiven them by now. Why haven't the Chinese done the same? The difference is that Japan holds a more central place in the historical memory of Chinese people, going back to the late nineteenth century and that Japan actually occupied China.

For more than a thousand years, China was the dominant country in Asia, respected by its neighbors for being superior culturally, as well as economically and militarily. Although Japan, unlike most of China's neighbors, was never a tributary state required to send gifts to recognize China's suzerainty, it had a subordinate place in the region—until the 1890s. As China became hobbled by massive internal problems that the inept Qing government couldn't solve, Japan humiliated China by defeating it in the Sino-Japanese War in 1894 to 1895. Although this was not China's first military defeat to foreign forces—it followed the loss to Britain in the Opium War in 1839 to 1842—it mortified the Chinese to be bested by an upstart Asian neighbor. The Western imperialist powers had forced open China and Japan at the same time in the mid-nineteenth century, but the Qing government failed to respond to the challenge with the same alacrity as Japan, which undertook a crash program to modernize its military and society. As China's 2004 senior high-school textbook puts it, "The Sino-Japanese War in 1895 exposed the Qing dynasty's incompetence and corruption and also showed the fearless spirit and strong will of patriotic Chinese military and civilians to defend against 'humiliation by foreigners.'"[42]

To add insult to injury, in the Treaty of Shimonoseki following the 1894–95 war, China lost Taiwan and its control over the nominally independent Korea to Japan. (The name of Li Hongzhang, the Qing official who ceded Chinese territory in the treaty, has gone down in infamy. To call a contemporary figure a "Li Hongzhang" is to condemn him as a traitor to his country.)

The Taiwan issue and the Japan issue are closely intertwined. Today's Chinese can't forgive Japan for dismembering China and ruling Taiwan as a colony until the end of World War II. Many older Taiwanese, including former president Lee Teng-hui, feel a close affinity to Japan and speak better Japanese than Mandarin, a fact that any Mainland Chinese taxi driver will tell you bitterly. The 2004 history textbook draws this connection between the Sino-Japanese War and the loss of Taiwan more explicitly than earlier versions. "Confronting the barbarous invaders, the Chinese civilians used all possible ways to defend the country, especially during the 'Anti-Taiwan Separation War.' The patriotic military and civilians fought a bloody war against the Japanese invaders, showing their strong will and high level of patriotic spirit of maintaining the territorial integrity of the homeland. Thereafter, during the five decades of Japanese rule of Taiwan the Taiwanese people never stopped their fight against the colonial rule and their pursuit of the return of the island to the homeland."[43]

As modern Chinese nationalism emerged in the early twentieth century, Japan was the "other" against which the Chinese people defined their identity. Following World War I, Japan (which had allied with Great Britain) issued the Chinese government an ultimatum claiming for itself the German concessions in China, including railroad and military garrison rights in Shandong Province. When the news reached Beijing that the Americans and Europeans had agreed to Japan's terms at the Versailles Peace Conference in 1919 and the Chinese representatives at the conference had caved in, mass demonstrations erupted in Beijing and throughout China. The May 4 movement, synonymous with modern Chinese nationalism, was born out of this anger against Japan.

By far the most traumatic episode in the history of Japan's aggression against China was its brutal invasion and occupation of China during the 1930s and 1940s. The Japanese armies occupied all of Eastern China and Manchuria (Northeastern China), driving the rival Communist and Guomindang governments to retreat to inland bases in Yanan and Chongqing respectively. The PRC government estimates that thirty-five million Chinese, mostly civilians, were killed during what it calls the Anti-Japanese War of 1931 through 1945.[44] (After Tiananmen, the government raised its estimate from the number of ten million that it had accepted after World War II to thirty-five million.[45]) Almost every family suffered in some way under the brutal onslaught, either by having someone killed by Japanese soldiers or by the hunger and illness caused by wartime chaos. Like families in the American South who suffered bitterly during the Civil War, Chinese families have passed down personal accounts of suffering and bravery from this ordeal to their children and grandchildren. A student told me, "I learned about the cruelty of the Japanese from the old people and it frightened me how such a small state wanted to conquer China and the world. Then I had a terrible dream about it. I still can remember the dream." President Jiang Zemin also had bitter personal experiences growing up in East China during the Japanese occupation. When his uncle was killed by the Japanese, he was adopted by his uncle's family to give them a male heir.

Of all the tragic stories from the wartime experience, the most horrific was the 1937 event that has come to be called the "Nanjing Massacre" or the city what historian Jonathan Spence has called "a period of terror and destruction that must rank among the worst in the history of modern warfare." According to Spence, approximately twenty thousand women were raped, and many of them killed; twelve thousand civilians were murdered; and thirty thousand Chinese soldiers were killed.[46] The official Chinese estimate is that three hundred thousand people lost their lives. A Chinese historian in Nanjing told me privately that the actual number of deaths was probably around one hundred thousand. The 1948 war crimes tribunal in Tokyo used the number of two hundred thousand. The true number may never be known.

After the war, Japan, under American occupation, adopted its new peace constitution and convicted twenty-seven political and military leaders in the Tokyo war crimes tribunal. But as a society, Japan never examined its responsibility for wartime atrocities as deeply and thoroughly as the Germans did.[47] (Beginning in 2005, the Chinese government began trying to shame the Japanese by highlighting the comparison to postwar Germany.[48]) Japanese schoolchildren learn a whitewashed version of the history of the war. A Japanese professor told me that when she and her students drove past an American military cemetery on a field trip to the island of Okinawa, now part of Japan, the students were surprised to learn that Americans had died in the Asian theater during World War II. Japanese museums dwell on the suffering of the Japanese victims of the American nuclear attacks on Hiroshima and Nagasaki in 1945 with hardly a mention of the Japanese aggression that provoked it. No historical museum in Japan gives anything close to an accurate rendering of the atrocities that the Japanese army inflicted on China and Korea, including forced sexual slavery of "comfort women" and experiments with chemical and biological weapons on prisoners. The museum attached to the Yasukuni Shrine glosses over the Japanese occupation of China and focuses on the Japanese fight against Western (especially American) colonialism in Asia. As a result, although Japan's prime ministers have repeatedly given "heartfelt apologies and condolences" for their country's "damage and pain inflicted by colonial rule and invasion" as Koizumi expressed it in 2005, these words have never sounded sincere to the ears of their Asian neighbors.

The Media Keep History Alive

Chinese rage against Japan's failure to acknowledge its wartime guilt has intensified instead of dissipating with time. Chinese young people are if anything more obsessed by the history question than are their parents or grandparents. The potent combination of official propaganda and the sensational popular media, both of which tend to exploit and heighten the notion of wartime suffering for their own purposes, have made people more conscious of this painful history than ever before. The popular media and Internet news sites trawl the international news for stories that will attract Chinese audiences. Anything related to Japan's wartime history or its current military development is sure to interest the young urbanites who are also the target audience of advertisers. Every reported outrage sparks excited discussions on Internet chat rooms. The media and Internet buzz gives leaders and officials, as well as ordinary people, the impression that anti-Japanese fervor is sweeping the country and encourages people to join in collective action like petitions and protests because they know they won't be alone.[49] It also makes policymakers—particularly the politicians—feel they are under intense pressure from public opinion and forces them to react publicly to even minor slights from Japan.

Every perceived slight by Japanese leaders, every revision of Japanese textbooks —as well as every misstep by Japanese students studying in China or Japanese visitors to China—is an opportunity for tabloid newspapers and Internet Web sites to attract audiences and whip up popular passions. Any event that connects Taiwan and Japan, such as a private visit to Japan by former Taiwan president Lee Teng-hui, is sure to arouse readers' interest. A South China orgy involving a large group of Japanese businessmen and Chinese prostitutes that took place in September 2003—the anniversary of Japan's invasion of Manchuria in 1931—first reported by *China Youth Daily* attracted more than seven thousand postings on prominent Web discussion sites in the first two days.[50] Even flaws in Japanese products—the brakes failing on Mitsubishi jeeps or poor reception with Matsushita cell phones—are grist for the media and the chat rooms. Advertisements for Japanese products that inadvertently affront Chinese consumers—such as a Toyota ad that showed a Toyota Prado (unfortunately transliterated as *Ba Dao*, "the way of the hegemon") driving in front of bowing Chinese stone lions under the line, "You cannot but respect the Ba Dao"—give people a chance to vent their anger toward Japan.

A magazine fashion spread featuring a Chinese actress wearing a short dress with a large imperial Japanese flag printed on it became the subject of an exposé by a Hunan newspaper and sparked a media and Internet frenzy (more than six thousand mostly angry messages were posted on the sina.com Web site the week after the exposé). The fashion magazine editor was forced to resign. Protestors smashed the actress's house with bricks and bottles. The actress apologized on the Internet and on television. Nevertheless, at a New Years' party, an enraged man hopped on stage and smeared excrement on her. Computer-generated nude pictures of her were circulated on the Internet. Each act of the saga further whipped up the mania.[51]

The Yasukuni Shrine is the focus of a great deal of Internet passion and even a little humor. For example, "I have already named my bathroom the 'Yasukuni Shrine,' I wish all of you guys would do the same."

Communist Party officials try to manage the media to keep Japan phobia from running amok. The Chinese government canceled the showing of the Hollywood film *Memoirs of a Geisha*, in which three Chinese movie stars play Japanese geishas, in order to avoid sparking media and public outrage. The State Council Information Office "guides" newspapers and online news sites to avoid broadsides against Japan and to criticize Japanese "rightists" instead. State Council Information Office head Zhao Qizheng promised Japanese reporters that "there will be no anti-Japan reporting by major news organizations," but he was unable to enforce his pledge.[52] Anti-Japanese stories are too good a draw for commercial media to give them up.

Cui Tiankai, the then head of the Asia Department of the Foreign Ministry, nervily complained to Japanese officials in 2006 that the Japanese media "only focuses on negative aspects of China. . . . In order to produce good coverage the government in China provides guidance to the media. The Japanese government should provide similar guidance." The Japanese officials replied bluntly that that Japan doesn't censor the media.[53]

In recent years, Chinese news media, like media elsewhere, have become enamored of stories about public opinion on hot topics. People are interested in knowing what other people think. Typically, the media use polls with highly unrepresentative samples, sometimes consisting only of those readers who feel strongly enough to take the trouble to answer the questions, and come up with dramatic conclusions. Whenever Japan is involved, public opinion is reported to be almost universally hostile toward Japan, reinforcing popular and elite impressions. For example, one April 2005 poll reported the unsurprising finding that 96 percent of people believe that the Japanese government's approval of new textbooks "has seriously hurt the Chinese people's feelings and is a slander and insult to their sentiments."[54] When the Communist Party tried to calm students after the April 2005 demonstrations, newspaper articles selectively quoted viewpoints posted on the Internet advocating calm, rational patriotism instead of simply invoking the authority of the Communist Party.[55]

Foreign Ministry officials complain about having to anticipate media coverage and public opinion on Japan policy all the time. Many of them go online themselves to read the debates.[56] The Internet sets the agenda and the diplomats react, trying to stay ahead of online opinion.

Mao Needed No Apology

In the earlier era of Mao Zedong (1949–1976), Chinese leaders had little need to mobilize popular sentiment against Japan. As the founder and dictatorial leader of the People's Republic, Mao had unchallenged authority on foreign policy matters. Mao Zedong and Premier Zhou Enlai, Mao's suave right-hand diplomat, promoted "peaceful, friendly relations" with Japan. As Chalmers Johnson notes, because Mao's and Zhou's "nationalistic credentials were unassailable [they] could on occasion ignore or deflect the nationalist issue when it suited their purposes to do so."[57] Whenever Mao wanted to mobilize the public with an international threat, he used the United States or later, the Soviet Union, instead.

"Everything was controlled by the top leaders. Good relations with Japan were a high-level political decision, the leaders had prestige, so the people followed them," one think-tank policy expert explained. It wasn't because they liked Japan, he added. In fact, the older generation hated Japan. "At a 1965 Japanese cultural exhibition in Beijing," he recalled, "when people came in and saw the Japanese flag, they fell to the floor in shock and dismay, they had such bad memories."

In the 1950s Mao and Zhou promoted good relations with Japan for international strategic considerations, to try to balance against the United States by seducing its ally to China's side. Despite the absence of diplomatic relations, China and Japan traded informally with one another. Sino-Japanese friendship was the theme in Mao-era political education and media propaganda. In the early 1970s Mao and Zhou made a strategic decision to cultivate political relations with Japan and the United States to counterbalance the Soviet Union, then viewed as China's greatest threat. They established diplomatic relations with Japan in 1972, seven years before establishing diplomatic relations with the United States, because the Japanese were more eager to increase trade and more amenable to sacrificing their political relations with Taiwan.

On the occasion of diplomatic recognition in 1972, Mao and Zhou willingly forswore any Japanese reparations from World War II, reaffirming the commitment that Chiang Kai-shek, the leader of the Republican government, had made following the war.[58] Their message explained that China did not want to use a wartime indemnity to construct their country; it would harm peace to force the losing country to be responsible for the huge indemnity; and it was unreasonable to require the generation that didn't fight the war to have to pay it.[59] Mao and Zhou were satisfied with Japan's statement of remorse in the joint communiqué. "The Japanese side is keenly conscious of the responsibility for the serious damage that Japan caused in the past to the Chinese people through war, and deeply reproaches itself." They believed that it settled permanently the issue of Japan's attitude toward its wartime aggression against China. As one Chinese scholar of relations with Japan said, neither Mao nor Zhou "thought it was necessary for Japan to apologize all the time."[60]

Deng Xiaoping's Deft Touch 1978-94

Deng Xiaoping, the veteran leader of the Long March generation who survived two purges during the Cultural Revolution to become China's preeminent political figure from 1978 to 1994, also had greater authority, particularly in the foreign policy realm, than today's leaders. Famous for advocating pragmatism—he stole Mao Zedong's slogan, "It doesn't matter if the cat is white or black, so long as it catches mice," and made it his own—Deng saw the relationship with Japan as crucial for his market-oriented economic reforms to succeed. Just months before he announced the reforms in December 1978, he visited Japan, making the first ever visit by a PRC leader. He later visited Japan a second time, and according to the *People's Daily*, he met with more guests from Japan than from any other foreign country.[61]

Shortly after the 2005 protests, a retired senior official in South China reminisced to me about the Deng era when relations with Japan were "sensible and friendly." He recalled that in the early 1980s, Deng Xiaoping asked Vice-Premier Gu Mu to invite several Japanese to serve as advisors to the PRC's economic modernization efforts and created the Sino-Japanese Economic Knowledge Exchange Association, an organization to help Chinese learn from Japan's development experience. China and Japan had some serious economic quarrels at the time. China had reneged on its contracts with Japan for building a modern steel plant outside Shanghai (to push Japan to import more Chinese oil to help pay for the plant and other technology goods that China wanted to buy), but the two countries remained "good friends."

In the 1970s and early 1980s, Japan had a positive image in China as an Asian economic and technological tiger worthy of emulation. In 1980 I spent a month doing research in Chongqing, the cloudy industrial city and former wartime capital in Sichuan Province, where I lived at a guesthouse for government officials. A roomful of Sichuan officials sat glued to the television set at night watching a weeklong documentary about Japan's economic miracle. What clearly impressed the Chinese officials was how the Japanese, even in such a modern society, took care of their elderly parents and celebrated traditional rituals.

Under Deng, China and Japan signed an agreement to increase trade and a Treaty of Peace and Friendship. And when the territorial dispute over the Diaoyu Islands threatened to disrupt friendly relations, Deng shunted it aside by stating that the issue would "be handled better by the next generation."[62] The Chinese government did react vigorously in 1982 when the first Japanese textbook controversy erupted, and in 1987 when a Japanese court handed ownership of a student dormitory, purchased in 1950 by the Republic of China, to the government on Taiwan instead of to the PRC. But as one policy advisor put it, "Deng kept it in control, he stopped the fever quickly." He noted that the Japanese attitudes of that time were different from today's as well. The Japanese Left—which by now has almost disappeared—was as critical of the textbooks as people in China were, and Prime Minister Nakasone, in 1985, was willing to ask the Ministry of Education to revise them. (Japanese textbooks have been revised several times since then, with some of the textbooks becoming more balanced, but some of the optional texts such as the one that stirred up the protests in 2005 moving further away from acknowledging the nation's wartime guilt.)

In 1993, relations between China and Japan were relaxed enough that the two countries had begun to talk about their militaries participating together in United Nations peacekeeping activities.[63]

The 1985 Student Protests

On the morning of September 18, 1985, school ceremonies at Beijing's elite universities to commemorate the anniversary of Japan's invasion of Manchuria turned into a large unsanctioned march to Tiananmen Square. The demonstrators shouted slogans like "Down with Japanese militarism!" "Down with [Prime Minister] Nakasone!" "Boycott Japanese goods!" and "Down with the second occupation!" The last slogan referred to the Japanese goods that at the time were a larger proportion of the foreign products reaching Chinese markets than they are today. Similar demonstrations erupted in other Chinese cities over the following weeks. (The Internet and cell phones hadn't been invented yet, but the word spread by telephone.) The triggers were the same as those twenty years later: Japanese textbooks and a prime minister's visit to the Yasukuni Shrine. A popular television serial, *Four Generations Under One Roof*, which dramatized the hardship and suffering of one family during the Anti-Japanese War, probably also contributed to the flood of emotions that led to the demonstrations.[64]

In 1985, however, the Japanese reactions were much more compliant. Japan was riding a wave of prosperity, and its government was confident of domestic support. Prime Minister Yasuhiro Nakasone, who was strongly committed to relations with China, ordered the education authorities to revise the textbooks to conciliate China. Even though he was in the midst of an election campaign, he committed not to visit the shrine again in order to "give appropriate consideration to the national sentiments of neighboring countries."[65]

Caught in the crossfire between international and domestic pressures, China's leaders at that time—Hu Yaobang was CCP general secretary and Zhao Ziyang was premier, but Deng Xiaoping, although not holding the top formal post, was the universally recognized preeminent leader—showed much more consideration for Japan than did their successors in 2005. A long, authoritative article prepared by the CCP propaganda czar, "Treasure the Hard-Won China-Japan Friendly Relations," strongly defended the Japanese people and stressed that only a handful embraced militarism.[66] Premier Zhao Ziyang met with Prime Pinister Nakasone in New York at the United Nations General Assembly without making a tough public statement even while the students were demonstrating against his visit to the Yasukuni Shrine.[67] And during the same period, Communist Party general secretary Hu Yaobang met with the China-Japan Twenty-First-Century Friendship Commission.

Although more willing than today's leaders to defend publicly the Japan relationship, the leaders then employed the same soft touch with the students that we saw in 2005, praising their patriotism but urging them to channel it into "diligent study" and "build[ing] our motherland into a strong and prosperous socialist power." These words were part of the speech presented by then vice-premier Li Peng to an assembly of six thousand youths on December 9 organized to prevent spontaneous demonstrations on that date, the fiftieth anniversary of student protests against Japan that had occurred in 1935.[68] Then, as now, no students were punished for participation in anti-Japanese demonstrations.

Deng and his lieutenants appeared to have ended the student demonstrations against Japan without paying any domestic or international price. But, in fact, the suppression of the protests set off a chain of political aftershocks that Chinese leaders may be studying today to avoid similar troubles in the future.

The Political Fallout of the Protests

After the 1985 anti-Japanese demonstrations, the students, having been reminded vividly of the strong arm of the Chinese state, reluctantly returned to their campuses. Beijing University students called for renewed demonstrations on the upcoming anniversary of the 1935 anti-Japanese protests by passing the word, "Bob up like a cork on December 9."[69] But the Communist Party made sure that there were no demonstrations on December 9. Campus wall posters (the low-tech antecedents of today's Internet postings) complained about a government that treated people as "donkeys to be herded" or "stupid yokels." The student postings derided a government that is so "afraid of the possibility that a friendly nation may be upset" that it doesn't care that "China [is] being degraded or the Chinese people [are] becoming numb and insensitive."[70]

The students' resentment continued to build, and when the December anniversary rolled around again in 1986, they strode out of their campuses in Hefei (the capital of Anhui Province), Shanghai, Wuhan, Shenzhen, Nanjing, and Beijing in demonstrations that lasted through the first days of 1987. This time, the students focused not on Japan, but on the shortcomings of their own political system. Signs and wall posters called for democracy and freedom. According to scholar Jeffrey Wasserstrom, who was on the scene in Shanghai, the main goal of the movement was to fight for the right to protest itself.[71] The students were particularly infuriated that their protests of 1985 and 1986 had never been reported in the press. They called on the official media "to tell the people what was really going on" and give the protestors air time to explain the reasons behind their actions.[72] Students in Beijing publicly burned official newspapers for criticizing the student struggle.[73] The number one goal of the Beijing University students, one Hong Kong periodical reported, was absolute freedom of the press and freedom to publish.[74]

(Although the 2005 student demonstrators did not openly criticize the Chinese government or raise issues of political reform, they were upset about a new rule that limited access to a university's Internet bulletin board only to students attending that university, and about other restrictions on the Internet. The contrast between China's still-censored media—which blacked out news about their protests—and international reporting has become increasingly apparent to students, especially the technically sophisticated ones who have found ways around the official filters. On the other hand, most of the nonpolitical grievances motivating student activism in the 1980s, such as state job assignment of college graduates, inflation, and poor living conditions on campuses, no longer existed in 2005.)

A third wave of protests in 1989 snowballed into the nationwide upheaval of Tiananmen that almost brought down the regime. In all three waves of protest (1985, 1986, and 1989), students felt little risk because some voices in the Communist Party leadership appeared to support them. The students looked behind the façade of Party unity and saw in newspaper editorials signs of divisions within the top elite over two issues that had become intertwined: policies toward Japan and China's political reform.

During the 1980s, CCP general secretary Hu Yaobang was the most outspoken proponent of both the China-Japan relationship and political reform. Acting on his own in 1984, he hosted three thousand Japanese youths in a high-profile and costly visit to China. Most unusual for a Chinese leader, he entertained Nakasone and his family in his own home.[75] (I was doing research in Beijing at the time, and my daughter, who was attending a Chinese preschool called "Number One Kindergarten" learned special songs and pom-pom moves to welcome the Japanese visitors to her school.) Hu also encouraged public discussion of political reform by intellectuals, some of whom became the leading figures in the demonstrations. Deng Xiaoping originally backed up Hu on both Japan and political reform. But infuriated by the 1986–87 demonstrations, Deng joined the more conservative faction in blaming them on Hu and in ousting him from power.[76] The firing of Hu Yaobang stands as an object lesson to present and future leaders of China. Since his fall, "no leader has attempted to soften their [*sic*] attitudes toward Japan."[77]

Deng Xiaoping's effort to stabilize relations with Japan was crucial to bringing the 1985 student demonstrations against Japan to a peaceful close. Deng met with the Japanese foreign minister in Beijing on October 10, a few weeks after the protests erupted, and reportedly reached an informal agreement that the Japanese prime minister would no longer visit the Yasukuni Shrine. In exchange, the Chinese government would no longer attack Nakasone.[78] PRC ambassador to Japan Wang Yi in a 2005 Tokyo speech revealed that a "gentlemen's agreement" had been reached between the two governments in 1985. If the top Japanese officials—the prime minister, the chief cabinet secretary, and the foreign minister—would refrain from visiting the shrine, in return China would not condemn pilgrimages there by lesser-known figures.[79] Nakasone in 2005 denied the existence of any previous "gentlemen's agreement."[80] The fact that after Nakasone's visit to Yasukuni in 1985 no Japanese prime minister visited the shrine for eleven years suggests that Deng probably did reach a private understanding with the Japanese prime minister.

I met with Wang Yi in 2005, and was not surprised to learn that he had been working hard to revive this informal agreement with Japan. He had no luck with Koizumi. By making its demand to stop visiting the shrine so public, the Chinese government made it impossible for Koizumi to acquiesce without looking weak to his own domestic audience. But Wang Yi hoped to do better with Shinzo Abe, who appeared to be the most likely choice to inherit the prime ministership. Abe's reputation as a nationalist hawk might provide political cover for him to be more flexible on the shrine issue—a dynamic similar to the one that enabled Richard Nixon to open up relations with Communist China.

Jiang Zemin's Patriot Games

Jiang Zemin succeeded Deng Xiaoping as a compromise choice after Tiananmen and began to take charge in 1994 through 1995 as Deng's health deteriorated. (Deng died in 1997 at the age of ninety-two.) Unlike Mao and Deng, Jiang lacked confidence. He worried about challenges from rival leaders and doubts from the public—memories of the Tiananmen crisis were fresh—and as a result, was much more attentive to nationalist public opinion. His intimidating face-to-face confrontations with anti-Japan student protestors when he served as mayor of Shanghai during the 1980s may also have made him fearful. When he spoke at his alma mater Jiaotong University in December 1986 to urge students to stop protesting, the students "heckled the mayor for spouting empty platitudes."[81] And his personal history had left him with bad memories of the Japanese occupation.

Over time Jiang became personally invested in improving ties with Washington, but when it came to Japan, he hammered away at the history issue much more aggressively than his predecessors had. A senior official in the Chinese Foreign Ministry acknowledged, "China used to be quite accommodating to Japan under Mao and Deng," but is much less so under Jiang. This official blamed the deterioration of Sino-Japanese relations on the dimming of Japan's economic miracle and Japan's growing resentment of China's rise, but others were not so forgiving toward Jiang. "Mao and Zhou had the greatest moral right to hate the Japanese, but they responsibly made good relations with Japan because they thought strategically. Jiang is just playing patriotic games," a think-tank expert told me.

Under Jiang, as China continued to move toward a capitalist-style economy, nationalism replaced communism as the rationale for people to support the Party. Beginning in 1994 the CCP Propaganda Department's "patriotic education campaign," designed to ensure the loyalty of its subjects—young people in particular—by nurturing their nationalist attachment to the state, became the dominant theme in school and media socialization.[82]

As the fiftieth anniversary of the end of World War II approached in 1995, schools and the media put the history of Japanese aggression against China front and center. President Jiang Zemin and his colleagues attended seventeen official celebrations of the Chinese victory over Japan during the summer of 1995.[83]

The Nanjing Massacre Memorial Museum, built in 1985, was expanded in 1995. (In 2005 the city government announced plans to further expand it—the expansions track perfectly the high points of nationalist mobilization.) It became a focal point of Chinese popular nationalism and a counterpoint to Japan's Yasukuni Shrine. A false rumor about the impending demolition of the museum in December 2000 sparked a violent local demonstration.[84] When a local figure proposed turning the Nanjing Massacre Memorial Museum into the Nanjing International Peace Center to signify a more forward-looking attitude in 2002, he was viciously attacked in local newspapers and Web sites for being unpatriotic. (In a positive sign, the latest expansion will both enlarge the museum and build an international peace square adjacent to it.[85]) The Chinese government commissioned two statues to commemorate the late Chinese-American writer Iris Chang, the author of the best seller *The Rape of Nanking: The Forgotten Holocaust of World War II*, one at the Nanjing memorial and one near her home in San Jose, California.[86] In July 2005, China's biggest Internet news site, sina.com, inaugurated its new Nanjing Massacre historical fact site in a ceremony at the Nanjing memorial attended by local propaganda department officials.[87]

Because of anti-Japanese feelings stirred up by Jiang's campaign, relations between China and Japan reached their lowest point in 1995 through 1996 since the reestablishment of diplomatic relations in 1972.[88] A vicious cycle developed. As scholar Gilbert Rozman described it, "China heightened Japan's alarm and then took that alarm as evidence of nefarious intentions."[89] China defied Japan's request to halt nuclear testing and tested three times in 1995. Japan showed its dismay by discontinuing its aid to China, and China cited its historic grievance, saying that the aid was a form of war reparation and therefore must continue. Tension over the Diaoyu Islands reemerged, and Japanese prime minister Ryutaro Hashimoto paid a personal visit to the Yasukuni Shrine, the first visit by a prime minister since 1985. (The visits by Nakasone and Koizumi were official.) When Washington and Tokyo redefined the guidelines governing their military alliance so that Japan could support American forces based in Japan if they had to respond to a regional crisis, the Chinese vehemently objected because they understood the implications for a fight over Taiwan. At the time, I proposed in a private meeting with a senior Chinese Foreign Ministry official that three-way talks between the United States, China, and Japan might help ease mutual suspicions, but he rejected the idea with astounding arrogance, saying, "But Japan isn't a *real* power like China and the United States, you know."

Not surprisingly, public attitudes on both sides grew more hostile. An unscientific poll of young people by the *China Youth Daily* conducted at the end of 1996 found that the word "Japan" "most easily" made 83.9 percent think of the Nanjing Massacre, and made 81.3 percent think of "Japanese denial" and the "war of resistance against Japanese aggression." When asked to label the Japanese, 56.1 percent chose "cruel."[90] According to Japanese government polls, the percentage of people who held "close feelings" toward China, which had already dropped from 68.5 percent (1988) to 51.6 percent in 1989 after Tiananmen, fell to 39.9 percent in 1996.[91]

Jiang's Visit to Japan

Jiang Zemin's disastrous state visit to Japan in 1998 exemplified his domestically oriented approach. Chinese and Japanese diplomats agree on their accounts of what happened:

Jiang went to Japan in November, following South Korea's president Kim Dae-jung's trip a month earlier. Originally, Jiang's trip was supposed to precede Kim's, but the schedules changed so that it followed Kim's. The Japanese government had presented Kim with a written apology for its wartime past in exchange for his promise that South Korea would never raise the history issue again.[92] In the original planning for Jiang's trip, the Chinese Foreign Ministry had not intended to request a written apology from Japan. Its original three themes for the visit were Taiwan, Japan's alliance with the United States, and history. But once Jiang saw that Kim had obtained a written apology, he was determined to get one too as a "deliverable" to bring home to the Chinese people. The two sides had little time for preparatory negotiations. The Chinese foreign minister, Tang Jiaxuan, a Japan expert, had to back up Jiang's demands for a written apology to show that Tang wasn't a Japan sympathizer. Some people in the Japanese government favored granting the written apology, but Japanese prime minister Keizo Obuchi called in his senior Foreign Ministry advisors and asked, "Why do you believe that China will put history behind it?" The Foreign Ministry officials recommended that Obuchi give Jiang only an oral apology because, unlike the South Koreans, the Chinese side had shown no sincerity at dropping the history issue even if it received the written apology. In their view, China and Jiang would always play the history card.

The Chinese debated canceling the visit, but Jiang, like many political leaders, overestimated his powers of persuasion and thought that once he arrived, he would get what he wanted. Jiang dropped the other two themes and concentrated like a laser on history. He pressed his case in every meeting, including the televised dinner with the emperor, which people in Japan, the left wing included, found extremely rude. In the end, Jiang came home empty-handed.[93] The *People's Daily* reported the visit as a great success, but the English-language *China Daily*, much to the irritation of the Foreign Ministry, criticized Japan for not giving Jiang a written apology. The public lambasted Foreign Minister Tang, who felt humiliated. Jiang himself blamed Tang for the fiasco.

After his trip, Jiang Zemin felt personally insulted by the Japanese. Foreign Ministry officials and other senior leaders, however, did some soul-searching. Japan experts reported to the Central Committee that the "situation was grave," because China's fixation on history was creating a backlash in Japan. Zhao Qizheng, the director of the State Council Information Office who was responsible for President Jiang's image overseas, visited Japan in early 1999, and was shocked at what he heard. He reported back to Jiang Zemin personally that China was making enemies of all the Japanese people.[94] Beijing needed to adjust its approach to promote broad-based cooperation with Japan instead. But Jiang was deaf to this logic, even when it came from his closest colleague, Zeng Qinghong, who traveled to Japan in 2000; Jiang criticized Zeng for meeting some conservative Liberal Democratic Party leaders. The Chinese Communist Party Leading Group on Foreign Affairs (chaired by Jiang) finally convinced him to allow the Foreign Ministry to try a somewhat more pragmatic approach to Japan, particularly on issues that did not receive much attention from the public.[95]

New Thinking on Japan

The essence of the new approach that China has adopted since 2000 was to ease Japanese suspicions by reducing the emphasis on history so that it would become only one of many issues on the agenda. The new line adopted a classical expression, "to take history as a mirror to look toward to the future" to give a nod to history while concentrating on improving future relations. Foreign Minister Tang Jiaxuan, in an interview with Japanese reporters (not reported in the Chinese press), said China would judge relations with Japan "from a long-term and strategic perspective."[96] China reacted with remarkable restraint when the Japanese parliament passed new laws to allow military responses to various kinds of international "emergencies." The Japanese noted the shift toward what it called China's "smile diplomacy."[97]

Premier Zhu Rongji's trip to Japan in 2000 employed the new approach to improving Japanese perceptions of China. Zhu conspicuously downplayed the history issue in his remarks—he raised it only in response to questions—and he held an amiable dialogue with Japanese citizens on live television. When asked about wartime history, the premier replied that because people of both China and Japan suffered, the Japanese people should not be blamed.[98] From the perspective of the Asia Department of the Foreign Ministry, whose top officials accompanied Zhu to Japan to fine-tune his messages on the spot, the visit was a great success.[99]

Chinese diplomats tried to stabilize relations with Japan by behaving calmly in reaction to incidents that otherwise might provoke crises. For example, in 2001, Japanese Maritime Self-Defense vessels in the East China Sea pursued and fired on an unidentified boat that turned out to be from North Korea. The North Koreans fired back and scuttled the boat so that it sank off the Chinese coast. Instead of making a fuss, the Chinese Foreign Ministry allowed Japan to salvage the ship.[100] According to a Chinese military officer, this issue was relatively easy to solve because "people were not paying much attention" to the North Korean mystery boat.

China also sought to intensify its cooperation with Japan in multilateral settings, much as France and Germany have done in Europe. Beijing proposed three-way consultations between China, Japan, and South Korea, focused first on economic issues and later on political and security issues. The first ASEAN Plus Three summit meeting was held in 1997 to address the Asian financial crisis, and by 2000 the group was meeting annually. The Chinese Foreign Ministry promoted these trilateral high-level contacts as a signal that it respects Japan as an equal and no longer wants to freeze it out of regional leadership. Such initiatives encounter little domestic interference because multilateral diplomacy rarely is front-page news.

At the same time, well-connected Chinese think-tank experts started to articulate a more relaxed attitude toward Japan in international symposia. I observed this evolution myself as the organizer of the Northeast Asia Cooperation Dialogue, an informal security forum among officials and academics from China, Japan, the United States, Russia, North Korea, and South Korea that has been meeting since 1993. Chinese participants for years had harangued the Japanese about the revival of militarism and cooperation on missile defense with Washington, but they changed their tune in 2001 and raised fewer criticisms of Japanese policy. In a China-Japan forum in 2002, the Japanese were amazed to hear the head of the think-tank connected with China's Ministry of State Security (its equivalent to the CIA) say openly that China didn't object to the U.S.-Japan security alliance.[101]

Media and Internet Blowback

The Chinese Foreign Ministry's pragmatic approach to Japan policy suffered a public relations catastrophe when Prime Minister Koizumi decided to visit the Yasukuni Shrine in August 2001. Shanghai was hosting the leaders of all the Asian countries and the United States at the Asia Pacific Economic Cooperation (APEC) summit in October—an event that would showcase China as a world economic and diplomatic power—and the Chinese government wanted to avoid having the event be overshadowed by conflict between China and Japan. So shortly following the September 11 terrorist attacks on the United States, Koizumi made a one-day visit to Beijing to meet with President Jiang and Premier Zhu to try to smooth things over. The visit followed a script negotiated by Japan expert and Vice–Foreign Minister Wang Yi with the Japanese ambassador to China.[102] The symbolic focus of the day was Koizumi's visit to the anti-Japanese war memorial at the Marco Polo Bridge outside Beijing, where the war began in 1937. He apologized to the victims of Japan's wartime aggression and placed a wreath on the large statue of a Chinese soldier that serves as a memorial to the soldiers killed in the war (see photograph in chapter 4).

But when Koizumi visited the Yasukuni Shrine a second time in spring 2002, no amount of stage managing by Chinese diplomats could stem the media and Internet backlash. President Jiang Zemin appeared to feel betrayed. He hinted that Koizumi had promised him not to go to the shrine again.[103] Koizumi wasn't ever again invited to China.

Balancing Act

China's present leaders, President Hu and Premier Wen, are trying to strike a balance between appeasing the nationalist sentiment mobilized during the Jiang era on the one hand, and preventing it from driving China into domestic instability or conflict with Japan on the other. This balancing act is a real struggle for leaders who may not yet have established firmly their authority even after four years in their positions. (One rumor reports that Jiang Zemin visited the Nanjing memorial shortly after the anti-Japanese demonstrations in 2005 to identify himself with the students' cause and implicitly criticize Hu.) An influential policy advisor told me that in the lead-up to the Seventeenth CCP Congress in 2007 when crucial decisions about the post-Hu leadership successor will be made, Hu Jintao is wary of appearing to renounce Jiang Zemin's tough approach to Japan. The Communist Party's uncertain straddle has been interpreted by the Chinese public as a green light for activism against Japan, and relations with Japan have gone from bad to worse.

The PRC Ministry of Education began in 2001 to revise senior and junior high school history textbooks for the first time since the early 1980s. It stripped away stale Marxist ideology, highlighted China's connections with the world by merging world history and Chinese history texts, and made the depiction of the United States less negative. The treatment of Japan, however, was made even more negative and more emotional. The new version dwells on Japan's invasions of China beginning with the Sino-Japanese War of 1894–95, its occupation of Manchuria in 1931, and the full-scale war between 1937 and 1945 that killed or wounded twenty-two million Chinese. The accounts are more vivid than the earlier versions.[104] In the place of dry descriptions of military campaigns, the new text has gruesome photographs of killing and burning in Nanjing, a destroyed and looted village, and the experiments with biological weapons on live prisoners. The discussion question for the section is "Japanese rightists strenuously deny that the Japanese military committed the atrocity of the Nanjing Massacre and say that it was just wartime behavior. What do you think?" The new version also makes the link between Japanese aggression and the loss of Taiwan more explicit.

The drafting group made a conscious decision not to improve the treatment of Japan. At the very first meeting of the interagency group on textbook revision, participants agreed with the proposition suggested by one official: "Topics related to our 'national sentiment,' such as the Sino-Japanese War, the Nanjing Massacre, and the American bombing of the Chinese Embassy in Belgrade, we have to keep. But anything else we can change to make it more historically accurate." A proposal by some scholars to introduce more material on Japan's postwar economic modernization was vetoed by the others.

The Japanese government has begun to make an issue of the Chinese textbooks in its diplomatic meetings with Chinese counterparts and to Japanese audiences. When the Chinese Foreign Ministry summoned Japan's ambassador to China to hear its objections to the newly revised Japanese textbooks in April 2005, the ambassador's rejoinder, related to the press by the Japanese Embassy, was that China's own education has created anti-Japanese sentiment among China's youths.[105] China denies this charge but has appointed a university expert on Japan as the head of the Ministry of Education's panel on Japanese issues.[106] Negotiating an end to the Sino-Japanese textbook wars will be difficult because no country wants to give other countries a say in what it teaches its children.

Historical Commemorations

The government's inciting of anti-Japanese feelings doesn't stop with the textbooks. The Chinese Communist Party continues to organize ceremonies in universities and schools to commemorate the important dates in the history of Japanese aggression against China: September 18, 1931, when Japanese troops blew up a section of the South Manchurian Railway and began their occupation of Manchuria; December 9, 1935, when university students in Beijing demonstrated to urge the Republican government to stop fighting Communists and unite with them to resist the Japanese; July 7, 1937, when a minor clash between Japanese and Chinese forces at the Marco Polo bridge west of Beijing escalated to full-scale war; and August 15, 1945, when Japan surrendered ending World War II (the Chinese call it "China's Victory in the War of Resistance Against Japanese Aggression," [107] as if the United States and the other Allies had nothing to do with it). Commemorative speeches celebrate the heroism of the Chinese people, criticize Japan's refusal to acknowledge its wartime atrocities, and warn against the danger of a revival of Japanese militarism.[108]

Every five years, the Propaganda Department leads a massive multimonth commemoration of the anniversary of China's 1945 victory against Japan in World War II. Preparing a year or more in advance, the propaganda officials blanket the television airwaves and movie theaters with vivid dramas of Japanese brutality and Chinese bravery. Several minutes on the 7:00 PM national nightly news are devoted to wartime history every night. Cultural life is saturated with anti-Japanese propaganda. It's inescapable. Foreign films are not allowed to open in the theaters during this period.

The 2005 commemoration of the sixtieth anniversary began in April on the eve of the anti-Japanese protests. According to the Communist Youth League, more than forty million young people logged on to more than one thousand Web sites about the history of foreign aggression in China to send flowers to those who gave their lives in the war. And in a televised ceremony at the Great Wall, students read the oath, "We will remember the unfulfilled wish of the martyrs and carry forward the national ethos. We shall never forget the national humiliation. We shall cherish peace."[109]

Anti-Japanese Activism

Chinese leaders tolerate more citizen activism against Japan than they do in any other foreign policy domain. Anti-Japanese Web sites survive for years while Web sites attacking the United States are shut down.[110] The

Web site of the Alliance of Patriots, www.1931-9-18.org, established in May 2002 by Beijing software engineer Lu Yunfei, has more than one hundred thousand registered members and has posted more than 1.5 million messages in all. On April 17, 2005, it posted a record 5,995 new messages commenting on the demonstrations, and surely attracted many times that number of hits.

Anti-Japanese activists like Tong Zeng hold small protests outside the Japanese Embassy in Beijing. Nothing similar is allowed outside the American Embassy.[111] Tong Zeng, who began his activism in 1991 with a letter demanding reparations from Japan, was fired from his job and sent out of Beijing by the authorities during the 1990s, but several years ago was allowed back, and now freely organizes anti-Japanese activities.[112]

Since Hu Jintao and Wen Jiabao came into office, the government also has allowed PRC nationalists to try to land fishing boats on the Diaoyu Islands to dramatize China's claim to the islands. Nationalists from Hong Kong and Taiwan made several highly publicized and dangerous voyages to the islands during the 1990s, but the Chinese government avoided confrontation with Japan by forbidding Chinese activists from going along. When a group of right-wing Japanese renovated a lighthouse on one of the islands and tens of thousands of outraged Chinese protested in Hong Kong, Macao, Taiwan, and Canada in September 1996, Beijing kept it quiet and prevented Mainland sympathizers from joining in.

The new leadership in Beijing, however, has decided to unleash the Diaoyu Islands nationalists. The Federation of Chinese Nongovernmental Organizations for Defending Sovereignty Over the Diaoyu Islands, a small but well-connected Chinese organization founded in 1996 (registered in Hong Kong but based in Xiamen on the coast of Fujian Province), has made three attempts to land on the islands, beginning in June 2003.[113] During the January 2004 expedition, according to the stirring account by China's official news agency, the patriot-sailors withstood an attack by ten Japanese warships with water cannons.[114] On its third try, in March 2004, the group made the first successful Chinese landing, but its members were arrested, questioned by Japanese police on the nearby Japanese island of Okinawa, and quickly deported back to China by a Japanese government anxious to avoid confrontation. In China, the group's preparations and their landings were dramatically publicized in the official press, a clear sign of approval by the Communist Party.[115]

The activists of the China Patriots' Alliance encountered no government interference to their organization of online petition drives against Japan in the high-profile controversies that have erupted repeatedly during the past several years. The Alliance used its Web site to gather more than one million signatures demanding that the Japanese government make amends for the Chinese injured by buried Japanese chemical weapons in August 2003. The following month, the Alliance collected more than eighty thousand signatures in just ten days to demand that the Ministry of Railroads not award any contracts for a planned bullet train between Shanghai and Beijing to Japanese companies.[116] Reports of these petitions in the official press signaled a tolerant attitude on the part of the Party authorities, who probably figured that collective action on the Internet was a less dangerous substitute for collective action in the streets. The nationwide demonstrations of spring 2005 proved, however, that virtual activism mobilizes actual activism instead of dampening it.

Mixed Messages

People in China know that the Communist Party still has ample tools to control the content of newspapers, Internet news sites, and even cell phone text messages. Netizens can deduce from what is blocked just what the Communist Party authorities agree or disagree with and draw inferences about what public behavior will be condoned. As one Chinese student recently told me, "Our generation thinks that anything that we're not told *not* to do it's probably OK to do."

In the months leading up to the April 2005 demonstrations, Chinese young people read the media and Internet signals to mean that the Communist Party would tolerate patriotic actions against Japan. An online petition initiated by Chinese people living abroad, urging the Chinese government not to support Japan's application to become a permanent member of the United Nations Security Council until it properly acknowledged its historical crimes, was prominently announced on the main officially guided Internet news sites. It was signed by more than forty million people. People in Chinese offices and factories rounded up signatures, with no hint of disapproval from Party authorities.[117] The Foreign Ministry spokesman Liu Jianchao replied to a journalist's question at the March 24 press briefing about the "anti-Japan petition" by saying, "I don't regard it as 'anti-Japan' sentiments; on the contrary, I think this is a request for Japan to adopt a right and responsible attitude on some historical issues." *People's Daily* noted the irony of Japan's desire to join the Security Council to represent the Asian people when millions of these same people were showing their lack of trust in Japan by signing the petition.[118]

Chinese tabloids and Web sites presented before-and-after comparisons of the revised Japanese textbook (which actually was adopted by only a small number of Japanese schools) to show that the facts in the 2005 version were even more distorted than in the 2001 version.[119] The official Xinhua news agency described the most egregious inaccuracies in inflammatory articles like "Distorted History Textbook Unacceptable," and "Lies in Ink Can Never Cover Up Facts in Blood."[120] Newspaper photographs of South Korean protests against the Japanese textbook inspired young Chinese to want to emulate them.[121]

The China Chain Store and Franchise Association announced a boycott of beer from Asahi, seasoning from Ajinomoto, and products from seven other Japanese companies because these companies had supported the Society for Textbook History Reform, the organization that had instigated the revision of Japanese textbooks to delete references to wartime atrocities by Japan.[122] Because Chinese trade associations like this one operate in close cooperation with government bureaucracies, the announcement was read as another signal of official support for mass action against Japan.

Whether the demonstrations actually received official permits or not is murky. The officials and journalists I have interviewed claimed that no permits had been requested or approved. Some of the announcements of demonstrations apparently tried to drum up a crowd by telling people that a permit had been granted.

Indecisive Response

In the days following the violent April 2005 demonstrations against Japan's application for permanent membership in the United Nations Security Council, no one in authority criticized them. Premier Wen Jiabao, traveling in India, identified himself with the protestors and satisfied their demands by announcing that China would not support Japan's membership in the Security Council.

When the Japanese foreign minister came to Beijing on April 17 to demand an apology for the damage the demonstrators had inflicted on the Japanese Embassy and consulates, Chinese foreign minister Li Zhaoxing retorted that it was Japan who should apologize, not China. The diplomatic shoot-out was well publicized in all the Chinese media.[123] Later that week, Prime Minister Koizumi formally expressed Japan's "deep remorse and heartfelt apology" for the "damage and suffering" its "colonial rule and aggression" had caused to Asian people,[124] at a large gathering of the developing world in Indonesia. He met privately with President Hu Jintao afterward. Following the meeting with Koizumi, a somber-faced Hu walked out and told reporters that Japan should "seriously reflect" on its wartime atrocities against the Chinese people.[125]

A month later, Vice-Premier Wu Yi, China's highest-ranking female leader, engaged in some public grandstanding of her own against Japan. She was sent to Japan as President Hu's envoy to ease tensions and try to convince Prime Minister Koizumi not to visit Yasukuni Shrine again, as well as to reach out to Japanese business people to urge them to lobby Koizumi against a shrine visit. A head of a Chinese think-tank provided an account of her trip. She had been reluctant to go and said publicly before her departure that her only purpose was to visit the World Expo being held in Aichi, Japan. President Hu summoned her to remind her that her primary mission was to mend bilateral relations. During her trip, Prime Minister Koizumi, appearing before a parliamentary committee, talked about his right to visit the Yasukuni Shrine. In a rare breach of diplomatic protocol, Wu Yi grabbed the excuse to cancel her meeting with the prime minister and leave for home. Chinese ambassador to Tokyo Wang Yi pleaded with her not to do it, but to no avail. The Japanese were offended by her obvious slap at their leader,[126] but the Chinese public lapped it up, as Wu Yi was pleased to learn when she asked her staff to go online to see how the press and public responded to her act. (One posting on Strong Nation said, "Every single patriotic Chinese should applaud Wu Yi's 'disrespectful' cancellation . . . without it Japanese leaders' evil characters would not be exposed.") "She should have been fired," the think-tank head said. But it would have been political suicide for Hu Jintao to do so.

Although the Chinese leaders continued to criticize Japan publicly, after three weeks of snowballing protests, they became alarmed that the unrest was threatening stability. Large-scale protests related to domestic problems were occurring at the same time. More than thirty thousand townspeople in southeastern China rioted against police and officials over pollution from local chemical plants.[127] Ten thousand workers went on strike at a Japanese-owned factory in Shenzhen to demand union representation.[128] Even the People's Liberation Army was showing signs of restiveness: two thousand retired military from about twenty provinces staged a sit-in outside the PLA's headquarters in Beijing to demand increases in their pensions.[129] Some of the anti-Japanese demonstrators in Shanghai carried signs against official corruption. Finally, over the weekend of April 16 to 17, the government moved to end the anti-Japanese protests.

According to one Hong Kong magazine, the Party Politburo and its Standing Committee convened three meetings and formed a special high-level subcommittee on Japan led by Luo Gan, the internal security chief.[130] Professors and security officials in plain clothes were dispatched to visit students in their dormitories to persuade them to settle down. The CCP Propaganda Department, the People's Liberation Army, the Ministry of Education, and several other important departments called an unusual meeting of thirty-five hundred senior officials in the cavernous Great Hall

Koizumi

of the People to hear the foreign minister explain why they should not allow the protests to disrupt stability or harm the friendly relations with Japan that are in China's national interest.[131] Teams of academic experts and former diplomats fanned out to universities throughout the country and went online to explain why in the age of economic globalization, China benefits from cooperation with Japan.[132] Top economic officials gave press interviews to explain that a boycott of Japanese goods would harm China because many of those goods are actually manufactured by Japanese firms in China.[133] The Public Security Ministry made its own public statement gently reminding young people that a license is needed for any demonstration and that it is inappropriate to use mobile phones or the Internet to alert people to a demonstration.

Showing ingenuity, the security organizations in some provinces and cities asserted control by using the very same technologies that had threatened to subvert it. They sent text messages to all cellular telephone subscribers to inform them that public demonstrations against Japan would not be tolerated.[134] The authorities also got the anti-Japanese activists who operate under official protection to urge calm on their Web sites.[135]

The Japanese press speculated that the slow reaction by the Chinese government toward the April 2005 protests reflected "conflict or vacillation in the leadership on policy toward Japan."[136] Communist Party leaders have a common stake in presenting a united front to protect the Party from a popular nationalist insurgency. Once protests erupt, however, leadership splits can emerge. As individual politicians competing with one another they must defend themselves against charges from their rivals and the public that they are too soft toward Japan. President Hu Jintao and Premier Wen Jiabao are the most at risk for being blamed for any perceived sellout to Japan. But any ambitious Politburo member waiting in the wings may view continued protests that discredit incumbents as an opportunity to rise within the Party. Herding demonstrators back to their campuses is possible only if the leaders can form a consensus to share the responsibility and the blame.

One hint of internal intrigue suggests that it was, in fact, hard to form such a consensus. A mysterious commentary published on April 26 in the newspaper run by the Shanghai Communist Party organization (associated with retired president Jiang Zemin) took a harsh line on the protests saying that "the illegal demonstrations were not patriotic actions . . . [or] . . . spontaneous mass actions but backstage conspiracies."[137] The Internet was abuzz with speculation about the meaning and import of this commentary, which contradicts the sympathetic view of anti-Japanese activism usually associated with Jiang. Students know that if different voices emerge from the top Party ranks, there may be an opening for future protests.

The New Leaders Hesitate

According to Chinese think-tank experts, Hu Jintao and Wen Jiabao have none of Jiang Zemin's emotional baggage about Japan and would like to prove to their colleagues in the political elite that they can handle this complicated relationship with more finesse than Jiang did. They came into office with plans to elevate the "new thinking" to official policy. But vociferous online reaction to two articles in the influential journal *Strategy and Management* (*Zhanlue yu Guanli*) in 2002 and 2003 gave them pause. Ma Licheng, in "New Thinking on Relations with Japan, Worries of People in China and Japan," criticized the xenophobia that had swept the country during the 1990s and argued that China should take a mature and confident approach to Japan. Sixty years after the war, it was time to move beyond history. China should understand Japan's aspirations to become a normal power, politically and militarily, said Ma.[138] Shi Yinhong's piece, "China-Japan Rapprochement and 'Diplomatic Revolution,'" argued that the growing mutual hostility between Chinese and Japanese people is dangerous to China's security. China's national interest requires that the government strengthen relations with Japan by, among other steps, shelving historical issues and supporting Japan's bid to become a permanent member of the U.N. Security Council. Improving relations with Japan will strengthen China's leverage with the United States.[139] Shi Yinhong is a professor, but because Ma Licheng was a senior editor of the Communist Party organ, *People's Daily*, his article was seen as a trial balloon from the new leaders to gauge reaction to a more pragmatic approach to Japan.

The Internet reaction to the articles by Ma and Shi was vicious. For months, postings attacking the authors as traitors crowded the news sites and university BBS. When the top leaders saw the Internet reaction, they hesitated. As one Foreign Ministry official explained, "They don't want to be labeled traitors themselves." The anti-Japanese protests of spring 2005, viewed by the leadership as a domestic crisis, drove this point home.

Prime Minister Abe's Visit to Beijing

Unnerved by the deterioration of relations with Japan but constrained by domestic public opinion from openly adopting a policy less focused on questions of wartime history, Hu Jintao and Wen Jiabao sought to head off disaster by dissuading Japan's incoming prime minister, Shinzo Abe, from visiting the Yasukuni Shrine. Chinese diplomats, working in concert with their South Korea counterparts, cultivated Japanese politicians and groups they viewed as potentially sympathetic to their cause. Influential Japanese business and media figures, perturbed by Japan's growing alienation from its Asian neighbors, urged that the prime minister no longer visit the shrine or that the shrine be modified by removing the memorials to the war criminals to another location.[140] Japanese public opinion took a sharp turn against shrine visits during the summer of 2006 after newspapers discovered records indicating that former emperor Hirohito had been reluctant to visit Yasukuni after the war criminals were enshrined there.[141]

The Chinese government's behind-the-scenes efforts to negotiate a deal apparently paid off. Prime Minister Abe arrived in Beijing in October 2006 less than two weeks after taking office. The visit occurred simultaneously with an important CCP Central Committee meeting at which Hu Jintao consolidated his domestic authority. In a break from precedent, Abe honored China by making Beijing rather than Washington the destination of his first foreign trip. The visit was the outcome of a compromise that allowed China to declare victory by announcing that Japan and China had come to "an agreement to eliminate the political obstacle." Everyone understood that these words were code for "no more visits to the Yasukuni Shrine." Prime Minister Abe would remain publicly noncommittal about whether he intended to visit Yasukuni. According to a Japanese newspaper analysis, he promised not to visit "for the time being."[142] It was a foreign policy coup for Hu Jintao, showcasing his ability to clean up a messy problem that his predecessor, Jiang Zemin, had created.

During and after the visit, the Propaganda Department warned the media not to publish anything that could "spoil the harmony." Chat room and Web site monitors quickly expunged critical postings while allowing the positive ones to remain. Even the positive messages, however, had undertones of caution ("We should pay attention not only to what Abe says, but also to what he does") and competition ("We should prepare two strategies: Maintain a good relationship with Japan while surpassing it in real power. That is the strategy for a great power!").[143]

North Korean leader Kim Jong Il rained on Hu Jintao's parade by choosing to test a nuclear bomb the day after Abe visited Beijing. The timing was one reason that the Chinese government reacted so angrily to the test. The North Korean nuclear threat, however, may open up a new arena for Sino-Japanese cooperation. During Abe's visit, he and the Chinese leaders declared their shared position that a nuclear North Korea cannot be tolerated. A common enemy can help unite countries that don't like each other much.

Japanese Prime Minister Shinzo Abe during his first visit to Beijing reviews the honor guard with Chinese Premier Wen Jiabao, October 8, 2006. (Itsuo Inouoy/AFP/Getty Images)

Prospects for the Future

Even if Prime Minister Abe actually desists from visiting the Yasukuni Shrine, China will not be able to negotiate a comprehensive resolution of history issues and an overall improvement in relations with Japan unless it can credibly commit to stop criticizing Japan's wartime history. The South Koreans, who pledged in writing to do so, couldn't keep their promise because of the same sort of domestic political pressures that roil China. Even if the Politburo Standing Committee somehow could agree to revise Chinese school textbooks and stop commemorating anniversaries, they still cannot control events in Japan or the Chinese tabloids that report on them. "The Foreign Ministry and the Party leaders want to change public opinion about Japan, and leave history behind, but it is too late," a PLA colonel told me. "We should have tried to change public opinion ten years ago when the Party could still control information. We can't do it now."

As China grows stronger and Chinese people become more self-confident, they are becoming increasingly intolerant of slights from Japan, related to history or otherwise. Deep down they believe that Japan is trying to keep China weak. A junior diplomat got huffy at an international meeting as he listened to a Japanese scholar. "The U.S. can accept China's rise, but Japan can't," he complained. "The U.S. can accept the peaceful reunification of Taiwan, but Japan can't."

The virulent anti-Japanese sentiment on the Web reflects the mind-set that China and Japan are engaged in a struggle for dominance in Asia, for example, "It is time to treat Japan as an enemy. We cannot wait until the Japanese hold bayonets over our heads; we cannot wait until we help the U.S. and Japan count the money after they sell Taiwan; we cannot ever allow Japan to become a permanent member of the Security Council and push China into the group of second-class countries."

Another netizen wrote that the pragmatic reason to maintain good relations with the United States was to "peacefully compete and surpass Japan. It is a highly probable outcome. Japan is stronger than China now, but its postwar miracle was mainly due to U.S. support. Japan's long economic stagnation shows how much of a bubble there was in the miracle."

A journalist writing in *Global Times* noted that during the two-thousand-year relationship between China and Japan, sometimes it was strong China and weak Japan, and sometimes strong Japan and weak China, but now, both are becoming strong and neither is weak. This leads to "a situation in which neither of the two sides would show its weakness. . . . Compromise made in the course of representation by either government might be seen as a sign of 'weakness' by some people, which constitutes quite a big pressure."[144]

A cosmopolitan young Ph.D. in finance predicted with alarming confidence that Chinese-Japanese relations were bound to improve as China grows stronger. "Right now there is close competition between China and Japan for leadership in Asia. When China is clearly number one then Japan will accept the situation and relations will be better."

7

Taiwan

"A Question of Regime Survival"

S ITTING IN THE BRIGHT COFFEE SHOP of my Beijing hotel, two retired military officers now working at a think-tank spoke anxiously about the upcoming presidential election in Taiwan. President Chen Shui-bian, running for reelection, had placed a referendum about policies toward the Mainland on the March 2004 election ballot. The Taiwan legislature, dominated by the two opposition parties (the Guomindang and the People's First Party), had tried unsuccessfully to stop Chen. Although President George W. Bush, standing next to PRC premier Wen Jiabao during his visit to Washington, had publicly rebuked Chen for taking a unilateral action to change the status quo in the Taiwan Strait, Chen nevertheless appeared determined to go ahead with the referendum. The specific questions on the ballot were innocuous. But the holding of a referendum itself created a dangerous precedent for a future vote on independence.

The retired military officers were worried less about Taiwan's actions than about the actions of their own government. "We are working hard to figure out how China can avoid using military force if Taiwan declares independence by referendum," one officer said. "People have very strong feelings about the Taiwan issue. If the leaders stand by and do nothing while Taiwan declares independence, the Chinese Communist Party will fall. But if the United States doesn't intervene to defend Taiwan, it will lose its international credibility. Neither country can back down for fear of damaging its credibility—international, for the U.S., and domestic, for China."

This pessimism about a confrontation between China and the United States over Taiwan is widespread in China. An American survey found that 74 percent of the Chinese population believes that China-Taiwan relations are likely to cause conflict.[1]

"Ordinary people take a very hard line on Taiwan," a well-known academic commentator explained later, "not because of the need to save

face, but because if Taiwan goes independent, it will trigger other secessionist movements in Tibet, Xinjiang, and maybe Inner Mongolia, and
national unity will be threatened." He contrasted people's feelings about
the three important issues of the United States, Japan, and Taiwan: Relations with America are a matter of "saving face and national interests,"
while Japan evokes strong nationalist feelings. But, he said, "Taiwan is a
question of regime survival—no regime could survive the loss of Taiwan."

If China's leaders believe the regime's survival is at stake, they would
feel compelled to react militarily to an independence referendum—even
if that means confronting America's military might—unless they can be
persuaded to do something else that looks just as forceful to the public
and other leaders. "Maybe they could say something new about China's
right to use force, instead of actually using it. Or use economic sanctions," the military men brainstormed. "The Americans and others
wouldn't recognize Taiwan as an independent country, but that won't be
enough to satisfy the Chinese people." Frustrated with always having to
react to Taiwan's actions instead of taking the initiative in their own hands,
they said, "We need to find a way to control the situation. Not give all the
control to the Taiwanese. We need to do something."

China's decision makers feel trapped between Taiwan and their own
public in an impossible situation. As one colonel put it, "People criticize
the government for not doing enough about Taiwan. If Chen Shui-bian
does something and the U.S. doesn't stop him, then the army will think it
should act to teach him a lesson. Then the U.S. will respond and the
Chinese people will support a harsh government reaction, showing muscle.
But the U.S. is the world's superpower, it has face to keep, so the U.S. will
have to respond. It will be impossible to control escalation."

As Taiwan has democratized, its relations with the Mainland have become more unpredictable and dangerous. Taiwan has metamorphosed
from an authoritarian regime almost as repressive as the one on the Mainland into a vibrant democracy. The Guomindang, the political party that
retreated to the island in 1949 after losing to the Communists in the Chinese civil war, originally embraced the goal of ruling a reunified China.
As they saw it, they had simply moved the capital of the Republic of China
from the Mainland to Taiwan. Taiwan's democratic politicians, however,
many of whom are native Taiwanese who never shared the Mainlanders'
optimistic expectation of returning to rule the Mainland, stimulated a
new sense of Taiwanese national identity that has taken root among the
descendents of the Mainland transplants as well as the native Taiwanese.
Responding to the Taiwanization of the island, the politicians step by step
have taken it down the path toward legal independence.

Both Lee Teng-hui, the native Taiwanese leader of the Guomindang who served as Taiwan's first elected president (1988–2000), and Chen Shui-bian, the former political activist from the Democratic Progressive Party who succeeded him in 2000, claim that because the Republic of China on Taiwan is already a sovereign, independent country, there is no need to actually declare independence. Instead, the government makes incremental changes—"salami tactics," such as revisions in its passport covers, textbooks, the name of its international representative offices, maps, etc. that in effect proclaim the island as a sovereign state. In addition to these small changes, President Chen Shui-bian and Lee Teng-hui before him from time to time surprise everyone with a major bombshell that could be construed as proclaiming Taiwan's independence. China's market-oriented media and Internet report these outrages to the Mainland public who demand that their government to do something to stop them.

Over time, China's military power vis-à-vis Taiwan and the United States is growing. But the Chinese Communist Party's ability, vis-à-vis its own public, to control information about Taiwan's actions is declining. The confluence of these two trends increases the danger of war.

As one journalist put it, "On Taiwan, China has no choice. We have to react. It's like we're a cow being led on a rope by Chen Shui-bian. There is no way to prevent disaster. Chen can raise whatever issues he wants, but China's leaders can't say anything, only react. Our leaders lack political resources, political wisdom."

Recognizing the huge costs of military action—at a minimum, it would set back the economy by three, five, or ten years, according to various Chinese internal studies—the CCP leaders seek to avert it, or at least postpone it until the military is ready.

They also try to win the trust of Taiwan people by reaching out to them with friendly overtures including economic links and political contacts. But the need to look tough domestically limits how much they can offer. To gain approval for a flexible, accommodating approach to Taiwan, the CCP leaders must convince people that the trends in the cross-Strait relationship are going the right way, or as Chinese often put it, "time is on our side." Without clear evidence for such optimism, a flexible approach just looks weak. The problem, however, is that many of the trends from Taiwan are going in the wrong direction—the economies of Taiwan and the Mainland are becoming increasingly integrated, but Taiwan is moving away from the Mainland politically instead of drawing closer. The CCP leaders, moreover, can't prevent information about these disturbing trends from reaching the public nor can they predict what Taiwan politicians will say or do next. For all they know, the day after they invite a Taiwan president to start a dialogue, he might embarrass them by telling a journalist that Taiwan is a sovereign state.

If the Beijing leaders rely on positive appeals to Taiwan, both Taiwan and their own people "mistake their restraint for weakness," as one expert put it, viewing China as a "paper tiger" that makes a lot of noise but needn't be feared. China's longtime threat to use force to stop Taiwan from declaring independence loses its credibility and the leaders are criticized at home. If the trends on Taiwan are going in the wrong direction, then a positive gesture to Taiwan is politically feasible only if it is paired with additional resources for military preparations or tough statements that strengthen deterrence. From the standpoint of a CCP politician, taking a tough, threatening stance is always safer.

The Role of the United States

The ideal solution from the standpoint of the leaders in Beijing is to solve the Taiwan problem through Washington—to have the U.S. government push Taiwan into reunification or at least stop it from moving further toward legal independence. The Chinese government has been trying to get the United States to do just that for decades, beginning with Premier Zhou Enlai's first discussions with Henry Kissinger about restoring U.S.-China diplomatic relations in 1971.[2] But the leaders in Beijing overestimate America's influence over the behavior of Taiwanese politicians. Beijing puts Taiwan front and center in all its dealings with Washington, trying to condition its commitments on issues such as nonproliferation with American promises to constrain Taiwan. In the eyes of China's policy experts, the "most important factor in the Taiwan matter is the state of China-U.S. relations . . . without good China-U.S. relations, the Taiwan matter will probably be essentially unresolved in the foreseeable future and its deterioration will be hard to stop."[3]

Because Taiwan is a vital interest to China but less so to America, every U.S. administration since Nixon has been willing to accommodate Chinese interests on this core issue to a certain extent, but not to abandon Taiwan entirely.[4] Taiwan has broad political support within the United States, particularly in Congress. During the Cold War, Congress and the American public sided with free Taiwan against "Red China." (That's why it took Richard Nixon, a Republican president with an impeccable reputation as an anti-Communist to open up relations with Beijing.) Americans feel a natural affinity with the twenty-three million people of Taiwan because of their democratic system and market economy, and many Americans believe mistakenly that Taiwan already is an independent country. In our eyes, Taiwan is a brave little David of a democracy standing up to the Communist Goliath of China. Taiwan also has one of the most formidable, well-funded lobbying organizations in the United States.[5]

When the United States shifted diplomatic recognition from the Republic of China (Taiwan) to the People's Republic of China in 1979, Congress passed the Taiwan Relations Act (TRA) to direct the executive branch to continue to defend the island. The TRA authorized the United States to sell weapons to Taiwan and committed it to view "any effort to determine the future of Taiwan by other than peaceful means, including by boycotts and embargoes, as a threat to the peace and security of the Western Pacific area and of grave concern to the United States." Although not a formal defense treaty—it does not pledge the United States to a specific course of action if hostilities break out with the People's Republic, which allows our response to be based on the specific circumstances at the time—the Taiwan Relations Act represents a strong American political commitment to Taiwan.

Why Is Taiwan So Important to the Chinese?

Americans often wonder why Chinese people care so much about Taiwan. Of course all countries find it hard to give up territory, no matter how insignificant. But how can the Chinese contemplate risking war with the United States and sacrificing all the economic progress they have made just to hold onto this small island of twenty-three million people ninety miles off its coast?

It's not because Taiwan is a threat to China's national security. During the Cold War the island was called America's "unsinkable aircraft carrier," but the United States hasn't had any military forces there since 1979. Nor does China worry about Taiwan's military power.

The roots of the Chinese fixation on Taiwan are purely domestic, related to regime security, not national security. The public cares intensely about Taiwan because the CCP has taught it to care—in school textbooks and the media. "The strong feelings about Taiwan are due to China's education," said one Chinese expert. "Public opinion about Taiwan has been created by fifty years of CCP propaganda," said another.

The island of Taiwan has not been an integral part of China for thousands of years. The Qing dynasty took control over it—along with Tibet, Xinjiang, Mongolia, and Manchuria—in the seventeenth century and then lost it after its defeat in the Sino-Japanese War two hundred years later.[6] In the 1940s, Mao Zedong actually told Edgar Snow, an American journalist, that after the CCP defeated the Japanese, it would let Taiwan become independent.[7]

The textbooks depict the history of Taiwan and China as a morality tale about China's exploitation by foreign powers during its period of weakness. Japan stole Taiwan from the Qing government in 1895. Under the CCP, China defeated Japan in World War II, and Taiwan should have been returned to China then. But the United States intervened with the Sixth Fleet during the Korean War to keep Taiwan permanently separated from China. The "century of humiliation" will not end until China is strong enough to achieve reunification. Like all irredentist claims, China's posture on Taiwan is not about territory—it is about national honor.

During the 1990s, the Communist Party sought to bolster its support by portraying itself as the defender of China's national honor on the world stage. As China scholar Tom Christensen observed, "the CCP is more beholden to its long-held nationalist mission [i.e., Taiwan reunification] than ever before. In fact, other than the raising of living standards, nothing is more important to the CCP's claim to rule than its nationalist credentials."[8]

China's market-oriented mass media play to popular emotions about Taiwan. "Taiwan sells," explains a journalist. "That's why you see so many front-page stories about Taiwan."[9] Articles based on public opinion surveys that show that over 90 percent of people are outraged by the latest provocation from Taiwan are very popular.[10] When President George W. Bush inadvertently referred to the "Republic of Taiwan," the media leapt on it. Newspapers took a line in a Pentagon report noting that if attacked, Taiwan might consider retaliating against high-value Mainland targets like the Three Gorges Dam, and turned it into a story that the United States had suggested attacking the dam.[11] "Our government can't afford to ignore any American mistake on Taiwan because people will see it as acquiescence. So the government spokesman has to respond," said a Beijing university professor.

It is universally believed in China that the CCP would fall if it allowed Taiwan to become independent without putting up a fight. A Beijing student put it this way, "If we can't get Taiwan back, the Chinese government may lose its power to control the people. It will show that the government is too weak to protect our territory—then people will want to change the government, maybe even demand democracy." This connection between the Taiwan issue and the survival of Communist Party rule makes the issue the "third rail" of Chinese politics. Mishandling the Taiwan issue means certain political humiliation, or worse. It also means that it may be impossible to prevent China from using force if Party leaders believe that it is necessary to preserve their power.[12]

People rarely specify how they think a Taiwan crisis would bring down the Communist Party—it takes more than a lot of angry unhappy people to overturn a government. And, in fact, once you get beyond the power elite in Beijing, you may find a "silent majority" who care more about

economic progress than Taiwan. (A small group of local government officials told me that, as one of them said, "The people don't really care
much about Taiwan. It's the government that cares.")

One Beijing professor confessed, "I believe that China could let Taiwan go independent. China is big enough to afford it. I can't say this to
anyone but my wife and maybe one or two other friends. My wife doesn't
agree with me." CCP leaders could change public opinion, he said, for
example by talking about new forms of sovereignty, but "first they would
have to believe it, and they don't. Also there are big political dangers to
them. They would be attacked as traitors. You can't talk like this in China
even during the time when soft policies dominate."

One daring Chinese author wrote that "if a large-scale military conflict
breaks out over the Taiwan matter . . . we probably should not have high
expectations that most of the Mainland Chinese people would forever
actively a support a military struggle that would have a huge cost and an
uncertain outcome."[13]

Yet the myth linking the political survival of the CCP regime to Taiwan is so pervasive that it creates its own political reality, especially in
Communist Party headquarters. And certainly, once the shooting starts,
people can be expected to rally round the PRC red flag.

While other foreign policy matters can be delegated to other top officials
or even the Foreign Ministry, Taiwan policy has always been considered
the responsibility of China's top leader (Mao, Deng, Jiang, and now Hu). A
leader's approach to Taiwan depends on three factors: domestic politics,
the current situation on Taiwan, and the current U.S. stance on cross-Strait
issues. The more confident a leader feels of his power, the better able he is
to take a restrained, flexible approach to Taiwan. But if the Taiwan president is lobbing verbal grenades over the Strait, then it becomes impossible
for anyone in Beijing to advocate moderation. The U.S. stance also can be
critical. If the White House actively discourages provocations from Taiwan,
it helps China's leaders restrain themselves and not overreact.

Every statement or action China's leaders make about Taiwan is aimed
first at the Chinese audience, second at the United States, which they
hope will restrain Taiwan, and only third at Taiwan itself. "Leaders can't
lose face with any of them," according to a Shanghai professor.

The 1995–96 Taiwan Strait Crisis

The combustible mix of domestic politics and Taiwan policy could have
ignited a war between China and the United States in the mid-1990s. I was
in the Pentagon for a meeting of the Defense Policy Board during the

harrowing March 1996 days when the Clinton administration was deciding how to respond to China's military intimidation of Taiwan. A grim-faced secretary of defense William Perry, the administration's foremost advocate of engaging China, argued persuasively for an unambiguous military signal to deter the Chinese from further escalation.[14] Fortunately, it worked. But a Sino-American confrontation over Taiwan could happen again. The People's Republic of China has a track record of going on the military offensive to achieve its objectives, especially when territorial issues are at stake.[15]

In January 1995, President Jiang Zemin, who had just begun to consolidate his power as China's top leader when elderly leader Deng Xiaoping became bedridden, made what by Chinese standards was a bold, positive proposal for peaceful reunification with Taiwan. In what became known as "Jiang's Eight Points," he offered to negotiate all issues with the Taiwan authorities on an equal basis "on the premise that there is one China." All Taiwan's leaders would have to do is acknowledge China's one-China principle, i.e., that there is one China and Taiwan is part of China. This had been the longtime position of Taiwan's governing party, the Guomindang. The return of the colonies of Hong Kong and Macao to Chinese rule was fast approaching (Hong Kong in 1997 and Macao in 1999), and Jiang raised expectations that Taiwan might follow soon after. Jiang embraced the agenda of reunification as the one historic achievement that might elevate him to the ranks of Mao Zedong and Deng Xiaoping.

nationalism

By leaning forward on Taiwan, Jiang took a real political risk at a time when his power was not yet firmly established and splits within the leadership could have destabilized the regime. According to the Hong Kong press, even before his January 1995 initiative, hard-line officials and PLA officers were criticizing his policies and those of Foreign Minister Qian Qichen toward the United States and Taiwan for being too soft.[16].7

Six months after making his offer, Jiang was blind-sided and humiliated by the United States. The Clinton administration, reversing a sixteen-year ban on visits by high-level Taiwan officials (because after 1979 the United States no longer had official diplomatic relations with Taiwan), gave Taiwan president Lee Teng-hui a visa to present a speech at his alma mater, Cornell University. American secretary of state Warren Christopher had told Chinese foreign minister Qian in April that the administration was opposed to issuing a visa to Lee because it would not be consistent with the United States' unofficial relationship with Taiwan. Foreign Minister Qian thought he had heard a commitment. Then the U.S. House of Representatives and Senate, with only one nay vote, demanded that President Clinton grant the visa. Lee used the Cornell platform to tout Taiwan as a democratic sovereign nation that for the first time he called "the Republic of China on Taiwan."

Jiang Zemin was subjected to intense internal criticism from his political rivals, Qiao Shi and Li Ruihuan (who despite—or because of—their reputations as domestic reformers, took a tough line on Taiwan),[17] and from the People's Liberation Army leaders. His conciliatory approach to Taiwan was blamed for sending a signal of weakness that Taipei and Washington had exploited.[18] Jiang had no choice but to go along with the hawks who advocated a strong military response. Not all the hawks were in uniform. Civilian officials flexed their muscles too. According to scholar Zhao Suisheng, the pressure for a military reaction came not just from the PLA, but also from the CCP ideologues who were pumping up nationalism as the Party's source of legitimacy, and central officials who hoped the crisis would justify enhanced control over the provinces.[19]

In July 1995, after a public warning, the PLA for the first time ever fired missiles close to Taiwan (eighty miles to the northeast). The following month, the PLA Navy carried out a second round of missile and artillery tests and conducted large-scale exercises north of the island. Other massive military exercises followed in October and November. The largest exercises, however, occurred in March 1996 on the eve of Taiwan's first presidential election. Two military regions mobilized their forces into a combined war-front command under a top Chinese general in Fujian Province facing Taiwan. Then, after giving warning, the PLA bracketed Taiwan with missile tests that temporarily closed the northeast port of Keelung and the southwest port of Kaohsiung.

The United States signaled its resolve to defend Taiwan by deploying not one but two aircraft carrier battle groups to the vicinity (not into the Taiwan Strait itself, which would have been "unnecessarily provocative" according to the thinking of senior American military officials).[20] China went ahead with huge exercises off the Fujian coast—televised to Mainland and Taiwan viewers—but no direct military engagement took place and the crisis came to a close.

During the 1995–96 crisis, the CCP broadcast bellicose threats and personal attacks on Lee Teng-hui through the media but decided not to mobilize mass demonstrations. Thousands of Chinese students—in New York City—protested against the Lee Teng-hui visit,[21] and demonstrations against Chinese bullying occurred throughout Taiwan. But on the Mainland itself, school authorities allowed only small demonstrations within the campus grounds.[22] The leadership consensus on how to handle the crisis was too fragile to risk a mass mobilization that could create a split. Large demonstrations also might push decision makers to escalate the military confrontation. The CCP facilitated public protests against the

United States after the Belgrade embassy bombing in 1999 and against Japan on several different occasions. Mao Zedong also mobilized the public behind the shelling of Taiwan's offshore islands in 1958 in order to galvanize support for his utopian scheme he called the Great Leap Forward.[23] But by the mid-1990s the CCP leaders didn't dare stir up protests that might spiral out of control in the Strait, or at home.

The Aftermath of the Crisis

Dangerous crises sometimes have a silver lining—they jolt people into recognizing the dire costs of military confrontation. Crises also provide the protagonists with information about each other's bottom-line positions.[24] Following the 1995–96 crisis, Beijing and Washington, with a new sense of urgency, intensified their efforts to avoid war by communicating better with one another—Presidents Jiang and Clinton exchanged state visits in 1997–98, and the two sides spent more time in open-ended "strategic dialogues" about the state of the world. The Clinton administration started to criticize Taiwan's moves toward independence as dangerously provocative. During his 1998 visit to China, President Clinton upset the Taiwan government (and the U.S. Congress) by stating what came to be known as the "Three Nos" (the United States does not support Taiwan independence, does not support "one China, one Taiwan" or "two Chinas," and does not support Taiwan's membership in international organizations that only states can join).[25]

The Chinese media portrayed the 1995–96 crisis as a great victory for China, but Mainland experts privately admitted that it had been counterproductive in its effect on Taiwan. Taiwan came away from the crisis more reassured about American protection than chastened by Mainland military action. Intimidation by the Mainland shocked the Taiwan economy, which depends heavily on foreign trade—the stock market tumbled and foreign businesspeople canceled trips. It probably also lost the Guomindang (the governing party) votes in the December 1995 legislative elections. But the voters' righteous anger toward Beijing after the March 1996 missile tests helped Lee Teng-hui win Taiwan's first direct presidential election by a surprisingly large margin.[26] Most important, the Americans had proven that they would rise to Taiwan's defense if need be. The United States and Japan had also reinvigorated their security alliance by revising their guidelines for defense cooperation. As a result, the crisis had the perverse effect of emboldening President Lee Teng-hui and the Taiwan public to continue to assert Taiwan's sovereignty.

Jiang is Impatient

The aftermath of the crisis put Jiang Zemin in a difficult position. He had tied his political legacy to the Taiwan issue. His 1995 Eight Points had been incorporated in the official canon of Taiwan policy and were commemorated in an annual ceremony. So he couldn't walk away from the issue despite the fiasco. In 1997, Jiang assumed leadership of the Taiwan Affairs Leading Small Group, consisting of the top decision makers from the government and the military responsible for Taiwan policy, reduced its size, and turned it into the main arena for Taiwan decision making.

Unlike Mao Zedong and Deng Xiaoping, who had taken a patient attitude toward reunification, "Jiang stirred up impatience toward Taiwan," as one expert put it. "He wanted a legacy of doing something great." He dreamed of going down in the history books as the Chinese leader who reunified the country. According to Chinese policy advisors on Taiwan, beginning in 1998, Jiang Zemin began to talk about timetables for reunification.

Jiang's sense of urgency about "the great cause of reunification" came through clearly in the government's major policy statement, its White Paper on Taiwan issued before the 2000 Taiwan presidential election.[27] (Shi Yinhong, a well-known Beijing academic expert on international security, described the White Paper, along with the 1996 missile tests and repeated military exercises targeting Taiwan, as examples of the "tough strategy" that Jiang adopted from 1995 to 2000.[28]) The White Paper repeated China's standard language about threatening to use force against Taiwan under two conditions, i.e., if Taiwan formally separates from China or if foreign countries invade Taiwan. But it added an ominous new threat. China would use force "if the Taiwan authorities refuse, sine die [indefinitely] the peaceful settlement of cross-Straits reunification through negotiations." It sounded like a PRC ultimatum to Taiwan: negotiate soon, or else. According to one well-connected insider, the "third if" was added by Jiang Zemin himself after the paper had been drafted by Taiwan experts and vetted by various departments. When I interviewed one of the drafters, he didn't deny this account.

I was in Beijing with the deputy heads of the U.S. State Department, National Security Council, and Defense Department for discussions about national missile defense on the gray February day when the White Paper was released. Our group was stunned by the audacity of the Chinese leaders' "in your face" timing, interpreting it as a major escalation of their threats to Taiwan and to us. The Chinese diplomats tried to convince us that the timing was the unintended result of poor interagency coordination in Beijing, but we had our doubts.

Bigger Sticks

Jiang Zemin's need to restore the PLA's trust in him as commander in chief after the humiliation of the Lee Teng-hui visit—and his determination to achieve reunification soon—led him to increase the military pressure on Taiwan beginning in 1995. The PLA received the green light for an accelerated program of military modernization with Taiwan as its strategic focus. Double-digit increases in the military budget gave the PLA the money to purchase advanced destroyers, fighter jets, and submarines from Russia. (Local production was not an option because most Chinese defense industries are out of date.) The PLA also started producing short- and medium-range missiles in quantity. It deployed these missiles in Fujian Province opposite Taiwan at a rate of fifty per year at first, then one hundred per year according to the Department of Defense.[29] PLA soldiers began to train more intensively, especially in the kind of joint operations that would be required to attack Taiwan from the air and the sea.

Military modernization got a second boost after another unpleasant surprise from Taipei in July 1999. Taiwan president Lee Teng-hui publicly asserted that relations between the Mainland and Taiwan were "state-to-state relations." To many in China—especially in the PLA—this sounded much like a formal declaration of independence. The military press reported, "All PLA soldiers and officers are very angry to hear Lee Teng-hui's secessionist statement."[30] The government warned Lee Teng-hui and the Taiwan government "not to underestimate the Chinese government's resolve to maintain sovereignty and territorial integrity, and not to underestimate the Chinese people's courage and power to combat secession and oppose Taiwan independence."[31] The pressure on Jiang Zemin to respond militarily was intense.

In Washington, we worried about a replay of the 1995–96 *High Noon*–style confrontation, and acted immediately to discourage Beijing from overreacting. President Clinton called President Jiang to reassure him that President Lee hadn't consulted us before making his statement and that we didn't endorse it.[32] At a White House press conference, President Clinton reiterated the U.S. adherence to "one China" but also reminded Beijing that the United States was bound by the Taiwan Relations Act to view with "grave concern" any use of nonpeaceful means in the Strait. By making clear that the United States rejected the "two states theory" of Lee Teng-hui, the United States helped Jiang manage the domestic reaction to Lee's statement.[33]

How to respond to Lee Teng-hui's assertion that Taiwan and China were two separate states became the hot topic at the 1999 annual summer gathering of China's political elite at the seashore resort of Beidaihe. The

Central Committee, expanded to include retired generals and Party leaders, discussed the problem. The mood of the group was somber because it had been a very trying year, what with Zhu Rongji's failure to bring a WTO agreement home from Washington, the Falun Gong sit-in, and the American bombing of the PRC Embassy in Belgrade. The bombing was interpreted by many as clear evidence of American hostility toward China, a pessimistic view that would require revising Deng Xiaoping's assessment that "peace and development are the main trends."[34] Although the Asian financial crisis did not affect China as severely as other more open Asian economies, it had slowed growth and caused deflation.[35] According to the accounts of policy advisors and military officers, at the meetings the generals argued emotionally that national honor was at stake in Taiwan and that China had to grab one of Taiwan's small off-shore islands or take some other military action to demonstrate resolve.

Jiang Zemin was loath to jeopardize China's economic progress and its relationship with the United States, but he couldn't afford to look weak, especially to his military constituency. He was in a tight spot. Jiang turned to the generals and asked the question, "If the United States intervenes to defend Taiwan, are you sure you can prevail?" The generals had to admit that they were not yet ready. Jiang then promised the PLA, "We are going to give you everything you need so that next time you are asked that question, you can say, yes. Go back and develop the capabilities to solve the Taiwan problem by force if peaceful methods fail."[36]

One commentator described the decision that came out of Beidaihe thus: ". . . avoid as much as possible a large-scale military action at present, pushing it off to the future when Mainland China's military and economic might develops to give us the overwhelming advantage, and decide then whether we still need to use force to contain or stop Taiwan independence."[37] A Chinese diplomat reported, "We are pursuing peaceful reunification, but we also are preparing to do it militarily, the decision has been made to do so." A colonel confirmed, "The PLA has speeded up its preparations. The government's job is to pursue peaceful reunification, but the military's job is preparation for war."

Jiang managed to exercise restraint by sounding tough, and by giving the military what it wanted most—the high-tech weaponry to become the kind of military a great power can be proud of. Other civilian leaders concurred, even those who favored a gentler approach to Taiwan. Under the circumstances, how could they not?[38] The media fulminated with bellicose rhetoric against Lee Teng-hui, PLA air force jet pilots flew aggressively close to Taiwan jets in the narrow Strait, and hackers attacked Taiwan computers. But all in all, the CCP exercised greater self-control in its reactions to Lee Teng-hui's affronts to China's national honor in

1999 than it did in the 1995–96 crisis. It managed to preserve good relations with Washington and to avoid a fight it was too weak to win.

After Lee Teng-hui's "two states theory" and the March 2000 Taiwan election of President Chen Shui-bian, who was the candidate of the proindependence Democratic Progressive Party, pessimism about the prospects for peaceful reunification pervaded the political atmosphere in Beijing. Time was not on the Mainland's side. Force would eventually have to be used.

The civilian leadership ordered the military high command to speed up preparations so that military options against Taiwan might be available by the end of the first decade of the twenty-first century. These options would include having the capabilities to deter the United States from intervening to defend Taiwan, as well as implementing a possible sea and air blockade against the island. Recognizing that it is starting from a very low base, and that the United States will always have superior firepower, the PLA is developing asymmetric capabilities it calls its "assassin's mace," that is, unconventional methods including information warfare that exploit the vulnerabilities of opponents and are difficult to respond to in kind.[39]

The 710 to 790 short-range ballistic missiles deployed on the coast opposite Taiwan, according to the Pentagon,[40] are China's most potent weapon to deter Taiwan independence or compel reunification on Beijing's terms. They could overwhelm Taiwan's missile defenses (even the most advanced theater missile defense does not provide total protection) and bring the island to heel by striking airfields and other military targets, terrorizing its civilian population, and devastating its trade-based economy. The military's goal is to have the capabilities to force Taiwan to capitulate and start negotiating before the United States can come to Taiwan's defense, or to convince the United States to stay on the sidelines.

China's leaders would prefer never to have to use any of these new military capabilities—to win without fighting, as Sun Tzu, China's ancient military sage, advised. The goal is to "keep the deterrence believable while doing all possible to draw our bows without shooting and keeping the pressure on without actually fighting."[41] Their hope is that as China grows militarily stronger and Taiwan becomes more economically dependent on China, Taiwan will fall into China's lap like a ripe plum. (Or as one Mainland Internet posting put it, "When China becomes the indisputable leader in East Asia, reunification with Taiwan will become the natural outcome.") At a time of its own choosing, Beijing will make Taiwan an "offer it can't refuse," with an implicit threat in the background. Taiwan's leaders will realize they have no choice but to negotiate some form of reunification and the United States will support the negotiated solution to avoid a conflict that has no winners. The difficult questions facing Americans are: Should we acquiesce to a "peaceful reunification" that is obtained because China has become militarily stronger than Taiwan? Or should we use our power to stop it by declaring China an enemy and going all out to contain it economically as well as militarily? And how can we be sure that China—especially the PLA—won't want to use its new capabilities once it has them?

Carrots and Sticks

A lesson that many Chinese took away from the 1995–96 and 1999 crises is that using military force alone against Taiwan is bound to fail. Force can backfire by estranging the Taiwanese, making them more dependent on the protection of the Americans, and reinvigorating the military alliance between the United States and Japan. Stopping Taiwan's slide toward independence and bringing it back into the fold will take carrots—positive inducements—as well as sticks. "It was clear that military pressure wasn't working, so we needed to try something else," said one policy advisor.

Jiang Zemin achieved a leadership consensus behind a two-track policy: build up military strength, but also reach out a hand of friendship to the Taiwanese compatriots, as Mainlanders call them. Use what the Communist Party calls "united front tactics" to build popular support in Taiwan, get the people to trust the Chinese government, and put pressure on the proindependence politicians. An additional benefit is that Washington will applaud Beijing's statesmanlike stance and blame cross-Strait tension on those Taiwan "troublemakers." President Hu Jintao has continued this two-track approach and has extended it to building ties with the opposition parties, in the hopes that when Chen Shui-bian's second term ends in 2008, the new president will be from one of these parties.

Domestic politics, however, limit how flexible and accommodating Chinese leaders can be toward Taiwan. In contrast with its pragmatic diplomacy toward other countries, China's approach to Taiwan is driven more by symbolic issues of principle that reverberate in domestic politics.

Political correctness requires any ambitious official to take a firm stand on issues related to Taiwan because they are matters of principle and not subject to compromise. "It would be suicide to suggest a creative idea that sounds soft," one policy advisor said. Any positive gesture toward Taiwan must be framed to look strong. For example, a journalist recalled a statement on Taiwan by Premier Wen Jiabao. "He said that they would pursue peaceful reunification as long as there is the slightest chance it could

succeed. He could say that because he first said that we will stop independence no matter the cost. So he paired the two points." The Hu Jintao
administration's positive initiatives were paired with efforts to make the
threat to use force more credible—or as strategic analyst Shi Yinhong put
it, to "sweeten the carrot" Hu also had to "harden the stick."[42]

In this stifling political atmosphere, creative ideas on Taiwan policy are
few and far between. Experts are consulted less often on Taiwan policy than
on Japan or the United States. According to one expert, "The leaders think
they understand Taiwan simply because they are Chinese." Not surprisingly, proposals for positive initiatives to Taiwan often come from senior
figures who are insulated from political criticism in one way or another.

Economic Links

Deng Xiaoping was the first leader with the courage to reach out in a
friendly manner toward Taiwan. In 1979, as he threw open China's door
to the world economy, he also included Taiwan. He demolished the wall
of hostility that since 1949 had blocked all economic and social contact
between the Mainland and Taiwan. China offered special incentives to
attract Taiwan investment and trade, and laid out the welcome mat for
family reunions and tourism. Since then, the ties between Taiwan and
the Mainland have multiplied dramatically. Taiwan firms, beginning with
small labor-intensive shoe and toy producers and gradually extending to
large high-tech companies like Taiwan Semiconductor (with banks and
services following), moved their factories to the Mainland to find cheaper
land, facilities, and labor. The economic attraction was so strong that
businesses evaded Taiwan government regulations designed to limit the
island's economic dependence on China. China has become Taiwan's
number one export market, and Taiwan the second-largest source of foreign investment in China,[43] even though there is no direct transport or
shipping across the Strait and all transactions have to go through Hong
Kong or other transit points. By the end of 2005, Taiwan's exports to China
(including Hong Kong) exceeded its exports to the United States, Japan,
and Europe combined.[44] The Taiwan information technology industry
migrated to China, bringing with it its entire network of supply and distribution infrastructure. More than one million of Taiwan's twenty-three
million people now live, work, go to school, and get married in China,
most of them in southeastern communities like Dongguan in Guangdong
Province and Kunshan outside Shanghai.

Political conflicts across the Strait cause hardly a pause in the inexo-
rable exodus of Taiwan money and know-how to China. With few excep-

tions, the Chinese government has protected Taiwan businesses from political flak during periods of tension. The presence of Taiwan businesses on the Mainland is not politically controversial, and local officials are keen to have the jobs these businesses create. Locally based representatives of the Taiwan Affairs Office run interference for Taiwan investors to keep them happy. PRC Chinese are glad to see Taiwan being pulled into China's orbit economically and socially[45] because it gives them hope that someday political integration will follow. Even so, after the 2000 and 2004 presidential elections in Taiwan, the domestic political reaction on the Mainland forced the CCP to state publicly that "green" business people — namely those who support Chen Shui-bian and the Taiwan independence movement, were not welcome in China.[46]

Jiang Zemin appointed his mentor, former Shanghai mayor Wang Daohan, to serve as cross-Strait negotiator. Wang was an influential voice on the Taiwan Leading Small Group advocating a conciliatory approach. As a respected elder with a close personal relationship with Jiang, he could ignore political correctness. In my discussions with him, I heard him mull over cutting-edge ideas like a freeze on missile deployments in Fujian to build confidence between the two sides. The coastal provinces viewed Wang as the representative of their interests in preventing cross-Strait strife from disrupting economic growth. The Taiwan Research Institute in Xiamen, on the Fujian coast, opposite Taiwan and far away from Beijing, also has a reputation for "more liberal views," according to one of its researchers.

Jiang stayed in touch with his Shanghai side by deepening the trade and investment ties between the two sides, promoting cross-Strait exchanges and dialogues, and offering what from China's perspective was a very generous autonomy package after reunification — labeled "one country, two systems" — that had originally been proposed by Deng Xiaoping. (For example, Taiwan would be allowed to keep its democratic political system and its own army.[47])

Words Get in the Way

Doctrinal rigidity and political correctness, however, impede CCP leaders from making offers to Taiwan that people there would find truly attractive. The Chinese media and public do not pay much attention to the precise wording of government statements about Taiwan, but the officials certainly do. The elite politics within the Chinese Communist Party, like those of the Vatican, result in the triumph of orthodoxy over change on issues regarded as matters of principle. Deng Xiaoping often bemoaned the fact that in internal debates, "left" always prevails over "right." Every official knows it is safer to hew to the maxims laid down by the founding fathers than to float an innovative idea. Once the CCP commits itself to a position on Taiwan, Chinese politicians are reluctant to change or abandon it for fear of being criticized as weak. The risk is multiplied because it is impossible to predict how the Taiwanese will react to any new formula. If the Taiwanese, driven by their own domestic politics, reject it and keep pushing toward legal independence, the Chinese politicians look like suckers. Even if Taiwan responds positively, any agreement looks suspect to the Chinese elite because it implies that their side must have conceded too much to achieve it.

An example of such rigidity is the "one country, two systems" shorthand proposed by Deng Xiaoping in 1979 to describe the home rule that Taiwan would enjoy after reunification with the Mainland. The Chinese government applied the same formula to Hong Kong during the reversion of the British colony to PRC rule in 1997, even though Hong Kong's autonomy was much more limited than what was originally offered to Taiwan. For example, the PLA now has bases in Hong Kong but Taiwan would have its own armed forces; Beijing has a veto over the pace of Hong Kong's political evolution from a colony to a democracy but, under Deng's plan, wouldn't interfere with Taiwan's democratic system. By associating "one country, two systems," with Hong Kong, the Beijing government tainted it in the eyes of the Taiwanese. (Taiwanese leaders have been highly skeptical of how Hong Kong has developed since the 1997 handover, pointing fingers especially whenever Beijing becomes involved in Hong Kong's political affairs.)

Speaking to a roomful of Chinese academics studying in America, I made the point that Beijing needed to create a new label, such as "one country, three systems" to differentiate it from Hong Kong and make it more appealing to Taiwan citizens. Taiwanese citizens will never support reunification unless it makes them better off than they are now. Officials and policy experts privately agree that "one country, two systems" should be junked. On any other foreign policy issue, Chinese pragmatism would prevail. But Deng Xiaoping's formula for Taiwan is sacrosanct.

Under Jiang Zemin, the "one-China principle"—there is only one China and Taiwan is part of China—became publicly enshrined as the absolute prerequisite for any cross-Strait discussions.[48] Beijing refuses to talk to Taiwan until its authorities accept this principle. By publicly insisting that the Taiwan president utter the magic words, "one China," they make it virtually impossible for him to comply without looking weak in the eyes of his own citizens. Either the Taiwan president loses face or the Chinese president loses face. The Clinton and Bush administrations urged

Beijing to initiate cross-Strait talks with no preconditions, but neither Jiang nor Hu Jintao dares to do it.

"Hu doesn't dare propose talks with Taiwan with no preconditions in view of his [limited] political authority now," a PLA officer said in 2004. "When Jiang was still around, he was the real boss but even he had no political power to do such a sensitive thing. And now Hu doesn't want to lose his reputation and get criticized by doing it."

The political elite in China is so obsessed with the "one-China principle," that until 2002, it made it a precondition for the opening of direct mail, transport, and trade with Taiwan (the "three links")—something it had craved since 1979 as a way to bind Taiwan more tightly to the Mainland.

Beijing makes a point of never recognizing the authority of the Taiwan government. The stubborn refusal to give the Taiwan government any face impedes discussion of even mundane practical issues like tourism or trade. Beijing insists that talks on economic issues be with private industry representatives—any government officials in the room must be present only as advisors to the industry. Although both China and Taiwan are WTO members, China will hardly speak to Taiwan in the WTO because it might imply that the Taiwan government has sovereignty over the island. It's difficult to see how peaceful reunification can move ahead until the Chinese government can swallow its pride and talk directly to the Taiwan government.

Jiang Zemin, in the last year of his term as CCP general secretary, was anxious to show progress toward reunification, and had some hope that Taiwan, then suffering an economic downturn, might agree to direct mail, transport, and trade links. Jiang also wanted to ingratiate himself with the new American president, George W. Bush, whom he was about to visit at his ranch in Crawford, Texas. After a decade serving as China's number one leader, his authority was solid. In this context, he finally managed to get an elite consensus to offer a somewhat more flexible formulation to Taiwan. The definition of "China" in the "one-China" principle was changed to make it less objectionable to Taiwan. China no longer is defined as the People's Republic of China with Taiwan relegated to the subordinate status of a province within it. The new mantra is "the Mainland and Taiwan are both part of one China."[49] This formulation aimed to show that reunification is based on equality and is "not an act of who is eating whom."[50] It opens up the possibility of a shared sovereignty arrangement between the two.

Beijing also offered an even more palatable alternative. Taiwan could accept the "1992 consensus," the ambiguous outcome of the first meeting of the two cross-Strait negotiators. Each side could repeat its own version of what "one China" means and ignore the other side's.[51] Or both sides could just say they embraced the "1992 consensus" without defining what they meant by it. Richard Bush, an American expert on cross-Strait relations, labels this a "symbolic fig leaf to justify resuming dialogue."[52] Yet Taiwan president Chen Shui-bian couldn't bring himself to say he supported the 1992 consensus and was not willing to send his negotiators to Beijing.

Significantly, neither of these two new formulations is widely used for domestic consumption—within China, Taiwan is still usually called a province, and "one China" is the absolute bottom line.[53] (In 2005, Hu Jintao tried again to contrive a phrasing of "one China" that Taiwan might accept—"two shores, one China." Chen Shui-bian rejected it, and Hu dropped it.[54])

Kenneth Lieberthal, a prominent American China scholar and former National Security Council staffer, has proposed that the two sides try to negotiate an "interim agreement" that would stabilize the status quo for a certain period of time, say fifty years.[55] A Beijing policy advisor said that although the idea itself had merit, China's leaders would never be able to publicly agree to it because the public and other officials would object to any compromise that gave up the hope of reunification for such a long period of time.

A New Taiwan President

Before Chen Shui-bian was elected president in March 2000, he visited Washington several times as mayor of Taipei and met informally with American officials like me. Chen appeared eager to differentiate himself from the proindependence fundamentalists within the Democratic Progressive Party, and intrigued with the possibility of making history by negotiating a modus vivendi with the Mainland.

When Chen was elected in a tight three-way race in 2000, we were apprehensive about a possible military reaction from Beijing, and warned Beijing not to make any provocative moves. But based on our previous impressions, we also had some hope that Chen might pull off a "Nixon to China" sort of coup. The American representative in Taipei urged Chen to move quickly to reassure Beijing about his intentions.[56]

Chen did float some carefully phrased positive messages in his acceptance speech and in his inaugural address two months later. Although he didn't say the magic words, "one China," he did promise not to declare independence unless the PRC showed its intention to attack, not to put the "two states theory" into the constitution, not to hold a referendum on independence, not to change the name "Republic of China," and not to abolish the National Reunification Guidelines and the National Reunification Council. (In typical Chinese fashion, these promises came to be called the "Four No's and One Will Not.") Inching closer to what Beijing demanded, Chen also talked about a *future* one China." But the Beijing leadership, still reeling from the shock of the election of a Taiwan president from the proindependence party and too twisted up in knots internally trying to figure out how to respond, couldn't take yes for an answer.

The CCP had tried to exercise some self-discipline in the period leading up to the presidential vote—the 1995 election taught it that military intimidation was counterproductive. As Chinese officials put it, they did not want to be Chen Shui-bian's campaign manager. Jiang Zemin, trying to appear strong while exercising restraint, reportedly rolled out a new internal report on accelerating preparations by the PLA for taking military action on Taiwan.[57] Still, the then-PLA-head general Zhang Wannian could not stop himself from threatening "Taiwan independence means war," in a speech to the national legislature that was published in *People's Daily*.[58] And on the eve of the election, Premier Zhu Rongji, perhaps to bolster his domestic position, which was still shaky after his disastrous 1999 trip to the United States, publicly warned the Taiwan people not to "act impulsively. Otherwise, it will be too late for regrets."[59]

After Chen's election, a cloud of pessimism descended over Beijing, and military preparations intensified, although the military exercises were kept modest so as not to provoke a confrontation before the PLA was ready. "Some people did advocate using force after Chen's victory," according to a Taiwan expert in Beijing, "But we tried to explain to them that Chen won because the Guomindang split and produced a three-candidate race, not because the proindependence party had expanded its support."

The government came out with a provisional line about the new Taiwan president that sounded open-minded, "we will listen to his words and watch his deeds," and refrained from criticizing him by name.[60] But no one in the leadership—certainly not Jiang Zemin—dared take the risk of responding positively to a president from the proindependence party. "If Jiang made unilateral concessions he would be viewed as a traitor and there would be demonstrations," a leading advisor on Taiwan policy said at the time. "If I talked about new concessions now, I certainly would be attacked." Once rebuffed, Chen Shui-bian never again tried in any serious way to bridge the gap with the Mainland.

Pessimism + Impatience = Danger

When Jiang Zemin retired as China's leader in 2002, his Taiwan policies were widely (but privately) condemned inside China as a complete failure.

One academic explained, "Students and other people are critical of Jiang's policy toward Taiwan for being too weak. Taiwan didn't reciprocate—it just took advantage of China's softness." The continuous stream of provocations from Taipei and Washington were blamed on Jiang's lack of spine. For example, one foreign policy think-tank expert said, "Everyone knows that the Taiwan defense minister just visited the U.S. It's a hot topic of taxi drivers and others." Another expert said, "Jiang is strongly and vocally criticized for being too accommodating to the U.S. and Taiwan. I have heard vice-ministers make such criticisms—for example, for not standing up when Bush said he would defend Taiwan by 'whatever it takes' and when the U.S. arms sales to Taiwan were so large." Jiang is also blamed for starting military preparations too late.

Experts affiliated with Wang Daohan, Jiang's cross-Strait negotiator based in Shanghai, tried to explain away the discouraging trends on Taiwan as "an unavoidable natural process, not the result of mistakes made by any state leader in his work."[61] But even those favoring reliance on economic integration and a positive approach to Taiwan had to admit that China's peaceful efforts were being outpaced by the momentum toward independence in Taiwan. As one Chinese advisor on Taiwan issues said, "Peaceful economic integration takes time, and Chen Shui-bian is giving us no time."

Meanwhile the People's Liberation Army was preparing to use force if need be. The investments begun earlier in the 1990s started coming online, and the buildup accelerated after 1999. China will be "ready" to solve the Taiwan problem militarily before the 2008 Olympics, according to the assessments of many Chinese, although most experts in Taiwan and the United States believe it won't be ready until the middle of the next decade. The speed by which the PLA has transformed itself from a ragged people's army into a modern force demonstrates that countries with one strategic focus can modernize their militaries very fast. It also helps to have generous—and paranoid—politicians who don't dare alienate the soldiers who guard them from domestic rebellion.

The pressure to put this modern military to use builds with each new provocation from Chen Shui-bian. According to one Chinese think-tank analyst, "The majority of policy people, Party people, and the military support using military force, military pressure, but it didn't happen in the Jiang period because Jiang, Premier Zhu Rongji, and Vice-Premier Qian Qichen had the political authority to enforce a more flexible line. Now all the leaders and policymakers are the same age. Hu Jintao and Wen Jiabao have less authority and are less willing to use the authority they have."

Pessimism Deepens

Jiang Zemin had stoked expectations that reunification could be achieved in the near term, and those expectations weighed heavily on Hu Jintao when he assumed office in 2002–03. As the People's Liberation Army grew more capable, China's range of aggressive options increased too. Hu Jintao came into office hoping to stabilize the Taiwan issue in domestic politics and foreign policy. He knew it was the one issue that could derail all his other plans.

The Taiwan issue forced itself on Hu Jintao before the official transition. He had to decide how to react before he had established his power over the military and the Party. In August 2002 Chen Shui-bian, without prior consultation with Washington or even with his own advisors, came out with his own version of Lee Teng-hui's "two states theory" — "one country on each side [of the Strait]." Simultaneously, he called for the Taiwan legislature to pass a law that would make it possible for the Taiwan people to hold a referendum. The PRC press reacted to Chen Shui-bian's bombshell with threatening words. In one week, August 5–12, 2002, *People's Daily* had more than thirty articles attacking Chen and warning him not to "play with fire" because China would not "sit idly by" as he separated

Front page of *World News Journal*, a Chinese newspaper, following Taiwan President Chen Shui-bian's call for a referendum. The headline over the photo of the People's Liberation Army soldiers reads: "Chinese military exercise intimidates the Taiwan independence movement," August 7, 2002. (Kevin Lee/Getty Images)

Taiwan from China. *Global Times* said "a referendum in Taiwan equals a declaration of war."[62] Hu Jintao let the media speak for him and kept a low profile on the Taiwan issue, trying to avoid a major error that could destroy his administration before it began.

War anxieties heightened during the 2003–04 presidential election campaign as Chen Shui-bian called for a referendum to revise the Constitution in 2006, and ratify it by 2008. This schedule was obviously timed to coincide with the 2008 Olympics to be held in Beijing. Chen was betting that the PRC wouldn't ruin its Olympic coming-out party by attacking Taiwan right before it.

Mainland newspapers published articles about possible war strategies, for example, "Under relentless and paralyzing strikes, the resistance of Taiwan's armed forces will cave in very quickly."[63] They also discussed China's ability to absorb the costs of war, which the papers said would include the economy plummeting 30 percent per year for two years and losing the Olympic Games—as echoed by one journalist who said, "to safeguard the motherland's unity, Chinese people are ready to pay any price."[64] Although no large-scale exercises were held, military men like former major general Wang Zaixi, now the vice-head of the government Taiwan Affairs Office, threatened that a referendum equals independence and independence means war.[65] The threats, in addition to bolstering Hu Jintao domestically, got the attention of the Bush administration, which went all out to try to prevent a military confrontation by stopping the referendum.

Many of China's normally pragmatic policy experts were exasperated with Chen Shui-bian and impatient to free China from the burden of its Taiwan problem, even if it meant war. As one usually liberal-minded think-tanker said to me in December 2003, "We have suffered internally and externally because of the unsolved issue of Taiwan. We have had to give too much to the U.S. just to hear the words 'one China.' We will have more leverage if the Taiwan issue disappears. Other issues with the U.S. are win-win issues. We need to get rid of this burden, sooner rather than later. We should be willing to sacrifice our foreign relations, investment, and economic growth . . . we could restore central planning, sell government bonds, and use the funds to create employment. It would unify society. China has robust domestic demand. It can withstand war and sanctions."

A Legal Alternative to Force

A number of policy advisors, like the ex-military men who introduced this chapter, were losing sleep over what they saw as a growing consensus behind use of force. With a sense of foreboding, they feared that if

China attacked Taiwan and forcibly imposed itself over a hostile Taiwanese population, the result would be just as disastrous as the American occupation of Iraq.

The political elite viewed the situation as all the more urgent after Chen Shui-bian was reelected in March 2004. The campaign ended like a bad movie—twenty-four hours before the election Chen was wounded in an assassination attempt that the opposition claimed was staged, and the opposition contested the close results in large postelection demonstrations. The Chinese media, seeking to discredit Taiwan democracy and attract audiences, reported all the gory details with relish. But in the end Chen's victory was confirmed—he would be in charge until 2008. There was no way for China's Taiwan watchers to explain away Chen's victory in the two-way election—it meant that "more than half of the people [in Taiwan do not support] . . . one China, they think they have the right to say no to China, have the right to call a referendum, and have the right to decide Taiwan's future on their own."[66] It also meant that Beijing's cross-Strait strategy was failing, and that even a public scolding from President Bush hadn't discouraged Taiwan voters from voting for Chen. If, as predicted, Chen's Democratic Progressive Party won a majority in the legislative election coming up in December 2004, a referendum to change the constitution appeared inevitable. At that point, Hu Jintao, to remain politically viable at home, would have to order an attack. As one Chinese article put it, "It is far harder for any Chinese decision maker to decide to tolerate Taiwan independence than to decide to wage war . . . even if China is bound to be defeated in war, Chinese decision makers will not necessarily have sufficient prestige (sometimes compromise needs still more prestige) and the will to tacitly allow and persuade the Chinese people to accept the fact of Taiwan independence."[67]

To give Hu Jintao a robust alternative to war, they came up with a creative notion. China could legislate its own legal riposte to Taiwan's referendum (and to the U.S. Taiwan Relations Act)—a law against Taiwan independence.[68] The trick was to come up with a law that looked strong to the public, Taiwan, and the United States without tying Beijing's hands and taking away all its wiggle room.

Chinese officials spun the contents to reassure worried Americans before the final draft was released. They stressed that the law would clarify China's threat to use force—never to coerce reunification, only to block independence. The law simply preserves the status quo, they said.[69] The original name, "Reunification Law," was changed to "Antisecession Law."[70] Hu Jintao had wanted to reduce the pressure on himself by cooling off the impatience Jiang Zemin had stirred up. But apparently not everyone was on the same page with Hu. When the final bill appeared, its authorization to use force was vague and expansive. It included the equivalent of the "third if" from the 2000 White Paper. Article 8 says that "the state shall employ nonpeaceful means" in three situations: if Taiwan secedes, if "major incidents entailing Taiwan's secession from China should occur," or if "possibilities for a peaceful reunification should be completely exhausted."[71] (The use of the euphemism, "nonpeaceful means" reflects the Chinese leaders' desire to strengthen the credibility of their threat to use force without taking any heat from the United States for doing so.)

When the opposition parties surprised everyone by winning a majority in Taiwan's December legislative elections, the rationale for the PRC antisecession law all but disappeared. The legislature would block Chen's plan to revise the constitution by referendum. President Bush, as well, had publicly criticized the referendum as a unilateral change in the status quo. But by then the draft bill was with the National People's Congress, and no Chinese—certainly not President Hu—dared call for it to be shelved.

Foreign observers were relieved that the law only authorized force instead of requiring it and that it included a long list of the standard positive offers to Taiwan. The U.S. government spokesman mildly criticized the law as "unhelpful." Still the U.S. Congress condemned the law, and the European Union—on the verge of lifting the embargo on arms sales to China it originally imposed after the Tiananmen crackdown—deferred its decision because of the law. Paying some cost internationally to defend the principle of reunification benefited Hu Jintao domestically, and helped make the threat to use force to prevent Taiwan independence more credible to Taiwan and the United States.

Although the law served as a short-term fix that helped Hu Jintao and his colleagues avoid using force at the time, it could make the use of force more likely in future crises. When debating how to react to some provocation from Taiwan, officials advocating a military response are likely to reference the law and argue the provocation is obviously a "major incident" toward secession that according to the law calls for the use of force.[72]

Tough Love for Taiwan

Hu Jintao has restored the elite consensus around a two-track approach to Taiwan: the Antisecession Law, accelerated military preparations, and firm statements of principle to show strength; combined with some friendly overtures toward the Taiwan people to try to win their hearts and minds.

Hu's instruction, circulated internally but not yet publicized openly, is "Prepare to fight, seek to talk, don't be afraid to delay." The last point stands in explicit contrast to Jiang Zemin's rush to achieve reunification. Policy advisors familiar with Hu's thinking say that he has learned from Jiang's failures that tying one's political fate to reunification is much too risky. Hu and Wen Jiabao are defining their legacy as helping China's poor instead. "Hu Jintao is more realistic than Jiang Zemin," one professor said. "He knows not to expect reunification any time soon."

Before taking any new positive initiatives, Hu sought to strengthen his reputation as a strong leader who would never lose Taiwan. (Hu already had earned considerable respect from the military and the control coalition for the strong fist he showed during his tenure as CCP secretary in Tibet, and for firing senior officials he held responsible for the SARS fiasco and the submarine accident in 2003.) In addition to the Antisecession Law, Hu authorized several new statements of principle. The May 17, 2004, statement won praise from China's policy community for being, as one policy advisor put it, "Our first new statement in twenty years that isn't just reactive to Taiwan." Another expert said it was the "most important statement [on Taiwan] issued since 2000."[73] The essence of the toughly worded statement was "The Chinese people will never compromise our stand of upholding the policy of one China . . . never tolerate 'Taiwan independence' . . . and will pay any price to resolutely and completely crush the secessionist 'Taiwan independence' scheme."[74] Hu also presented his own guidelines for handling Taiwan when China's National People's Congress held its annual meeting in March 2005 and passed the Antisecession Law. The guidelines combined firmness and friendliness toward Taiwan, but the Chinese government emphasized their firm side by calling them the "Four Nevers."[75]

On this foundation of firm adherence to principle, the Communist Party renewed its effort to build a united front with Taiwan's opposition parties and economic interest groups. The Party aimed to isolate politically Chen Shui-bian and the Democratic Progressive Party while encouraging other groups to block Chen's drive toward independence, as well as lay the groundwork for forward progress after 2008 when a new president will be elected. During an exciting two-week period in May 2005, the Communist Party hosted first the Guomindang head Lien Chan and then, the People's First Party head James Soong—the Lien-Soong ticket had lost to Chen in the 2004 election. Neither of the two had stepped on Mainland soil since they had left as children in 1949, and their homecoming tours were emotional and widely televised events. Beijing's gesture of friendship resonated well with Chinese, Taiwanese, and Americans. The Chinese government sent Lien Chan home with gifts—promises to

import many varieties of Taiwan fruit tariff free and to provide easier entry for Taiwan tourists, and to give Taiwan two pandas. The offer of the
pandas, which received extensive publicity in the Mainland and Taiwan
(including contests to name them and jokes about "Trojan bears") was
rejected by the Chen Shui-bian administration, which explained that the
animals would not receive suitable care in the Taiwan zoos.

By allowing the two Taiwan politicians to address the Chinese public
on live TV (like the live address by President Clinton in 1998 on which it
was modeled), the Chinese leaders looked confident. (Lien Chan, although viewed by Taiwanese as a stiff, unsympathetic political figure, came
across to Mainlanders as a warm, articulate, and very Chinese politician
who put their own leaders to shame.)

Following the visits, the benevolent gestures continued. Hu Jintao, in
his speech on the sixtieth anniversary of the end of World War II, shared
credit with Guomindang forces for the defeat of the Japanese, and invited
some Guomindang veterans to join the ceremonies.[76] Chinese universities announced that they will now charge Taiwan students the same tu-
ition fees as Mainland students. The Beijing government will recognize
Taiwan college degrees and allow Taiwan medical doctors to be licensed

Taiwan Guomindang chairman Lien Chan delivers a speech at Beijing University
during his visit to the Mainland, April 29, 2005. (Liu Weibing/Xinhua)

on the Mainland. Mainland tourists can start visiting Taiwan. The first direct cargo flight between China and Taiwan arrived in Shanghai in July 2006.[77] The CCP utilized "fruit diplomacy" to ingratiate itself with Taiwan's farmers. It negotiated with the Guomindang a purchase of two thousand metric tons of Taiwanese bananas to support the price of the fruit, which had plunged due to overproduction.[78]

The publicity surrounding the Antisecession Law and the visits of Lien Chan and James Soong helped dispel the dangerously pessimistic mood about cross-Strait relations, created the impression that "time is on our side," and for the time being, reduced the pressure on China's leaders to react to Taiwan provocations by using force. Still, Hu does not yet feel sufficiently secure to propose direct talks with the Taiwan government, to drop the "one-China" precondition for contacts, or to allow lower-level academics and officials from the Democratic Progressive Party to visit China. When Wang Daohan, China's former cross-Strait negotiator, passed away, the Chinese government refused to permit any Taiwan representatives to attend his funeral.

A Weakened Taiwan President

In February 2006, Chen Shui-bian surprised everyone again by suddenly announcing plans to abolish the symbolically important National Unification Council. Chen may have hoped to shore up his sagging popularity at home. The Taiwan public was losing confidence in the president's ability to handle mounting domestic problems, cross-Strait issues, and relations with Washington.

If that was Chen's intention, he miscalculated. The Bush administration reacted with alarm, publicly demanding that the Taiwan government "clarify" its position to explain that it wasn't actually "abolishing" the council and that it stood by President Chen's previous pledges not to abolish it. Behind the scenes the administration frantically negotiated with the Taiwan government to get it to restate its position to be consistent with its previous pledges. Failing in that effort, the State Department spokesman simply issued a statement that expressed the American "understanding" that "the announcement did not abolish the council, did not change the status quo, and that Chen's previous assurances remain in effect."[79]

Mainland Chinese were exasperated with Chen Shui-bian's latest tactic. According to one policy advisor, participants in internal meetings expressed tremendous anger and frustration that no matter how well they managed cross-Strait relations, they were powerless to prevent Chen from taking such outrageous actions. All they could do was to react with critical statements. The media were told to downplay the issue to reduce public pressure to react with something stronger than words.

The most important factor in reinforcing Beijing's relatively restrained response was Washington's unusual public chastisement of Chen Shui-bian's actions. President Hu Jintao's meeting with President Bush at the White House in April 2006 further bolstered his confidence in American support. President Bush, whose patience with Chen Shui-bian was wearing thin, implicitly encouraged Hu not to let Chen's surprises deflect him from his steady course in cross-Strait relations. According to one Beijing policy advisor, "Bush told Hu, 'My policy toward the Taiwan issue will not change. If you have any problems in the future [with Taiwan], just call me.'"

Meanwhile Chen Shui-bian's political fortunes were dimming. Besieged by corruption scandals involving his family, associates, and himself, he survived several votes in the Taiwan legislature to recall him but remained under intense pressure to resign. Large-scale demonstrations led by Shih Ming-teh, a revered elder from the same political party as the president, continued for months and disrupted the government's National Day ceremonies. The first lady and three staff members from the presidential office were indicted, and the prosecutor said he will indict the president too as soon as Chen leaves office and loses his immunity. Even if Chen manages to survive until his term ends in March 2008, he is too hobbled to accomplish anything on his domestic agenda.

On the Mainland, the Hu Jintao administration, although undoubtedly feeling some satisfaction at Chen's domestic troubles, remains on edge because Chen persists in calling for a referendum to revise Taiwan's constitution that would effectively establish its sovereignty as an independent country. In Beijing's eyes, a weak and desperate Taiwan president is just as dangerous as a strong one. The fundamental problem facing Chinese leaders is that since Taiwan's democratization, they cannot predict what Chen will do next or what Taiwan's next president might do.

The Risk of War

Former secretary of defense William Perry, in a 2005 Hong Kong speech, worried out loud that PLA generals might be urging China's top leaders to take action against Taiwan because "the U.S. is pinned down in Iraq and will not be able to come to the defense of Taiwan." Meanwhile in Taiwan, Chen Shui-bian might be considering "making a bold movement in the direction of independence" because the United States would "feel compelled" to come to Taiwan's defense if it did. "History is replete with wars that were started with miscalculations," Secretary Perry warned.[80] Chinese analysts are unanimous in predicting that "changes in the situation in the Taiwan Strait are more likely than anything else to drag China into a conflict."[81]

The danger is compounded by the volatile mixture of domestic politics and foreign policy in China and Taiwan. In China, leaders are under increasing domestic pressure to use force as the military becomes stronger and the Party's control over information reaching the public becomes weaker. Growing economic interdependence does not make war unthinkable. The economic ties across the Strait appear to influence policy more in democratic Taiwan than in authoritarian China where the private businesses, coastal provinces, and the "silent majority" who value economic progress over the "one-China principle" have no political voice. Some brave Chinese scholars suggest the only answer is to somehow get people to pay less attention to Taiwan. The CCP should not "push mass feelings deeper" on the Taiwan problem, and should defer its resolution into the future. The Taiwan issue should take second place to China's modernization drive.[82] "Now is the best time for China's rapid economic growth so we should not impetuously talk about war."[83] But it is hard to imagine China's leaders feeling secure enough to try to persuade people that the Taiwan issue isn't as important as they once thought it was.

8

The United States

"External Troubles Can Become Internal Troubles"

May 7, 1999, Washington, D.C.

A S I WAS DRIVING HOME from the State Department on a balmy Friday evening, my cell phone rang. The State Department Operations Center informed me that American military planes had struck the Chinese Embassy in Belgrade, Yugoslavia. Jerking my car around and speeding back to the office, I anxiously reviewed the possibilities in my mind. It must be a case of "collateral damage," I decided, caused by stray fragments from a nearby target. The U.S. Air Force, under NATO command, had been bombing Belgrade intensively to press the Yugoslav government to stop its persecution of Albanians in Kosovo. Some hours later, I was shocked to learn that in fact an American B-2 bomber had targeted and directly attacked the embassy, mistaking it for a Yugoslav military office building. The plane had struck the embassy with five guided JDAM bombs, killing three Chinese and injuring twenty. Because of our own tragic error, we had a major crisis on our hands. As the deputy assistant secretary of state responsible for relations with China, I was responsible for coordinating our efforts to defuse the crisis and salvage American relations with the PRC.

My first impulse was to have us apologize immediately and profusely, from the president on down. I knew that the Chinese people would never forgive us—or let us forget it—if they felt our apologies were inadequate, just as they have never stopped pressing the Japanese for a proper apology for their World War II atrocities. President Clinton telephoned President Jiang Zemin, but Jiang refused to accept the call. Clinton had to send an apology through American ambassador James Sasser instead. The president also apologized on television, spoke by telephone with President Jiang a few days later, and signed the condolence book from the Chinese Embassy in Washington. The night after the bombing, Secretary Madeleine Albright went to the Chinese Embassy to apologize to Ambassador Li Zhaoxing and on her way out was jostled by a crowd of shouting, fist-waving Chinese journalists who had been invited in by the ambassador.

We adjusted the air traffic around Belgrade to enable a Chinese plane to retrieve the remains of the dead and evacuate the injured. Ambassador Sasser asked permission to attend the airport ceremony when the plane landed, but the Chinese government turned him down. We sought to send a high-level delegation to Beijing immediately, but the Chinese government told us to wait. Our embassy in Beijing and our consulates in other Chinese cities flew their flags at half staff. In every way we could think of, we sought to express our remorse to the Chinese government and the Chinese people.

Much to my frustration, our sincere regret had no effect on the Chinese reactions. The streets of Beijing soon were filled with the largest mass demonstrations since the 1989 prodemocracy protests in Beijing's Tiananmen Square. Tens of thousands of young people, mostly students, protested outside the U.S. Embassy in Beijing and consulates in Guangzhou and Chengdu, shouting anti-American slogans and throwing bricks and Molotov cocktails. Protestors burned the consul general's residence in Chengdu. The American media carried pictures of Ambassador

A demonstrator throws a rock at the U.S. Embassy in Beijing while the police stand by following the U.S. bombing of the Chinese Embassy in Belgrade, Yugoslavia, May 9, 1999. (Peter Rogers/Getty Images)

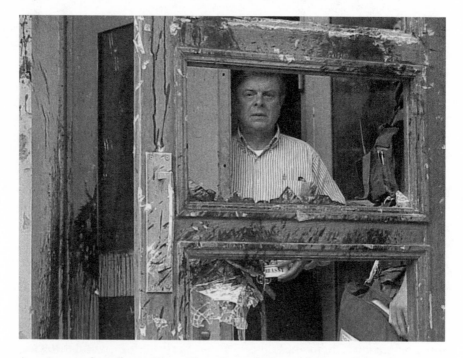

American Ambassador to China James Sasser looks out from inside the U.S.
Embassy in Beijing damaged by demonstrators, May 9, 1999. (AP Photos)

Sasser, who remained in the embassy under siege, looking like a prisoner
in the battle-scarred building. Students also attacked McDonald's and
Kentucky Fried Chicken restaurants in Beijing.

China's Communist Party leaders deflected the students' nationalist
outrage away from themselves onto the United States. From the first report of the incident, China's official media described it as intentional, a
"brazen" and "barbarian" act. The media delayed reporting the apologies
from the U.S. president, secretary of state, and other senior officials and
reported favorably on the demonstrations as expressions of youthful patriotism. At government request, universities provided the buses that transported the students to demonstrate outside the American Embassy. The
police stood by and allowed the violence, stepping in only to block the
demonstrators from entering the U.S. compounds. President Jiang Zemin
avoided the limelight by sending Vice President Hu Jintao to appear on
television to express the government's support for the protestors but to
warn them not to go too far, "to conduct all activities in good order and
according to law." The Chinese government canceled all diplomatic
meetings with the United States for the rest of the year.[1]

A Chinese study of the crisis explains: "Facing heavy pressure, the government and university administrations had to allow students and civil-

ians to protest. President Jiang Zemin later told American officials that 'It is unstoppable when 1.2 billion people are angry.'"[2]

The timing of the accident triggered the leaders' defensive reflexes. Several major anniversaries of historical events fell during 1999, and past anniversary gatherings had snowballed into mass protest. In spring 1999, the Chinese Communist Party was anxiously preparing for two anniversaries of historical protests that might bring students out on the streets against the regime again: the eightieth anniversary of the May 4, 1919, demonstrations against the Republican government's concessions to Japan, and the tenth anniversary of the June 4, 1989, prodemocracy demonstrations in Tiananmen Square.

Jiang Zemin and the other Chinese leaders already felt a sense of heightened tension because just two weeks before the Belgrade embassy bombing they had awakened to the alarming sight of more than ten thousand members of the Falun Gong sitting silently on the pavement outside their windows. The Falun Gong is an apolitical organization of people who practice a type of traditional Chinese breathing exercises called *qigong* that they believe are beneficial for their health. It is led by a guru who lives in New York City. The protestors, mostly middle-aged, white-collar professionals, quite a few of them Communist Party members and government officials, had mysteriously appeared overnight without any forewarning from the police or internal security agencies. They silently surrounded Zhongnanhai, the compound where the Communist Party leaders live and work. Using cell phones and the Internet, the group had stealthily organized the sit-in to petition the Party for recognition as a legitimate organization.

President Jiang Zemin seemed to be personally traumatized by the Falun Gong sit-in even though the public security officials and Premier Zhu Rongji had persuaded the group to disperse by the end of the day. According to one account, President Jiang wrote an angry letter to the other leaders blaming the public security departments for dereliction of duty and insinuating that Falun Gong had backing from abroad. At a meeting of the Politburo Standing Committee he lost his temper, accusing the head of public security of endangering Communist Party rule.[3]

Two weeks later, when the Belgrade embassy bombing occurred, President Jiang reacted from fear as if he were facing a coordinated attack from the American government, the Falun Gong, and the students. He ordered the universities to provide buses to take the students to the American Embassy after the Belgrade embassy bombing, probably figuring that if the students didn't go there, they would head straight for Tiananmen Square or Zhongnanhai.[4] The Chinese admit that the government gave permission for the demonstrations and provided the buses that transported

Ten thousand Falun Gong practitioners peacefully demonstrate outside the Chinese government compound at Zhongnanhai, April 25, 1999. (Greg Baker/AP Photo)

the students to demonstrate outside the American Embassy.[5] A student from Chengdu whom I interviewed said that in her city, senior high school students as well as university students were organized by the government to protest outside the U.S. consulate.[6]

A Communist Party insider told me that President Jiang stayed up late on the night after the Belgrade embassy bombing, writing a long memo—not on how to respond to the bombing, but on how to crush the Falun Gong. In what other Chinese officials confided they thought was a ludicrous overreaction, Jiang ordered an all-out nationwide campaign to suppress the Falun Gong, imprison its leaders, and arrest any members who practiced the breathing exercises in parks or other public places.

China's mass media, which by the late 1990s included market-oriented outlets as well as the Party mouthpieces, reported extensively and emotionally on the Belgrade bombing. The Chinese analysis of the event highlights the role of the commercial media in aggravating the crisis. "While the government tried to lead public opinion, the marketization of China's mass media and the growth of the Internet made it difficult for the government to prevent some tabloids from promoting their own news. These nonmainstream voices increased the pressure on the Chinese government in handling the crisis."[7]

One newspaper compared the bombing to a "Nazi war crime."[8] A front-page story in *People's Daily* lambasted the attack as a modern version of the imperialist invasion of China during the Boxer Rebellion.[9] But even after the *People's Daily* had shifted into lower gear, the popular *Beijing Youth Daily* continued to fulminate against the United States. The paper's dramatic headlines aroused the emotions of young readers, for example, "The strongest protest, the loudest voice, the angriest action, the darkest midnight, the most barbarous outrage, the deepest pain, and strongest support. . . ."[10] (The Propaganda Department later awarded the *Beijing Youth Daily* a special award for its coverage.[11])

Southern Weekend (*Nanfang Zhoumo*), the Guangdong newspaper identified with the coastal business class, was the sole sober-minded voice that dared to question the plausibility of the assertion that the American government had intentionally bombed the Chinese Embassy, saying, "If NATO sought to provoke China by intentionally bombing the Chinese Embassy in spite of the obvious fact that it would gain nothing from the bombing, the conclusion would be but one: NATO is insane."[12] *Southern Weekend* also called for a rational perspective on America. "Since the Opium War, some Chinese have either extremely hated America or extremely admired America. Both of them are harmful for the development of the Chinese nationalist spirit, the maturation and progress of Chinese society, and the objective knowledge of the West and America."[13] Yet one piece in the newspaper by a military expert said that the attack was intended by the United States and NATO "to probe the Chinese government's reaction to international crises, especially sudden accidents, as well as its mass reaction, public opinion, and related policies."[14]

I coordinated the U.S. government interagency investigation to discover how our country could have made such a horrific blunder. What we found was a combination of errors including a CIA employee using the wrong method to locate the Yugoslav military agency we intended to strike and the military checking and double-checking the target with databases that were outdated and not as independent of one another as they were supposed to be.[15] We presented the explanation to the Chinese Foreign Ministry, posted it in Chinese on the Web site of the U.S. Embassy in Beijing, and paid compensation for the deaths and injuries and the massive damage to the building.

But despite our best efforts, the Chinese people—in awe of American technology and management methods—did not believe it was possible for the United States to commit such a stupid mistake. Therefore the bombing must have been intentional. If President Clinton didn't have any reason to attack the Chinese Embassy, then the bombing must have been planned by a lower-level anti-China conspiracy.[16] According to the Chinese postmortem of the crisis, few academic experts dared to cast doubt on the theory that the bombing was intentional. "Scholars supporting the 'conspiracy hypothesis' gradually dominated the debate while those who believed the 'mistaken bombing hypothesis' had to keep silent."[17]

"We believed it was intentional," said a college student who was in junior high school at the time, "because that is what the newspapers and TV said and we had no access to any other opinions. The experts on TV without exception said it was intentional and they gave a lot of reasons that were very convincing. All the information pointed to one purpose." She also recalled the feeling of solidarity with friends and family the bombing produced. "We felt bound together, we had an enemy."

"Pretty much all the intellectual and policy elite now believes the bombing was intentional, the result of a conspiracy," one policy expert told me years after the incident. Most everyone I meet in China still believes the same thing, although I do my best to convince them otherwise based on the facts of the incident. The bombing profoundly damaged trust in America's intentions toward China. As the Chinese postmortem concludes, "The change of public opinion toward the U.S. was one of the most serious and profound consequences. The embassy bombing turned China into a direct victim of U.S. and NATO's new strategy, imposing a strong impact on ordinary people's perspective."[18]

Which Face to Show the United States?

China's leaders confront a difficult dilemma in dealing with the United States. On the one hand, China's success, and the leaders' own power, depend on cooperation with the United States. If the United States declared China the enemy in a new Cold War and tried to tie an economic noose around it, China's economic growth and job creation would be slowed and domestic problems would mount even if few American allies joined the U.S. effort. A hostile U.S. military posture would drive the PLA and the public to demand that the government put more resources into building China's own military, and increase the risk of war. As one Chinese scholar explained, "The experiences and lessons of history prove that a latecomer power can only eventually rise through cooperation with the dominant power in the international system." That is the way the United States was able to rise without causing conflict with Great Britain in the nineteenth century.[19] The best way for China to rise peacefully is to behave like a responsible power and accommodate to the current superpower, the United States.

But on the other hand, inside China, other leaders, the public, and the military expect Chinese leaders to stand up to the United States. Nationalist ardor runs high, fanned by government propaganda and the commercial media and Internet. The United States, as the dominant power in the world, is the natural target of suspicion and resentment in China, just as it is in many other countries, particularly after the American invasion of Iraq. A Chinese political leader who takes a principled stand against the United States always wins more points than one who gives in to it. Compromise is likely to be viewed as capitulation. "Looking weak in the face of foreign pressure can doom you," is the lesson today's leaders learned from the fall of the Qing Dynasty and the Republic of China. An international crisis can trigger a domestic challenge. America expert Wang Jisi put it this way: The factors in Sino-U.S. relations "that pose a serious threat to China's national security are the issues that may turn 'external troubles' into 'internal troubles.'"[20]

How do China's leaders resolve this quandary? Jiang Zemin first tried to have it both ways, improving relations with the United States while simultaneously pumping up nationalism to bolster his domestic standing. But making progress with the United States was stymied by congressional insistence on improvements in human rights, the one area in which the CCP was most afraid to bend. Then several unpredictable events such as the Chinese Embassy bombing in Belgrade triggered destabilizing domestic reactions. China's leaders learned the hard way that when public opinion has been inflamed, international crises can become dangerous domestic crises.

After a heated internal debate, the Chinese government decided that from then on, it would swallow its pride to preserve good relations with the United States and try to minimize the domestic fallout. A major effort to improve crisis management and tone down nationalist rhetoric with the goal of insulating Sino-U.S. relations from the pressures of domestic politics resulted. And superficially, China's relations with the United States improved significantly. Under the surface, however, the Chinese public and the military continue to suspect U.S. intentions and the gap between nationalist public opinion and pragmatic foreign policy remains.

Domestic Considerations

When Jiang Zemin first arrived in Beijing, the political elite were at loggerheads over how to salvage the regime after the close call of Tiananmen and the collapse of the Soviet Union. The ideological diehards wanted the patriotic education campaign, designed to revive young people's support for the Chinese Communist Party, to target the threat of Western capitalism and values. They viewed the United States as an enemy that was trying to do to the CCP regime just what it had done to the Soviet Union—attempting to subvert it by promoting "peaceful evolution."[21]

The Tiananmen protests showed the positive image of American democracy held by Chinese students. The symbol of the student movement was the twenty-one-foot statue of the Goddess of Democracy, modeled on the Statue of Liberty monument in New York Harbor, which the students had wheeled into the square a few days before the PLA tanks entered with guns blazing (see photo in chapter 3).

Although Deng Xiaoping was the architect of China's 1979 diplomatic normalization with the United States, he felt no personal attachment to the relationship with the United States especially after the Tiananmen crisis. Deng saw Washington's hand behind the prodemocracy student movement.[22] Ever the pragmatist though, he also believed that the regime's survival rested on whether it could deliver jobs and better living conditions to people. The Chinese economy was becoming increasingly internationalized and dependent on trade and investment from the United States. Inciting people to hate America and provoking an American backlash would jeopardize China's economic progress and political stability. The quick victory of America's high-tech military against Iraq in Desert Storm (1991) confirmed the judgment that it would be suicidal to overreact against the United States. Deng expressed his prudent attitude in 1991.

China's leader Deng Xiaoping attends a rodeo during his state visit to the United States after the establishment of diplomatic relations between the two countries, February 2, 1979. (Dirck Halstead/Time Life Pictures/Getty Images)

"We should firmly stick to economic construction and continue along this line unless there is large-scale foreign aggression . . . we should not be afraid of peaceful evolution."[23] Directed by Deng, officials instructed the media in 1991 not to use loaded phrases against the United States or attack American leaders by name.[24]

In the end, the patriotic education campaign targeted Japan instead of the United States because the risks of conflict with the United States were just too high. School textbooks since Mao's day taught American history as if it had been written by Karl Marx—as the story of capitalist exploitation of the working class, black people, and the poor. But American history lessons taught in classrooms could never be as affecting as the bitter tales of Japan's wartime occupation that young people learned on the knees of their parents and grandparents. Nevertheless, patriotic education reinforced a general suspicion of foreign intentions toward China that in turn spilled over into public opinion toward the United States.

Within the Communist Party oligarchy, President Jiang Zemin's moves to improve ties with the United States faced opposition from Premier Li Peng, who was reviled by Americans as the "butcher of Beijing" for his role in the Tiananmen crackdown. Jiang didn't establish his full authority over foreign policy until 1997, when Li Peng stepped down after two terms as premier and handed over the Foreign Affairs Leading Small Group to President Jiang. Even after that, Li remained in the Standing Committee of the Politburo and was a voice of skepticism about America until he retired along with Jiang in 2002. In the planning for President Clinton's visit to China in 1998, Vice-Premier Qian Qichen purposely scheduled the meeting to decide key issues at a time when Li Peng was out of the country, according to a policy advisor.

The CCP Propaganda Department remained in Cold War mode, hammering away at what it called American "hegemonism." For the Chinese, "hegemonism" refers to America's desire, as the most powerful nation in the world, to remain dominant by keeping down emerging powers like China. Over the course of the 1980s, use of this Mao-era polemical term in the leading CCP newspaper *People's Daily* diminished. It increased again in the aftermath of Tiananmen, rose after the 1995–96 Taiwan Strait crisis, dropped during the exchange of presidential visits in 1997 through 1998, and then more than doubled during the tension-ridden year of 1999 (see graph in chapter 4).

When I traveled to China during 1997 through 2000 to negotiate with my Chinese counterparts I noticed the disjunction between China's harsh media rhetoric and its flexible diplomacy. After a long day in the bowels of the Foreign Ministry—either over-air-conditioned or overheated depending on the season—and a long evening in the equally uncomfortable U.S. Embassy writing reporting cables to Washington, I returned to the haven of my hotel room and turned on the television. I was struck by the contrast between the television news commentary, which sharply criticized American actions in various parts of the world, and the businesslike tone of the negotiations I had just been part of. The public rhetoric toward the United States and the official interactions with the United States that were hidden from public view were completely at odds. The media, guided by the Communist Party Propaganda Department, criticized the United States to arouse popular support for the Party, while at the same time Chinese diplomats were making compromises with the U.S. government.

"Because the media never criticizes any country other than America, it seems like the only wrong country is the U.S.," said a foreign policy expert. "The media never explains why the U.S. might attack other countries, so it just looks like U.S. bullying."

Satisfying the People's Liberation Army was another constraint Jiang had to deal with, especially when making policy regarding Taiwan. As Robert Suettinger observes, "The military, by tradition and ideological training, was the most nationalistic and xenophobic segment of the regime, and by habit one of its most outspoken."[25] Military writings, consistently more hard-line in their condemnation of American hegemonism than civilian ones, reflect the PLA view that the United States is the greatest long-term threat to national security.[26] The military officers and civilian officials I've interviewed insist that there is a range of opinion within the Chinese military. For one thing, military officers are cautious about picking fights they don't think they can win, as they are in all countries. And many of the most aggressive voices come from civilians, not soldiers. That said, Chinese generals have no qualms about criticizing foreign policy when they think it is too timid. For example, in 1994, eighty generals reportedly wrote a letter to the Central Committee calling on China to "uphold its principles" in the face of American "attempts to subvert, penetrate, interfere in, and undermine China."[27] Diplomats report that in internal meetings PLA officers often criticize them for gutlessness and "selling out the country."

Concessions to Washington, But Not on Human Rights

Despite these domestic constraints, the Chinese leaders made some significant concessions to help improve relations with the United States during the 1990s, particularly concerning issues like nuclear and missile nonproliferation that don't attract much attention from the Chinese public. As one of the five recognized nuclear powers, China became increasingly supportive of the nuclear nonproliferation regime. It also started to realize that its own security interests as an oil importer were jeopardized by missile and nuclear sales to countries like Iran, which destabilized the Middle East by supporting terrorists. American negotiators effectively used the threat of additional sanctions to obtain new commitments from China not to transfer nuclear or missile technologies to countries like Pakistan and Iran. In the lead-up to President Jiang's 1997 state visit, Foreign Minister Qian Qichen pleasantly surprised Secretary of State Madeleine Albright by agreeing to the U.S. request that China stop selling antiship cruise missiles (not regulated by any international rules) to Iran just because they threatened U.S. Navy ships patrolling the Persian Gulf. China also agreed to terminate all nuclear cooperation with Iran, although not required to do so by the Nuclear Nonproliferation Treaty.

In the 1990s, the U.S. Congress started to assert itself as much on foreign policy as on domestic policy, with China policy being a textbook case. Once the risk of nuclear war subsided, Congress saw less reason to defer to the president as the man with his finger on the button. And after Tiananmen, Congress viewed China primarily through human rights lenses. The image of a PLA tank facing one brave student in central Beijing during the Tiananmen massacre had become permanently etched in Americans' minds as a symbol of communist tyranny more vivid than anything we had seen since the anti-Soviet revolts in Hungary or Czechoslovakia. Yet human rights was the one issue on which Chinese officials could bend the least because it was intertwined with the survival of the Communist Party autocracy.

Beginning in 1990, Congress debated every year whether to strip China of its treatment as a normal trading partner (mislabeled "most-favored nation" trading status) because of its human rights abuses. U.S. administrations tried repeatedly to negotiate with Beijing to release people imprisoned for political acts, improve treatment of prisoners, and reform other features of human rights. We set the bar low in the expectation that these steps wouldn't be difficult for the Chinese government to take. Instead of seeking elections or other steps toward democracy that China was sure to reject, we targeted the persecution of political dissidents, which was also the number one issue for influential human rights groups like Amnesty International and Human Rights Watch, the mass media, and Congress. Congress threatened punitive tariffs on Chinese imports if China didn't show tangible progress on human rights.

Even so, the Chinese repeatedly ignored the U.S. government's ultimatums.[28] If China did free a political critic (e.g., Fang Lizhi, Wei Jingsheng, or Wang Dan), and allow him or her to leave China, it usually did so after the congressional debate or summit meeting, not before—to make clear it was not caving into American bullying. The timing of the gesture was designed to protect the Chinese leader who approved it from being disgraced in the eyes of his Politburo colleagues. Even China's signature on the United Nations Covenant on Civil and Political Rights, negotiated ahead of time, had to come after Clinton's 1998 visit to China.

Although most Chinese don't know the names of political prisoners or care much about their fate (news of political cases is always blacked out of the domestic media), Chinese leaders nevertheless worry that information about the releases could leak out and embolden other groups to challenge the Communist Party. A political decision to release a prisoner also encroaches on the prerogatives of the powerful internal security agencies within the Party and the government. Whenever I protested to Chinese diplomats about arrests of individuals for purely political offenses and reminded them about how damaging such arrests were to U.S.-China relations, they threw up their hands. "The Foreign Ministry can't do anything about it. The Ministries of State Security and Public Security are much more powerful. They won't even give us information about the cases," they complained.

President Bill Clinton, eager to end the annual China bashing in Congress over China's trade status and confident in his persuasive powers, took on his own shoulders the responsibility of improving human rights conditions in China when he came into office. The administration announced in 1993 that from now on the extension of China's trade status would be done not by congressional action, but by executive order, with human rights conditions clearly attached. (The Congress would still have the power to vote on the president's annual decision). When the Chinese government still failed to meet the minimal conditions—and actually made new arrests—the Clinton administration faced reality and announced in 1994 that it was decoupling trade and human rights issues in order to "place our [U.S.-China] relationship into a larger and more productive framework."[29]

Congress continued to press human rights causes like Tibet. Foreign Relations Committee chairman Jesse Helms—the powerful Senator who controlled the confirmation of all diplomatic appointments—ordered the State Department to create the post of American Ambassador to Tibet even though the U.S. government has long recognized Tibet as part of China. Helms finally agreed to a compromise that would create a "special coordinator" for Tibet, but his staff insisted that the State Department appoint the Tibet coordinator at the very moment when Jiang Zemin was paying his first state visit to the United States in October 1997. I had the awkward responsibility of informing Foreign Minister Qian Qichen about the appointment.

Losing Face to the United States

Jiang Zemin straddled the line between trying to look strong domestically and developing friendly relations with Washington. But this uphill battle was shaken by a series of incidents provoked by domestic politics in the United States that no Chinese leader could have predicted, much less controlled. Each of these events dealt a stinging slap in the face to Jiang and to Chinese pride, discredited China's experts on America as "America lovers,"[30] and made it hard for Jiang to defend the relationship domestically.

The Olympic Bid

What better way to revive national pride and popular identification with the Communist Party after Tiananmen than to bring the Olympics to China? Japan's economic miracle began when it hosted the Olympics in

1964, and Korea's emergence as an economic power was heralded by its hosting the games in 1988. Now it was China's turn.

China launched its bid to host the 2000 Olympic Games at the 1990 Asian Games in Beijing. During the closing ceremony, a huge banner appeared in the stands that read, "With the success of the Asian Games, we look forward to hosting the Olympic Games."[31] For the next three years, billboards with slogans like "A more open China awaits the 2000 Olympics" appeared everywhere. The government organized massive rallies with thousands of people at historic sites like the Temple of Heaven and the Great Wall to excite the public and demonstrate to the International Olympic Committee the widespread support for the bid.[32] The Communist Party put its prestige on the line. Every time I drove into Beijing from the airport and saw the 2000 Olympics billboards and signs in the taxicabs, I worried, "What if China doesn't win the bid?"

One month before the International Olympic Committee decision, the U.S. House of Representatives passed a bill opposing China's bid. The bill's sponsor, Representative Tom Lantos said, "China's abominable human rights record violates the spirit of the games and should disqualify Beijing from consideration." Lantos, the only Holocaust survivor serving in Congress, said that China shouldn't receive the international esteem that Hitler and the Nazi regime obtained by hosting the 1936 Olympics.[33] American groups like Human Rights Watch campaigned hard to persuade the International Olympic Committee (IOC) to reject China's bid. But the Chinese government, confident that it had sewed up the votes on the IOC (for one thing, the president of the IOC had publicly discounted the importance of human rights issues in the decision), paid little heed to the non-binding congressional action. China's overconfidence and blindness to its political handicap were reflected in its choice of Chen Xitong, the hardline mayor of Beijing who had played a central role in the violent suppression of the Tiananmen demonstrators, as the head of its Olympic bid.

When the IOC rejected Beijing's bid and awarded the games to Sydney by two votes, the Chinese government and the public reacted with shock and anger. They blamed Americans for campaigning against China's bid.[34] (In fact, it was later revealed that the Australians had offered bribes to two IOC members.[35]) Jiang Zemin, still struggling to establish himself as Deng's successor, lost face.

The Chinese government, smarting from the IOC's rejection, didn't compete for the 2004 games. When China won the competition to host the 2008 Olympics by a large margin, it celebrated with a huge nationally televised rally in Beijing, complete with lavish fireworks. I happened to be in the city to experience the excitement. Although the celebration was stage-managed, the public elation and sense of vindication were genuine. Still, the earlier rejection left a lasting legacy of resentment toward the United States for trying to rob China of its Olympic glory.

A U.S. Visa for Taiwan President Lee Teng-hui

The Clinton administration humiliated Jiang Zemin and sparked a Chinese political crisis in June 1995 when it permitted the Taiwan president to visit the United States. The visit made Jiang, who had offered a conciliatory proposal to Taiwan only six months before, look like he'd been duped. The hawks in the People's Liberation Army and the Communist Party lambasted the Foreign Ministry and Jiang for misreading American intentions and harming the country. They called for resignations and demanded a forceful reaction against the United States and Taiwan. Province and ministry officials pleaded for clear direction from the center about the correct approach to take to the Taiwan issue. Jiang reportedly made a self-criticism to the Politburo and acknowledged his disillusionment with the United States. The country, he said, needs to be more "sober-minded . . . and understand that the United States and Western forces will never give up their strategy of Westernizing and disintegrating China."[36] As Deng Xiaoping lay gravely ill, the controversy threatened to provoke a succession struggle within the Communist Party.

Because the internal situation was so precarious, Party leaders didn't allow the public to go to the streets to vent its anger at Taipei or Washington. Tiananmen had taught them that the combination of leadership conflict with mass protest could be fatal. Protestors, spontaneously or at the instigation of one of the elite protagonists, might have taken a U-turn and toppled the fragile regime. Jiang Zemin decided it was safer to appease the hawks in the army, the government, and the public by holding live-fire missile exercises toward Taiwan and risking a war with America than allow public protests—an ominous precedent for future Taiwan-related crises.

In the aftermath of the 1995–96 Taiwan Strait crisis, "Sino-U.S. relations [sank] to their lowest level since the normalization of diplomatic relations between the two countries in 1979," according to the official press.[37] Jiang Zemin asserted, "The United States is responsible for the current problems in Sino-U.S. relations . . . [and should] take definite actions to remove problems lying between the two nations."[38] Newspaper articles lashed out at America for "hegemonism and power politics" and for using Taiwan to contain China and keep it weak.[39] And students and policy experts became convinced that the United States was determined to keep the island of Taiwan separated from the Mainland in order to keep the PRC from growing stronger. To try to reverse deteriorating Sino-U.S. relations the two governments organized state visits between their presidents, President Jiang to the United States in 1997 and President Clinton to China in 1998.

The WTO Fiasco

Premier Zhu Rongji's scheduled visit to the United States in April 1999 came at a tense time in Sino-American relations. American Air Force jets under NATO command were bombing Yugoslavia, and the U.S. government had accused Wen Ho Lee, a Taiwan-born scientist at the Los Alamos National Laboratory, of passing nuclear secrets to China (accusations that ultimately were rejected by the American courts). Negotiations on China's accession to the World Trade Organization, having gone nowhere during thirteen years of on-again, off-again talks, now were on the brink of success and were expected to culminate in a bilateral agreement between the two countries during Zhu's visit.[40] Although Zhu was apprehensive about the timing of the trip, he recognized the importance of WTO membership for promoting China's domestic economic reforms and making its firms internationally competitive. Li Peng and a number of other leaders urged postponing the trip, but Jiang Zemin disagreed, and so Zhu departed for Washington. When he arrived, he said, "I was really reluctant to come . . . the current political atmosphere in the United States is so anti-China, I really lack the guts to pay the visit. But President Jiang decided that I should come according to schedule."[41]

The afternoon before Zhu's arrival in Washington, President Clinton, after meeting with his advisors, decided not to sign the WTO agreement during the visit. In a speech given that same morning he had said, "The bottom line is this: if China is willing to play by the global rules of trade, it would be an inexplicable mistake for the United States to say no."[42] But Clinton's domestic advisors, including National Economic Council head Gene Sperling and Treasury Secretary Robert Rubin (Rubin's views, in particular, carried a lot of weight with the president), made a case that critics in Congress would assume that any agreement "rushed to conclusion" in time for Zhu's visit must have given away too much.[43] Congress would have to, in effect, ratify the WTO agreement by voting to give China permanent normal trade relations. No matter how good the substance of the deal, congressional approval was going to be an uphill battle, as all trade legislation is. Better to wait until a month or so after the visit, they argued, and then finalize the deal.

The China hands in the government, backed up by Secretary of State Madeleine Albright, National Security Advisor Sandy Berger, and U.S. Trade Representative Charlene Barshefsky who had negotiated the agreement, argued strenuously that any delay could cause us to lose what was an excellent deal. If we bailed on the proposed agreement now, Zhu Rongji would face censure at home and China's offers might very well disappear once Chinese interest groups found out about them. The clever tactic proposed by the White House advisors, initially conceived to avoid losing a congressional battle, ignored the domestic political context on the other side.

President Clinton told Zhu the bad news when they met informally in the White House residence the evening before their formal session. The next day the American side compounded the damage by releasing the draft agreement on the Internet to gain support from our own industrial and agricultural interest groups.

The premier and the rest of the Chinese team were visibly upset. They disavowed the document posted on the Internet. At his joint press conference with President Clinton, Zhu came out and said that the agreement hadn't been signed not because the two sides hadn't agreed on the terms,

U.S. President Bill Clinton and Chinese Premier Zhu Rongji confer at their joint news conference at the White House, April 8, 1999. (Pool/Getty Images)

but because of "the political atmosphere."[44] As the American representative accompanying Zhu on his travels I squirmed with mortification as the premier spoke bluntly to groups in New York, Boston, Chicago, and Denver about his disappointment and the benefits American business could have gained from the deal. On the plane, the Chinese group anxiously pored over the Hong Kong press to get a reading of how the Chinese public was reacting to Clinton's slap in Zhu's face.

President Clinton, recognizing his mistake almost immediately, telephoned Zhu in New York City. Hoping that Clinton might be able to pull a rabbit out of the hat, I stood at Zhu's side in a small room at the Waldorf Astoria as he took the call. President Clinton proposed that the Chinese team complete the negotiations while Zhu continued his travels in Canada so that the deal could be concluded before he departed from North America. Zhu sadly rejected the idea as infeasible because it would be too rude to the Canadians who were also in WTO negotiations with China.[45]

When Premier Zhu Rongji returned to Beijing, he was met by a firestorm of criticism from agriculture and industry, the Internet public, and other leaders. Zhu was attacked as a "national traitor," and the WTO commitments he had made were condemned as the contemporary version of the "Twenty-One Demands," the notorious agreement imposed by the Japanese on China during World War I.[46] With Li Peng in the forefront, the CCP leaders accused Zhu of being naïve about the United States and selling out China's interests. Jiang Zemin, who had approved China's offers ahead of time, shifted the blame to Zhu. "A field commander must make decisions, even if these go against the king's orders," he said.[47] According to the account of one of the premier's advisors, his boss was the victim of Jiang's "mean power game."[48]

By a miserable coincidence, it was just a month after this debacle that the United States accidentally bombed the Chinese Embassy in Belgrade and sent U.S.-China relations into a tailspin.[49] President Clinton implored President Jiang to salvage relations by concluding the WTO negotiation as soon as possible. It took a meeting between Clinton and Jiang at the margin of the Asia-Pacific Economic Cooperation forum in Auckland, New Zealand, two phone calls from Clinton to Jiang, and a trip by Treasury Secretary Larry Summers to meet Zhu in China, to convince the Chinese leaders to resume the negotiations. Public and elite suspicions of American intentions—and the political risk to China's leaders of another failure—were high.

The last round of negotiations in November 1999—in which I participated—was harrowing. The Chinese claimed their pound of flesh for the April humiliation by retracting a number of previous commitments. Several times our team members packed our bags and prepared to leave. One surreal night, the Chinese trade officials locked the gate to stop us from leaving the ministry. Finally, Zhu Rongji broke the impasse by mustering the support of Jiang and other Politburo Standing Committee members for the critical compromises and a final agreement. (Beijing University scholar Wang Yong notes that separate side-payments to economic interest groups in China were required for Zhu to impose the agreement on them.[50]) After throwing away the WTO agreement in April, we retrieved it in November by the skin of our teeth, and on somewhat worse terms.[51]

Mistrust of America

The cumulative effect of the 1990s shocks to Sino-U.S. relations was to deepen mistrust of American intentions at both the mass and elite levels. In the words of one Chinese living in the United States, "When I came to the U.S. from China in 1996, the general Chinese public was very friendly toward the U.S. and admired Americans in almost every way, for good or bad. In the last ten years, this friendly feeling has been incrementally reversed."

Because of the lack of reliable nationwide survey research or any information about baseline attitudes before the mid-1990s, it is impossible to draw definitive conclusions about how these shocks affected public opinion toward the United States. The only scientific data about attitudes toward the United States over time comes from the Beijing Area Study, analyzed by Alastair Iain Johnston, which shows that friendly feelings toward the United States declined markedly from 1998 to 1999, recovered slightly in 2000, and then declined again from 2000 to 2001 (probably in reaction to the military plane collision in April 2001).[52] Johnston attributes the loss of goodwill to the external shocks to the relationship.[53] He found no evidence that that younger people were more negative toward the United States than older ones, but he did find that the better educated, more cosmopolitan middle class were less hostile toward America than lower-income people.[54]

Other less scientific surveys conducted only among young people showed more dramatic alienation from America. Based on more than 100,000 questionnaires distributed to its young readers in the newspaper, a national poll conducted right after the Taiwan president visited the United States in 1995 by the *China Youth Daily* found that 87.1 percent of respondents saw the United States as the country "least friendly" to China, 57.2 percent as the country toward which they felt most negative, and 74.1 percent as the country with the greatest influence on China.[55] A survey of high school students in six large cities done right after the U.S. bombing of the Chinese Embassy found that the United States had the highest negative rating of any country, higher even than Japan.[56] An unscientific survey by Chinese scholars organized by the Kettering Foundation also conducted after the bombing found positive opinions of American domestic achievements but negative ones of its international behavior, a pattern familiar from other countries.[57]

Six young authors wrote a 1996 best seller, *The China That Can Say No* that emotionally describes how events like the loss of the Olympics and the Taiwan president's visit to America disillusioned them about American ideals over the decade. The book struck a chord with the public—one survey found it was the most influential book published after 1993.[58] The authors wrote a sequel a few years later—*The China That Still Can Say No*—that inspired numerous books of the same genre.

The 1999 Debate

The 1999 summer seaside session of the CCP leadership was filled with tension. In just half a year, the Party had been humiliated and shaken by a series of unforeseen events that shattered what little confidence it had: Clinton's deferral of the WTO agreement, the Falun Gong sit-in, the Belgrade embassy bombing and student demonstrations, Taiwan president Lee Teng-hui's statement about "special state-to-state relations." There was strong sentiment in favor of some dramatic military gesture against Taiwan, to show that China would not be pushed around. But in the end, cooler heads prevailed. Jiang Zemin managed to postpone any use of force against Taiwan by appeasing the military with more budget increases. He also won agreement, despite Li Peng's reported efforts to the contrary, that Deng's optimistic assessment that "peace and development remain the main trends" still held despite all the discouraging events. Among academics and researchers, however, the debate about American international strategy continued, with the range of views skewed toward the pessimistic.[59] Even the most benign interpretations of American behavior said that the United States engaged with China in order to restrain it domestically and internationally. Wang Jisi, one of the leading Chinese experts on America, put it bluntly. "For more than half a century since the founding of the People's Republic of China (PRC), it is still widely believed among China's political elites that the United States, joined by other hostile external forces, is intent on efforts to conquer, divide, destabilize, and demonize China."[60] Chu Shulong, another prominent America hand, wrote that U.S. strategy is "to Westernize China," and that "U.S. strategists and politicians firmly believe that the phenomenon of 'the fall of the Berlin Wall' will happen in China sooner or later."[61] For elites as well as masses, the Belgrade bombing, coming on top of the previous incidents, shattered any remaining illusions about America's good intentions toward China.[62]

Crisis Management

The crises during the 1990s taught China's leaders that arousing the public's nationalist feelings is not cost free. When an unexpected international event injures Chinese national pride, domestic reactions can spiral out of control and provoke violent conflict both at home and abroad. And since they couldn't count on the United States, which was hamstrung by its own domestic politics, to carry the burden of preserving good relations, they would have to do more of it themselves. Beginning in 1999, the Chinese leaders tried to subdue public opinion and learn to react to crises in a more rational manner. The CCP's new guideline for international affairs was "cool observation and calm dealing."[63]

China's leaders recognized as early as Tiananmen that they had a crisis management problem and quietly started studying how to fix it.[64] Air Force colonel Hu Ping published a 1993 book, *International Conflict Analysis and Crisis Management*, which synthesized American research on how successfully to manage different kinds of domestic and international crises.[65] The book includes handy dos and don'ts like "preserve limited goals, sacrifice unlimited ones," "avoid excessively ideological 'lock-in' positions," and "think ahead about the unintended consequences of your actions." After the Taiwan Strait crisis of 1995–96, the China Foundation for International and Strategic Studies, an influential think-tank affiliated with the PLA, initiated a project on crisis management limited to international crises like the Cuban missile crisis. After the Belgrade bombing, however, the Chinese government pursued knowledge on crisis management with greater urgency, permitting experts to analyze Chinese crises as well as international ones, and involving a number of different think-tanks including the China Institute for Contemporary International Relations, a think-tank connected to government intelligence agencies. The 2003 SARS epidemic served as an additional warning about the importance of crisis management, according to Xue Lan, the Tsinghua University professor who is a leader in the national study of the subject.[66] America hand Wang Jisi repeatedly called for strengthening crisis prevention and management "to prevent any abrupt incident from affecting bilateral ties" between China and the United States.[67]

The experts involved in these studies identified several big problems with China's crisis management practices. First, it's hard to get a timely authoritative decision out of the Chinese system. The Chinese government makes decisions by consensus. As one military officer put it, "no individual wants to be the one held responsible."[68] To make interagency coordination more efficient, China established a National Security Leading Small Group in 2000. It includes the internal security departments as well as the military and Foreign Ministry. But the Politburo Standing Committee members, only four of whom sit in the group, refuse to delegate crisis decisions to it, so the NSLSG simply adds another layer to the process.

Second, coordination with the Communist Party Propaganda Department is poor. The Propaganda Department goes off on its own and lays down a line for the media that can complicate the resolution of the crisis. "It was a mistake in the Belgrade bombing and EP-3 crises to come out right away saying that the U.S. did it on purpose, that it was the U.S. fault," according to one Chinese expert. "That got us into a 'commitment trap' too early."

Third, according to the same expert, "The leaders have to balance domestic and international pressures. There is too much information, but a lack of critical information and uncertainty is great. The leaders don't know the consequences of their decisions." The leaders' first instinct is to be responsive to what they think the public is feeling. Consider, for example, the initial statements after the Belgrade bombing. "The leaders knew how people felt and they felt the pressure and had to respond. They had to show people that they would maintain international respect for China. Even then, people thought the statement was too insipid."

Another Accident, Another Crisis

Chinese leaders' determination to react calmly to crises was tested when another unfortunate accident put China and America into an eyeball-to-eyeball confrontation once again. The morning of April 1, 2001, a lumbering U.S. turbo-prop EP-3 military surveillance plane with twenty-four in crew was flying one of its regular reconnaissance missions over international waters in the South China Sea seventy miles southeast of the large Chinese island of Hainan. A PLA Naval Air Force F-8II fighter jet, instead of making an interception at a safe distance—the normal minuet of militaries as they interact in international space—collided with the American spy plane and crashed into the sea, killing the Chinese pilot. The American plane, seriously damaged, radioed a Mayday and limped into the PLA Navy airfield on Hainan where its crew was held prisoner for eleven days.

According to four policy advisors who participated in meetings during the crisis, China's immediate reaction was both too slow (because it took some time to contact Jiang Zemin, who was traveling outside Beijing, and get him back to the city) and too dominated by the military (because it was their plane involved). The information on the accident came from the Hainan naval air base, whose interest was in protecting its own pilots from blame. The PLA said unequivocally, just as it had in the Belgrade embassy bombing, that the American military had caused the incident. The government adopted the military version as the official version of the incident and designated the pilot, Wang Wei, as a martyr.[69] The very first Chinese statement, issued thirteen hours after the collision, said the American EP-3 had "suddenly veered" toward the Chinese fighter jet and crashed into it. It also accused the American plane of entering China's airspace without permission. The PLA did not permit any U.S. contact with the American crew for almost forty hours, until midnight, the night of April 3.

When Deputy Secretary of State Richard Armitage tried to open communication by telephoning Vice-Premier Qian Qichen, Qian refused to take the call. "How could he take the call? Qian is too astute to take too much risk on to himself," said a participant who blamed President Bush for not calling President Jiang himself.

After President Bush made a public statement calling for the safe return of the crew, Jiang felt he had to make a public statement too. He locked China into a set of demands by insisting the United States take full responsibility for the collision and halt its surveillance flights. The Chinese Foreign Ministry spokesman added a demand for an apology from the United States and claimed that the United States had violated international law and threatened China's sovereignty with its "spy flights" over waters close to China that fall under its exclusive economic zone.[70] This extensive claim of sovereignty over the two-hundred-mile exclusive economic zone (which according to the law of the sea gives a state special rights over marine resources) was asserted by the Propaganda Ministry and the military and wasn't coordinated with the rest of the government, according to interview accounts. Later, the Foreign Ministry and State Council Information Office advised editors to drop it because it didn't accord with international law and they "didn't want the world to think that China claimed that far out."

"The decision to demand an apology probably came from Jiang himself or his staff," speculated one participant. "Once Jiang insisted on an apology, we had to find a way to satisfy it." The Chinese rebuffed oral statements of regret for the loss of life by Secretary of State Colin Powell and President Bush as inadequate, and insisted on a formal written apology in order to show the public that their leader could defend China's honor.

According to a Chinese analysis, the crisis would have been easier to resolve if it had received less publicity and been handled in a more low-key way. The two sides "should have investigated the cause jointly and drawn a conclusion later."[71]

"In the first few days the leaders were tempted to take a dramatic public position against the U.S. and considered a big public rally at the Great Hall of the People," said one advisor. In the fevered discussions about what to do, the military and the internal security bureaucracies pressed for a more extreme response. Some military officers said that the pilot in the plane that accompanied Wang Wei's plane should have attacked the EP-3; others talked about preparing to fight the United States. "We're a country of laws, we should put the American crew on trial in our courts," the internal security officials said. "Or we should release the crew gradually over time, with the women first, then the rest of the crew, and finally the pilot." The experts from think-tanks advised restraint. "We will get the same international reaction if we hold one person as if we hold them all," they said. "Instead we should get the crew out quickly and keep the plane." They had to frame their advice with a lot of tough rhetoric against the United States to protect themselves from being attacked as weak. "The internal negotiations were much more difficult than the negotiations with the U.S.," said one advisor.

The PLA held the American crew for eleven days, until it received a written apology. It refused to allow the United States to repair the plane and fly it home, and insisted instead that it be disassembled and transported as freight. A senior PLA general explained, "We couldn't agree to let it fly out because public opinion wouldn't accept it. But we agreed to let it be shipped out in parts. We didn't go to extremes."

Still, Jiang made a perceptible effort to prevent the situation from spinning out of control internationally or domestically. "Jiang was clear from the beginning about not doing anything to negatively impact the long-term relationship with the U.S.," said a policy advisor. According to a military officer, "Jiang Zemin didn't want things to get out of control. The upper level was very cautious in this crisis. They didn't want to harm Sino-American relations." From the American perspective, however, the Chinese side hardly looked cautious. The Bush administration (especially the Pentagon) and the public were steaming that the Chinese were holding hostage our servicemen and -women (although the administration carefully avoided calling the American crew "hostages"). K-Mart received thousands of calls from angry consumers demanding the chain store stop selling Chinese goods.[72]

I was in Shanghai right after the accident, and the emotions it evoked from university students and faculty were palpable. One professor I had known for years had difficulty speaking civilly to me. Another professor had just come back from speaking at an inland university where the students were all demanding a military response. "They said they were ready to die to defend the honor of the nation." A Shanghai physicist brave enough to try to explain to students and colleagues the technical reasons why the U.S. plane, larger and slower than the Chinese fighter, could not have caused the accident, said he met heavy resistance to his analysis.[73] A PLA colonel I talked to later told me that military officers "were angry that the government was bowing down to America," and that "if the university authorities hadn't stopped the students from taking to the streets, there would have been demonstrations everywhere."

After the incident was resolved, Secretary of Defense Donald Rumsfeld revealed in a press conference that pilot Wang Wei was known to the American EP-3 crews as a *Top Gun*–style hotdogger. Just weeks before the collision he had taunted the U.S. crews by flying by and pressing a piece of paper with his e-mail address on it up to the window of his plane. (Rumsfeld showed the photograph to the TV cameras.) In late December 2000, the United States had complained to the Chinese government about PLA pilots flying too close.[74] The PLA Navy's more aggressive interceptions may have been in retaliation for the increased frequency of American surveillance flights over the waters south of China during the second half of 2000.[75]

The public reaction, according to the participants, was driven less by the faulty military intelligence about the American plane crashing into the Chinese one than by the alarm people felt at the sudden discovery that the U.S. military regularly had been flying so close to China. (To gain a sense of China's perspective on the incident, imagine the reaction were Americans to learn that the Chinese Air Force was patrolling regularly off the California shoreline.)

To prevent a repeat of the kind of anti-American demonstrations that followed the Belgrade embassy bombing, the government ordered university authorities to keep students on campus. The Propaganda Department directed the media to exercise restraint in reporting the incident. (According to a Chinese study of the crisis, "The instructions for the official mainstream media were much better than in the 'Embassy bombing' incident."[76]) The State Council Information Office held background briefings to help editors understand that the EP-3 collision was a kind of traffic accident, not a deliberate attack on China. The official press stressed the importance of relations with the United States and reassured readers that the majority of Americans were friendly toward China, but at the same time it demanded that the United States make amends for the accident.[77] Xinhua didn't report aggressive statements by President Bush or the commander of the U.S.

Front page of *World News Journal*, a Chinese newspaper, following the collision of a Chinese fighter jet and a U.S. EP-3 spy plane. The headline reads: "American military plane don't even think about flying home," May 12, 2001. (Kevin Lee/ Getty Images)

Pacific Command, Dennis Blair, a journalism professor said, "Because if they printed them people would see the contrast between Bush who was strong and Jiang who was weak." The tabloids dramatized the crisis to attract readers (e.g., *Beijing Youth Daily* ran photographs of the damaged American plane under the headline, "The Evidence of Arrogance," on April 4), but were directed by Party authorities to use less enflamed rhetoric than they had used during the Belgrade embassy crisis.

The Chinese leaders asked the diplomats in the Foreign Ministry—not the PLA—to take the lead in negotiating an agreement with the American side.[78] Once Jiang obtained a consensus not to do anything to damage relations with the United States, he departed for a trip to Europe, delegating leadership to Vice President Hu Jintao and Vice-Premier Qian Qichen, but in fact, he managed the crisis from abroad with the foreign minister who accompanied him on the trip. While traveling, Jiang hinted that both sides might have caused the accident by saying that China asked for an apology because it was what people say to one another when they bump into one another in the street.[79]

Most significantly, the Chinese side agreed to a diplomatic compromise to resolve the crisis. The American side provided a written statement that said it was "very sorry" (*qianyi*) for the loss of the pilot and for entering Chinese airspace without clearance to land in Hainan but did not use the word apologize (*daoqian*). The United States did not agree to cease its surveillance flights. The America hands advising the Chinese government sold the compromise by showing that the first definition of "sorry" in the concise *Oxford English Dictionary* is "a way to apologize." The successful outcome of the negotiation also was due to the diplomatic skills and credibility of American ambassador Joseph Prueher, a retired admiral who had spent the first twenty-four years of his service in the U.S. Navy as a fighter pilot.

Blocked from acting out their anger toward the Americans and dissatisfied with the passivity of the government, young people vented their frustration on the Internet. As the journalism professor put it, "Because the print media failed to follow public sentiment, the Internet comments turned against the government." He gave an example. "One day the Foreign Ministry spokesman said, 'We have to take an appropriate [*tuoshan,* which implies being careful] position on the collision.' He was strongly criticized online, 'Why do we have to be 'appropriate'?' When the spokesman talked the next day, he didn't use the word 'appropriate.'" A content analysis of one Web site, Strong Nation Forum, run by *People's Daily,* found that during April 1 through 13, 63 percent of the postings were about the collision, and 79 percent of those were strongly nationalistic. Some accused the Chinese government of acting like the Qing Dynasty, too cowardly to take a stand against foreign aggression.[80] People criticized Jiang, saying that he "turned on the left signal light but turned right" (meaning that he sounded like a revolutionary but acted like an America lover) and "Mao Zedong would have been stronger."

"These two events [the embassy bombing and the plane collision] showed us that when you are strong, you can do whatever you want. They laid the foundation for our hope that China will rise so we won't have to experience such bad things again," a Beijing college student told me.

Sino-U.S. Relations are the Best in History

Secretary of State Colin Powell, in a remarkable 2003 statement, declared that U.S.-China relations were the best they'd been since Nixon's visit in 1972.[81] When I asked an influential Chinese America hand if he agreed with this assessment, he went even further. "Best in history," he replied, "if you consider the economic ties too and the fact that under Chiang Kai-shek [pre-1949] China and the U.S. weren't really equal partners."

Relations between China and the United States during the first decade of the twenty-first century are indeed much smoother than those of the last decade of the twentieth century. Both sides are responsible for the improvement.

The terrorist attacks of September 11, 2001, on New York City and Washington, D.C., focused the fears of Americans on the real and immediate threat of Al-Qaeda and related terrorist networks instead of the possible

China's President Jiang Zemin greets U.S. President George W. Bush at the meeting of Asia-Pacific Economic Cooperation (APEC) leaders in Shanghai, October 21, 2001. (Joe Marquette/AP Photo)

future threat of a rising China. In American politics, relations with China always do better out of the political spotlight than when voters and politicians are paying a lot of attention to them. "Bin Laden saved China," one Beijing student observed. "Before 9/11 China was acting aggressive and provoking the U.S. But then the terrorists became America's number one enemy, and China came back to 'taoguang yanghui' [Deng Xiaoping's low key foreign policy]."

In China, Jiang Zemin and Hu Jintao learned over the course of the turbulent 1990s that arousing the public against the United States carries real risks. American politics are volatile. Accidents happen. Crises occur. And stirring up the emotions of the public makes it much harder to make the compromises necessary to resolve a crisis before it causes domestic upheaval or war. Economic progress and continued Communist Party rule, moreover, depend on not provoking an American backlash. To accomplish this, China must do everything possible to reassure Americans than China is not a threat. And it must protect relations with the United States from the nationalist public, deflecting its attention instead to Japan, which is less crucial to China's stability.

Kinder, Gentler Propaganda

The CCP leaders instructed the Propaganda Department to tone down the anti-American rhetoric in the mass media beginning at the end of 1999. Stirring up popular antipathy toward America had complicated their tasks of managing crises and steering a steady foreign policy course. Foreign Ministry officials felt pressured by the public criticisms that deluged them by mail, phone, and the Internet for not standing up to the United States. The name calling in Chinese newspapers, reported by foreign journalists abroad, also was making Americans suspect that China's true intentions were not friendly. The Clinton administration had started to complain about the hostile media rhetoric, and the Bush administration continued to do so. After the U.S. ambassador complained about the biased version of American history being taught to students, the Education Ministry revised the high-school textbooks.

The impact of the new propaganda line was immediately apparent in the media. Alastair Iain Johnston's content analysis of Chinese journals shows a clear reduction of use of the negatively loaded term "multipolarity" and an increase in the use of the more evenhanded term "globalization."[82] My analysis shows that mentions of "hegemonism" in *People's Daily* also have declined since 2000, with an uptick after the 2001 airplane collision much slighter than the one after the Belgrade bombing (see Figure 4.1).

Newspapers toed the more positive line when they reported on President Bush's November 2005 visit to China. *Global Times* ran a picture of president and Mrs. Bush surrounded by smiling Chinese children waving American flags under a headline, "Bush's Third China Visit for Cooperation," and an article that noted that "Bush has paid more visits to China than did his predecessor and his attitude toward China has a more pragmatic spirit."[83] *People's Daily* did not report in its Chinese version, but only in its English version, on Bush's speech delivered in Japan before arriving in Beijing, which criticized China—both the substance and the location of the speech would have angered Chinese readers.

Whereas once the Chinese press leapt upon every distasteful word out of Washington and heaped condemnation on it, after 1999 it often didn't react at all. The CCP leaders started to play deaf in the hopes that the restive public wouldn't hear anything either. To protect the relationship, they ordered newspapers and Web sites to play down American actions that would upset people. For example, when in 2002 Chinese engineers discovered listening devices on the Boeing 767 airplane intended to be President Jiang's Air Force One—devices that may have been planted when the plane was refitted in Texas—the government kept the story out of the media and ordered Web masters to remove comments about it.[84] Embarrassing gaffes during the ceremony welcoming President Hu Jintao to the White House in 2006—the interpreter mistranslated China's name as the Republic of China, which is Taiwan's name, and a reporter from a Falun Gong newspaper shouted out at Hu—were excised from all Chinese television and media reports.

However, now that the public gets more of its information from the commercialized media and the Internet than from the official press, this shift in the Party's line on the United States was not as effective as it once might have been. A PLA colonel observed, "In the 1970s we could normalize relations with the U.S. even when the U.S. was so hostile to China because we could educate the public. Now we can't. It's too late."

Learning to Live with the Hegemon

Since 1999, Chinese foreign policymakers have bent over backward to avoid public fights with Washington that would anger the Chinese public as well as the Americans. The goal is not only to convince Americans that China is not a threat, but also to prevent anti-American sentiments in China from disrupting relations with the United States or from turning against the CCP regime. In recent years, the Chinese government has found it safer to quietly accommodate U.S. policies than to get into a high-profile battle. It would rather hide its conflicts with Washington from the public than highlight them. This may be why the Chinese side declined the American request for a live televised press conference like the Clinton-Jiang one when President Bush visited Beijing in 2005.

In a remarkably self-conscious way, Jiang Zemin, Hu Jintao, and their colleagues set about trying to repair the dangerous misperceptions that are created when a rising power challenges the dominant power. In two special study sessions (November 2003 and February 2004) the entire twenty-four-member Politburo heard from academic experts about the rise and fall of nations since the fifteenth century and the implications for China's current situation.[85] The negative examples of Germany and Japan were discussed. The lesson drawn from the fall of the Soviet Union was that if you try to challenge the United States militarily, you will bankrupt yourself and collapse from internal problems.

The slogan "peaceful rising" was designed by Hu Jintao's advisor Zheng Bijian primarily to ease American fears of a China threat. A Shanghai academic explained that the slogan "should have a positive ring in U.S. ears. It delivers a message: China does not base its growth on challenging U.S. authority."[86]

Beijing University scholar Jia Qingguo notes that the Chinese government "has tried to limit the damage to Sino-American relations concerning issues about which the two countries do have significant conflicts of interests and views.[87] The American invasion of Iraq strained Sino-U.S. relations beginning in 2002. But Jiang Zemin was determined not to let Iraq get in the way of improving relations with the United States—or of his 2002 farewell visit to the Bush ranch in Crawford, Texas. Therefore Beijing took a low-key approach to the war in Iraq, allowing the media to express different points of view and people to organize both pro- and antiwar petitions on the Internet.[88] As America expert Wang Jisi described it, China's foreign policy approach was to stick to its principles on trying to work the crisis through the U.N. but "not engage in head-on diplomatic conflict with the U.S., with the result that the U.S. government further understood that China does not deliberately damage U.S. strategic interests."[89] The experts who appear on TV as commentators about the war in Iraq are instructed by the Propaganda Department not to mention Bush, Cheney, or Rumsfeld by name or criticize the U.S. military operation.

According to a policy advisor who was helping prepare President Hu for his visit to the United States in September 2005 (because of hurricane Katrina, the trip was limited to a meeting with President Bush in New York City), Hu intended to articulate a new set of "three nos" to reassure the American president: China will not challenge the United States globally, China will not seek to exclude the United States from Asia, and

China will not confront the United States on bilateral issues like trade. In short, the new rules were "no challenge, no exclusion, no confrontation."

International relations experts published defenses of China's accommodating attitude toward America. They said that although the principle of resolutely opposing hegemonism must be maintained, "opposing hegemonism does not mean that China should clash and conflict head-on at any time with all countries pursuing a hegemonistic policy."[90] It must have been frustrating for nationalist commentators to hold their tongues against the United States at a time when it was acting more "hegemonistically" than ever in the Middle East. As one professor at the CCP Party School wrote, the Western critics of the American intervention in Iraq have adopted the term "unilateralism" instead of "hegemonism." "Even though it represents a criticism, it is far more diplomatic." China's opposition to hegemonism also should "refrain from becoming emotional, simplistic and one-sided . . . stress restraint and tactics . . . stress cooperation and win-win propositions . . . the safeguarding of world peace should be placed above the opposition to hegemonism."[91]

Some Chinese foreign policy experts were seriously worried that "irrational nationalistic feeling" might drive China into a war with the United States.[92] They observed that feelings that China should say no to the United States and make a big push to build up military capabilities are well received among older people and young students.[93] One interesting anonymous essay, buried in a technical journal on shipbuilding, argued that "emotional nationalism" and "reverse racism" could drive China into a military confrontation with America. China should adopt a "constructive nationalism" instead, "adopting a calm and rational approach to handling hostile and isolating attempts made by other countries, such as the United States." That is the way to "avoid the fate of Germany and Japan."[94] A 2005 article by sociologist Zhou Xiaozhen criticized "a handful of generals within the army for impetuously talking about war" to reunify Taiwan, "which is terrible."[95]

President Jiang Zemin, in his last major statement before retiring, framed the restrained approach to foreign policy in language most likely to gain widespread Communist Party support—as a smart strategy for China to strengthen its national power. "Taking an overall view, for us the first twenty years of the twenty-first century are a period of important strategic opportunity which we must tightly seize and in which we can get a lot done," Jiang said in his report to the Sixteenth CCP National Congress in November 2002.[96] In an ironic twist, the Chinese appropriated the term "period of strategic opportunity" from the U.S. National Security Strategy of 1999, which said (as the Chinese rendered it), that because no large country would catch up with it before 2015 or 2020, America had the opportunity to mold a new order and realize U.S. global leadership.[97]

But after the September 11, 2001, terrorist attacks on America, Jiang Zemin realized that China had been handed its own period of strategic opportunity that it could exploit to improve relations with the United States and accelerate its domestic economic development. "After the 9/11 incident, the U.S. strategic focus has been somewhat readjusted . . . with the result that China may win a correspondingly longer lasting environment of peace and development and concentrate more of its strength on developing the country."[98] (Military strategists take a more cynical view of 9/11 and argue that "the fundamental aim of U.S. national security strategy is to use the war against terrorism as the means to make full use of the current 'period of strategic opportunity' . . . to seek . . . superiority in the new century and ensure and maintain the unipolar world under U.S. hegemony.")[99]

The former prime minister of Singapore, Lee Kwan Yew, a sage observer of China's rise, highlighted the learning process that the Chinese leaders had experienced. "I believe the Chinese leadership have learnt: If you compete with America in armaments, you will lose. You will bankrupt yourself. So, avoid it, keep your head down, and smile, for 40 or 50 years."[100]

National Missile Defense and the Nuclear Relationship

China's restrained approach to the United States was reflected in the manner it dealt with the issue of U.S. national missile defense (NMD). Beginning in 1998, the Clinton administration considered deploying a national missile defense shield to protect the U.S. mainland against a nuclear attack from North Korea or an accidental launch by another country. It would begin on a small scale, with the deployment of interceptors in Alaska—to defend against missile threats from North Korea and other Asian countries who remained unmentioned. The early tests of the NMD technology had not been encouraging, however.

One of the president's declared criteria for making a decision was how the reactions of other countries to NMD would affect U.S. security. Administration officials had already begun consultations with Russia, whose reactions were considered the most crucial because Clinton wanted to have NMD without tearing up the U.S.-Soviet Antiballistic Missile (ABM) Treaty. Russia, with an arsenal of thousands of nuclear-tipped missiles, would retain its second-strike capability to deter an attack if the United States built the shield. Strategic relations would remain stable. Neither country would attack first because the other would certainly retaliate if attacked.

"What about China?" I kept asking my colleagues in the government. "Shouldn't we be talking with the Chinese about their views too?" Because of the tiny size of China's strategic nuclear arsenal (about twenty long-range missiles armed with warheads), Chinese strategists might fear that even the smallest-scale version of national missile defense would deprive them of their second-strike capability. Theoretically, we could launch a first strike, wipe out most of China's nuclear weapons and then have NMD to protect us from any we might have missed. And there would be no way to credibly assure China that we wouldn't do so. From China's perspective our shield was actually a dangerous weapon aimed at them. To restore strategic stability, China would have to accelerate the buildup of its nuclear forces and make its strategic missiles more mobile until once again it had a secure survivable deterrent.[101] But if China engaged in a nuclear arms race with America, Chinese analysts worried, it could "exhaust its resources and harm its economic development,"[102] ruin its international reputation as a responsible power, and destroy mutual trust with the United States.

Chinese officials told me that the Russians had already begun trying to persuade them to make common cause against NMD. But the Chinese were wary of climbing out on a limb with the Russians. They suspected (correctly as it turned out) that the Russians would eventually acquiesce to the American national missile defense plans because they didn't harm their security in any tangible way.

When we finally took a high-level interagency team to Beijing in 2000 to start discussions about NMD, we assured the government that the system wasn't aimed at countering the Chinese nuclear threat.[103] The Chinese officials were still uneasy and accused the United States of harming China's security in order to try to achieve perfect security for itself.[104]

The Chinese government, however, was not as anxious about U.S. national missile defense as it was about the local version, called "theater missile defense," that the United States was considering deploying to protect Taiwan from Mainland missile attacks.[105] Theater missile defense for Taiwan would require the United States to share its intelligence and coordinate its command and control with Taiwan, resulting in a close, alliance-type relationship of the two militaries. What worried China even more was that U.S.-Taiwan joint development of theater missile defenses would encourage the Taiwanese to push toward independence because it would give them the "illusion of safety."[106] From the Chinese perspective, the combination of Taiwan theater missile defense with U.S. national missile defense would very destabilizing. Taiwan would be emboldened to act provocatively, and then the United States could intervene without worrying about nuclear retaliation from China.

After President Clinton chose to delay a decision about deployment of NMD until the next administration, and President Bush decided to abrogate the ABM treaty and go full-steam ahead, the issue of NMD could have become even more contentious. According to Chinese scientists, NMD had become a hot topic on the Internet, with as many Web sites devoted to it as devoted to McDonald's restaurants.[107]

The Chinese side, however, was making up its mind to cope quietly with NMD instead of making it a major public controversy. As a Chinese officer at a military think-tank explained in 2001, "The relationship with the U.S. is the most important to China and its security . . . China will respond to NMD in proportion to the threat and refrain from a vicious cycle or arms race with the U.S." "China doesn't know for sure what it will do," he continued, "expand our arsenal or develop penetration aids instead. We seek assurance that NMD isn't aimed at us, that the U.S. doesn't intend to undermine China's deterrent." I asked how the United States could convince China that it doesn't intend to reduce its security. "If the U.S. would limit its deployment of NMD radars [i.e., keep the shield small and thin]," he answered, "That would show a sense of responsibility for our bilateral relations. We also should discuss how to control the damage this issue could do to bilateral relations."

The Bush administration was unwilling to adjust its NMD deployment plans to take Chinese concerns into account. Forced to plan for a thick, robust missile shield around the United States (even though the technology may never succeed), China has sought to minimize the damage to bilateral relations. The PRC is opting to make its small arsenal more mobile and therefore more survivable, and to rely on penetration aids like decoys instead of engaging in a nuclear arms race that would arouse American fears of a China threat.

Economic Interdependence

Zhu Rongji, speaking at Tsinghua University in 2000, was asked what he considered the greatest international threat to China. He replied, "Problems in the U.S. economy."

The growing interdependence of the Chinese and American economies has transformed the way Chinese leaders think about bilateral relations. According to U.S. statistics U.S.-China trade was $285.3 billion in 2005, as contrasted with $5 billion in 1980.[108] The United States is also one of the most important sources of foreign direct investment in China, although it provides less than Hong Kong, Taiwan, Japan, and South Korea.

Before China started buying up big chunks of U.S. government debt in 2001, the economic relationship was asymmetric.[109] For one thing, a smaller share of American exports was bought by China than the share of Chinese exports bought by America. Foreign investment flows were almost entirely in one direction. China had more to lose if the American economy stumbled than America did if the Chinese economy stumbled.[110] China also had a stronger motivation to protect the bilateral political relationship. If Americans declared China an enemy that must be contained, they could inflict massive damage to China's economic growth and domestic stability.

China's economic dependence on the United States inspired Chinese caution in managing relations with its biggest customer, but at the same time, it also created a host of new frictions. "I look forward to the day when the biggest problem in U.S.-China relations is trade conflict," I said to U.S. Trade Representative Charlene Barshefsky as we were negotiating China's WTO accession in November 1999. Little did I know that we would reach that point so soon.

China's entry into the WTO did not eliminate the trade deficit or even narrow it. As a WTO member, China allowed more imports to enter its markets—China became America's fastest-growing export market—but it

Chinese President Hu Jintao with Microsoft Chairman Bill Gates during Hu's visit to Microsoft headquarters in Redmond, Washington, April 18, 2006. (Andy Clark/ AFP/Getty Images)

also gave foreign companies the confidence to move their export-oriented manufacturing plants to China. As a result, China's exports kept growing, and America's trade deficit with China ballooned to politically explosive proportions. In 2000, America's trade gap with China exceeded its gap with Japan, and it has remained the biggest bilateral trade deficit ever since. The deficit grew from $3.5 billion in 1980 to $83.8 billion in 2000 and an enormous $200 billion in 2005.[111] The loss of American jobs to China became a hot issue in the 2000 and 2004 presidential campaigns. Rampant piracy of DVDs, CDs, prescription drugs, and other intellectual property frustrated American producers. Members of Congress accused China of underpricing exports and overpricing imports by manipulating its currency, i.e., pegging it to the U.S. dollar instead of allowing it to float. They threatened sanctions if Beijing didn't raise the value of the renminbi.

China started recycling the huge amount of foreign currency reserves it earned from exports and foreign investment to buy up U.S. government debt. The primary motive is economic — U.S. government securities are considered the safest place to keep foreign currency holdings — but the political benefit of linking the two economies surely has not escaped China's decision makers. The two sides need each other now — as one Chinese writer put it, they have become economic "Siamese twins."[112] According to one 2005 Chinese estimate, China bought U.S. treasury bonds with over 70 percent of its massive reserves.[113] Chinese capital flows to America allowed American consumers to enjoy low interest rates and high levels of consumption. Yet reliance on China to keep our economy afloat triggers the anxiety that one day China could pull the plug. The day after the Democratic Party won control over both houses of Congress in November 2006, the head of China's central bank said that the bank intended to diversify more of its $1 trillion reserves into currencies other than dollars. The value of the dollar tumbled as international investors sold their dollars.[114] The timing may have been coincidental, but it was a vivid reminder that American prosperity and global influence increasingly depend on decisions made in Beijing.

Chinese analysts, while welcoming economic interdependence for making the interests of the two countries inseparable, question whether the United States can handle bilateral economic and trade issues "according to a non-politicized principle."[115]

CNOOC's Failed Bid for UNOCAL

In an atmosphere of economic Sinophobia, the news in summer 2005 that the Chinese state-owned oil company, China National Offshore Oil

Corporation (CNOOC), had bid to buy the Union Oil Company of California (UNOCAL) set off cries of alarm in Washington. The acquisition by the Chinese firm Lenovo of IBM's personal computing division and the bid by Haier to acquire Maytag had sparked relatively mild concern in previous months. But the media and politicians went into a white-knuckle panic at the thought that the Chinese government might buy up a U.S. oil company and get a chokehold on our energy security. Chevron, who had offered a competing bid for UNOCAL, launched an intensive lobbying campaign to defeat CNOOC's bid by exaggerating the security risks it would pose. The Chinese firm hired its own lobbyists and applied for a normal review from the interagency committee under the Treasury Department that reviews foreign acquisitions of American companies. Its $18.5 billion bid was substantially larger than the $16.4 Chevron had offered. CNOOC insisted that the anxiety about American energy security was unfounded as 70 percent of UNOCAL's reserves were in Asia. Less than 1 percent of U.S. oil and gas consumption came from UNOCAL. CNOOC promised that all the energy UNOCAL produced in the United States would remain here and that the company would retain all of UNOCAL's U.S. employees. Nevertheless, the House of Representatives voted 398 to 15 that allowing CNOOC to buy UNOCAL would "threaten to impair the national security of the U.S."[116]

Meanwhile, in Beijing, the Chinese government was stunned and demoralized by the political explosion the CNOOC bid had ignited. CNOOC is internationally known for its independence from the government and its sophistication in the global marketplace. Although CNOOC had obtained approval from the government agency that supervises it — the government's policy is to encourage Chinese companies to go abroad to find new sources of energy — the company had not consulted with government leaders or foreign policy officials.

A Foreign Ministry official responsible for relations with the United States learned about CNOOC's bid when he read about it in the newspaper. He immediately telephoned CNOOC CEO Fu Chengyu and went to see him. Fu was very confident — after all, he had Goldman Sachs and other international financial institutions advising him — and as he said in an interview, they "were following a system that was set up by Western leading companies."[117] Fu explained that because almost all UNOCAL's assets were outside the United States, it shouldn't be a problem for Americans. "Never underestimate the political reaction of Congress," the Foreign Ministry official said to Fu. Because the United States defines its strategic interests globally, he explained, Congress was likely to react even though the assets weren't in the U.S. proper. But his advice came too late.

The Chinese Embassy in Washington also was worried that the controversy over the CNOOC bid could spoil Hu Jintao's first visit to the White House, planned for that fall. At the embassy's recommendation, CNOOC announced on August 2, 2005, that it was retracting its bid because of "the unprecedented political opposition" it had engendered.

The CNOOC effort to buy UNOCAL tested American responses to the entry of China as a player in the international corporate arena. America failed the test by showing that even when China plays by normal commercial rules, America would block it. CNOOC Chairman Fu, crushed by the American backlash, said that he had discovered "that what Westerners taught us is not the way the West wants to go."[118]

The incident also deepened the cynicism of Chinese intellectuals about American market principles. One student said, "The U.S. is always promoting free trade but then it uses its political power to stop [CNOOC]. It says one thing and does another. China supports the international market system more than the West does."

"People's hopes in the U.S. were dashed," said one government official. "They think the U.S. will try to contain us no matter if we behave responsibly." (Two officials told me they suspected that it was the Bush administration—specifically the oil industry interests connected with Vice President Cheney—not Congress that killed the deal.)

The Chinese government, worried about an angry outcry from the public, directed the media to publish only the official Xinhua news agency accounts of the CNOOC's controversy.[119] Ironically, the fiasco prompted the Chinese government to strengthen its oversight of the international activities of Chinese corporations to avoid similar political flaps in the future—it established a high-level group to vet future acquisitions by Chinese companies. By treating competition for energy as a geopolitical "great game" instead of a commercial matter, the United States is driving China to do the same.

Future Risks

Since Hu Jintao became president and CCP head, he has continued China's prudent, accommodating approach to the United States. Differentiating himself somewhat from his predecessor, who had been criticized in policy circles for being too eager to please the Americans, he is focusing more on China's relations with its Asian neighbors than Jiang did. Hu also has tacked to the left by tightening Party control over the media and nongovernmental groups in an apparent effort to consolidate his authority and head off political unrest. But he has resisted the temptation to bolster himself domestically by bashing Washington. Cooperation between Beijing and Washington is relatively smooth. And no major crises have disrupted relations since the 2001 plane collision. During this time, China's international image also has improved. Surveys show that China is viewed more positively throughout the world than the United States is.[120]

Yet Sino-American relations are far from relaxed. In America, as the fear of terror attacks recedes, older fears about the China threat may reemerge and be heightened by anxieties about job loss and the trade deficit. American political reactions to the rise of China could combine the worst features of the Cold War fears of the Soviet Union and the economic fears of Japan before its growth slowed. According to 2006 polls, people remain evenly divided between those who see China favorably and those who see it unfavorably.[121] And the majority of people view China's economy catching up with the American economy as both good and bad.[122] (Citizens in states like Michigan and Ohio undoubtedly are less sanguine about competition from China.) But Americans feel cooler toward China than China's neighbors do and view China more as a rival than as a partner.[123] Three-quarters of the public is concerned about China becoming a military power.[124] China's pleasant rhetoric about "peaceful rising" and "responsible power" hasn't convinced Americans that China's true intentions toward them are entirely friendly. When polled, 58 percent of Americans say they do not trust China at all or very much to act responsibly in the world, and 60 percent of them say they don't trust China to take the interests of the United States into account when making their foreign policy decisions.[125]

For one thing, if China's leaders are not accountable to ordinary citizens or to economic interests with a stake in good relations, what is to prevent them from changing their tune as soon as they are strong enough to challenge the United States? The country as a whole has a very strong interest in avoiding conflict with the United States, but who in the domestic arena can effectively make the case if tensions rise? The Chinese interest groups who benefit most from the economic relationship with the United States and from globalization more broadly—private companies and coastal provinces—do not yet have a voice in the foreign policy process, nor do they lobby for particular foreign policies. Provincial officials, who want to stimulate growth and create jobs by attracting foreign investment and exporting local products, constitute the largest bloc in the CCP Central Committee to whom the top leaders are accountable.[126] But in a crisis, such as one provoked by Taiwan or Japan that arouses patriotic zeal, can we count on these provincial officials to check and balance the CCP leaders and the military?

For over five years, China's official media have communicated a kinder, gentler view of America. Education authorities have revised textbooks to present a less critical account of American history. No accidents have caused crises to incite the public against America. The Chinese leaders have reacted calmly to the U.S. war in Iraq. Even so, recent surveys indicate that the Chinese public remains highly mistrustful of America, possibly even more mistrustful than they were right after the Belgrade embassy bombing or the airplane collision. Alastair Iain Johnston found that friendly feelings toward America declined among Beijing residents during 2002, 2003, and 2004 even without the stimulus of a crisis. In a pattern similar to other countries especially since the war in Iraq, Beijingers differentiate between the United States as a state and Americans as a people, and feel more positive toward the people than the state.[127]

The Pew Center for the People and the Press conducted surveys of urban China as part of its Global Attitudes Project. In 2005, 42 percent of the Chinese surveyed had a favorable view of the United States, while 53 percent had an unfavorable view.[128] (The views of Japan were much more negative: 17 percent favorable and 76 percent unfavorable.) The Chinese were also the least likely people in sixteen countries to consider Americans as hardworking (44 percent) and only 35 percent see Americans as honest. A majority of Chinese believe Americans are violent (61 percent) and greedy (57 percent).[129] In a 2006 BBC poll, 62 percent of Chinese said that the United States was having a negative influence in the world, twenty points higher than a year before (the Chinese negative views of the United States are twenty-one points higher than the world average).[130]

Other less scientific surveys of cities in China also find that people are mistrustful of the American government. A 2005 poll conducted by *Global Times* with the Chinese Academy of Social Sciences Institute of American Studies found that about two-thirds of people said they liked American people but more than half said that the U.S. government was containing China and only 10 percent believed that the United States was a friendly government.[131] Surveys by the Horizon Company found that 70.3 percent (1999) and 74.4 percent (2004) of people consider the United States the country least friendly to China.[132]

The war in Iraq is eroding respect for America in China as it is in other countries. An economics graduate student said to me, "The U.S. is democratic at home, but hegemonic abroad. There are really two Saddam Husseins: Saddam in Iraq and Bush in the international system. Iraq is a hot topic. We follow it on Phoenix TV."

The Chinese elite still suspects that America intends to keep China in a weak, subordinate status so the United States can remain the world's sole superpower. In an internal speech, statesman Qian Qichen described the American war on terrorism as an excuse to use its military might to dominate the world.[133] When former deputy secretary of state Robert

Zoellick said in a 2005 speech that he hoped China would become an international "stake-holder," and President Bush adopted the term too, their intention was to signal that America was ready to share power with China if it behaved responsibly. Some Chinese experts, however, have interpreted the concept as a tactic for America to slow down China's rise by shunting some of the burden of global management to China.[34]

Despite the Chinese government's efforts to paint its relations with Washington in a more positive light, popular suspicions of American intentions appear to have become deeply rooted in the political culture of this rising power. A future crisis with the United States, especially one involving Taiwan or Japan, could arouse the public's ire to the degree that China's leaders might believe that the regime would fall unless they respond militarily to the insult to national honor. In Wang Jisi's words, "Despite obvious improvements in bilateral relations in the last year or two, it must be admitted that the two countries' political image in each other's society remains principally negative . . . once unexpected incidents appear in their bilateral relations, the 'enemy state image' latent in the two societies will probably resurface to create major political and security crises."[35]

9

China's Weakness, America's Danger

W HEN PRESIDENT HU JINTAO met with President George Bush in fall 2005, he sought to reassure the American president that China was not a threat by describing the many difficult domestic problems he was struggling to juggle at home. Although China looks like a powerhouse from the outside, to its leaders it looks fragile, poor, and overwhelmed by internal problems. But China's massive problems, instead of reassuring us, should worry us. It is China's internal fragility, not its growing strength that presents the greatest danger. The weak legitimacy of the Communist Party and its leaders' sense of vulnerability could cause China to behave rashly in a crisis involving Japan or Taiwan, and bring it into a military conflict with the United States. If economic growth slows and problems multiply, there is a possibility that China's leaders could be tempted to "wag the dog"—mobilize domestic support by creating an international crisis. More likely, however, is that when confronted with a crisis, the leaders make threats they can't back away from because of their fear of appearing weak to the domestic audience. Only by understanding the dangers of China's domestic fragility and incorporating this understanding into their policies can Chinese and American decision makers avoid a catastrophic war.

Domestic Challenges

Twenty-five years of market reform and opening to the world economy have radically transformed Chinese society and created potential threats to Communist Party rule. The Party can no longer keep track of the population, much less control it. Over one hundred million farmers have moved to cities. Three-quarters of the workforce is employed outside the state sector where there is little political supervision. Thirty million people traveled abroad in 2005.[1] Of those people with college degrees, 90 percent access information through the Internet.[2] Whenever the CCP leaders intensify their censorship of the media and Internet it signals to the public just how nervous they are. As President Clinton observed in an April 1999 speech about China, "A tight grip is actually a sign of a weak hand."[3]

The glaring gaps between the lavish lifestyles of the rich and the struggles of poor farmers and urban migrants who cannot afford heavy school fees and medical bills make people mad. People suspect that official corruption, not hard work or ingenuity, is the real source of most of the wealth. Angry urban mobs have assaulted the affluent drivers of fancy cars who accidentally hit pedestrians.

The state-run medical system has disintegrated now that China is a market economy, and most people do not have any insurance to cover medical expenses. China's once-impressive public health system also has fallen apart. More than three hundred citizens died during the 2003 SARS epidemic, and an avian flu epidemic could decimate the country. China's air and water pollution are among the worst in the world. Industrial poisoning of rivers has become a major cause of mass protest. A large-scale environmental disaster could spark a revolt.

Protests by workers laid-off by state factories are a daily occurrence, and rural unrest is spreading. Legal advocates from the cities are beginning to go down to the countryside to organize rural resistance. Well aware that Chinese dynasties traditionally were toppled by peasant rebellions, the Communist Party leaders are trying to ease the dangerous strains in rural society by channeling more funds to the countryside.[4]

Another lesson from Chinese history is that nationalism is the emotional platform that can meld various discontented social groups into a revolutionary movement. The Qing Dynasty and the Republic of China fell to nationalist movements that turned against the government for not standing up to foreign aggression. In recent years, anger against the United States and Japan has brought hundreds of thousands of students out on the streets. If China's leaders lose control of this nationalist fervor it could drive them into war or turn against the Communist government just as it did against the two governments that preceded it. As the Chinese always say, "internal disorder and external pressure" go together.

Singapore former prime minister Lee Kuan Yew, an astute observer of China, says that although he is confident that the current leaders want to concentrate on economic development and avoid the mistakes made by Germany and Japan when they were rising powers, he worries about "whether the next generation will stay on this course. . . . We know the mind of the leaders but the mood of the people on the ground is another matter. Because there's no more communist ideology to hold the people together, the ground is now galvanized by Chinese patriotism and nationalism."[5]

Party leaders know their political survival depends as much on keeping the oligarchy unified and the military loyal as on preventing widespread protest. So far they have succeeded with a package that gives something to everyone: a pragmatic foreign policy that sustains domestic economic growth; tough rhetoric on Japan, Taiwan, and sometimes toward the United States; and double-digit increases in the People's Liberation Army's budget. But leadership competition is a constant fact of life, and policy differences are bound to emerge.

The two faces of Chinese foreign policy are both rooted in the nation's internal fragility. China behaves as a responsible power to signal its moderate aims and head off an international backlash that potentially could disrupt its economic growth, throw millions of workers out of their jobs, and inflame urban and rural unrest. At the same time, China's sometimes impetuous emotional responses to Japan, Taiwan, and the United States are the unfortunate result of the need to prove to the public, the military, the "control coalition" (internal security and propaganda agencies), and to one another that they are staunch defenders of national pride and sovereignty. Hence, compromise on hot-button issues involving Japan, Taiwan, or the United States might be cast as capitulation and become politically suicidal.[6] In the end, China's emotional responses may undermine its more moderate aims and get it, and us, into trouble.

How Can China Help Itself?

Chinese leaders have boxed themselves into a dangerous corner. They are their own worst enemy. As one Chinese policy advisor says, "If China's rise is certain to bring about challenges, then the challenges first of all come from China itself."[7] Whenever political figures from Japan, Taiwan, or America make statements that sound insulting to China, Chinese leaders feel compelled to respond in kind to protect themselves from domestic criticism, even though they know that nonconfrontational relations with all three governments are in China's economic and security interests.

Yet there are some steps that Chinese leaders could take to escape from this predicament that are politically practicable and would not require wholesale change of their authoritarian political system. The leaders recognize that their system reacts to crises both too slowly and too impetuously. But instead of focusing on organizational fixes to improve crisis management, they would be better off reducing, or providing counter-weights to, the domestic pressures for bellicose actions.

Stop official sponsorship of assertive nationalism

The Communist Party's post-Tiananmen effort to rebuild its legitimacy through the patriotic education campaign is largely responsible for the increase in antiforeign nationalism among today's youth. Now the CCP ought to start cooling nationalist passions instead of inflaming them. The Ministry of Education has revised school textbooks to portray American history in a more balanced manner. It should do the same for the textbooks' treatment of Japan, for example by including information on post-war Japan's economic miracle and its peace constitution. Textbooks should also stop glorifying the xenophobic violence of the Boxer Rebellion in 1900 if the Party doesn't want to see it repeated. The CCP further should cease sponsoring campus and media commemorations of the historical humiliations inflicted by Japan. These memorial activities only serve to fan the flames of assertive nationalism.

Cultivate positive nationalism

From the standpoint of CCP leaders, it's safer to inculcate a positive identification with China than hostility toward foreigners. School text-books, instead of depicting modern China only as a victim during the "century of humiliation," should highlight the successes of its statesmen, reformers, entrepreneurs, and scientists. Contemporary China also has a lot to be proud of, including the honor of hosting the 2008 Olympic Games. Celebrating China's achievements—such as sending a man into space and other economic and technological strides—is a less risky way to win political support than nurturing a victim mentality.

Empower private business

The groups who benefit the most from China's globalized economy and peaceful foreign relations—provincial officials and private businesspeople—should have a voice in foreign policy. At present, foreign policymaking is highly centralized, and there is no counterweight to the nationalist pub-lic, the military, and the intelligence and control bureaucracies that might push China's leaders to take rash action. Provincial officials do serve in the CCP Central Committee to which Party leaders are formally account-able. And Jiang Zemin took a step in the right direction by urging that private businesspeople be admitted as Party members. But as yet only one private businessperson is an alternate member in the Central Commit-tee. The disenfranchisement of the group with the greatest interest in avoiding international conflict is a dangerous disconnect between China's reformed economy and its unreformed political system.

Strengthen civilian control of the military

Today's CCP leaders are less confident of the People's Liberation Army's support than the Long March generation who fought side by side with the military in the revolution. Although the military no longer sits in the Politburo Standing Committee and appears more preoccupied with military matters than politics, civilian control over the military remains incomplete. Therefore, the leadership can't say no to the PLA's budget requests for fear of alienating the people with the guns, as double-digit annual increases in official military spending make clear. Even though military officers as a rule are more conscious of the human costs of war than civilian politicians, eventually the generals may want to use the destroyers, submarines, and jet fighters that these big budgets have bought. War could be the by-product of the military buildup.[8] A good way to put speed bumps in the path would be to make the budget more transparent and openly debate the budget in China's legislature, the National People's Congress. Right now the central government budget and the military budget are treated as state secrets. Allowing a legislative debate about the relative priority of military and domestic programs (a "guns vs. butter" debate) would provide better oversight of military spending and build up domestic constituencies for meeting domestic needs first.[9]

Decontrol the media

A mass media that is market oriented but still controlled by the government is a recipe for increased nationalist pressure on decision makers. While China's commercialized newspapers, magazines, television, and Internet news sites compete for audiences, the themes of their news reporting still are orchestrated by the CCP propaganda maestros. Publications attract readers with vivid stories about threats or insults from Japan, Taiwan, and the United States, in a sensational style that is much more gripping than the stale prose of the Mao-era Party press. The contents of the media are heavily skewed toward nationalist mythmaking, without exposing people to countervailing arguments.[10] The views expressed in newspapers and the Internet then blow back on the leaders, creating the impression that everyone is a passionate nationalist. The way to break this perverse syndrome is to shackle the Propaganda Department and decontrol the marketplace of ideas to allow people a broader range of information, which will in turn give China's leaders more accurate information about public opinion. Loosening their grip on the media will also make the leaders look more confident and gain legitimacy. A free press, moreover, is essential for curing corruption, the insidious disease eroding support for the regime. (Some might argue that it's impossible to have a free press without democracy—but that's what people used to say about a market economy without democracy, until China pulled it off.)

Open up dialogue with the Taiwan government

Taiwan's democratization is strengthening the island's sense of a separate identity and driving its politics toward formal independence despite its growing economic ties with the Mainland. Inside China, the widespread belief that the Communist Party would be overthrown if Taiwan declared independence and the Mainland didn't put up a fight, puts China's leaders in an impossible situation. Their political fate hinges on the actions of Taiwan's president, which they cannot control. Nor can China count entirely on Washington, which is constrained by Americans' strong popular support for Taiwan, to squelch Taiwanese proindependence gestures.

How can China's leaders forestall a Taiwan crisis that would force them to choose between political humiliation and a military confrontation with Taiwan and the United States? The current formula—economic links, relations with opposition parties, the Antisecession Law, and tough rhetoric—may play well at home, but it offers Taiwan's president no incentive to reverse the drive to establish Taiwan as a sovereign nation. A military demonstration of resolve like the 1995–96 show of force would be popular at home, but it would be hard for the Chinese to stop it from escalating into war.

The conflict between Taiwan and the Mainland grows more dangerous as China's military power vis-à-vis Taiwan and the United States improves, but the CCP's ability to control the information flowing to the public and insulate decision making from public opinion declines. The combination of these two vectors intensifies the domestic pressure to use force in the Taiwan Strait.

Initiating direct talks with the Taiwan government without preconditions would be the best way for President Hu Jintao and his colleagues to escape from their domestic dilemma and take the air out of Taiwan's movement toward independence. There is a precedent for putting aside preconditions in order to talk. In 1997 China dropped the "one China" requirement and invited Taiwan's cross-Strait negotiator to get on an airplane to China. It wouldn't be an easy step for President Hu to take now, however. China's leaders for years have refused on principle to talk directly to the Taiwan government until its president utters the magic words "one China." Consequently, Hu would be criticized by his peers as well as by some members of the control coalition and the military if he retreats from the "one-China principle" and gives face to Taiwan's president. The

Chinese government is counting on Taiwan electing a new president from the Guomindang in 2008, most likely Taipei mayor Ma Ying-jeou, who they expect to endorse the one-China principle. Yet wouldn't it be better to compromise now and take the domestic heat than to run the risk of ruining everything—economic progress, domestic stability, relations with the United States, and the 2008 Olympics—if the current Taiwan president provokes a major crisis before 2008 or if Ma is not as compliant as they expect? On the plus side, the United States and the rest of the world would applaud President Hu's statesmanship, and would lean on Taiwan to reciprocate with concessions of its own.

China's leaders also might be surprised by the domestic reaction to their brave about-face on the one-China precondition. Although some of the elite and the military and passionate young netizens would carp, the silent majority would greet the resumption of cross-Strait talks with a positive sense of relief that the danger of war has receded and progress is being made. The broad public cares more about not losing Taiwan than specific formulations about it. The leaders, freed from their paranoid assumptions, would discover that they have more domestic latitude than they realized to handle Taiwan as flexibly as they handle other foreign policy issues.

What Can Americans Do?

We cannot control whether China's leaders heed our advice to them. But we can control how we ourselves think about and behave toward China, which is all the more important because we can't count on China always to act responsibly or in its own best interest.

Everything Americans say and do regarding China reverberates through Chinese domestic politics. Just as Americans are wondering if a rising China will threaten us, the Chinese are wondering about America's intentions toward China. Can America learn to live with rising China? Or as the number one power in the world, is America bound to try to keep China weak to maintain its own position? China's people, and its leaders, are listening to what we say and watching what we do.

Historically, rising powers cause war not necessarily because they are innately belligerent, but because the reigning powers mishandle those who challenge the status quo in one way or another. Based on history, the prognosis for relations between rising powers like China and reigning powers like the United States is poor. It could produce direct conflict between two nuclear powers. The costs of such a conflict would be devastating not just for the two societies but for the rest of Asia and the entire world.

It will take smart statesmanship that recognizes the complexities of domestic politics on both sides to get us through this power transition without stumbling into war. But by keeping in mind how our words and actions resonate inside China, Americans can enable China's leaders to act like the responsible power they claim China to be, instead of being driven into aggressive actions by the nationalist passions of the public, the control coalition, and the military.

Put priority on China's international behavior

Former secretary of state Madeleine Albright used to call U.S. relations with China "multifaceted" because of the many contentious issues on the table. Different groups of Americans feel upset about China's various laws, behaviors, and practices—from its limits on religious and labor rights to its forced abortions, its role in global warming, its treatment of Tibet, its threat to American manufacturing jobs, and its pirating of Hollywood movies.

But America's overriding national interest lies in averting a war by inducing China to behave cooperatively and not aggressively toward other countries. Other goals, even democratization and the promotion of human rights, must take second place, much as we find China's still-repressive practices abhorrent. Constant finger pointing at China's failings triggers resentful reactions from the Chinese public, making it more difficult for Chinese leaders to act in concert with America instead of at cross-purposes with it. As Henry Kissinger put it, "A prudent American leadership should balance the risks of stoking Chinese nationalism against the gains from short-term pressures."[11]

Our hopes for political reform in China, moreover, will never be realized through outside pressure. Domestic demand, not foreign prodding, gives rise to political transformations. We inspire more progress on the ground by the example of our vibrant democratic society than by preaching or punishments that evoke a backlash. My own experience in government taught me that Washington's typical approach to human rights in China—which involves public shaming and threats of sanctions—wins points with American domestic audiences but is counterproductive in China. Most Chinese, even those committed to democratization, resent American interference in the country's domestic affairs and believe that in order to avoid chaos political change must be gradual. Heavy-handed efforts to push democratization look to the Chinese like a form of containment designed to keep China weak. Overplaying the human rights issues also undercuts the Chinese voices who advocate a cooperative relationship with the United States by casting doubt on their patriotic credentials.

Maintain a strong U.S. military presence

Keeping U.S. forces deployed in the Asia-Pacific region to deter potential aggression is all the more necessary once we are aware of the domestic pressures that could drive China's leaders to behave rashly. We want Chinese decision makers, when faced with a crisis, to look out to the Pacific and see a U.S. military with the will and capacity to defend Taiwan, our allies in Japan and South Korea, and our other Asian friends. Because restraining themselves may cost Chinese leaders domestic popularity, we need to balance that cost with the even greater cost they will pay if they act belligerently internationally and are defeated by our forces. To quote Henry Kissinger again, "The challenge to American foreign policy is how to deal with Chinese nationalism without inflaming it while standing firm when it turns to threats."[12] Maintaining our overwhelming military superiority also helps the doves in China argue that if the country tries to compete militarily with the United States just as the Soviet Union did, then it will collapse from within just as the Soviet Union did.

Don't flaunt U.S. military strength

While showing that we are capable of responding swiftly to military adventures, we must be careful to avoid saber rattling. Quiet strength is the best formula for a reigning power to handle the rise of a new power. The less we say about how strong we are—provoking prickly reactions from within the rising power—the better.

America is the strongest military power in China's backyard. As China rises, this anomalous situation will cause increasing angst among Chinese, especially those in military uniforms. So far, China's leaders have not enunciated a Monroe Doctrine for Asia—similar to U.S. president James Monroe's 1823 declaration that outside powers from Europe were not welcome in North and South America. In fact, Jiang Zemin and Hu Jintao have privately told President Bush that they have no intention of trying to push the United States out of Asia. Chinese leaders will have a hard time maintaining their equanimity toward the U.S. presence, however, if Americans go in for the kind of military chest thumping that arouses a hostile response from the Chinese public and the military.

The U.S. Pacific Command in Honolulu, which has done an exemplary job of organizing cooperative activities with the Chinese and other Asian militaries, should expand its high-visibility collaborations with the PLA. Television and newspaper photographs of Chinese and American navies exercising together would go a long way to diluting opposition to our military presence in China's neighborhood. We could encourage the Southeast Asian navies to invite Chinese and American naval vessels to join them in joint patrols to keep the Strait of Malacca and other choke points in the sea-lanes of communication free of pirates and terrorists. While maintaining a strong military presence, we should go the extra mile to reassure the Chinese that the region is big enough for both of us.

Don't build up Japan as a military power

Japan has become the most volatile foreign policy issue for any Chinese politician. Yet the Bush administration—with an eye on burden sharing and power balances rather than the potential political reactions from inside China and South Korea—has actively encouraged Japan to become America's military partner in Asia and in our other theaters in Afghanistan and Iraq. Thanks to American sponsorship, Japan is now well on its way to abandoning the self-imposed military limits that America encouraged after its defeat in World War II. In the next few years Japan is likely to revise its "no war" constitution and come out of the closet as a formidable military power; some establishment Japanese are even starting to talk about nuclear weapons.

Americans might feel completely relaxed about a rearmed Japan, but the Chinese and South Koreans certainly don't. Any benefit the United States gains from having Japan share the expense of deterring China and preserving stability in Asia is offset by the cost of inflaming public opinion in China, which makes it almost impossible for its leaders to mend relations with Japan. The more unpopular Japan becomes in China and South Korea, the less value America's obtains from its alliance with Japan.

Making a show of involving Japan in the defense of Taiwan has a particularly incendiary effect. The Clinton administration quietly renegotiated its military arrangements with Japan to make sure that U.S. forces based in Japan would be able to respond to regional contingencies—which could include an attack on Taiwan—but it did not throw this in China's face by explicitly stating that the scope of the agreement extended to Taiwan. The Bush administration, by being much more forthright about enlisting Japan to defend Taiwan—even to the point of a joint training exercise on the California coast for an amphibious landing on an island—risks placing China's leaders under public pressure to make threats against Japan from which it cannot retreat.

Deteriorating relations between China and Japan create a serious security risk for Americans. The seething public animosity between the two countries could goad their politicians into moves that lead to a naval clash over oil and gas fields in the East China Sea. If that happens, the United States, as Japan's military protector, could feel compelled to intervene. Although neither China nor Japan would welcome American mediation in finding face-saving ways to shelve the contentious history issues, the

United States should open the door to three-way talks. Regular dialogues between China, Japan, and the United States, which the Clinton administration proposed but the Chinese didn't accept at the time, would help prevent mutual suspicions from degenerating into overt conflict.

Work the China-Taiwan problem

No matter how reasonable Chinese foreign policy becomes, the Taiwan issue remains an emotional blind spot. The assumption that CCP rule could not survive a Taiwan declaration of independence compels China's insecure leaders to react to steps toward formal independence by threatening the use of force—and makes it costly for them to back down. Chinese leaders used force in 1995–96 and would do so again, even at the price of sacrificing the 2008 Olympics, if they felt their hold on power required it. The tense stand-off between China's nervous leaders and Taiwan's proindependence ones represents a serious risk to U.S. national security. Under the Taiwan Relations Act, the United States is pledged to help Taiwan defend itself.

Oddly, the Taiwan Strait, one place in the world where American forces are most likely to be called upon to fight, is also the place where we always told ourselves we mustn't intervene diplomatically. For decades, American presidents have limited themselves to declaratory policy. They repeat ad nauseum an evenhanded mantra—"One China, the three U.S.-China communiqués (signed in 1972, 1979, and 1982), and the Taiwan Relations Act"—that is aimed at maintaining the status quo by deterring China from attacking Taiwan and deterring Taiwan from provoking a fight by declaring independence. Even after Presidents Clinton and Bush amended the mantra to include explicit statements that the United States doesn't support independence for Taiwan or unilateral actions to change the status quo, it nevertheless has failed to curb incremental steps toward formal independence by the last two Taiwan presidents. It also has failed to prevent China from building up its military forces to solve the Taiwan problem by force if need be—including the seven-hundred-plus missiles on the Fujian coast opposite the island. Because politicians on both sides have found that they look stronger and gain more popularity by standing tough than by listening to America, the U.S. government has lost control over this dangerous situation.

The American public is not keen to send our soldiers and sailors into battle with the PLA in the defense of Taiwan. According to a 2006 poll, almost two-thirds of Americans oppose using U.S. troops if China invaded Taiwan.[13] A failure to defend Taiwan, however, would drastically reduce American credibility and influence in Asia. With so much at stake, it's time for the United States to untie its hands and use some of its diplomatic muscle to keep the politicians on the two sides from jeopardizing peace in the Strait. The State Department took a welcome step in this direction in March 2006 with an unprecedented public ultimatum to Taiwan president Chen Shui-bian that it will hold him to all the promises he made after the 2000 and 2004 elections about not changing the island's political status.[14] The State Department statement hinted at possible retaliation if the Taiwan president takes further steps to change the status quo, perhaps by withholding approval for arms sales, denying Taiwan officials visas to visit or transit through the United States, or some other sanction. The Bush administration demonstrated the credibility of this threat by denying President Chen approval to transit anywhere in the mainland United States on his way to visit Latin America.[15]

As for China, the U.S. president should take a walk in the woods with the Chinese president and talk with him candidly about the China-Taiwan issue and how it has long bedeviled U.S.-China relations. A peaceful resolution of the standoff—or a long-term agreement to put it on the shelf—would create possibilities for closer relations, perhaps even including military cooperation, between Beijing and Washington, and reduce the risk that actions by Taiwan could sabotage China's peaceful development. Discussions about Taiwan with the Chinese government generally stick closely to scripted talking points because back in 1982 the State Department promised Taiwan that it wouldn't consult with China on its arms sales to Taiwan or mediate between China and Taiwan.[16] But Taiwan's own security, as well as our own, requires that we overcome this inhibition and explore through open-ended discussions what carrots and sticks it would take to get China to begin a genuine process of political reconciliation with Taiwan.

Provide respect

After a century of sitting on the sidelines, the Chinese leaders and public crave respect and approval from the world community, especially from the United States. China has pressed all its neighbors to sign formal bilateral statements declaring not just friendship but partnership. The Chinese also view expressions of respect like high-profile state visits as reassuring signs that the world is ready to accept China as a major power.

Fortunately, respect is easier for Washington to deliver than other types of inducements to cooperate that Congress might find difficult to swallow. President Jiang Zemin's 1997 state visit to Washington left him personally invested in his relationship with President Clinton and in improving relations with the United States. President Hu Jintao wanted his own state visit to the White House complete with a state dinner and all the trimmings, instead of the weekend on President Bush's ranch in Texas that had originally been offered. In China the formal ceremonies connote more respect than informal intimacy does. The Bush administration erred in turning down the Chinese request and making Hu Jintao settle for lunch at the White House instead. We should lavish respect on China's leaders. Each of these well-publicized occasions flatters the leaders and deepens their commitment to the relationship with the United States. The symbolism of the ceremonies also bolsters the leaders back home, thereby diminishing the need for them to make themselves popular by whipping up assertive nationalism.

Making China a member of all important multilateral forums enhances the prestige of China and its leaders, as well as giving them a stronger sense of responsibility for maintaining world order. China considered WTO membership an important expression of international recognition, and it has joined almost every arms control and nonproliferation regime as well. Isn't it about time to invite China, the fourth-largest economy in the world, to join the G-8, the elite grouping of the United States, Canada, France, Germany, England, Italy, Japan, and Russia, that leads the international economy? Bringing China into the global establishment would strengthen domestic support in China for acting responsibly instead of emotionally.

American policymakers are having some difficulty adjusting to the new reality that we cannot solve any of the most pressing problems in the world today, including nuclear proliferation in North Korea and Iran and the genocide in Sudan, without China's help. We should be discussing these issues and coordinating our diplomatic efforts more actively with China. By holding frequent "strategic dialogues" with their Chinese counterparts, American officials also would signal our welcome of China's emergence as a power with interests and influence all over the world.

Don't overreact to China's economic rise

China's revival as a world economic power is causing a near panic in some quarters of American society. America has been the leading economy for a century and we have come to think of it as our divine right.[17] We had a similar hysterical reaction when Japan began competing head-to-head with us in automobiles and electronics and injured our national pride by purchasing real-estate icons like Rockefeller Center. China is causing an even more mortifying psychological adjustment because we are heavily in debt to it as well as competing with it. At the same time, China's rise triggers our old Cold War reflexes. We wring our hands over China's expanding influence in various regions and its military modernization program much as we did over expanding Soviet influence and the "missile gap" between the United States and the Soviet Union during the Cold War.

The challenge from China could have a salutary effect if it stimulates us to cure our own weaknesses, including ballooning government deficits and personal debt, a failing educational system, and stagnant government investment in basic science. In the 1950s, Sputnik (the first satellite launched into space by the Soviet Union in 1957) inspired America to make major investments in science education. In the 1980s and '90s, to meet the Japanese challenge, our companies restructured and the U.S. government fixed policy problems, and it worked. Today, America still has many strengths that China doesn't have—we should be able to maintain our edge if we focus on getting our own house in order instead of blaming and punishing China. The question is, as columnist Tom Friedman put it, will China be America's "scapegoat or Sputnik?"[18]

Unfortunately, Cold War fears and protectionist instincts are clouding Americans' economic reason. Our overreactions, which are read by the Chinese public and its leaders as an expression of our hostile intentions toward China, could turn China from an economic rival into an all-out enemy. Members of Congress are trying to narrow the trade deficit by threatening sanctions against China's currency "manipulation," even though economists estimate that the exchange rate is one of the least important sources of the gap. The firestorm of paranoia that greeted CNOOC's (China National Offshore Oil Corporation) bid to acquire Unocal, forced CNOOC to withdraw from the deal. The CCP plays down these affronts in the media to prevent them from angering the Chinese public, but news of them filters in from abroad anyway.

By politicizing normal commercial dealings and turning them into matters of national security we tell China's leaders and citizens that even when they follow the rules, we will fight dirty to block their economic rise and preserve our own dominance. This message not only inflames Chinese public reactions but also robs China's leaders of any incentive to act responsibly. If Americans are going to try to keep them down no matter how they behave, then why bother to behave as a responsible power?

Concluding Thoughts

Preventing war with a rising China is one of the most difficult foreign policy challenges our country faces. Are we up to it? We have our own complicated domestic politics, with a multitude of groups each responding to China's rise from the standpoint of its own short-term interests and politicians tempted to play to voters' fears of China to help them get elected. Our policies toward China, moreover, don't exist in a vacuum. How we pursue our foreign policy objectives in Iraq, Iran, North Korea, and other parts of the world, and how well we cooperate with other countries in achieving these objectives will influence China's willingness to cooperate with us too, especially now that Chinese people avidly follow international news in the tabloids and on Internet news sites.

Seeing China objectively by recognizing the domestic fragility of this emerging superpower can help us avoid mistakes that could provoke a confrontation: overreacting to China's economic rise, drawing down our military presence in Asia, inflaming nationalist public opinion by public hectoring or chest thumping, and mishandling our relations with Japan and Taiwan.

Our best hope is that as China's leaders address their domestic problems, they will be able to deal with the world in an increasingly responsible way. It won't happen automatically. Prosperity and progress inside China could make its Communist leaders feel all the more politically vulnerable. That is why our own words and actions are so crucial. The way America approaches China's rise can either reinforce its responsible personality or inflame its emotional one. If the responsible China succeeds, then we can expect that China will put its growing power and influence behind our common efforts to preserve peace, fight terrorism, maintain global economic stability and openness, reduce poverty, and slow global warming. Some optimistic Chinese even believe that someday the relationship between the United States and China could become as close as the alliance of the United States and Great Britain: China would lead Asia and the United States would lead the world. So long as China remains a communist state it's hard to imagine such perfect harmony between our two countries. America also would expect Japan, Russia, and India, as the other major powers in Asia, to share regional leadership with China. But the vision of a partnership in which the United States and China share responsibility for regional and global leadership can be realized if America has the wisdom to appreciate China's fragility and the maturity not to try to go it alone.

Appendix

Chinese and Japanese Periodicals

Chinese Periodicals with English Translation

Apple Daily (Pingguo Ribao) (Hong Kong)
Asia Weekly (Yazhou Zhoukan) (Hong Kong)
Beijing News (Xin Jing Bao)
Beijing Times (Jinghua Shibao)
Beijing Youth Daily (Beijing Qingnian Bao)
China Construction News (Zhongguo Jianshe Bao)
China Economic Times (Zhongguo Jingji Shibao)
China Education News (Zhongguo Jiaoyu Bao)
China Newsweek (Zhongguo Xinwen Zhoukan)
China Review (Zhongguo Pinglun) (Hong Kong)
China Times (Chung-Kuo Shih-pao) (Taiwan)
China Youth Daily (Zhongguo Qingnian Bao)
Chinese Population Science (Zhongguo Renkou Kexue)
Contemporary Asia-Pacific (Dangdai Yatai)
Contemporary International Relations (Xiandai Guoji Guanxi)
Economic Daily (Jingji Ribao)
Economic Journal (Hsin Pao) (Hong Kong)
Economics Weekly (Jingji Xue Zhoubao)
Fortnightly Review (Banyue Tan)
Freezing Point (Bing Dian)
Global Times (Huanqiu Shibao)
Guangming Daily (Guangming Ribao)
Liberation Army Daily (Jiefang Jun Bao)
Liberation Daily (Jiefang Ribao)
Naval and Merchant Ships (Jianchuan Zhishi)
Observe and Think (Guancha yu Sikao)

Open (Kaifang) (Hong Kong)
Oriental Daily News (Tong Fang Jih Pao) (Hong Kong)
Oriental Morning News (Dongfang Zaobao)
People's Daily (Renmin Ribao)
People's News (Renmin Bao)
Research in International Issues (Guoji Wenti Yanjiu)
Sanlian Life Weekly (Sanlian Shenghuo Zhoukan)
Seek Truth (Qiushi)
Shanghai Daily (Shanghai Ribao)
Southern Weekend (Nanfang Zhoumo)
Strategy and Management (Zhanlue yu Guanli)
Study Times (Xuexi Shibao)
Wide Angle (Kuang Chiao Ching) (Hong Kong)
World Economic Herald (Shijie Jingji Daobao)
World Economics and Politics (Shijie Jingji yu Zhengzhi)
World Knowledge (Shijie Zhishi)
World News Journal (Shijie Xinwen Bao)
Zhejiang Daily (Zhejiang Ribao)

Chinese Periodicals with No Common English Translation

Caijing (Beijing)
Cheng Ming (Hong Kong)
Liaowang (Beijing)
Ming Pao (Hong Kong)
Sing Tao Daily (Hong Kong)
Ta Kung Pao (Hong Kong)
Wen Wei Po (Hong Kong)

Japanese Periodicals

Asahi Shimbun
Chunichi Shimbun
Mainichi Shimbun
Nikkei Weekly
Sankei Shimbun
Sentaku
Yomiuri Shimbun

Notes

Individual author preference has been followed regarding the order (traditional vs. Western) of Chinese and Japanese surnames.

Chapter 1

1. Angus Maddison, *The World Economy: A Millennial Perspective* (Organization for Economic Cooperation and Development [OECD]: 2001).
2. According to the World Bank, www.worldbank.org, China's gross domestic product in 2005 was $2.23 trillion according to current exchange rates, putting it in fourth place. When the World Bank adjusts this figure for the lower price of goods and services in China, using a method called "purchasing power parity," it becomes $8.57 trillion, making China the second-largest economy in the world behind the United States. The Central Intelligence Agency's 2004 *World Factbook*, www.cia.gov/cia/publications/factbook/index.html, describes China as the second-largest economy in the world, as do the *Economist* and other magazines. When we are trying to compare the economic and military power of different countries, however, it doesn't make sense to use purchasing power parity calculations because they apply only to output sold and bought in China and not to output sold and bought abroad. Of course, international comparisons of national economies not adjusted for purchasing power parity are sensitive to changes in official exchange rates. If the Chinese government raises the value of its currency from the 2005 rate of 8.2 to the dollar to, say, 7 to the dollar, the size of the economy would increase to $2.60 trillion as a result, 17 percent larger than its current size of $2.23 trillion.
3. Thucydides, *History of the Peloponnesian War*, trans. Rex Warner (Harmondsworth, U.K.: Penguin, 1972).
4. According to the World Bank, China's per capita GDP in 2005 was $1,445, or $5,878 using the purchasing power parity method. *World Development Indicators*, 2006.
5. Reuters, March 4, 2003, www.cnn.com/2003/BUSINESS/asia/03/04/china.zhu.reut.
6. Xinhua, "Chinese Communist Party's Central Committee Decision on Enhancing the Party's Ability to Govern," September 26, 2004, Foreign Broadcast Information Service (FBIS), CPP20040926000042.

7. CCTV-1, "PRC Premier Wen Jiabao News Conference," March 14, 2006, FBIS, CPP20060314070001.

8. Paul Kennedy, *The Rise and Fall of the Great Powers* (New York: Vintage Books, 1989), xvi.

9. For 2005, Department of Defense, *Annual Report to Congress: The Military Power of the People's Republic of China*, www.dod.mil/news/Jul2005/ d20050719china.pdf; Central Intelligence Agency, "Rank Order: Military Expenditures," *The World Factbook* 2005, www.cia.gov/cia/publications/factbook/ rankorder/2067rank.html.

10. For 2003, International Institute of Strategic Studies, *Military Balance* 2006.

11. For 2003, RAND Corporation, "Modernizing China's Military: Opportunities and Constraints," www.rand.org/news/press.05/05.19.html.

12. Central Intelligence Agency, *The World Factbook*, 2004, www.cia.gov/cia/ publications/factbook/index.html, (March 15, 2005); Council on Foreign Relations, *Chinese Military Power*, 2003, 5.

13. Alastair Iain Johnston, "Is China a Status Quo Power?" *International Security*, vol. 27, no. 4, Spring 2003, 14.

Chapter 2

1. National Statistics Bureau of China, *China Statistical Yearbook*, 2004.

2. If China revalues its currency, the *renminbi* (RMB), its ranking could change. But as its GDP is still substantially below that of Germany, the third-largest economy, even a large appreciation of the RMB is unlikely to move it up to number three.

3. World Bank, 2006. At the end of 2005 the Chinese government revised its statistical estimates of GDP to better account for the service sector. Foreign economists believe the change made Chinese estimates more accurate. The 2004 GDP was revised upward 16.9 percent to $1.93 trillion at 2004 exchange rates. The revised 2004 per capita income was $1,490. Annual growth rates for 2001 through 2005 were revised upward, but no annual growth data based on the new measure was provided for before 2001. Judging from the changes in the 2001 through 2005 growth rates, China's average annual growth from 1979 to 2005 would likely be approximately 10 percent. For an explanation see the briefing by the head of National Bureau of Statistics of China, December 20, 2005, www.stats.gov.cn/english/newsandcomingevents/t20051220_402297118.htm.

4. International Iron and Steel Institute, www.worldsteel.org.

5. Oxford Economics and the Signal Group, "The China Effect: Assessing the Impact on the U.S. Economy of Trade and Investment with China," *Chinese Business Forum*, January 2006.

6. OECD, "China number one exporter of ICT goods in 2004," www.oecd.org/ document/8/0,2340,en_2649_201185_35833096_1_1_1_1,00.html.

7. Yungkai Yang, "The Taiwanese Notebook Computer Production Network in China: Implication for Upgrading of the Chinese Electronics Industry," The Personal Computing Industry Center (PCIC), University of California–Irvine, www.pcic.merage.uci.edu/pubs/2006/TaiwaneseNotebook.pdf.

8. *Wall Street Journal*, March 31, 2005.

9. *China Education Yearbook*, 2004. U.S. figures (2002) from National Science Foundation, www.nsf.gov/statistics/seind06/c2/c2h.htm/. Educational standards in China for an engineering graduate, however, are lower than in the United States.

10. *Financial Times*, February 7, 2005.
11. *Wired*, January 2003.
12. U.S. figures are $313 billion (2004) and $184 billion (1995). Japanese figures are $113 billion (2004) and $82 billion (1995). OECD, *OECD Science, Technology, and Industry Scoreboard*, 2005, www.sourceoecd.org/sti/scoreboard. The R&D spending estimate based on exchange rates is $29.4 billion (2005), *Wall Street Journal*, March 14, 2006. The State Council's February 2006 national guidelines for science and technology development set a target of raising R&D expenditures from 1.23 percent (2004) to 2.5 percent of GDP by 2020, english.gov.cn/2006-02/09/content_184335.htm.
13. *China Daily*, February 6, 2006, www.chinanews.cn.
14. China tops the list of countries where companies are likely to establish an R&D facility according to the U.N. Conference on Trade and Development, *World Investment Report*, 2005.
15. *Wall Street Journal*, March 13, 2006.
16. *People's Daily Online*, February 8, 2006, www.people.com.cn.
17. "China: Promoting Growth with Equity," World Bank, October 15, 2003, ii.
18. *New York Times*, May 3, 2006.
19. Barry Naughton, *The Chinese Economy: Growth and Transitions* (Cambridge, Mass.: MIT Press, 2006), 127.
20. On cars, *China Facts and Figures*, 2005, www.china.org.cn/english/en-sz2005/index.htm; on cell phones, Ministry of Information Industry, *Statistical Report of Telecommunication Development*, 2005, www.mii.gov.cn/art/2006/02/09/art_169_6243.html.
21. A May 2005 poll of Chinese citizens conducted as part of a seventeen-country survey by the Pew Global Attitudes Project found that China is "the world leader in hope for the future on a composite index of optimism," http://pewglobal.org.
22. "China Aims to Quadruple GDP, Build a Well-Off Society and Become the World's Largest Economy by 2020," *China Economic Times*, December 17, 2002, FBIS, CPP20021217000175.
23. Before 1978, the economy grew annually at a respectable 6 percent and per capita income at 4 percent. Naughton, *The Chinese Economy*.
24. Naughton, *The Chinese Economy*, 165.
25. Deng Xiaoping, "Building a Socialism with a Specifically Chinese Character," *Selected Works*, vol. 3 (Beijing: People's Publishing House, 1993), 64; and "Hold High the Banner of Mao Zedong Thought and Adhere to the Principle of Seeking Truth from Facts," *Selected Works*, vol. 2 (Beijing: People's Publishing House, 1994), 127, quoted in Wu Jinglian, *Understanding and Interpreting Chinese Economic Reform* (Mason, Ohio: Thomson Southwestern, 2005), 294.
26. Wu, *Understanding and Interpreting*, 291.
27. Ibid., 313.
28. Nicholas R. Lardy, *Testimony before the House Committee on International Relations, U.S. House of Representatives*, October 21, 2003.
29. Wu, *Understanding and Interpreting*, 315.
30. Naughton, *The Chinese Economy*, 3.
31. "There is no economic reason why China will stop adding manufacturing capacity until it reaches 15 percent of the world total, and quite possibly 20 percent or more." Arthur Kroeber, "How long can it last?" *China Economic Quarterly*, fourth quarter, 2004.

32. Of the working age population, 83 percent is actually employed—752 million people as of the end of 2004. Almost all Chinese women work. Naughton, *The Chinese Economy.*

33. Naughton, *The Chinese Economy,* 176.

34. Ibid.

35. The notion was introduced at the fifth plenum of the Fifteenth CCP Central Committee in October 2000, but wasn't elaborated until Jiang Zemin's speech to the Sixteenth CCP Congress in November 2002.

36. A Chinese index of economic and military strength that it uses to rank all the countries of the world.

37. Hu Angang, "China's Development Plan for 2020: Build a Well-Off and Harmonized Society China." December 8, 2005, www.chxk.org/2005/news/ view.asp?id=75.

38. Ibid.

39. Susan L. Shirk, *The Political Logic of Economic Reform in China* (Berkeley: University of California Press, 1992), 149–196.

40. Total tax revenues increased from 9.9 percent of GDP (1995) to 15.9 percent (2005). World Bank Office, Beijing, *Quarterly Update,* February 2006, www.siteresources.worldbank.org/INTCHINA/Resources/318862-1121421293578/ cqu_feb06.pdf.

41. Even if total military spending is estimated at three times the official budget as it is by the U.S. Department of Defense, however, it would constitute 4.2 percent of GDP (2004), not a massive mobilization of national resources.

42. *Global Times,* February 21, 2003, FBIS, CPP20030225000049.

43. According to Gary Saxonhouse, "The Integration of Giants into the Global Economy," American Enterprise Institute, no. 1, 2006, American manufacturing jobs fell during 1969 through 1971 as Japanese imports surged. But the drop turned out to be more due to macroeconomic causes than to Japanese competition. Manufacturing jobs in the United States have been declining for twenty-five years, but the rate of decline has accelerated since 1998 when Chinese imports began to increase rapidly. Close industry-by-industry analysis, however, makes it hard to see a connection between Chinese imports and large-scale job losses.

44. The United States retaliated with safeguards that have brought South Asia back into play in the U.S. textile and garment market.

45. Natural-resource-rich countries like Canada and Australia also are benefiting.

46. Saxonhouse, "Integration of Giants."

47. *Wall Street Journal,* October 24, 2005.

48. Yet China imports only 6 percent of its energy needs compared to 30 percent in the United States and only 8.2 percent of its energy consumption consists of petroleum.

49. Energy Information Administration (EIA), Country Analysis Briefs, www.eia.doe.gov/emeu/cabs/china.html.

50. Saxonhouse, "Integration of Giants."

51. World Bank Office, Beijing, *Quarterly Update,* February 2006, siteresources.worldbank.org/INTCHINA/Resources/318862-1121421293578/ cqu_feb06.pdf.

52. *Financial Times,* June 29, 2005. Taxes on gas guzzlers and other measures to limit private cars are already provoking complaints in the media from China's urban middle class. *China Youth Daily* editorial reported in *China Daily,* December 19, 2004.

53. *Oil and Gas Journal Online*, February 8, 2006, ogj.pennnet.com/articles/article_display.cfm?Section=ONART&C=Genin&ARTICLE_ID=247605&p=7.

54. The strategic logic also is flawed as China lacks the naval capabilities to protect its oil tankers in the far-flung sea-lanes of communications.

55. U.S. Department of Energy, *Section 1837: National Security Review of International Energy Requirements*, February 2006, resourcescommittee.house.gov/subcommittees/emr/issues/GlobalDemand/DOEChinaStudy.pdf.

56. Xia Liping, "Sino-U.S. Relations in the Early 21st Century, Asymmetrical Interdependence," *Contemporary Asia-Pacific*, December 15, 2005, FBIS, CPP20060124455001.

57. Because China agreed to enter the WTO in 2001 as a nonmarket economy for fifteen years, antidumping cases against China are easy to win if the price of the Chinese good is low. Wu, *Understanding and Interpreting*, 318.

58. *Straits Times*, October 29, 2005.

59. Taiwan runs a trade surplus with China, and Japan has run a deficit since 1988.

60. Thomas Lum and Dick K. Nanto, *China's Trade with the United States and the World*, Congressional Research Service, April 29, 2005. Much of Taiwan foreign direct investment (FDI) is routed through Hong Kong and offshore havens like the Virgin Islands and Cayman Islands.

61. Lum and Nanto, *China's Trade*.

62. Institute for International Education, "Chinese Students at American Colleges and Universities," January 26, 2005, www.iienetwork.org/?p=56814.

63. Bloomberg, January 6, 2006.

64. *Independent*, January 27, 2006.

65. Chinese estimates of the trade deficit always are lower than the U.S. estimates because of the different ways we treat products to and from China that pass through Hong Kong.

66. *China Daily*, "China forex reserves rose to US$ 818.9b in 2005," January 16, 2006, chinadaily.com.cn/english/doc/2006-01/16/content_512635.htm.

67. Lawrence H. Summers, "America Overdrawn," *Foreign Policy*, July–August 2004.

68. Lum and Nanto, *China's Trade*.

69. *New York Times*, February 9, 2006.

70. Council of Economic Advisors, *Economic Report of the President*, February 2004. China's share of U.S. imports grew from 3 percent in 1990 to 13 percent in 2004 while the rest of East Asia's share fell from 36 percent to 21.6 percent. Lum and Nanto, *China's Trade*.

71. Saxonhouse, "Integration of Giants."

72. *Financial Times*, November 6, 2006.

73. Economist Gary Saxonhouse ("Integration of Giants") notes that the United States, Germany, and Japan all ran large foreign exchange surpluses during their periods of rapid growth.

74. Nicholas R. Lardy, *Testimony before the House Committee on International Relations*, October 21, 2003, www.iie.com/publications/papers/paper.cfm?researchid=268. Lardy estimates that a 20 percent appreciation of the renminbi would result in a $10 billion reduction in the U.S. bilateral trade deficit with China and is actually more likely to be reflected in a slowdown of the rate of increase of the deficit instead of a reduction in its absolute size. Also see "Collective China Wisdom," *International Economy*, Spring 2005.

75. Major General Peng Guangqian, "China's Peaceful Development Path and Sino-U.S. Relations," *China Review* (Hong Kong), February 1, 2006, FBIS, CPP20060208510011.

76. *Economist*, "A great big bank gamble: China's banking industry," October 29, 2005. The nonperforming loans constitute 10.7 percent of GDP. *People's Daily Online*, December 28, 2005, www.people.com.cn.

77. *New York Times*, "International business: the two faces of China," December 6, 2004.

78. *People's Daily Online*, March 7, 2004, www.people.com.cn.

79. *People's Daily Online*, June 25, 2004, www.people.com.cn. According to the 2000 census, seventy-nine million people (6 percent of the population) are long-distance migrants. Liang Zai and Ma Zhongdong, "China's Floating Population: New Evidence from the 2000 Census," *Population and Development Review*, 30(3), September 2004, cited in Naughton, *The Chinese Economy*.

80. *Beijing Youth Daily*, "China Academy of Science describes the well-off society in 2020," September 18, 2003.

81. China Construction News, "China Housing Report," July 4, 2006, www.creva.org.cn/show.aspx?id=1913&cid=7.

82. As of 2003, only 68,670,000 of the 256,390,000 urban employees worked in state-owned enterprises. "Development of Non-State-Owned Economy 2002–2003," July 4, 2005, www.china.org.cn/chinese/zhuanti/scjj/906206.htm.

83. Based on Chinese official figures cited in John Giles, Albert Park, and Fang Cai, "How Has Economic Restructuring Affected China's Workers?" *China Quarterly*, no. 185 (March 2006), 61–95. State enterprise employment dropped by 46 percent and collective enterprise urban employment dropped 60 percent.

84. Xinhua, "China's urban unemployment rate declines for the first time in a decade," February 2, 2005, news.xinhuanet.com/newscenter/2005-02/02/content_2538341.htm.

85. Barry Naughton estimates that overall unemployment peaked from 1997 to 2000 at about fifteen million (10 percent of the urban labor force), *The Chinese Economy*, 186. See Giles et al., "Economic Restructuring" for unemployment rates in five large cities determined by sample surveys.

86. Xinhua, January 1, 2006.

87. *Guangming Daily*, October 18, 2005.

88. National Statistics Bureau of China, *China Statistical Yearbook*, 2004.

89. Reuters, October 27, 2006.

90. Between 1978 and 2004, 814,884 people studied abroad, and 197,884 of them returned to China. 20,100 returned in 2003, a 12.3 percent increase over the previous year. In 2004, 25,116 returned, a 24.6 percent increase. Over 35 percent of the 2003 returnees had difficulty finding work back in China. *China Today*, May 12, 2004, www.china.org.cn; *China Education News*, February 28, 2005.

91. *People's Daily Online*, June 21, 2005, www.people.com.cn.

92. Xinhua, January 27, 2006.

93. *China Daily*, June 19, 2005.

94. Xinhua, July 7, 2005.

95. Report by research institute of the Ministry of Labor and Social Security, *China Daily*, August 22, 2005.

96. *China Daily*, June 19, 2005. According to this article, China's Gini coefficient is "over .48." More recently the government states that the Gini is .46, *China Daily*, October 9, 2006.

97. *People's Daily*, May 11, 2002. According to this article, China's Gini coefficient was .33 in 1980 and exceeded .45 in 2002.

98. World Bank, *World Development Indicators*, 2004, which estimates China's Gini coefficient at .447.

99. Xinhua, July 7, 2005.
100. *China Daily*, March 8, 2004.
101. *People's Daily*, May 11, 2002.
102. *Wide Angle* (Hong Kong), June 16, 2005, FBIS, CPP20050621000075; *People's Daily Online*, December 7, 2004 reports on a study comparing China and other countries that identified special obstacles impeding China's future growth including the expanding income gap.
103. Transparency International, "Survey sources for the TI corruption perceptions Index 2005," ww1.transparency.org/cpi/2005/cpi2005.sources.en.html.
104. *China Daily*, July 1, 2006.
105. *Financial Times*, October 29, 2002.
106. Xinhua, August 8, 2005, FBIS, CPP20050808000212.
107. David Dollar, "China's Economic Problems (and Ours)," *Milken Review*, 2005, www.milkeninstitute.org/publications/review/2005_9/48_58mr27.pdf.
108. Xinhua, September 23, 2005, www.chinaview.cn.
109. Ibid.
110. *Independent*, October 19, 2005.
111. *China Daily*, February 12, 2006.
112. Elizabeth C. Economy, *The River Runs Black: The Environmental Challenge to China's Future* (Ithaca: Cornell University Press, 2004), 72.
113. For example, Hu Jintao's speech, "Comprehensively Implement and Fulfill Scientific Development Concept," *Seek Truth*, January 1, 2006, FBIS, CPP20060106501022.
114. *Financial Times*, February 7, 2006.

Chapter 3

1. James Tong and Elaine Chan, eds., *Fire and Fury: The Democracy Movement in Beijing, April–June 1989* (Armonk, N.Y.: M. E. Sharpe, 1990), 317.
2. *People's Daily*, editorial, April 26, 1989.
3. My retelling of the Tiananmen story draws from the most authoritative insider's account of the crisis. Andrew J. Nathan and Perry Link, eds. (compiled by Zhang Liang), *The Tiananmen Papers* (New York: Public Affairs, 2001).
4. *Tiananmen Square, 1989, The Declassified History*, National Security Archive, www.gwu.edu/~nsarchiv/NSAEBB/NSAEBB16/documents/19-01.htm.
5. Nathan and Link, eds., *Tiananmen Papers*, 255.
6. Ibid., 438.
7. Ibid., 423.
8. Douglas McAdam says that a protest movement only develops when there is a "political opportunity structure." *Political Process and the Development of Black Insurgency* (Chicago: University of Chicago Press, 1999).
9. H. Lyman Miller, "Hu Jintao and the Party Politburo," *China Leadership Monitor*, no. 9 (Winter 2004).
10. *New York Times*, September 18, 2005.
11. *New York Times*, August 31, 2005.
12. Past Standing Committees had five to nine members. During the Deng Xiaoping era, the retired elders made many of the most significant decisions in Deng's living room. Today, the only retired leader who still participates in some important international decisions is retired president and CCP general secretary, Jiang Zemin. The Chinese, when referring to the "Party and government

leaders" use a broader definition that includes more than one hundred positions in the CCP, government, National People's Congress, National People's Political Consultative Congress, Supreme People's Court, Supreme People's Procurate, and the Central Military Commission. Lu Ning, *The Dynamics of Foreign-Policy Decisionmaking in China* (Boulder: Westview Press, 1997), 95.

13. Susan L. Shirk, *The Political Logic of Economic Reform in China* (Berkeley: University of California Press, 1993).

14. Ibid.

15. Frederick C. Teiwes, "Normal Politics with Chinese Characteristics," in Jonathan Unger, ed., *The Nature of Chinese Politics from Mao to Jiang* (Armonk, N.Y.: M. E. Sharpe, 2002), 254.

16. Shirk, *Political Logic of Economic Reform*.

17. Jack Snyder argues that "cartelized systems" in which power assets are concentrated in the hands of parochial groups with narrow interests, are prone to international expansion. *Myths of Empire: Domestic Politics and International Ambition* (Ithaca: Cornell University Press, 1991), 31.

18. A third interagency group, the National Security Leading Small Group, has not yet played a significant role.

19. Robert L. Suettinger, *Beyond Tiananmen: The Politics of U.S.-China Relations, 1989–2000* (Washington, D.C.: Brookings Institution Press, 2003), 182; Patrick Tyler, *A Great Wall: Six Presidents and China* (New York: Public Affairs, 1999), 401.

20. Wang Chien-min, "Story behind the Truth of Submarine No. 361 Accident," *Asia Weekly* (Hong Kong), no. 20, May 12, 2003, FBIS, CPP20030513000079; *Washington Post*, June 13, 2003.

21. *Open* (Hong Kong), December 2004, www.open.com.hk/2003_12news1.htm.

22. *Globe and Mail* (Toronto), September 8, 2005.

23. *Asia Times Online*, December 7, 2004.

24. FBIS Media Analysis, December 10, 2004, CPF20041210000197.

25. It is called the educational campaign "to preserve CCP's advanced nature." *People's Daily*, September 2, 2005, FBIS, CPP20050905000009.

26. *Washington Post*, April 24, 2005.

27. *South China Morning Post*, August 18, 2005.

28. *People's News*, July 28, 2001, FBIS, CPP20010802000183. For an example of a split in the Iranian leadership played out on the Internet see the *New York Times*, June 21, 2005.

29. *New York Times*, March 9, 2001.

30. *Seek Truth*, December 16, 2002, FBIS, CPP20021218000098.

31. Alice Miller notes, however, that at the Sixteenth CCP Congress, every one of the Politburo members not required to retire due to age was promoted to the Standing Committee, which may indicate a new standard practice instead of Jiang's packing the body with his followers. "The 16th Party Congress, Implications for Understanding Chinese Politics," *China Leadership Monitor*, no. 5, Winter 2003, 50.

32. *Straits Times*, September 21, 2004.

33. Xinhua, September 20, 2004.

34. For example, the document of the Fourth Plenum of the Fourteenth Central Committee in 1994. See Joseph Fewsmith, *China Since Tiananmen: The Politics of Transition* (Cambridge: Cambridge University Press, 2001), 163.

35. Some entrepreneurial politicians already have started playing to mass publics in anticipation of future changes in the political game. Li Ruihuan, as mayor and CCP secretary of Tianjin in the 1980s, squeezed money out of the state industrial

enterprises that have traditionally been favored by the CCP in order to build parks and other public works desired by ordinary citizens. The current CCP secretary of underdeveloped Henan Province is leading a well-publicized effort to eliminate discrimination against people from Henan who are often stereotyped as criminals. Xinhua, May 26, 2005.

36. Posted October 4, 2005, www.qglt.com/bbs/ReadFile?whichfile= 29119&typeid=41&openfile=0. An excerpt was translated by the blogger Anti chinathinkbase.com/archives/16. Also see Jonathan Huang, "The Future of Education on Economics in Mainland China," December 1, 2005, China Elections and Governance, www.chinaelections.org/en/ readnews.asp?newsid=%7BF61AAA0D-F41C-437D-A.

37. *Liaowang*, December 5, 2005, FBIS, CPP20051214510008.

38. *People's Daily Online*, June 5, 2006, english.peopledaily.com.cn/200606/05/ eng20060605_271081.html.

39. More than one contender for the top job may be moved into the Politburo Standing Committee at the Seventeenth Party Congress in fall 2007 if no one individual can win enough support, which would heat up the competition during the 2007–12 term. Several Standing Committee slots may become available because although only one current member will be over the seventy retirement age (Luo Gan) in 2007, two others will be sixty-nine, one will be sixty-eight, and one will be sixty-seven. The retirement age for CCP leaders has never been formally announced, and some Chinese analysts believe that it actually may have been lowered to sixty-eight at the Sixteenth CCP Congress in 2002.

40. Li Junru, deputy head of the Communist Party School. Quoted in Reuters, March 10, 2006.

41. *New York Times*, May 15, 2002.

42. Fei-ling Wang, "Self-Image and Strategic Intentions: National Confidence and Political Insecurity," in Yong Deng and Fei-ling Wang, eds., *In the Eyes of the Dragon: China Views the World* (Lanham, Md.: Rowan and Littlefield, 1999), 31.

43. David Shambaugh, "Containment or Engagement of China? Calculating Beijing's Response," *International Security*, vol. 21, no. 2 (Autumn 1996), 206.

44. Samuel P. Huntington, *The Third Wave: Democratization in the Late Twentieth Century* (Norman: University of Oklahoma Press, 1991).

45. *People's Daily Online*, September 20, 2005.

46. Jiang Zemin, "Hold High the Great Banner of Deng Xiaoping Theory for an All-round Advancement of the Cause of Building Socialism with Chinese Characteristics to the 21st Century—Report at the 15th National Congress of the Communist Party of China," *People's Daily*, September 22, 1997.

47. *People's Daily*, commentary, July 27, 2005.

48. *China Daily*, March 8, 2004. In fact, the 2004 unemployment rate declined to 4.2 percent. *People's Daily Online*, January 26, 2005; *China Daily*, March 6, 2005.

49. What China is experiencing is an extreme form of what political scientist Karl Deutsch called "social mobilization," Karl Deutsch, *Nationalism and Social Communication* (Cambridge, Mass.: M.I.T. Press, 1953).

50. Suzanne Lohmann, "The Dynamics of Informational Cascades: The Monday Demonstrations in Leipzig, East Germany, 1989–91," *World Politics*, vol. 47, no. 1 (October 1994), 42–101; Timur Kuran, "Now Out of Never: The Element of Surprise in the East European Revolution of 1989," *World Politics*, vol. 44, no. 1 (October 1991), 7–48.

51. Murray Scot Tanner, "China Rethinks Unrest," *Washington Quarterly*, vol. 27, no. 3 (Summer 2004), 143. *The Social Blue Book* produced annually by the Chinese Academy of Social Sciences provides analyses of different types of

protests and their causes. *Zhongguo: Shehui Xingzhi Fenxi yu Yuce* [China: Analysis and Forecast of the Social Situation] (Beijing: Chinese Social Sciences Press).

52. The police released a statistic of eighty-seven thousand "public order disturbances" during 2005, a number that Western journalists are now using as a
   measure of the increase in protest activity. The category "public order disturbances" (*raoluan gonggong zhixu*), however, is not the same as the category
   "mass incidents" (*qunti xing shijian*) according to Murray Scot Tanner (personal
   communication).

53. The 2003 statistics are from *Liaowang* (Beijing), June 7, 2004. The 2004 statistics
   are from *South China Morning Post*, July 7, 2005. The earlier numbers are from
   Tanner, "China Rethinks Unrest," 138–139.

54. Public Security Minister Zhou Yongkang's report to the Chinese People's
   Political Consultative Congress, quoted in *Ta Kung Pao* (Hong Kong) and
   reported in Reuters, July 27, 2005.

55. *Democracy and Law*, issue 16 (August 2005). The term "mass incidents" was
   publicly introduced at a news conference held by the CCP Organization
   Department July 7, 2005. "Mass Incidents Challenge China," *Globe*, August 1,
   2005.

56. *Open* (Hong Kong) reports that the Propaganda Department forbade reporting
   on demonstrations, strikes, riots, and acts of sabotage after Hu Jintao's tough
   speech to the CCP Central Committee in September 2004, www.open.com.hk/
   2003_12news1.htm.

57. "PRC Civil Disturbances 1 Jan–15 Dec 04," FBIS Report, CPP20041223000120,
   December 23, 2004.

58. *Social Blue Book* 1993–94, 269.

59. Tanner, "China Rethinks Unrest," 144.

60. *Economist*, March 15, 1997.

61. Chien-peng Chung, "China's 'War on Terror': September 11 and Uighur
   Separatism," *Foreign Affairs*, July–August 2002.

62. *New York Times*, November 26, 2004.

63. The labor market is working to diffuse the discontent of employed workers.
   Workers unhappy about low wages and poor working conditions in Guangdong
   factories just pick up and move to Zhejiang or Jiangsu. Faced by an unprecedented labor shortage, Guangdong industry now has to offer more.

64. Cai Yongshun, *State and Laid-Off Workers in Reform China: The Silence and
   Collective Action of the Retrenched* (London and New York: Routledge, 2006).

65. *Cheng Ming* (Hong Kong), January 1, 2003, in *BBC Monitoring*, January 10, 2003.

66. *International Herald Tribune*, November 8, 2006.

67. *Apple Daily* Web site (Hong Kong), February 4, 2006.

68. *New York Times*, July 19, 2005.

69. *South China Morning Post*, July 1, 2005.

70. Associated Press, August 21, 2005.

71. Reuters, June 29, 2005.

72. Suisheng Zhao, *A Nation-State by Construction: Dynamics of Modern Chinese
   Nationalism* (Stanford, Calif.: Stanford University Press, 2004), 213.

73. Jiang Zemin, "Strengthening Education in Patriotism," *People's Daily*, May 11,
   1997, quoted by Zhao, *Nation-State by Construction*, 227.

74. From 1978 to 1988 there were 181 articles in *People's Daily* that included the
   terms "social stability" and "patriotism." From 1989 to 2002, there were 1,286
   articles with both terms.

75. Xinhua, October 22, 1996, cited by Zhao, *Nation-State by Construction*, 222.
76. Benedict Anderson, *Imagined Communities* (London: Verso, 1991). The nationalist sentiments widely expressed by Chinese living abroad are evidence that not all contemporary Chinese nationalism is engineered by the CCP.
77. Zhang Xudong, "Nationalism and Contemporary China," *East Asia: An International Quarterly*, vol. 16, no. 1–2 (Spring–Summer 1997), 4.
78. Edward Friedman, *National Identity and Democratic Prospects in Socialist China* (Armonk, N.Y: M. E. Sharpe, 1995).
79. Zheng Yongnian, *Discovering Chinese Nationalism in China: Modernization, Identity, and International Relations* (Cambridge: Cambridge University Press, 1999), 15.
80. As historian Jonathan Spence observed, "The damaging defeats inflicted on China by the British during the first half of the nineteenth century were part cause and part consequence of China's own domestic instability." Jonathan D. Spence, *The Search for Modern China* (New York: W. W. Norton and Co., 1990), 165.
81. In 1905 Washington demanded that Beijing issue a proclamation against the boycott of American goods. The Qing government superficially complied but signaled its ambivalence by posting the proclamation upside down in many cities. Spence, *Search for Modern China*, 238.
82. Joseph Esherick, *The Origins of the Boxer Uprising* (Berkeley: University of California Press, 1987), 289.
83. The Guomindang did fight hard against the Japanese in the Shanghai and Nanjing areas, but lost to superior Japanese forces.
84. Chalmers Johnson, *Peasant Nationalism and Communist Power: The Emergence of Revolutionary China* (Stanford, Calif.: Stanford University Press, 1963).
85. *People's Daily*, August 15, 2005.
86. *Cheng Ming* (Hong Kong), January 1, 2003, in *BBC Monitoring*, January 10, 2003.
87. *South China Morning Post*, July 4, 2005.
88. *People's Daily* front-page commentary quoted in *South China Morning Post*, July 29, 2005.
89. *South China Morning Post*, August 17, 2005.
90. Barbara Geddes observes that single-party states like China survive longer than authoritarian regimes under military or personalistic rule because they co-opt potential challengers. Geddes, Barbara, "Authoritarian Breakdown: Empirical Test of a Game Theoretic Argument," unpublished paper, 1999. The Falun Gong claims that there have been massive resignations from the CCP, signaling that regime change is imminent, but there is no evidence to support the claim. Such resignations occurred in Hungary in the years before its Communist government fell.
91. Xinhua, October 28, 2003, FBIS, CPP20031028000087.
92. *China Daily*, July 1, 2006.
93. Andrew G. Walder, "The Party Elite and China's Trajectory of China," *China: An International Journal*, vol. 2, no. 2 (September 2004), 200.
94. *China Education News*, May 11, 2006.
95. In the often-quoted words of historical sociologist Barrington Moore, "no bourgeoisie, no democracy." *Social Origins of Dictatorship and Democracy: Lord and Peasant in the Making of the Modern World* (Boston: Beacon Press, 1966).
96. *People's Daily Online*, January 27, 2001.
97. Surveys conducted in 1995, 1996, and 1999 by Jie Chen, *Popular Political Support in Urban China* (Washington, D.C.: Woodrow Wilson Center Press, 2004), table 2.1, 30–33. Chen also finds that about 50 percent of people say they

would not criticize the government because of their fear of political persecution, but there is very little relationship between how fearful people say they are and how much they say they support the system. Shi Tianjian also found that over 40 percent of people he surveyed were concerned about being reported to the authorities if they criticized the government. "Cultural Values and Political Trust: A Comparison of the People's Republic of China and Taiwan," *Comparative Politics*, July 2001, 405.

98. Pei Minxin, *China's Trapped Transition* (Cambridge, Mass.: Harvard University Press, 2006), 18.

99. Lieutenant General Wang Zhiyuan, deputy director of the Science and Technology Commission of the PLA, said to the Hong Kong newspaper *Wen Wei Po* (March 10, 2006, FBIS, CPP20060310508004), "As China is such a large country with such a long coastline and we want to protect our maritime interests, aircraft carriers are an absolute necessity." The story also reports that China has learned to make catapults for carrier-based aircraft so it will be able to build horizontal deck carriers like the American ones.

100. Office of the Secretary of Defense, *The Military Power of the People's Republic of China*, 2005, executive summary.

101. Department of Defense, *Quadrennial Defense Review Report*, February 6, 2006, www.defenselink.mil/pubs/pdfs/QDR20060203.pdf.

102. Ibid.

103. Snyder, *Myths of Empire*, 142.

104. Frederick Teiwes, "The Chinese State during the Maoist Era," in David Shambaugh, ed., *The Modern Chinese State* (New York: Cambridge University Press, 2000).

105. Andrew Scobell, "China's Evolving Civil-Military Relations: Creeping *Guojiahua*," *Armed Forces and Society*, vol. 31, no. 2 (Winter 2005), 233.

106. PLA head Lin Biao, who had been chosen by Mao as his successor, attempted unsuccessfully to seize power and was killed fleeing to the Soviet Union in 1971.

107. "The State Military System," in Pu Xingzu, ed., *Zhonghua Gongheguo Zhengzhi Zhidu* [Political System of the People's Republic of China], (Shanghai: Shanghai People's Publishing House, 2005); Scobell, "China's Evolving Civil-Military Relations," 227–244.

108. *Liberation Army Daily*, December 8, 2005, FBIS, CPP20051208510020.

109. Zhongguo Tongxun She (Hong Kong), October 23, 2005, FBIS, CPP20051023057019.

110. You Ji, "The Supreme Leader and the Military," in Unger, ed., *The Nature of Chinese Politics*, 276.

111. Whereas Germany and Japan modernized their economies by starting with heavy industries like steel, machinery, and shipbuilding closely tied to the military, China's pattern of economic modernization began with agriculture and light industry, which are less related to military strength.

112. I am grateful to Tai Ming Cheung for this information.

113. David Shambaugh, *Modernizing China's Military: Progress, Problems, and Prospects* (Berkeley: University of California Press, 2002), 191.

114. The 1981 figure is from Harlan W. Jencks, *From Muskets to Missiles: Politics and Professionalism in the Chinese Army, 1945–1981* (Boulder: Westview Press, 1982), 146, and the 2001 figure is from Shambaugh, *Modernizing China's Military*, 154.

115. Thomas Christensen suggested framing the trends in this way.

116. Office of the Secretary of Defense, *The Military Power of the People's Republic of China*, 2005, 21.

117. Xinhua, March 5, 2006.
118. The Wilhelmian German government sought to strengthen the fiscal authority of the center over the provinces to build up national military strength. I have found only one instance in which a Chinese leader justified the 1994 recentralization of fiscal revenues in the same terms. Jiang Zemin, in a 2000 speech, made the case that the central government could control more fiscal resources, reclaiming them from the provinces, "in order to strengthen the construction of national defense." *People's Daily*, April 17, 2000.
119. Xinhua, March 5, 2006.
120. Ibid., 57.
121. The 1998 order requiring the PLA to divest itself of all its commercial businesses was welcomed by the military brass. Commercialization had corrupted the military and impeded its professionalization, and the government's budget increases more than compensated for the foregone profits.
122. James Mulvenon, "They Protest Too Much (Or Too Little), Methinks: Soldier Protests, Party Control of the Military, and the 'National Army' Debate," *China Leadership Monitor*, no. 15 (Summer 2005).
123. The 1991 Gulf War was the first impetus to spur military modernization, but the Taiwan issue is its strategic focus.
124. Andrew Scobell, "Show of Force: Chinese Soldiers, Statesmen, and the 1995–96 Taiwan Strait Crisis," *Political Science Quarterly*, vol. 115, no. 2 (Summer 2000), 227–246.
125. *Ming Pao* (Hong Kong), April 11, 2006, FBIS, CPP200604111477.
126. *China Daily*, May 9, 2006.
127. Alastair Iain Johnston (personal communication) reports that the Beijing Area Study 2003 and 2004, conducted by the Research Center on Contemporary China at Beijing University, found that in 2003, 62 percent disagreed with the statement that military spending should be decreased in order to establish a better welfare system, a proportion that increased to 73 percent in 2004.
128. Pew Global Attitudes Project, "Publics of Asian Powers Hold Negative Views of One Another," 2006, http://pewglobal.org.
129. Xinhua, March 5, 2006.
130. *China Daily*, March 9, 2006.
131. *Liberation Army Daily*, January 9, 2006, FBIS, CPP20060215502001.
132. *Liberation Army Daily*, April 28, 2006, FBIS, CPP2006050252001.
133. Shen Dingli, "Compete with the United States in a Justifiable Way," *Oriental Morning News*, February 7, 2006.
134. Ji, "The Supreme Leader and the Military," 289.
135. Ibid., 295.
136. *China Daily*, July 17, 2005.
137. *Financial Times*, July 25, 2005.
138. *Boston Globe*, December 22, 2005.
139. George Yang, "Mechanisms of Foreign Policy-Making and Implementation in the Ministry of Foreign Affairs," in Carol Lee Hamrin and Suisheng Zhao, eds., *Decision-Making in Deng's China: Perspectives from Insiders* (Armonk, N.Y.: M. E. Sharpe, 1995), 92.
140. Allen Whiting, "Chinese Nationalism and Foreign Policy after Deng," *China Quarterly*, no. 142 (June 1995), 295–316.
141. Thomas J. Christensen, "Tracking China's Security Relations: Causes for Optimism and Pessimism," *China Leadership Monitor*, no. 1 (Winter 2002), 1.

Chapter 4

1. Yuan Weishi, "Modernization and History Textbooks," *Freezing Point*, January 11, 2006, trans. EastSouthWestNorth, www.zonaeuropa.com/20060126_1.htm.
2. China Youth League Central Propaganda Department, "Concerning the Handling Decision with Respect to *China Youth Daily Freezing Point* Weekly Wrongly Publishing 'Modernization and History Textbooks,'" EastSouthWestNorth, www.zonaeuropa.com/20060126_1.htm.
3. Li Datong, "A public protest against the illegal stoppage of the *Freezing Point* weekly magazine," EastSouthWestNorth, www.zonaeuropa.com/20060126_3.htm.
4. *Epoch Times*, February 14, 2006, www.epochtimes.com/gb/6/2/14/n1223760.htm.
5. *Sing Tao Daily* (Hong Kong), March 2, 2003, EastSouthWestNorth, www.zonaeuropa.com/200603.brief.htm. Chinese journalist-critic Dai Qing repeated the report of Hu Jintao's intervention in dwnews.com, March 4, 2006.
6. Ithiel de Sola Pool, "Communication in Totalitarian Societies," in Ithiel de Sola Pool et al., *Handbook of Communication* (Chicago: Rand McNally, 1973), 463.
7. Ibid., 488.
8. Benjamin L. Liebman, "Watchdog or Demagogue? The Media in China's Legal System," *Columbia Law Review*, vol. 105, no. 1 (January 2005), 17.
9. Wang Guoqing, "Annual Report of Newspaper in China 2005," August 5, 2005, *People's Daily Online*, media.people.com.cn/GB/40710/40715/3595542.html; Yu Guoming, "Summary of China Media Industry Annual Report 2004–2005," June 30, 2005, www.china.org.cn/chinese/zhuanti/chuanmei/903486.htm.
10. The economic logic was the same as that applied to schools and offices, namely, reduce the government's financial burden, improve the efficiency of the units, and meet the needs of China's nascent market economy. I am puzzled, however, about the political logic of the decision. Did Deng Xiaoping and his Party colleagues feel so politically secure by the 1980s that they could risk surrendering their monopoly control of the information reaching citizens? Or did they think that they could retain control over the marketized media?
11. China had a genuinely free *People's Daily* and CCTV for six days, May 13–19, 1989, during the Tiananmen demonstrations. The Communist Party leaders were as worried about the journalists' rebellion as they were about the students' (see Nathan and Link, eds.,*Tiananmen Papers*). After the crackdown, Party conservatives closed several liberal newspapers—the *World Economic Herald* in Shanghai and *Economics Weekly* in Beijing. They also criticized the former leaders Zhao Ziyang and Hu Yaobang for making the mistake of loosening control over the press. See Liu Xiaobo, "The Tragedy of Hu Yaobang and Zhao Ziyang," Chinese Newsnet.com, March 2005, www5.chinesenewsnet.com/MainNews/Opinion/2005_2_1_19_11_58_68.html.
12. Gallup, February 2005.
13. *The Age*, December 31, 2006, www.theage.com.au/news/web/chinas-internet-population-boom/2006/12/29/1166895509752.htm.
14. Gallup, February 2005.
15. Ibid.
16. Ibid.
17. Li Xiguang and Qin Xuan, "Who Is Setting the Chinese Agenda in the Recent Chinese-U.S. Collision?" unpublished paper, 2001.
18. He Qinglian, *Media Control in China: A Report by Human Rights in China*, 2003, www.hrichina.org/public/contents/20205.

19. *Financial Times*, March 4, 2002.
20. For a discussion of how the speed of the Internet makes it impossible to stop dissent from spreading see *Washington Post*, February 20, 2006.
21. The foreign press uses the number thirty thousand for the size of the Internet censorship operation. This number never had any reliable basis and certainly underestimates the current size of the operation, which according to the Chinese press has expanded especially at the local level.
22. Open Net Initiative, www.opennetinitiative.net/studies/Singapore.
23. Jack Snyder, *From Voting to Violence: Democratization and Nationalist Conflict* (New York: Norton, 2000), 59.
24. Thomas C. Schelling, *The Strategy of Conflict*, second ed. (Cambridge, Mass.: Harvard University Press, 1980), 144.
25. The newspaper published as a weekly until 2001, twice a week from 2001 to 2003, three times a week from 2003 to 2005, and all five weekdays since 2005.
26. *People's Daily Online*, November 5, 2004, www.people.com.cn/GB/14677/21963/22063/2969220.html.
27. The paper's treatment of Clinton was not unsympathetic. For example, its front-page headline on November 15, 1998, was "Sexual affairs and national affairs are two different things. The president and ordinary people are all human beings."
28. FBIS Media Survey Report, China, February 2004.
29. *Economist*, February 5, 2005.
30. Liebman, "Watchdog or Demagogue?" 32.
31. Ibid., 39.
32. Associated Press, September 15, 2001.
33. Joseph Man Chan, "Administrative Boundaries and Media Marketization," in Chin-Chuan Lee, ed., *Chinese Media, Global Contexts* (London: Routledge Curzon, 2003), 167.
34. According to interviews with two of the Phoenix anchor people in *Sanlian Life Weekly*, no. 15, April 12, 2004.
35. Peter Hessler, "Straight to Video," *New Yorker*, October 15, 2001.
36. *New York Times*, January 8, 2001.
37. According to a CCTV director, CCTV-4, its international news channel, increased its commercial advertising from less than one minute per hour to three minutes every half hour since it began to broadcast reports about the U.S. attack on Iraq. *Wall Street Journal*, March 27, 2003.
38. Yin Lijuan and Xiong Lei, "Chinese Media Coverage of War in Iraq, *World Press Review*, April 9, 2003.
39. *New York Times*, March 8, 2006.
40. See Ashley Esarey, "Speak No Evil: Mass Media Control in Contemporary China," February 2006, Freedom House Special Report.
41. Hu Shuli, "Let a Thousand Newspapers Bloom," Project Syndicate, February 20, 2005, www.project-syndicate.org/commentaries/commentary_text.php4?id=1081&lang=1.
42. Xiao Qiang, "Testimony before the U.S.-China Economic and Security Review Commission," June 5, 2003.
43. "Internet Filtering in China 2004–5," www.opennetinitiative.net/studies/china.
44. *China Digital Times*, August 30, 2004, www.chinadigitaltimes.net/2004/08/the_words_you_n.php.
45. See "Living Dangerously on the Net," Reporters without Borders, May 12, 2003, www.rsf.org/article.php3?id_article=6793.

46. A SCIO official said that the nation's "mainstream Internet media" consisted of eight central level Web sites and twenty-four local level ones. FBIS report, November 28, 2004, CPP20041206000038.

47. Agence France Presse, April 4, 2004, www.story.news.yahoo.com/news?tmpl=story&ncid=1212&e=2&u=/afp/20050404/tc_afp/vaticanpopechinainternet&sid=96001018.

48. *Washington Post*, December 17, 2005.

49. "New Survey in Mainland China Paints a Detailed Picture of Which People Are Using the Internet and Why," Markle Foundation, www.markle.org/resources/press_center/press_releases/2005/press_release_1117200.

50. *Wall Street Journal*, February 13, 2006.

51. *Asia Weekly* (Hong Kong), March 12, 2006, www.zonaeuropa.com/20060305_1.htm.

52. Xinhua, "CPC Official Li Changchun Advocates Improving Propaganda Work," January 8, 2003.

53. BBC News, July 14, 2005.

54. *Public Interest Times* (reported in *South China Morning Post* [Hong Kong] February 13, 2006); *Beijing News* (reported in Agence France Presse, December 30, 2005).

55. Xinhua, December 12, 2005, english.sina.com/china/1/2005/1202/56460.html.

56. *Global Times*, May 28, 2004; *Oriental Daily News* (Hong Kong), August 24, 2004, FBIS CPP20040824000115.

57. Foreign Minister Li's Web dialogue was December 24, 2003.

58. "Living Dangerously on the Net," Reporters without Borders, May 12, 2003, www.rsf.org/article.php3?id_article=6793.

59. *South China Morning Post*, May 19, 2003.

60. *Guardian*, March 4, 2003.

61. I repeated the analysis of Alastair Iain Johnston, "The Correlations of Beijing Opinion toward the United States, 1998–2004," in Alastair Iain Johnston and Robert S. Ross, eds., *New Directions in the Study of China's Foreign Policy* (Stanford, Calif.: Stanford University Press, 2006).

62. The Internet discussion of Abu Ghraib on Strong National Forum, although about 45 percent anti-American, included 25 percent praise for the U.S. press for exposing the abuse and criticism of China's press for not being able to do the same for problems at home. More than one-third of all the postings praised America's democratic system. Anthony J. Spires, "Some Chinese See Positive Lessons in Iraqi 'Torture Gate,'" *Yale Global*, May 14, 2004, www.yaleglobal.yale.edu/display.article?id=3871.

63. This was the formula Deng Xiaoping adopted to assess Mao Zedong following the Cultural Revolution. It is considered damning with faint praise, not a compliment.

64. On the perception that the media reflects public opinion see Liebman, "Watchdog or Demagogue," 121.

65. *China Daily*, January 21, 2005.

66. Xinhua, March 5, 2006.

67. Spires, "Some Chinese See Positive Lessons."

68. He Qinglian, *Media Control in China, A Report by Human Rights in China*, 2003, Chapter 3, www.hrichina.org/public/contents/20205, has a description of the CCP's internal reporting system.

69. As of a few years ago, Xinhua journalists were paid five thousand yuan if their internal report was selected for the daily briefing of Politburo members and ten

thousand yuan for Politburo Standing Committee members. If a Standing Committee member responded to the report, they got twenty thousand yuan.

70. *New York Times*, August 10, 2001.
71. Zhang Kunsheng, "Unconventional Visit: Memorandum of Li Zhaoxing's Visit to Japan and South Korea," *Observe and Think*, September 1, 2003.
72. Liu Xiaobo, "Me and the Internet," EastSouthWestNorth, www.zonaeuropa.com/20060224_2.htm.
73. http://english.gov.cn/official/2005-07/26/content_17166.htm.

Chapter 5

1. Translation of speech distributed at the conference.
2. Susan L. Shirk, "Asia Pacific Regional Security: Balance of Power or Concert of Powers," in David A. Lake and Patrick M. Morgan, eds., *Regional Orders: Building Security in a New World* (University Park: Pennsylvania State University Press, 1997), 245–270.
3. *China Youth Daily*, May 21, 2003, FBIS, CPP20030521000060.
4. Ma Xiaojun, "Transforming Concepts and Proactively Responding to Factors," *Contemporary International Relations*, November 20, 2002, FBIS, CPP20021209000250.
5. "Chinese Diplomacy Oriented Toward the 21st Century: Pursuing and Balancing Three Needs," *Strategy and Management*, December 30, 1999, FBIS, CPP20000215000115. The phrase became more prominent in 2003, as China struggled to salvage its international reputation after the fiasco of the initial cover-up of the SARS epidemic. See *Southern Weekend*, May 29, 2003 and *China Youth Daily*, May 21, 2003.
6. Alastair Iain Johnston, "Is China a Status Quo Power?" *International Security*, vol. 27, no. 4 (Spring 2003), 5–56.
7. *World Knowledge*, June 16, 2002, FBIS, CPP20020708000168.
8. *People's Daily Online*, December 12, 2003, www.people.com.cn.
9. Xinhua, March 26, 2004.
10. Robert L. Suettinger, "The Rise and Descent of 'Peaceful Rise,'" *China Leadership Monitor*, no. 12 (Fall 2004).
11. Xinhua, August 12, 2005.
12. "Multilateralism" is usually defined as "coordinating national policies in groups of three or more states." Robert O. Keohane, "Multilateralism: An Agenda for Research," *International Journal*, vol. 45, no. 4 (Autumn 1990), 731. Bilateralism involves relations between only two states.
13. 2005 Pew Global Attitudes Survey. http://pewglobal.org; BBC, March 5, 2005, news.bbc.co.uk/2/hi/asia-pacific/4318551.stm; Program on International Policy Attitudes, University of Maryland, March 7, 2005, www.pipa.org/OnlineReports/BBCworldpoll/030505/html/bbcpoll3/html.
14. Pei Minxin, *Financial Times*, September 12, 2004.
15. Bin Yu, "China and Its Asian Neighbors: Implications for Sino-U.S. Relations," in Yong Deng and Fei-Ling Wang, eds., *In the Eyes of the Dragon: China Views the World* (Langham, Md.: Rowman and Littlefield, 1999), 186.
16. Ma Xiaojun, "Transforming Concepts and Proactively Responding to Factors," *Contemporary International Relations*, November 20, 2002, FBIS, CPP20021209000250.
17. Zhang Yunling and Tang Shiping, "A More Self-Confident China Will Be a Responsible Power," *Straits Times*, October 2, 2002.

18. Avery Goldstein, *Rising to the Challenge: China's Grand Strategy and International Security* (Stanford: Stanford University Press, 2005).
19. Xinhua, September 1, 2005.
20. M. Taylor Fravel, "Regime Insecurity and International Cooperation: Explaining China's Compromises in Territorial Disputes," *International Security*, vol. 30, no. 2 (Fall 2005), 47–83.
21. "China's Growing Influence in Southeast Asia: Interim Findings," Institute for National Strategic Studies, National Defense University, April 21, 2004.
22. *Summary Report of the U.S. Department of State, Bureau of Intelligence and Research Conference on China-Southeast Asia Relations*, Singapore, August 22–24, 2005.
23. Michael G. Gallagher, "China's Illusory Threat to the South China Sea," *International Security*, vol. 19, no. 1 (Summer 1994), 172.
24. Gerald Segal, "East Asia and the 'Constrainment' of China," *International Security*, vol. 20, no. 4 (Spring 1996), 159–187.
25. Ibid.
26. Association of Southeast Asian Nations (ASEAN), www.aseansec.org/13163.htm. Beijing floated the idea of a clause prohibiting joint military exercises in the area (clearly aimed at the United States), but ASEAN rejected the proposal. *China-Southeast Asia Relations: ASEAN Hedging Strategy*, Singapore, August 22–24, 2005, U.S. Department of State, Bureau of Intelligence and Research, 3.
27. Xinhua, March 15, 2005.
28. *People's Daily Online*, November 1, 2005, www.people.com.cn.
29. Amitav Acharya, "Will Asia's Past Be Its Future?" *International Security*, vol. 28, no. 3 (Winter 2003/04), 153. Also see *China-Southeast Asia Relations*, U.S. Department of State, Bureau of Intelligence and Research.
30. *Global Times*, December 8, 2003.
31. Speech delivered at Johns Hopkins University School of Advanced International Studies, April 25, 2005.
32. T. N. Srinivasen, "Economic Reforms and Global Integration," in Francine R. Frankel and Harry Harding, eds., *The India-China Relationship—What the United States Needs to Know* (Washington, D.C.: Columbia University Press and Woodrow Wilson Center Press, 2004), 254. Srinivasen notes that this amount was scarcely more than the $2.45 billion when trade reopened in 1977 after being suspended from 1962 through 1977.
33. Xinhua, December 22, 1988, quoted in Hu Weixing, "India's Nuclear Bomb and Future Sino-Indian Relations," *East Asia: An International Quarterly*, vol. 17, no. 1 (Spring 1999).
34. John W. Garver, *Protracted Contest: Sino-Indian Rivalry in the Twentieth Century* (Seattle: University of Washington Press, 2001), 228.
35. Satu P. Limaye, "India-East Asia Relations: India's Latest Asian Incarnation," *Comparative Connections* (Pacific Forum CSIS, Third Quarter 2000).
36. Susan L. Shirk, "One-Sided Rivalry: China's Perceptions and Policies Toward India," in Frankel and Harding, eds., *The India-China Relationship*, 93.
37. Ibid., 75.
38. *Global Times*, March 30, 2005.
39. Ibid., April 25, 2005.
40. Ibid., May 7, 2004.
41. *Wall Street Journal*, April 27, 2006.
42. Alastair Iain Johnston, "China and Arms Control in the Asia-Pacific Region," in Frank C. Langdon and Douglas A. Ross, eds., *Superpower Maritime Strategy in the Pacific* (London: Routledge, 1990), 173–203.
43. The Chinese saw that ARF was "on the verge of death," in the words of one Foreign Ministry diplomat, and that regional energies were being diverted into

the ASEAN Plus Three grouping that excludes the United States. To reassure Washington and keep it involved in regional cooperation, China tried to revive the ARF by extending it into military security issues.

44. China contributed over $4 billion according to the Chinese government, www.fmprc.gov.cn/eng/ziliao/3602/3604/t18037.htm.

45. President Clinton said in the televised press conference with President Jiang, "China has shown great statesmanship and strength in making a strong contribution to the stability not only of the Chinese people and their economy but the entire region by maintaining the value of its currency," June 27, 1998, www.zpub.com/un/china27.html. Prime Minister Blair said at the G-8 summit that the leaders had "paid particular tribute . . . to the work that China has done in the aftermath of the Asian financial crisis and to its very strong commitment to financial stability." Quoted in John Kirton, "The G-7 and China in the Management of the International Financial System," University of Toronto G-8 Information Center, www.g8.utoronto.ca/scholar/kirton199903/chinaintro.htm.

46. Chinese Japan expert Tang Shiping described ASEAN Plus Three as "an excellent platform by which China and Japan can leave history behind and reach a more extensive common understanding." *Strategy and Management*, October 1, 2002, FBIS, CPP20021017000169.

47. Fu Ying, "China and Asia in the New Period," *Foreign Affairs Journal*, no. 69 (September 2003), 6.

48. Iran, India, Pakistan, and Mongolia are now invited as observers.

49. The Chinese media concurred with this view. They attributed the intervention of the United States to its intention "to squeeze the SCO and contain China and Russia." *Wen Wei Po* (Hong Kong), March 26, 2005, FBIS, CPP20050326000026.

50. *China Youth Daily*, July 18, 2005, FBIS, CPP20050718000072.

51. *People's Daily*, May 25, 2004; *People's Daily*, September 27, 2005.

52. The one exception was the massive joint exercises China held with Russia in 2005 that while ostensibly for counterterrorism, included the same type of amphibious landings that would be used in a Taiwan conflict.

53. Xinhua, September 29, 2005. China proposed to the ARF that its members "before conducting any bilateral or multilateral joint military exercises . . . should notify each other well in advance and invite other ARF members to participate as observers," www.fmprc.gov.cn/eng/wjb/zzjg/gjs/gjzzyhy/2612/2614/t15318.htm#.

54. The bureaucracies got approval to join in the PACOM multilateral exercises in 2001 but did not put it in Foreign Minister Tang Jiaxuan's speech at the ARF that summer because they were not sure that after the April collision between the American military spy plane and the Chinese fighter jet off the southern coast, the U.S. invitation to China was still good.

55. Reuters, May 24, 2006.

56. Zhu Feng, "China's Policy on the North Korean Nuclear Issue," *China Strategy*, vol. 3, July 20, 2004.

57. Bob Woodward, *Bush at War* (New York: Simon and Schuster, 2002), 340.

58. A June 4, 1994, article in the pro-Beijing newspaper *Ta Kung Pao* (Hong Kong) said that the PRC would cut off oil and food aid to Pyongyang if the U.N. Security Council imposed sanctions on North Korea. Joel S. Wit, Daniel B. Poneman, and Robert L. Gallucci, *Going Critical: The First North Korean Nuclear Crisis* (Washington, D.C.: Brookings Institution Press, 2004), 199. A *Ta Kung Pao* article entitled "North Korea Harming Own Interests with 'Capricious' Foreign Policy," January 13, 2003, sent a similar signal of Beijing's intentions in the later North Korean nuclear crisis.

59. Susan L. Shirk, "China Gets Tough with North Korea," *Yale Global*, October 26, 2006, yaleglobal.yale.edu/display.article?id=8341.

60. *New York Times,* October 31, 2006.
61. *Wall Street Journal,* October 24, 2006.
62. *Guardian Unlimited,* October 20, 2006.
63. China Peace Forum (Zhongguo Heping Luntan), forum.china.com.cn/ciicbbs/ read.php?tid=35136&page=e&fpage=1. The influential journal *Strategy and Management* reportedly was forced to cease publication by Party authorities in 2004 when it published an article critical of Pyongyang. *South China Morning Post,* September 22, 2004.
64. Secretary of State Madeleine Albright used this term during the Clinton administration to describe how for any international coalition to achieve its objectives, it had to include the United States. (See the transcript from the ABC television show, *Nightline,* February 18, 1998, www.fas.org/news/iraq/1998/02/20/ 98022004_tpo.html.)
65. *People's Daily Online,* September 14, 2005, www.people.com.cn.
66. Qian Qichen, "International Relations in the New Century," *Study Times,* October 18, 2004, FBIS, CPP20041020000203.
67. Robert B. Zoellick, "Whither China: From Membership to Responsibility?" September 21, 2005, www.state.gov/s/d/former/zoellick/rem/53682.htm.
68. *Global Times,* May 30, 2003.
69. Alastair Iain Johnston, "Socialization in International Institutions: The ASEAN Way and International Relations Theory," in G. John Ikenberry and Michael Mastanduno, eds., *International Relations Theory and the Asia-Pacific* (New York: Columbia University Press, 2003), 131.
70. "Jiang Zemin's speech at the Conference on Disarmament," March 26, 1999, un.fmprc.gov.cn/eng/7275.html.
71. Johnston, "Socialization in International Institutions," 130.
72. Wu Xinbo, "The End of the Silver Lining: A Chinese View of U.S.-Japanese Alliance," *Washington Quarterly,* 29:1 (Winter 2005–06), 119–130; also see Michael Pillsbury, *China Debates the Future Security Environment* (Washington, D.C.: National Defense University Press, 2000).
73. *Global Times,* December 15, 2003.
74. Kyodo World Service, May 11, 2005. Cui Tiankai, then head of the Asia Department of the Foreign Ministry, stated at a Singapore meeting, "China is not seeking exclusive strategic interest in the region, and will not exclude the strategic existence and interests of other concerned major countries in this region." Xinhua, June 4, 2005.
75. Theoretically, the United States could have joined the summit if it had agreed to sign the ASEAN Treaty of Amity and Cooperation that includes pledges of noninterference in internal affairs. The United States was not invited to be an observer, but Russia was.
76. Only SCO members and observers were invited.
77. Zoellick, "Whither China: From Membership to Responsibility?"
78. G. John Ikenberry, *After Victory: Institutions, Strategic Restraint, and the Rebuilding of Order after Major War* (Princeton: Princeton University Press, 2001).
79. International Monetary Fund, www.imf.org/external/np/speeches/2005/ 011005.htm; World Bank, *World Development Indicators,* 2005.
80. *Global Times,* February 21, 2003, FBIS, CPP20030225000049.
81. Department of Finance, Canada, November 2005, www.fin.gc.ca/ec2005/agenda/ agc6e.html.
82. World Bank, *World Development Indicators,* 2005. China's share of world imports increased from 1.5 percent of world imports (1990) to 3.6 percent (2000), and 5.7 percent (2005). International Monetary Fund, www.imf.org/external/np/ speeches/2005/011005.htm.

83. The intraregional trade of the fifteen East Asian economies together (ASEAN, China, Japan, Korea, Hong Kong, and Taiwan) reached 57 percent of their total trade in 2002, compared to 48 percent for the North America Free Trade Agreement countries and 62 percent for the fifteen European Community countries. Asian Development Bank, *Asian Economic Cooperation and Integration: Progress, Prospects, and Challenges,* 2005, 9. The percentage is lower if Hong Kong trade is combined with China's to avoid double counting.

84. Asia Development Bank news release, April 28, 2004, www.adb.org/Documents/News/2004/nr2004031.asp.

85. China's share of total foreign direct investment to ASEAN plus China went from 36 percent (1988–92) to 72 percent (1999–2000). Andrew MacIntyre and Barry Naughton, "The Decline of a Japan-Led Model of the East Asian Economy," in T. J. Pempel, ed., *Remapping East Asia: The Construction of a Region* (Ithaca: Cornell University Press, 2005), 87.

86. *Summary Report of the U.S. Department of State Bureau of Intelligence and Research Conference on China-Southeast Asia Relations,* Singapore, August 22–24, 2005.

87. Prime Minister Koizumi's intervention to force agricultural interests to lower some market barriers so that Japan could conclude a bilateral free trade agreement with Mexico may indicate that agricultural protection is no longer a political sacred cow in Japan.

88. *Times* (London), July 1, 2006.

89. Chinese officials note that the United States imports approximately 2.4 million barrels a day from Africa compared with China's approximately 771,000 barrels a day. *Wall Street Journal,* October 24, 2006.

90. *Financial Times,* October 23, 2006.

91. *Wall Street Journal,* November 6, 2006.

92. *International Herald Tribune,* November 11, 2006.

93. *New York Times,* November 17, 2006.

94. U.S. Senate Foreign Relations Committee hearing, September 28, 2005, foreign.senate.gov/hearings/2005/hrg050928a.html.

95. *International Herald Tribune,* November 3, 2006.

96. *Daily Telegraph,* March 10, 2006.

97. Phillip C. Saunders, "China's Global Activism: Strategy, Drivers, and Tools," Institute for Strategic Studies, National Defense University, June 2006, 1.

98. Kenneth Lieberthal and Mikkal Herberg, "China's Search for Energy Security: Implications for U.S. Policy," National Bureau of Asian Research, April 2006, 21.

99. Flynt Leverett and Jeffrey Bader, "Managing China-U.S. Energy Competition in the Middle East," *Washington Quarterly,* vol. 29, no. 1, 194.

100. China is building a port in Pakistan and looking at building a canal across Thailand because right now almost half of its imported oil has to go through the Malacca Strait, one of the busiest shipping lanes in the world located between Malaysia, Singapore, and India, which is vulnerable to terrorists, pirates, or a chokehold by the U.S. Navy.

101. Lieberthal and Herberg, "China's Search for Energy Security," 20.

102. *New York Times,* June 27, 2005.

103. Saunders, "China's Global Activism," 7.

104. Zoellick, "Whither China: From Membership to Responsibility?"

105. *Los Angeles Times,* October 13, 2006.

106. *Der Spiegel,* August 8, 2005.

Chapter 6

1. The shrine served as the "spiritual pillar for Japanese nationalism" during the 1930s and '40s. In 1978 the Shinto priests at the shrine secretly enshrined the names of the class-A war criminals, including the wartime leader Hideki Tojo, a fact that only became public in 1979. Prime ministers Masoyoshi Ohiro (December 1978 to June 1980) and Zenko Suzuki (July 1980 to November 1982) visited the shrine, but with little media attention or international reaction. Sean Curtin, "Yasukuni Shrine: Old Wounds Still Fester," *Asia Times*, July 22, 2005.

2. The eye-witness accounts of the demonstrations come from personal communications from Michael Pettis and Willem van Kemenade, and from my April 2005 interviews in Beijing.

3. *South China Morning Post*, Internet version, April 25, 2005.

4. *Cheng Ming* (Hong Kong), May 2005.

5. *Zhejiang Daily*, April 24, 2005, FBIS, CPP20050504000075.

6. *International Herald Tribune*, April 18, 2005.

7. Xiao Qiang, "Control Mechanism Cracked in the Face of Technology," *Asian Wall Street Journal*, April 27, 2005.

8. Xinhua (English version), April 16, 2005.

9. *Observer*, April 17, 2005.

10. Xinhua lifted the embargo in its English service on April 16.

11. Zheng Yongnian, *Discovering Chinese Nationalism in China: Modernization, Identity and International Relations* (Cambridge: Cambridge University Press, 1999), 134.

12. Some Western scholars like Chalmers Johnson do attribute the Communists' victory in the Chinese civil war against the Guomindang to their superior ability to win popular support with nationalist anti-Japanese appeals. Chalmers Johnson, *Peasant Nationalism and Communist Power: The Emergence of Revolutionary China 1937–1945* (Stanford: Stanford University Press, 1962).

13. Zheng, *Discovering Chinese Nationalism*, 95.

14. I am grateful to Yinan He for bringing this comparison to my attention.

15. Tomohiko Taniguchi, "A Cold Peace: The Changing Security Equation in Northeast Asia," *Orbis*, (Summer 2005), 449.

16. *Yomiuri Shimbun*, May 18, 2005.

17. *China Daily*, October 7, 2005. "Results of Opinion on Poll on Japan's Diplomacy," Tokyo Cabinet Office, December 26, 2005, FBIS, JPP20060201016001. The Chinese poll was conducted by the Institute of Japanese Studies of the Chinese Academy of Social Sciences in fall 2004, *People's Daily Online*, November 28, 2004, FBIS, CPP20041129000077. A *Yomiuri Shimbun* poll conducted with Gallup in December 2005 found that 72 percent of respondents said they didn't trust China. *Yomiuri Shimbun*, December 15, 2005.

18. The Japanese opinion of China has grown markedly more negative. In 2002, over half (55 percent) viewed China favorably. The Pew Global Attitudes Project, 2006, "Publics of Asian Powers Hold Negative Views of One Another," http://pewglobal.org.

19. *Times* (London), August 16, 2005.

20. Japan's Ministry of Foreign Affairs reports that from 1979 to 2005, Japan gave 3.1331 trillion yen (approximately $27.5 billion) in loans, 145.7 billion yen ($1.3 billion) in grant aid, and 144.6 billion yen ($1.3 billion) in technical cooperation to China, www.mofa.go.jp/policy/oda/region/e_asia/china/index.html.

21. *China Daily*, October 7, 2005, english.people.com.cn/200510/07/eng20051007_ 212982.html. Some Chinese scholars apportion blame for deteriorating relations more equally, e.g., Li Wen says that some Chinese are "arrogant" and their reactions in some incidents involving Japan are "excessive or extreme." *Contemporary Asia-Pacific*, July 15, 2005, FBIS, CPP20050916000238.

22. *Economist*, October 8, 2005.

23. *Sankei Shimbun*, February 21, 2006, FBIS, JPP20060222036001.

24. Xinhua, July 18, 2005, english.people.com.cn/200507/18/eng20050718_ 196799.html.

25. *People's Daily*, July 15, 2005, FBIS, CPP20050715000121.

26. *Chunichi Shimbun*, October 15, 2005.

27. According to *People's Daily* (*People's Daily Online*, December 24, 2004), the "cold politics and hot economics" of China-Japan relations in recent years have started to chill the economic relationship, which hurts Japan more than China. The Japanese recognize this trend as well. See Chi Hung Kwan, "Japan Is Missing the 'China Express' While China Is Distancing Itself from Japan," *China in Transition*, February 18, 2005, www.rieti.go.jp/en/china/05021801.html.

28. The difficulty in obtaining student visas to the United States after 9/11 was one explanation. Taniguchi, "A Cold Peace," 446.

29. Poll by Teikoku Databank Ltd. Quoted in the *New York Times*, May 25, 2005.

30. From 86 percent in December 2004 to 55 percent in May 2005. *New York Times*, June 27, 2005.

31. Wu Xinbo, "The End of the Silver Lining: A Chinese View of the U.S.-Japanese Alliance," *Washington Quarterly* (Winter 2005–06), 119–120.

32. Chinese government and media have been silent about these involvements probably to avoid antagonizing Washington.

33. *New York Times*, September 10, 2005.

34. Eric Teo Chu Cheow, "Southeast Asians Worry About Northeast Asia's Feuds," *PacNet Newsletter*, no. 21, May 19, 2005, www.csis.org/component/option,com_ csis_pubs/task,view/id,245/type,3/.

35. *New York Times*, May 25, 2005.

36. *People's Daily Online*, May 12, 2005, compares this to Germany and France's less than 40 percent share of the European Union's economy.

37. *Fortnightly Review*, August 8, 2005, FBIS, CPP20050822000133.

38. Alastair Iain Johnston, "The Correlates of Nationalism in Beijing Public Opinion, 2000–2003," unpublished paper, March 2005.

39. *Japanese Studies*, no. 6 (2002); *People's Daily Online*, November 28, 2004.

40. For example, Zhao Hongwei, "China and Japan Should Establish a Special Relationship," *Global Times*, March 23, 2005.

41. *China Daily*, July 6, 2005.

42. *History: High School Textbook*, version 1, vol. 1 (Beijing: People's Education Press, 2004), 32.

43. Ibid.

44. *People's Daily Online*, September 12, 2005, www.people.com.cn.

45. Edward Friedman, "China's Nationalist Narrative," *Dissent* (Winter 2006).

46. Jonathan D. Spence, *The Search for Modern China* (New York: Norton, 1990), 448.

47. Ian Buruma, *The Wages of Guilt, Memories of War in Germany and Japan* (New York: Farrar, Straus, and Giroux, 1994).

48. For an example of this, see Xinhua, April 22, 2005, news.xinhuanet.com/english/ 2005-04/22/content_2864759.htm.

49. Michael Suk-young Chwe calls this kind of information that facilitates collective action, "common knowledge." *Rational Ritual: Culture, Coordination and Common Knowledge* (Princeton: Princeton University Press, 2001).

50. I am grateful to Lu Xiaobo for this information.

51. Peter Hays Gries, "China's 'New Thinking on Japan,'" *China Quarterly*, December 2005, no. 184, 831–850. Ma Licheng, "New Thinking on Relations with Japan, Worries by People in China and Japan," *Strategy and Management*, vol. 55, no. 6, 2002, 41.

52. *Yomiuri Shimbun*, October 4, 2004.

53. *Asahi Shimbun*, January 10, 2006, www.asahi.com/english/Herald-asahi/TKY200601100361.html.

54. Xinhua, April 19, 2005.

55. Ibid., and Xinhua, April 22, 2005.

56. Zhang Kunsheng, "Unconventional Visit: Remembering Li Zhaoxing's Visit to Japan and South Korea," *Observe and Think*, September 1, 2003.

57. Chalmers Johnson, "The Patterns of Japanese Relations with China, 1952–1982," *Pacific Affairs*, vol. 59, no. 3 (Autumn, 1986), 427.

58. Allen S. Whiting, *China Eyes Japan* (Berkeley: University of California Press, 1989), 4.

59. Zheng Yi, *Deng Xiaoping Biography* (Hong Kong: Ming Bao Publishing Company, 1996).

60. Zhang Xiangshan, "Looking Back on the Negotiation on Restoring Relations Between China and Japan," *Journal of Japanese Studies*, Institute of Japanese Studies, Chinese Academy of Social Sciences, vol. 1 (1998). According to this author, the two Chinese leaders had objected to the original wording of Prime Minister Kakuei Tanaka's apology made in a September 1972 dinner speech in Beijing—Japan "brought big trouble" to China during World War II—because they believe it trivialized Japan's crimes. So they persuaded the Japanese side to change the wording to what appeared in the communiqué.

61. *People's Daily Online*, August 18, 2004.

62. Zheng, *Deng Xiaoping Biography*, 233.

63. *Nikkei Weekly*, June 7, 1993.

64. Whiting, *China Eyes Japan*, 195.

65. Ibid., 62.

66. Zhang Tuosheng, "China's Relations with Japan," in Ezra F. Vogel, Yuan Ming, and Tanaka Akihiko, eds., *The Golden Age of the U.S.-China-Japan Triangle, 1972–1989* (Cambridge, Mass.: Harvard University Press, 2002).

67. Kyodo, October 29, 1985.

68. Whiting, *China Eyes Japan*, 74.

69. "The Cause and Effect of the December Students' Demonstration," *Cheng Ming* (Hong Kong), January 1987, 12.

70. *Inside China Mainland* (Hong Kong), January 1987, 5.

71. Jeffrey N. Wasserstrom, *Student Protests in Twentieth-Century China: The View from Shanghai* (Stanford: Stanford University Press, 1991), 300.

72. Ibid.

73. Ibid., 304.

74. *Inside China Mainland* (Hong Kong), March 1986.

75. "3000 Messengers Sow the Seeds of Friendship," *China Newsweek*, October 8, 2002.

76. Luo Bing, "Insights into the Hu Yaobang Incident," *Cheng Ming* (Hong Kong), February 1987, 8.

77. Zheng, *Discovering Chinese Nationalism*, 132.
78. Lin Siyun, "Looking Back on the Question of Japan's Yasukuni Shrine," May 21, 2001, unpublished paper.
79. Agence France Press, April 27, 2005. Notably, the Chinese report of Wang Yi's speech in *Global Times*, April 29, 2005, does not refer to this "gentlemen's agreement."
80. Agence France Press, April 28, 2005.
81. Wasserstrom, *Student Protests*, 301.
82. *People's Daily*, September 6, 1994.
83. Lee Fuzhung, "A Re-Examination of Nationalism and the U.S. China Policy," *China Strategic Review*, vol. 1, no. 6, September 5, 1996, cited in Suisheng Zhao, *A Nation-State by Construction: Dynamics of Modern Chinese Nationalism* (Stanford, Calif.: Stanford University Press, 2004), 220.
84. Muzi.com, December 15, 2000, latelinenews.com/ll/english/1030165.shtml.
85. *China Daily*, March 1, 2005.
86. *San Jose Mercury News*, June 23, 2005.
87. *Kyodo Clue II*, July 7, 2005, FBIS, JPP20050707000037.
88. Zhang Tuosheng, "Sino-Japanese Relations at the Turn of the Century, 1992–2001," unpublished paper, March 2004; Kazuo Sato, "The Japan-China Summit and Joint Declaration of 1998: A Watershed for Japan-China Relations in the 21st Century?" Brookings Institution, Fall 2001.
89. Gilbert Rozman, "China's Changing Images of Japan, 1989–2001: The Struggle to Balance Partnership and Rivalry," *International Relations of the Asia-Pacific*, vol. 2 (2002), 107.
90. *China Youth Daily*, March 18, 1997, cited in Joseph Fewsmith and Stanley Rosen, "The Domestic Context of Chinese Foreign Policy: Does 'Public Opinion' Matter?" in David M. Lampton, ed., *The Making of Chinese Foreign and Security Policy in the Era of Reform* (Stanford: Stanford University Press, 2001), 162.
91. Sato, "The Japan-China Summit and Joint Declaration of 1998," 3–4.
92. Prime Minister Tomiichi Murayama of Japan's Socialist Party, who headed a coalition with the Liberal Democratic Party during 1995, issued a full, unambiguous apology of Japan's wartime "colonial rule and aggression" for the first time. Emperor Akihito visited China in 1992 and said that he "deeply deplore[d]" the "great sufferings" Japan inflicted on the Chinese people during the war, but the Emperor had never visited or made a similar statement in South Korea. (Sato, "The Japan-China Summit and Joint Declaration of 1998," 9.) President Roh Moo-hyun broke South Korea's promise to shelve the history issues in 2005 when he lashed out publicly at Japan over the disputed Tokdo Islands, history textbooks, and the prime minister's visits to Yasukuni Shrine.
93. The communiqué did refer to history but did not include a full formal apology such as that provided to South Korea. The Japanese also failed to get the Chinese to agree to include statements on Japan's postwar contributions to peace (included in the ROK document) or give their support to Japan's effort to become a permanent member of the U.N. Security Council. Sato, "The Japan-China Summit and Joint Declaration of 1998," 13–15.
94. *Sentaku*, April 1, 2000, FBIS, JPP20000404000049.
95. *Mainichi Shimbun*, July 8, 2002, FBIS, JPP20020710000028.
96. Ibid.
97. Rozman, "China's Changing Images," 113.
98. *People's Daily*, October 14, 2000.

99. During Zhu Rongji's visit to Japan in 2000, the official newspapers were filled with the good news of Sino-Japanese friendship, but *Global Times* was running stories like "Japanese Navy Flaunts Its Military Force Outside Its Territory." *Global Times*, October 21, 2000.

100. For the military's less calm reaction to the incident see *Liberation Army Daily*, December 31, 2001, FBIS, CPP20011231000070.

101. *Mainichi Shimbun*, July 8, 2002, FBIS, JPP2002710000028.

102. James J. Prystrup, "From Precipice to Promise," *Comparative Connections*, October–December 2001.

103. Kyodo, April 29, 2002.

104. *History: High School Textbook*, version 1, vol. 1 (Beijing: People's Education Press, 2004), 35–41. On previous versions, see Whiting, *China Eyes Japan*, 37.

105. Kyodo News International, April 5, 2005. The Chinese version of the meeting is Xinhua, April 5, 2005.

106. Xinhua, March 16, 2005.

107. For example, Xinhua, April 1, 2005.

108. Whiting, *China Eyes Japan*, 53.

109. Xinhua, April 1, 2005.

110. For a list of over twenty anti-Japan sites see www.zhao369.com/dir/politics_law/diplomacy/chinese_diplomacy/sino_japan/.

111. *China Daily*, February 17, 2005.

112. Information from the Web site of the Federation of Chinese Non-governmental Organizations for Defending Sovereignty Over the Diaoyu Islands, www.cfdd.org.cn. I thank Alastair Iain Johnston for bringing the Web site and its contents to my attention.

113. *South China Morning Post*, June 24, 2003.

114. Xinhua, January 15, 2004, www.chinaview.cn.

115. *Shanghai Daily* on sina.com, March 3, 2004; *People's Daily Online*, March 18, 2004.

116. *People's Daily Online*, September 9, 2003. This campaign was modeled on the "safeguard the railway movement" in 1911 when hundreds of people protesting the Chinese government's contracts with Japanese companies to build a railroad in Sichuan were killed by the police.

117. *International Herald Tribune*, April 18, 2005.

118. *People's Daily Online*, April 14, 2005, www.people.com.cn.

119. *Beijing News*, March 25, 2005, www.thebeijingnews.com/news/2005/0325/05@020917.html, see also www.peacehall.com/news/gb/intl/2005/03/200503270511.shtml.

120. Xinhua, March 31, 2005; Xinhua, April 5, 2005. For a good comparison of the 2005 and 2001 textbook versions of history, see www.zonaeuropa.com/20050321_2.htm.

121. *Beijing News*, March 25, 2005, www.thebeijingnews.com/news/2005/0325/05@020917.html; *People's Daily Online*, April 6, 2005.

122. *Times Online* (London), April 6, 2005; Associated Press, April 6, 2005.

123. *Beijing Times*, April 18, 2005.

124. *China Daily*, April 22, 2005.

125. *Crienglish.com*, April 24, 2005.

126. *New York Times*, May 25, 2005.

127. *South China Morning Post*, April 12, 2005.

128. *Washington Post*, April 26, 2005.

129. Reuters, April 15, 2005.

130. *Cheng Ming* (Hong Kong), May 2005, 6. The April 15 Politburo meeting was reported in Xinhua, April 20, 2005.

131. Xinhua, April 19, 2005.

132. Xinhua, April 20, 2005.

133. On the statement by Minister of Commerce Bo Xilai, see Xinhua, April 22, 2005, and *South China Morning Post*, April 23, 2005.

134. Apparently some people had spread on the Internet the false information that the authorities had approved a demonstration during the national holiday beginning on May 1. Xinhua, April 29, 2005.

135. Jiji-Web, April 14, 2005; also see article on Web site of the China Federation of Defending Diaoyu Islands, www.cfdd.org.cn/web/Article/200504/20050407103233.html.

136. Kyodo Clue II, May 25, 2005, FBIS, JPP20050526000012.

137. *Liberation Daily*, April 25, 2005.

138. Ma Licheng, "New Thinking on Relations with Japan, Worries by People in China and Japan," *Strategy and Management*, vol. 55, no. 6, 2002, 41–47.

139. Shi Yinhong, "China-Japan Rapprochement and the 'Diplomatic Revolution,'" *Strategy and Management*, vol. 57, no. 2, 2003, 71–75.

140. *Yomiuri Shimbun*, editorial, June 4, 2005; *Asahi Shimbun*, editorial, June 5, 2005.

141. *Asahi Shimbun*, July 25, 2006.

142. *Yomiuri Shimbun*, October 6, 2006.

143. Comments from www.sina.com and www.people.com, October 9 and 10, 2006.

144. *Global Times*, April 6, 2005; and *People's Daily* April 9, 2005, FBIS, CPP20050409000044.

Chapter 7

1. Chicago Council on Global Affairs, *The United States and the Rise of China and India*, 2006, www.thechicagocouncil.org/curr_pos.php.

2. The memoranda from these meetings show clearly that Taiwan was the primary objective of Premier Zhou and the other Chinese negotiators, although Kissinger hid this fact in the account he provided in his memoirs to deflect domestic criticism for his "selling out" Taiwan. William Burr, ed., *The Kissinger Transcripts, The Top Secret Talks with Beijing and Moscow* (New York: The New Press, 1998), 66–68, 115–117.

3. Shi Guhong, "Difficulties and Options: Thoughts on the Taiwan Matter," *Strategy and Management*, October 1, 1999, FTS19991119000349.

4. Robert S. Ross, *Negotiating Cooperation: The United States and China 1969–1989* (Stanford, Calif.: Stanford University Press, 1995).

5. The effectiveness of the Taiwan lobby has been impeded by the domestic political divisions within Taiwan during Chen Shui-bian's two terms as president. Kerry Dembaugh, *Taiwan-U.S. Political Relations: New Strains and Changes*, Congressional Research Service, October 10, 2006, 23.

6. See Peter Perdue, *China Marches West: The Qing Conquest of Central Eurasia* (Cambridge: Belknap Press, 2005) and Emma Jinhua Teng, *Taiwan's Imagined Geography: Chinese Colonial Travel Writing and Pictures, 1683–1895* (Cambridge, Mass.: Harvard University Press, 2004).

7. Edgar Snow, *Red Star Over China*, first revised and enlarged edition (New York: Grove Press, 1968), 110. Mao told Khrushchev on October 2, 1959: "We don't

want to take over Taiwan in one night. It doesn't matter if it remains in the hands of Jiang Jieshi [Chiang Kai-shek] for 10, 20, or 30 years. We don't want to fight [with KMT] over Jinmen and Mazu." Ministry of Foreign Affairs and CCP Central Literature Studies Office, ed., *Mao Zedong Waijiao Wenxuan* (Selected Works of Mao Zedong on Diplomacy) (Beijing: Central Literature Studies Press and World Affairs Press, 1994), 381.

8. Thomas J. Christensen, "PRC Security Relations with the United States: Why Things Are Going So Well," *China Leadership Monitor*, no. 8 (Fall 2003), 2.

9. According to one journalist, articles about Taiwan by scholars, but not by regular journalists, have to be cleared through the State Council Taiwan Affairs Office.

10. For example, see the four polls in 2003 through 2004 by the Social Survey Institute of China: www.chinasurvey.com.cn/freereport/chenshuibian.htm (11/03), www.chinasurvey.com.cn/freereport/320weixian.htm (03/04), www.chinasurvey.com.cn/freereport/320houxu.htm (04/04), www.chinasurvey.com.cn/freereport/diaochaindex.htm (11/04).

11. For example, *Global Times*, June 11, 2004; *China Youth Daily*, June 16, 2004.

12. Thomas J. Christensen, "Posing Problems Without Catching Up: China's Rise and Challenges for U.S. Security," *International Security*, vol. 25, no. 4 (2001), 5–40.

13. Shi Guhong, "Difficulties and Options."

14. Robert L. Suettinger, *Beyond Tiananmen: The Politics of U.S.-China Relations 1989–2000* (Washington, D.C.: Brookings Institution Press, 2003), 255.

15. Alastair Iain Johnston, "China's Militarized Interstate Dispute Behavior 1949–1992: A First Cut at the Data," *China Quarterly*, no. 153 (March 1998), 1–30; Alastair Iain Johnston, "Cultural Realism and Strategy in Maoist China," in Peter J. Katzenstein, ed., *The Culture of National Security: Norms and Identity in World Politics* (New York: Columbia University Press, 1996), 15–16; Allen S. Whiting, "China's Use of Force, 1950–96, and Taiwan," *International Security*, vol. 26, no. 2 (Fall 2001), 103–131.

16. Suettinger, *Beyond Tiananmen*, 207–208.

17. Ibid., 262.

18. Richard C. Bush, *Untying the Knot: Making Peace in the Taiwan Strait* (Washington, D.C.: Brookings Institution Press, 2005), 182.

19. Zhao Suisheng, introduction to his edited *Across the Taiwan Strait: Mainland China, Taiwan, and the 1995–1996 Crisis* (New York: Routledge: 1999), 8.

20. Suettinger, *Beyond Tiananmen*, 255.

21. *People's Daily*, September 22, 1995.

22. Sheng Lijun, *China's Dilemma: The Taiwan Issue* (London: I. B. Tauris, 2001), 34.

23. Chen Jian, *Mao's China and the Cold War* (Chapel Hill: University of North Carolina Press, 2001), 59. Thomas J. Christensen, *Useful Adversaries: Grand Strategy, Domestic Mobilization, and Sino-American Conflict, 1947–1958* (Princeton: Princeton University Press, 1996), chap. 6. Mao believed that if he could get people to work harder by organizing them into big collective farms and inspiring them with ideological appeals, he could overtake the West economically. The failed campaign produced a three-year-long nationwide famine in which 32.6 million people died. (Cao Shuji, "The Deaths of China's Population and Contributing Factors in 1959–61," *Chinese Population Science*, issue 1, 2005, observechina.net/info/artshow.asp?ID=35550&ad=6/23/2005.) By "attempting to stir up international tensions short of war," as scholar Tom Christensen put it, Mao hoped to use the Taiwan issue to arouse popular fervor behind the Great Leap Forward (Christensen, "Posing Problems," 9). Mao explained his thinking, "A tense [international] situation could mobilize the population, could particu-

larly mobilize the [politically] backward people, could mobilize the people in the middle, and could therefore promote the Great Leap Forward in economic construction." (Chen, *Mao's China*, 175.)

24. Zhao, *Across the Taiwan Strait*, 13.

25. This statement was intended to reassure Beijing about American intentions as well as to discourage the pro-independence proclivities of Taiwan politicians.

26. Suettinger, *Beyond Tiananmen*, 260.

27. Taiwan Affairs Office of the State Council, *The One-China Principle and the Taiwan Issue*, February 21, 2000. The Chinese government has issued two Taiwan white papers, one in 1993 and one in 2000.

28. Shi Yinhong, "An Analysis on the New Tactics the Chinese Mainland Employs in Handling the Taiwan Issue," *China Review* (Hong Kong), February 1, 2005, FBIS, CPP20050201000100.

29. U.S. Department of Defense, *Security Situation in the Taiwan Strait*, 1999, www.defenselink.mil/pubs/twstrait_02261999.html; Philip C. Saunders, "Taiwan's Response to China's Missile Buildup," October 2002, Center for Nonproliferation Studies, Monterey Institute for International Studies; Office of the Secretary of Defense, *Annual Report to Congress, Military Power of the People's Republic of China*, 2006, www.defenselink.mil/pubs/pdfs/China%20Report%202006.pdf.

30. *People's Daily*, July 15, 1999.

31. *People's Daily*, July 13, 1999.

32. Suettinger, *Beyond Tiananmen*, 382.

33. Alan D. Romberg, *Rein In at the Brink of the Precipice: American Policy Toward Taiwan and U.S.-PRC Relations* (Washington, D.C.: The Henry Stimson Center, 2003), 189.

34. In the end, Jiang Zemin succeeded in getting the group to agree that Deng Xiaoping's optimistic assessment that "peace and development are the main trend," still held despite a series of setbacks to China during 1999. The green light to the military to speed up its modernization efforts may have been needed to obtain this consensus. David M. Finkelstein, *China Reconsiders Its National Security: "The Great Peace and Development Debate of 1999,"* Project Asia, The CNA Corporation, December 2000.

35. Lin Chong-pin highlights this domestic backdrop to Beijing's reaction to Lee Teng-hui's statement in an unpublished paper, "Tactical Adjustment and Strategic Persistence," Taipei, 2002 (cited with permission of the author).

36. Every military officer who tells me this story says, "Solve the Taiwan problem by force if need be," with the clear implication that the PLA is preparing to compel Taiwan to reunify with the Mainland. But when I ask explicitly if that is the PLA's mission, they suddenly realize that they have revealed too much, and hasten to assure me that their mission is only to prevent Taiwan independence, not to force reunification. My own hunch is that Jiang Zemin's true goal was unification, and for most of the military, it still is.

37. Shi Guhong, "Difficulties and Options."

38. Zong Hairen's account quotes all the Standing Committee members as advocating a tough military response to Lee Teng-hui's statement. "Responding to the 'Two States Theory,'" *Zhu Rongji in 1999*, trans. in *Chinese Law and Government*, vol. 35, no. 2 (March/April 2002), 14–36.

39. Office of the Secretary of Defense, *The Military Power of the People's Republic of China*, 2005, 26. Michael Pillsbury's collections of Chinese military writings first identified the "assassin's mace" in Chinese strategy. Michael Pillsbury, ed., *Chinese Views of Future Warfare* (Washington, D.C.: National Defense University Press,

1997) and *China Debates the Future Security Environment* (Washington, D.C.: National Defense University Press, 2000).

40. Office of the Secretary of Defense, *The Military Power of the People's Republic of China*, 2006.

41. Shi Guhong, "Difficulties and Options."

42. Shi Yinhong, "An Analysis on the New Tactics."

43. According to PRC official statistics, Taiwan is the fifth-largest source of international investment (behind Hong Kong, United States, Japan, and the European Union). But if you include half of the investment from tax havens based on the assumption that much of that investment comes from Taiwan, then Taiwan is the second largest.

44. U.S.-Taiwan Business Council, "Taiwan Business Topics," November 2005.

45. Bush, *Untying the Knot*, 78.

46. The Taiwan Affairs Office spokesman singled out Hsu Wen-lung, the billionaire who is chairman of the Chi Mei group, in a front-page article in the *People's Daily*, June 1, 2004. According to T. J. Cheng, individuals like Hsu, who were put on the blacklist, were not penalized and since then, actually have invested more on the Mainland. ("China-Taiwan Economic Linkage: Between Insulation and Superconductivity," in Nancy Bernkopf Tucker, ed., *Dangerous Strait: The U.S.-Taiwan-China Crisis* [New York: Columbia University Press, 2005], 107.)

47. Some senior officials have said privately that Taiwan also would be allowed to continue to purchase weapons systems from the United States.

48. Wang Daohan invited Taiwan's cross-Strait negotiator to come to the Mainland to meet with him in 1998. After a months-long tussle with Taipei over the agenda for the talks (Beijing wanted political talks, Taipei wanted talks about practical issues related to trade and exchange) and its precondition that Taiwan first embrace the "one China principle," Jiang Zemin simply held his nose and allowed the envoy to come "informally" with no preconditions. Such flexibility was unprecedented, and it has never again been repeated.

49. Vice-Premier Qian Qichen rolled out this new version in September 2000 (www.sina.com.cn, September 11, 2000) and used it in a March 2001 meeting with Taiwanese legislators (*People's Daily*, March 9, 2001) on the eve of his first meetings with Bush administration officials in Washington later that month. He showcased China's new flexibility toward Taiwan in his speeches during the visit to the United States. *People's Daily*, March 24, 2001.

50. Zhang Nianchi, "The 16th CCP National Congress and Cross-Strait Relations," *China Review* (Hong Kong), December 1, 2002, FBIS, CPP20021204000033.

51. The PRC had previously rejected the notion of a "1992 consensus" that might serve as the basis for dialogue, and Taiwan before Chen Shui-bian had embraced it. By 2001, however, the two sides had flipped their positions.

52. Bush, *Untying the Knot*, 286.

53. An English-language official yearbook acknowledges the change. "In political terms, the mainland has adjusted the statement on the one China principle, 'Taiwan is a part of China,' to that of 'both the mainland and Taiwan are part of China' so the statement can be better accepted by Taiwan compatriots," www.china.org.cn/english/shuzi-en/en-shuzi/zz/htm/tw-zs.htm.

54. *Washington Post*, May 13, 2005; *China Times* (Taiwan), August 7, 2005, FBIS, CPP200508000127.

55. Kenneth Lieberthal, "Preventing a War Over Taiwan," *Foreign Affairs*, March-April 2005.

56. *Washington Post*, May 12, 2000.

57. Suettinger, *Beyond Tiananmen*, 402.

58. *People's Daily*, March 6, 2000.
59. CCTV, March 15, 2000, FBIS, CPP20000315000134.
60. The press did make personal attacks on Vice President Annette Lu, a proindependence fundamentalist, and former president Lee Teng-hui.
61. Zhang, "The 16th CCP National Congress and Cross-Strait Relations."
62. *Global Times*, August 8, 2002.
63. Ibid., November 26, 2003.
64. Ibid., November 24, 2003; Yan Xuetong, a well-known academic commentator, laid out the arguments for using force to prevent Taiwan independence in "The Pros and Cons of Using Force to Constrain Law-based Taiwan Independence," *Strategy and Management*, May 1, 2004. One of his arguments against the "new thinking" that Beijing should deal with Chen Shui-bian by peaceful methods, is "Following Gorbachev's new thinking, the Soviet Union broke up."
65. Xinhua, November 18, 2003.
66. Zhang Nianchi, *Ta Kung Pao* (Hong Kong), March 28, 2004, FBIS, CPP20040328000019.
67. Zhang Xuezhong, "Reflections on Measures to Guard Against Worst Case Scenarios for the Taiwan Issue," *Strategy and Management*, May 1, 2004, FBIS, CPP20040702000238.
68. The official story was that the idea of the law was suggested to Premier Wen Jiabao by a Chinese living in England in May 2004 (*China Daily*, May 11, 2004). Think-tank experts told me that they had started discussing it beginning in late 2003. One Hong Kong article reports that discussions about a Taiwan Basic Law began in 1995. *Wen Wei Po* (Hong Kong), March 6, 2005.
69. For example, see the report of the interview with Shanghai scholar Huang Renwei in *People's Daily Online*, January 26, 2005.
70. *Wen Wei Po* (Hong Kong), March 6, 2005.
71. *China Daily*, March 14, 2005.
72. By predelegating the decision to use force in a crisis to the State Council and Central Military Commission, the law also puts the number one leader, who chairs the CMC, in the position of having to take personal responsibility for the decision instead of being able to hide behind an opaque collective decision process within the Politburo Standing Committee.
73. Shi Yinhong, "An Analysis on the New Tactics."
74. Ibid. In an interview with the *Washington Post* published on November 23, 2003, Premier Wen Jiabao had said that Chinese people were prepared to "pay any price to safeguard the unity of the motherland." Also see General Peng Guangqian, "The Reorientation and Development of China's Taiwan Policy," Center for Strategic and International Studies, *China Strategy*, vol. 3, July 20, 2004.
75. "Never sway in adhering to the one China principle, never give up in efforts to seek peaceful reunification, never change the principle of placing hope on the Taiwan people, and never compromise in opposing the Taiwan independence secessionist activities." *China Daily*, March 4, 2005.
76. According to Hu's speech, the CCP was the "mainstay" of the resistance, but the Guomindang army organized "a series of major campaigns, which dealt heavy blows to the Japanese army." Xinhua, September 3, 2005.
77. The flight did not have to stop in Hong Kong, but still was required to fly over Hong Kong.
78. *China Post*, October 23, 2006.
79. State Department Press Statement, March 2, 2006.
80. *Asian Wall Street Journal*, January 14, 2005.

81. Meng Xiangqing, "Domestic Security and International Security Will Become More Interwoven and Interdependent in the Future as China Faces Growing Traditional and Nontraditional Security Threats," *World Knowledge*, June 1, 2005, FBIS, CPP20050617000196.

82. Jia Ziqi, "Concerned About Chaos," *Strategy and Management*, June 1, 2000, FBIS, CPP20000623000121.

83. *Ta Kung Pao* (Hong Kong), August 5, 2005.

Chapter 8

1. One of the very few diplomatic channels that the Chinese government agreed to continue was consultations on North Korea.

2. Wu Baiyi, "China's Crisis Management during the Incident of 'Embassy Bombing,'" *World Economics and Politics*, no. 3 (2005).

3. Zong Hairen, *Zhu Rongji in 1999*, trans. in *Chinese Law and Government*, vol. 35, no. 1 (January–February 2002), 58 and 61.

4. A survey of Beijing students found a sizable minority who kept their distance from the officially facilitated demonstrations because they didn't want to be "used." The students who had been prevented by the government from protesting the 1998 violence against ethnic Chinese in Indonesia all were in this category. Dingxin Zhao, "Nationalism and Authoritarianism: Student-Government Conflicts During the 1999 Beijing Student Protests," *Asian Perspective*, vol. 27, no. 1 (2002), 21.

5. Wu, "China's Crisis Management."

6. The Chengdu newspaper also reported positively on the demonstrations. See *Sichuan Daily*, May 9 and 10, 1999.

7. Wu, "China's Crisis Management."

8. Wang Zuxun, "The Impact of Kosovo War on International Security," *Outlook Weekly*, no. 20, 1999, 8, cited in Wu, "China's Crisis Management."

9. Guan Chajia, "Humanitarianism or Hegemonism?" *People's Daily*, May 17, 1999, cited in Wu, "China's Crisis Management."

10. *Beijing Youth Daily*, May 9, 1999.

11. Stanley Rosen, "Chinese Media and Youth, Attitudes Toward Nationalism and Internationalism," in Chin-chuan Lee, ed., *Chinese Media, Global Contexts* (London: Routledge Curzon, 2003), 111.

12. *Southern Weekend*, May 11, 1999.

13. Ibid., May 21, 1999.

14. Ibid.

15. *State Department Report on Accidental Bombing of Chinese Embassy*, hongkong.usconsulate.gov/uscn/state/1999/0706.htm. (As of publication, this document is temporarily not available on the Web site of the U.S. Consulate in Hong Kong. State Department officials say, however, that it will soon be available on both that Web site and the Web site of the U.S. Embassy in Beijing.)

16. Some people believe that the Chinese Embassy probably was aiding and abetting the Serbian war effort and that that is why the Clinton administration attacked it.

17. Wu, "China's Crisis Management."

18. Ibid.

19. Xia Liping, "Sino-U.S. Relations in the Early 21st Century, Asymmetrical Interdependence," *Contemporary Asia-Pacific*, December 15, 2005, FBIS, CPP20060124455001.

20. *Ming Pao* (Hong Kong), November 22, 2002.

21. Suisheng Zhao, *A Nation-State by Construction* (Stanford: Stanford University Press, 2004), 215.

22. Andrew J. Nathan and Perry Link, eds. (compiled by Zhang Liang), *The Tiananmen Papers* (New York: Public Affairs, 2001), 358.

23. *People's Daily*, October 10, 1991.

24. Allen S. Whiting, "Chinese Nationalism and Foreign Policy after Deng," *China Quarterly*, no. 142 (June 1995), 308.

25. Robert L. Suettinger, *Beyond Tiananmen: The Politics of U.S.-China Relations 1989–2000* (Washington, D.C.: Brookings, 2003), 203.

26. Michael Pillsbury, ed., *Chinese Views of Future Warfare* (Washington, D.C.: National Defense University Press, 1998); Michael Pillsbury, *China Debates the Future Security Environment* (Washington, D.C.: National Defense University Press, 2000).

27. *Economic Journal* (Hong Kong), July 8, 1994, quoted in Suettinger, *Beyond Tiananmen*, 208.

28. Robert Suettinger suggests that in the year following Tiananmen, the threat of not renewing or adding conditions to China's most favored nation trading status may have induced the Chinese government to release people imprisoned for Tiananmen related "crimes," over 500 of them in January 1980 and 211 in May 1980. After President Bush announced his decision to renew MFN, the Chinese released 97 more and allowed Fang Lizhi, the dissident scientist who had taken refuge in the U.S. Embassy in Beijing, to leave the country. Suettinger, *Beyond Tiananmen*, 110.

29. "Press Conference of the President," May 26, 1994, quoted in Suettinger, *Beyond Tiananmen*, 197.

30. The equivalent term of opprobrium in the United States is "panda-hugger."

31. Official Web site of the Chinese Olympic Committee, en.olympic.cn/china_oly/olympic_bids/2004-03-27/121850.html.

32. Zhao, *A Nation-State by Construction*, 233.

33. International Relations Committee Democratic Office, www.house.gov/international_relations/democratic/press_beijing08.html.

34. Zhao, *A Nation-State by Construction*, 233.

35. In 1999, the head of the Australian Olympic Committee revealed that the night before the vote he had offered $35,000 inducements to Kenya and Uganda, www.cnn.com/WORLD/europe/9901/22/olympics.03/. Another factor suggested by the head of China's Olympic Committee was that the Australian press had started a rumor that China had threatened to boycott the Atlanta Olympics because the vice-mayor of Beijing had said that although the U.S. congressional resolution would be sufficient reason for China to boycott the Atlanta Olympics, China wouldn't actually boycott. Liang Lijuan, *He Zhenliang: Wuhuan Zhi Lu* [He Zhenliang and the Five Rings] (Beijing: World Knowledge Press, 2005).

36. *Economic Journal* (Hong Kong), January 17, 1996, and *Cheng Ming* (Hong Kong), July 1, 1995.

37. *Guangming Daily*, September 14, 1995, FTS, 19950914000596.

38. Interview with *Asahi Shimbun*, August 13, 1995.

39. For example, Xinhua, August 22, 1995.

40. To join the WTO, a country must negotiate separate bilateral agreements with each of its main trading partners, but the terms of the agreements are applied to all WTO members.

41. See www.pub.whitehouse.gov/uri-res/I2R?urn:pdi://oma.eop.gov.us/1999/4/9/3.text.1. Also see Zong, *Zhu Rongji*, 41.

42. President Clinton's April 7, 1999, speech on U.S. policy toward China, www.cnn.com/ALLPOLITICS/stories/1999/04/07/clinton.china/transcript.

43. *New York Times*, September 10, 1999.

44. See http://clinton4.nara.gov/WH/New/html/19990408-1109.html.

45. *New York Times*, April 15, 1999, and November 17, 1999; and Suettinger, *Beyond Tiananmen*, 368–369.

46. Wang Yong, "China's Stakes in WTO Accession, the Internal Decision-making Process," in Heike Holbig and Robert Ash, eds., *China's Accession to the World Trade Organization* (London: Routledge Curzon, 2002), 33.

47. Zong, *Zhu Rongji*, 50.

48. Ibid., 52.

49. Wang, "China's Stakes," 32.

50. Ibid., 34–35.

51. U.S. Trade Representative Charlene Barshefsky did a masterful job of trying to gain a new benefit for every one we lost so that the overall agreement could be said to be just as good as the original one.

52. On a standard 100-degree-feeling thermometer with 0–49 cool, 50 neutral, and 51–100 warm, the mean levels were 62.08(1998), 53.31(1999), 56.53(2000), 46.75(2001), 52.39(2002), 47.37 (2003), and 39.25 (2004). Alastair Iain Johnston (co-authored with Daniela Stockmann), "Chinese Attitudes toward the United States and Americans," in Peter Katzenstein and Robert Keohane, eds., *Anti-Americanisms and World Politics* (Ithaca: Cornell University Press, forthcoming in 2007), 157–195.

53. Alastair Iain Johnston, "Chinese Middle-Class Attitudes towards International Affairs: Nascent Liberalization?" *China Quarterly*, no. 179 (September 2004), 627.

54. Ibid., 603–628.

55. Yang Yu, *Zhongguo Ren de Meiguo Guan, Yige Lishi de Kaocha* [Chinese People's Views of the United States, A Historical Investigation] (Shanghai: Fudan University Press, 1996), 302. For a discussion of the survey methodology see Joseph Fewsmith and Stanley Rosen, "The Domestic Context of Chinese Foreign Policy: Does 'Public Opinion' Matter?" in David M. Lampton, ed., *The Making of Chinese Foreign and Security Policy in the Era of Reform* (Stanford, Calif.: Stanford University Press, 2001), 161 and note 30, 433.

56. Horizon Research Report, December 15, 1999, cited in Fewsmith and Rosen, "Domestic Context," 161. Sociologist Dingxin Zhao argues that student anger toward the United States was "more a momentary outrage than a reflection of a long-term development of popular anti-U.S. nationalism," but his survey of Beijing students conducted just months after the Belgrade bombing cannot determine how long lasting the anger will be, although the responses show a nuanced and ambivalent attitude toward the United States, instead of total negativity. "An Angle on Nationalism in China Today: Attitudes among Beijing Students after Belgrade 1999," *China Quarterly*, no. 172 (December 2002), 885–905.

57. Zhao Mei and Maxine Thomas, eds., *China-United States Sustained Dialogue 1986–2001* (Dayton, Ohio: The Kettering Foundation, 2001).

58. Fewsmith and Rosen, "Domestic Context," 163.

59. By allowing such an open foreign policy debate, the Chinese government kept credible its threat to use force by signaling that elite opinion would support a military response.

60. Wang Jisi, "China-U.S. Relations at a Crossroads," in Zhao and Thomas, eds., *China-United States Sustained Dialogue*.

61. *Strategy and Management*, October 26, 1999, FBIS, FTS19991026000196.

62. Suettinger, *Beyond Tiananmen*.

63. Xinhua, "CCP Central Committee Decision on Enhancing the Party's Ability to Govern," September 26, 2004, FBIS, CPP20040926000042.

64. According to one crisis management expert, in the Tiananmen crisis, "the leaders waited too long to act and then felt they had to use force."

65. Hu Ping, *Guoji chongtu fenxi yu weiji guanli yanjiu* [Studies of International Conflicts and Crisis Management] (Beijing: Junshi Yiwen Chubanshe [Military Friendship and Culture Press], 1993).

66. Xinhua, February 4, 2004, cited in "China: State of Emergency Law Raises Speculation of Use Against Hong Kong, Taiwan," FBIS Report, CPP20040510000179, May 10, 2004.

67. *People's Daily*, June 14, 2004, english.people.com.cn/200406/14/end20040614_146259.html; *Global Times*, May 28, 2004.

68. Also see, U.S. Army War College, "Chinese Crisis Management," Crisis Brief, 2004.

69. James Mulvenon, "Civil-Military Relations and the EP-3 Crisis: A Content Analysis," *China Leadership Monitor*, no. 1 (Winter 2002).

70. Xinhua, April 4, 2001.

71. Zhang Tuosheng, "US-China Airplane Collision and Its Lesson," *World Economics and Politics*, no. 3, 2005.

72. *New York Times*, April 11, 2001.

73. According to one policy advisor speaking in 2005, "One hundred percent of the Chinese elite know that the Chinese pilot not the EP-3 was to blame for the accident."

74. Shirley Kan et al., *China-U.S. Aircraft Collision of April 2001: Assessments and Policy Implications*, Congressional Research Service, October 10, 2001.

75. Ibid., 14.

76. Zhang, "US-China Airplane Collision."

77. Mulvenon, "Civil-Military Relations." For example, see the *People's Daily* commentary, April 12, 2001.

78. Secretary Powell on CBS *Face the Nation*, April 8, 2001, cited in Kan et al., *China-U.S. Aircraft Collision of April 2001*.

79. *China Daily*, April 6, 2001.

80. Zhou He, "How Do the Chinese Media Reduce Organizational Incongruence? Bureaucratic Capitalism in the Name of Communism," in C. C. Lee, ed., *Chinese Media, Global Contexts* (London: Routledge Curzon, 2003), 204–205.

81. George Washington University, September 4, 2003.

82. Alastair Iain Johnston, "The Correlates of Beijing Public Opinion toward the United States, 1998–2004" in Alastair Iain Johnston and Robert S. Ross, eds., *New Directions in the Study of China's Foreign Policy* (Stanford, Calif.: Stanford University Press, 2006), 340–378.

83. *Global Times*, November 14, 2005.

84. *New York Times*, January 26, 2002.

85. H. Lyman Miller, "Party Politburo Processes under Hu Jintao," *China Leadership Monitor*, no. 11 (Summer 2004).

86. Wang Yiwei, "China and the United States Should Realize Strategic Mutual Trust," *Global Times*, August 27, 2004, FBIS, CPP20040901000133.

87. Jia Qingguo, "Learning to Live with the Hegemon," *Journal of Contemporary China*, vol. 14, no. 44 (August 2005), 403–404. The heading of this section is taken from the same article.

88. See *Southern Weekend*, March 27, 2003.

89. *Study Times*, August 16, 2004, FBIS, CPP20040823000245.

90. Ye Zicheng, "Carrying Forward, Developing and Pondering Deng Xiaoping's Foreign Policy Thinking in the New Situation," *World Economics and Politics,* November 14, 2004, FBIS, CPP20041123000200.

91. Li Zhongjie, "Understanding and Promoting the Process of World Multi-polarization," *Liaowang* (Beijing), June 3, 2002, FBIS, CPP20020802000160.

92. For example, Ye Zicheng and Li Bin, "The Great Power Foreign Policy Psychology that China Must Construct," *Global Times,* July 20, 2001, and Yang Fu, "China's Grand Strategy as Seen from Jiang Zemin's Visit to the United States," *Wide Angle* (Hong Kong), October 16, 2002, FBIS, CPP20021018000058.

93. Yang, "China's Grand Strategy."

94. *Naval and Merchants Ships,* June 10, 1999, FBIS, FTS19990722000820.

95. *Ta Kung Pao* (Hong Kong), August 5, 2005, FBIS, CPP20050805000105.

96. *Jiang Zemin on Socialism with Chinese Characteristics,* a collection of Jiang's essays, discussed the "period of strategic opportunity to achieve China's greatness" prior to the Party Congress speech. *People's Daily,* September 17, 2002, FBIS, CPP20020917000039.

97. *People's Daily,* June 30, 1999, FTS19990630001117; *People's Daily,* February 1, 2000, FTS20000202000090.

98. Xinhua, October 23, 2002, cited in Yang Jiemian, "U.S. Global Strategy and China's 'Period of Responsibility,'" *Research in International Issues,* March 13, 2003, FBIS, CPP20030418000203. Also see Liu Jianfei, "The Period of Strategic Opportunity and Sino-U.S. Ties," *Liaowang* (Beijing), January 20, 2003, FBIS, CPP20030207000061.

99. *Guangming Daily,* December 10, 2002, FBIS, CPP20021210000027.

100. *Der Spiegel,* August 8, 2005, service.spiegel.de/cache/international/Spiegel/0,1518,369128,00.html.

101. China began a program to modernize its strategic missile forces because of doubts about the survivability of its small nuclear deterrent beginning in the 1980s after President Reagan's announcement of the first attempt to create a missile shield—called the Strategic Defense Initiative—but the program had been moving at a modest pace.

102. Some Chinese scholars believed NMD was an American trick to draw China into a debilitating arms race and get the regime to collapse as it had done with the Soviet Union. Li Bin, Zhou Baogen, and Liu Zhiwei, "China Will Have to Respond," *Bulletin of the Atomic Scientists,* vol. 57, no. 6 (November–December 2001), 25–28. In fact, nuclear weapons development is less expensive than many other types of military programs.

103. Charles Ferguson, "Sparking a Buildup: U.S. Missile Defense and China's Nuclear Arsenal," *Arms Control Today,* March 2000.

104. *USA Today,* "China Warns Against Amending the ABM Treaty," July 7, 2000; Sha Zukang, "Briefing on Missile Defense Issue," March 23, 2001, www.chinaembassy.se/eng/xwdt/t101262.htm.

105. Thomas J. Christensen, "Theater Missile Defense and Taiwan's Security," *Orbis,* vol. 44, no. 1 (Winter 2000), 79–90. As Christensen notes, Taiwan TMD is more consequential politically than militarily—the Mainland's large number of missiles could easily overwhelm any missile defense system envisioned for Taiwan.

106. Ibid., 86.

107. Li, Zhou, and Liu, "China Will Have to Respond," 25–28.

108. U.S. International Trade Commission, U.S. Department of Commerce. Because the United States calculates trade figures to include Hong Kong, its totals are typically about 20 percent higher than the Chinese figures.

109. "The Choice of China's Diplomatic Strategy," *People's Daily*, March 19, 2003. Also see Xia, "Sino-U.S. Relations in the Early 21st Century."

110. Wang Jisi observed that ". . . an economic downturn in the United States would bring about a series of negative consequences that will make China's economic situation grimmer." "Interview with Wang Jisi, 'Prevent External Troubles From Becoming Internal Troubles,'" *Ming Pao* (Hong Kong), November 22, 2002, FBIS, CPP20021122000025.

111. Wayne M. Morrison, *China-U.S. Trade Issues*, Congressional Research Service, April 13, 2001. The U.S.-China Business Council, 2006, www.uschina.org/statistics/tradetable.html.

112. Fu Mengzi, "China Also Needs 'Speech Power,'" *World Knowledge*, February 1, 2006, FBIS, CPP2006022345001.

113. Zheng Bijian, "Four Strategic Opportunities for Sino-U.S. Relations," *People's Daily*, July 12, 2005, FBIS, CPP20050712000056.

114. Reuters, November 11, 2006.

115. Zheng, "Four Strategic Opportunities."

116. *New York Times*, July 7, 2005.

117. *Washington Post*, July 7, 2005.

118. Ibid.

119. *Wall Street Journal*, August 5, 2005.

120. The Pew Global Attitudes Project, June 23, 2005, http://pewglobal.org. The two exceptions are Poland and India. The BBC World Service poll, www.pipa.org/OnlineReports/China/China_Mar05/China/Mar05_rpt.pdf.

121. Pew Global Attitudes Project, 2006, "Publics of Asian Powers Hold Negative Views of One Another," http://pewglobal.org.

122. Chicago Council on Global Affairs, "The United States and the Rise of China and India," 2006, www.thechicagocouncil.org/curr_pos.php.

123. Ibid.

124. Ibid.

125. Ibid.

126. If Central Committee alternate members are included. If they are not included, central Party and government officials are a larger bloc. Yumin Sheng, "Central-Provincial Relations at the CCP Central Committee: Institutions, Measurement and Empirical Trends, 1978–2002." *China Quarterly*, no. 182 (2005), 338–355.

127. See note 52.

128. When the question was repeated in 2006, the favorable percentage had increased to 47 percent. Pew Global Attitudes Project, 2006, "Publics of Asian Powers Hold Negative Views of One Another." http://pewglobal.org.

129. The Pew Global Attitudes Project, June 23, 2005, http://pewglobal.org.

130. "Chinese Become Sharply Negative About US, Americans Mildly Negative About China," www.worldpublicopinion.org/incl/printable_version.php?pnt=189.

131. *Global Times*, March 2, 2005.

132. *Horizon Report*, no. 724 (April 11, 2005).

133. Qian Qichen, "International Relations in the New Century," *Study Times*, October 18, 2004, FBIS, CPP20041020000203.

134. Wang Yiwei, "The U.S. Wants to Lighten Its Hegemonic Burden," *Global Times*, July 7, 2006, FBIS, CPP20060721329001.

135. *Global Times*, May 28, 2004, FBIS, CPP20040602000264.

Chapter 9

1. *Asia Times*, February 9, 2006.
2. Markle Foundation, November 17, 2005.
3. See www.cnn.com/ALLPOLITICS/stories/1999/04/07/clinton.china/transcript.
4. The *New York Times* (March 5, 2006) noted, however, that the 14.2 percent increase in spending for rural needs the government promised for 2006 is less than the 19.8 percent central and local government revenues rose in 2005.
5. *Der Spiegel*, August 8, 2005.
6. David Shambaugh, "Containment or Engagement of China? Calculating Beijing's Responses," *International Security*, vol. 21, no. 2 (Autumn 1966), 190.
7. Fu Mengzi, "China Also Needs 'Speech Power,'" *World Knowledge*, February 1, 2006, FBIS, CPP20060223455001.
8. Steven Van Evera, "Causes of War," Ph.D. dissertation, University of California, Berkeley, 1984, quoted in Jack Snyder, *Myths of Empire: Domestic Politics and International Ambition* (Ithaca: Cornell University Press, 1991), 33.
9. The U.S. government has been pressing China to make its military budget more transparent. But the domestic demand for transparency is likely to have greater effect than international pressure.
10. Jack Snyder, *From Voting to Violence: Democratization and Nationalist Conflict* (New York: W. W. Norton, 2000), 59.
11. Henry Kissinger, *Does America Need a Foreign Policy? Toward a Diplomacy for the 21st Century* (New York: Simon and Schuster, 2001), 148.
12. Ibid., 136.
13. Chicago Council on Global Affairs, "The United States and the Rise of China and India," 2006, www.thechicagocouncil.org/curr_pos.php.
14. U.S. Department of State, Press Statement, March 2, 2006. In February 2006, President Chen announced he was "ceasing" the National Unification Council and the Guidelines, but the U.S. side insisted that this was not the same as "abolishing" them, and that it intended to hold Chen to all his earlier commitments.
15. *Straits Times*, May 13, 2006.
16. These are the "Six Assurances," www.indiana.edu/~easc/security_issues/china/six_assurances.pdf.
17. Charlene Barshefsky and Edward Grasser, "Revolutionary China, Complacent America," *Wall Street Journal*, September 15, 2005.
18. *New York Times*, November 10, 2006.

Index

Note: Page numbers in *italics* indicate photographs and illustrations.